LORD NORMAN

THE GOVERNOR: 1942

From a photograph by Howard Coster

LORD NORMAN

BY

SIR HENRY CLAY

LONDON

MACMILLAN & CO LTD

NEW YORK · ST MARTIN'S PRESS

1957

MACMILLAN AND COMPANY LIMITED
London Bombay Calcutta Madras Melbourne

THE MACMILLAN COMPANY OF CANADA LIMITED
Toronto

ST MARTIN'S PRESS INC
New York

PRINTED IN GREAT BRITAIN

FOREWORD

BY

MR. C. F. COBBOLD, GOVERNOR OF THE BANK OF ENGLAND

SIR HENRY CLAY was killed in a motor accident when he had done some three-quarters of the work he had planned on Lord Norman's Life. The arrangements made for completing the book after his death are explained in the Editorial Note.

Inevitably the picture of Lord Norman is less finely drawn than if Sir Henry Clay had lived to complete his work. The great public servant, the financial statesman and the fascinating individual emerge clearly enough, as do the breadth of interest, the industry and the creative and searching mind. What perhaps emerges less clearly is the degree to which work and personality were interwoven. To work with or for Lord Norman was always an intense personal experience — nothing was dull, nothing was routine — he infused drama and fun into everything, important and trivial alike.

Many things which are to-day taken for granted in our own financial arrangements and in our financial relationships with the Commonwealth, with Europe and with the United States, were in fact created and fostered by Lord Norman. To a new generation of Central Bankers, both in this country and in many other parts of the world, the instruments and practice which he devised have become a part of daily life. They and their successors will remain in Lord Norman's debt for his technical contribution to their trade and even more for the values and standards which his personality implanted.

A Governor of the Bank has few closer contacts than with the Chancellor of the Exchequer of the day. It is of interest to recall two paragraphs from a reference to Lord Norman in Lord Snowden's autobiography:

'It was said of a great statesman in the Victorian Age that he had the "international mind". How truly that may be said of the present Governor of the Bank of England!

To him, more than to any statesman of Europe, is the credit due for the partial restoration of the economic conditions of Europe from the utter collapse in the years following the War.

'Whether Mr Norman's policy and actions have been right or wrong, whether he has made mistakes or not, one thing is indisputable — no man with great responsibilities ever tried more faithfully to discharge them with the single aim of promoting national and international well-being.'

EDITORIAL NOTE

In May 1950, at the request of the Court of the Bank of England and of Lord Norman's family, Sir Henry Clay started work on a life of Lord Norman, Governor of the Bank from 1920 to 1944. The records of the Bank — voluminous for the later years — were thrown open to him, and he quarried much in the papers of Benjamin Strong, sometime Governor of the Federal Reserve Bank of New York. Basing himself primarily on these two sources, he was already beginning to speak of his task with a sense of growing achievement, but with much still to be done, when on 30 July 1954 he was killed in a road accident while on holiday in Holland.

It proved that Clay had written the first draft of his work up to the year 1939, needing (as he himself had said) some revision and compression. Two chapters only were not yet in draft, one covering the Second World War, the other and final chapter an appraisal to be called 'The Man'. The sponsors had to decide how the work should be finished. Should the material be turned over to another author and a fresh start made? Should an attempt be made to complete the book in a similar treatment? Or should Clay's work be left to stand on its own and the gaps be filled by others, in a treatment admittedly different from Clay's own work?

It was decided to adopt the third solution, partly because the most active and creative part of Lord Norman's career had been covered, and partly because of the evident difficulty of absorbing Clay's work at so advanced a stage into a new book by another author. With the agreement of his own family, the editorial task of preparing his draft for publication has been undertaken by his friends and former colleagues at the Bank of England. Two of them, who had also worked most closely with Lord Norman, have contributed postscripts to take the place of the two intended final chapters, one dealing with the concluding period and the other giving a short personal appreciation of Lord Norman.

How much has been done to Clay's own work should be made clear. The opinions expressed are entirely his and remain as he wrote them : but the quotations, references and figures have been checked, a little overlapping has been removed and in places the argument has been condensed. Every effort has been made to avoid rewriting and to preserve the balance of emphasis and of judgment. Footnotes have been added only where some technical explanation seemed necessary, or to place the personalities referred to. The result is intrinsically Clay's work in his own words, although it cannot be exactly in the form in which he would have left it had he lived to complete and polish the draft himself.

Clay was an intimate adviser of Lord Norman at the Bank from 1929 : he is the unnamed 'economist whose interests had been in industrial, not banking questions' of Chapter VIII. The reader will accordingly be hardly surprised to find that this book is primarily a study of Lord Norman as Governor of the Bank, not a biography of conventional pattern. 'I have not attempted', he wrote, 'a history of the inter-war period ; but have felt it would be of more use to include as much as was relevant and necessary for judging the Governor's decisions in preference to seeking to pass judgment on them myself.' Purely biographical material is to be found only in the earlier chapters covering the years before Lord Norman began his life's work at the Bank. It follows that there are aspects of his life which receive small mention, and would doubtless have been covered if Clay had lived to finish his work. Two of these must be mentioned here.

Lord Norman's mother had a lasting influence upon him. She was very musical, and her artistic sense showed itself also in her love of a beautiful house. The furnishings of all kinds were chosen with care and with a delight in fine materials, and her house was always admirably administered. She liked younger people and attracted them : and was at least abreast, if not ahead, of the next generation. She knew her own mind clearly and decisively, having arrived at her conclusions intuitively and not by reasoning, and expressing them with the utmost frankness. Although Lord Norman lived very little at home with his parents after his schooldays, the impalpable influences of heredity, both physical and spiritual, were strong and enduring. Physically, his long loose figure and his slender hands and fingers came from his mother : so, too, did his artistic sense and his love of music and of beautiful things : so, too, did his forward-looking and intuitive mind and his attraction for young people. Still alert in mind and decisive in judgment, Mrs. Norman died at the age of ninety-nine, only one month before her eldest son.

Secondly — in point of time — Lord Norman married in January 1933, when he was in his sixty-second year and had already been Governor of the Bank for thirteen years, Priscilla Worsthorne, daughter of Major Robert and Lady Alice Reyntiens. Suffice it to say that all those who were privileged to enjoy their friendship in the later years of Lord Norman's life know full well how happy and fortunate that marriage was.

It remains to acknowledge (as he would have wished to do) the help which Clay received in the writing of this book, help which has been generously renewed in the task of preparing it for publication, even though the list cannot be made complete. For material he owed much to Lady Norman and other members of Lord Norman's family; to directors and senior officers of Brown, Shipley and Co., Lord Norman's old firm; to Lord Norman's old associates and friends in this country and in the United States. The Federal Reserve Bank of New York gave him access to and permission to use the papers of Benjamin Strong; a handsome grant from the Rockefeller Foundation enabled him to take full advantage of this and other material. For their assistance in ordering the great mass of papers which with their help he had collected, Clay would have wished to thank Mrs. Lloyd Prichard who was his assistant for more than a year : Mrs. Broadley, his secretary at Oxford, and the staff of the Secretary's Office at the Bank, particularly Miss C. M. Perry.

The reader should bear in mind the circumstances here explained in judging how far the following pages do justice to the subject and the author.

CONTENTS

ILLUSTRATIONS

xi

CHAPTER I

THE FORMATIVE YEARS

(i)

THE founder of the family of merchants and bankers to which Montagu Collet Norman belonged was a Richard Norman, born in Rotherfield Greys, Oxfordshire, in 1646. This Richard left a home of yeomen farmers in 1661 to become apprentice to a London carpenter. He prospered, becoming a Member of the Carpenters' Company and, in 1706, Master. The Company in 1681 still claimed to incorporate a 'Handicraft Trade and Manual Occupation'; but the numbers engaged in the industry of building were outrunning the number who became freemen of the Companies, and members of the Carpenters' Company had already made the transition from self-employing craftsmen to employers of others. Richard Norman at the end of a long life described himself as of the parish of St. Ann's, Blackfriars, although he resided in the parish of St. Botolph's on the other side of the City; and in St. Ann's was the site of the timber-merchanting business which his descendants were to carry on for more than a century.

It was an age of expanding opportunities for anyone of enterprise engaged in the building industry, particularly for a timber merchant. The great fire of 1666 was followed, it is true, by the substitution of brick for timber as the chief material of building; but against this was the great expansion in the demand for timber and for the work of carpenters in the rebuilding of the city. As that was exhausted, a new and growing demand sprang up in the expansion of London outside its old limits. Throughout the century there were recurrent complaints of the depletion of indigenous woods and forests. The chief sources of imported timber were Scotland and the Baltic, and London, both by the facilities it offered to shipping and by its own need of timber, was the greatest port of entry for the trade.

Richard Norman was succeeded by his son, another Richard, also Master of the Carpenters' Company, but a merchant beyond question with a substantial business, who was able to leave a considerable fortune to his children. His successor, James Norman, third of seven sons of whom four died in infancy, marked a further stage in the growth of the family fortunes. He is described as 'a merchant trading chiefly with Norway'. In the course of the eighteenth century the firm developed an important connection with Norway, maintaining extensive wharves and timber yards there. The timber yard in Blackfriars was acquired soon after 1700, and an adjoining house, 13 Earl Street (a continuation of Upper Thames Street West), was used first as a residence and then as offices. A neighbouring property in Liquorpond came from the family of another timber merchant, of the name of Ward, who had married a sister of the second Richard Norman's wife. The firm also acquired wharves in Blackfriars, which James's grandson, George Warde Norman, continued to own after he retired from the business, selling many years later St. Ann's Wharf and Lee's Wharf to the London, Chatham and Dover Railway, and Hood's Wharf to the Metropolitan Railway. The family also acquired scattered properties in London, sometimes involuntarily, taking them as security for timber supplied and having them left on their hands.

James Norman was a man of cultivated tastes, a collector of books and prints, a keen gardener and the friend of scientists. He shared the ambition which Adam Smith noted in the successful merchants of that time of becoming country gentlemen. In 1754 he leased, and ten years later purchased, The Rookery, a house and thirty-seven acres in Bromley Common, Kent. At that time Bromley was far enough from London for him to carry pistols in his holsters and take an armed servant with him when he rode into London. His second wife belonged to a family of the name of Innocent, long established in Bromley and possessed of property there which passed to her husband's children. He himself added a farm to the estate and enlarged and improved the house ; his son and grandson made further improvements, and the house remained the home of the senior line of the family until the present century.

By his first wife, Henrietta Wroughton of Wilcot, Wiltshire,

James Norman had three sons. The eldest died in childhood. The youngest married a daughter of the fourth Duke of Rutland, and left eight surviving sons, of whom three took Holy Orders and three entered the armed services. The second son, George, succeeded to the timber business and The Rookery on his father's death in 1787. He added extensively to the estate in Kent, and served as High Sheriff in 1795. Unlike the capitalist landowner of popular tradition, he resisted the proposal to enclose Bromley Common until resistance became useless, though there were obvious economic advantages to be gained; one objection which weighed with him was the consequent loss of the cricket ground used by the local club. His investments in land and in the improvement of his house were, however, suspended when trade with Norway was interrupted by Napoleon's Berlin Decrees and the British Orders in Council. Some imports continued under licence; but the trade was subject to violent fluctuations, and it was not until four or five years after the end of war that he was able to disengage any of his capital from financing his business. He married a daughter of the Rev. Edward Beadon, who held the living of North Stoneham, Hampshire, for forty-nine years and was succeeded in it by a son, who held it for sixty-nine years.

George Warde Norman, the eldest son of George Norman, was born in 1793. On leaving Eton in 1810 he went into the family business; he made long visits to Norway, where he had many friends, and succeeded his father when the latter retired in 1824. His ability had already received recognition in his election to the Court of the Bank of England in 1821, but his interests did not lie in the active conduct of affairs. He retired from his own business in 1830 (the year of his father's death), transferring it to Sewell and Co., of which his brother, Richard, became a partner. Though a Director of the Bank of England for fifty years, and a member of the Committee of Treasury [1]

[1] The Committee of Treasury is a Committee of the Court of Directors first appointed in August 1694 and until 1918 consisting almost exclusively of the Governor and Deputy Governor, former Governors and (in later times) the prospective Deputy Governor. In 1918, as will be seen in Chapter III, the field of selection was widened. As Sir Ernest Harvey told the Macmillan Committee in 1929: '. . . It is a body of nine members, and except that the Governor and Deputy Governor are *ex-officio* members, it is elected by ballot of the whole Court, by secret ballot. They act as a special body with whom the Governors can consult regarding all the more important business of the Bank, and can

for much of the time, he did not serve as Governor; his colleagues explained to a Parliamentary Committee that 'the ordinary preliminary Condition (for membership of the Committee) of having filled the Chair was dispensed with when the Health of the Party rendered his Appointment as Governor inexpedient'. On the same pretext he avoided the office of High Sheriff, though his Liberal principles did induce him to take an active and long-continued interest in the administration of the new Poor Law. On the other hand, he was a man of unusually wide reading, especially in history, and not only in English but Norwegian, French and Italian literature, medieval and contemporary, and the later Latin poets. With his neighbour and intimate friend, George Grote, he shared an interest not only in banking and history, but in the promotion of cricket in West Kent. Later in life, Charles Darwin valued the wide reading and acute mind of 'my clever neighbour Mr. Norman'. His estate and his children, who settled round him, and the affairs of his neighbourhood, met any need for more active interests.

In one field he did play an active part — in the reshaping of the currency and banking system. Unlike his grandson's, his contribution was not one of policy and execution but of ideas and propaganda. The main principles of the Bank Act of 1844 were suggested by the Bank itself. Norman in that year had been a Director for over twenty years and was a member of the Committee of Treasury. He had set forth his views in a pamphlet written in 1832 (though not published till 1838) and in evidence before the committee of inquiry into the Bank's Charter in 1832 and the committee on Banks of Issue in 1840–41. They were those of the 'Currency' school — a name he coined — aiming at the control of monetary conditions by the automatic adjustment of the note-issue to the inflow and outflow of bullion, so that the note circulation, above a fixed fiduciary issue, would fluctuate exactly like a metallic currency. As an original member of the Political Economy Club Norman saw the logic of Ricardo's proposal for entrusting a monopoly of note-issue to a Government

consider matters to be submitted to the Court and make recommendations, it being, of course, open to the Court to question any recommendation made and to open a discussion on any matters submitted to them. . . .'

corporation, performing no other function; as a Director of
the Bank he saw the disadvantages of a complete break with
existing practice. He advocated instead a separation of the
distinct functions of note-issue and banking in two departments.
He neglected the parallel influence of other banks' deposits
with the Bank of England, though he recognised it in discussing
the action the Bank was forced to take in providing assistance
in a crisis; but London bankers' deposits accounted for less
than £1 million in 1844, only a ninth of private deposits and
less than a twelfth of total deposits, and even this use of balances
with the Bank of England in place of notes in their cash reserves
was a recent growth. Similarly, while he argued that the
widely diffused right of note-issue by private banks — 'the
inherent vice of issues made in competition and upon securities
bearing interest' — was wrong in principle, he recognised that
it could not be suddenly taken away, and proposed only that
it be subjected to a terminable licence and not extended to new
banks. Again, while arguing for an automatic control of note-
issue, he recognised the possibility of emergencies in which
exceptional action was called for, and proposed that an extension of the Fiduciary Issue should be possible on the authority
of three Ministers.

He was thus no doctrinaire, but worked out his ideas in
relation to actual practice. His colleagues relied on him and
continually re-elected him to the Committee of Treasury, successive official committees of inquiry invited his evidence, and
Chancellors of the Exchequer — notably Wood in the commercial crisis of 1847 — sought his advice. Though he avoided
responsibility and action, whereas his grandson, the Governor,
always sought them, they have something in common in their
thinking, possibly because both observed actual transactions
from the same viewpoint of a central bank. George Warde
Norman's insistence on the country's dependence on an international order, typified in the rejection of all criteria for the
regulation of the currency except movement of bullion and
exchange rates; his fear of speculative excesses if there was no
automatic check on the expansion of currency; his insistence
that, while a sound currency policy was essential, it could not
prevent fluctuations in business due to waves of excessive optimism and depression among business-men; his belief in the

B

'practical knowledge, spirit of economy, and concentrated interest of individuals in private partnerships', his distrust of deposit banking carried on in overseas countries by banks in London — all remind the student of his descendant. And in a wider field as well; in his dislike of the tendency of a democracy, not only to control the appointment of the Government, but 'to administer details, as well as to rule in the last resort, through organs of public opinion, which do not possess the acquaintance with the subject-matter or the responsibility' — 'a democracy may carry on war successfully, but it can never carry on war democratically with success'; in his insistence on the limitations and dangers of the fashionable principle of Nationality as a guide in foreign policy, and on the danger of democratic diplomacy encouraging hopes among oppressed nationalities which it had no intention of satisfying.

George Warde Norman was not a banker; but he was the friend and neighbour of bankers — Hankey, Grote, Jones Loyd, Hay Cameron, Lubbock, Stone, Martin and later Mark Collet — and one of his brothers was a partner first in Bouverie's and then in Jones, Loyd & Co. His marriage to Sibella, one of the three daughters and co-heirs of Henry Stone, a partner in Stone and Martin (later Martin & Co.) brought his children into one of the oldest of English banking families and two of them into partnership in the oldest of the Clearing Banks. The eldest son entered the Army and died of wounds in the Crimea. The second son, Charles Loyd, inherited The Rookery. He was a partner in the banking firm of Finlay Hodgson, and, when it was absorbed by Baring Bros., a partner in Barings. Frederick Henry, the fourth son, the father of Montagu Collet Norman, was a partner, and when it became a company a director, in Martin & Co., as was also the seventh and youngest son, Edward.

Writing in 1873 Bagehot doubted whether the class of private banker could continue. The change in the conditions of banking, especially the growth of deposits and the increase in the detail of the business involved, favoured joint-stock banking, and the private banks would be driven, either first to reorganise their external management on the lines of the joint-stock banks, and then to complete the transition by becoming joint-stock banks themselves, or to lose their independence. His forecast in the main has been realised; Frederick Henry Norman's working life spanned the transition. After being called to the Bar, and serving as an assistant-commissioner of the Royal Commission which reported in the years 1867 and 1871 on the employment of Women and Children in Agriculture and later of the Boundaries Commission, he gave up his practice at the Bar to enter Martin's Bank. He was admitted a partner in 1880. Bagehot's description of the London Private Banker would have fitted him: 'a certain union of pecuniary sagacity and educated refinement which was scarcely to be found in any other part of society . . . the calling is hereditary: the credit of the bank descends from father to son; this inherited wealth soon brings inherited refinement. Banking is a watchful, but not a laborious trade. A banker . . . can feel pretty sure that all his transactions are sound, and yet have much spare mind. A certain part of his time, and a considerable part of his thoughts, he can readily devote to other pursuits.' But private banking was becoming more exacting. As a youth he had been a great cricketer, captain of Eton and Cambridge and playing for the Gentlemen at Lord's; but he dropped quickly out of first-class cricket. A student of architecture and history, he took an active part in hospital administration and he was Chairman of the Sun Fire Office for over thirty years; but on the whole he was absorbed in the work of his bank. When his younger brother was admitted to partnership in 1884 there were two Martin and two Norman partners, who all had a common ancestor in Richard Stone, a brother-in-law of Sir Francis Baring. Barings had an account with Martin's Bank from 1764 and Frederick Norman's son remembered the anxiety caused his father by the crisis in Baring's affairs in 1890. Martin's was incorporated as a company in that year, but retained much of the character of a private bank.

Frederick Henry Norman married in 1870 Lina Susan Penelope, the only daughter of Mark Wilks Collet, a banker living not far away at Croydon. Montagu Collet Norman was the eldest of their three children. Mark Collet's career showed that, though bankers might inter-marry and form a caste, it was not a closed caste. He was born in 1816 in Highbury, the son of a merchant of Manx descent who was ruined by the

Napoleonic Wars and died young, leaving his widow to bring up their three sons. She was Wendelina van Brienen, the daughter of a Dutch merchant settled in Archangel and, like Collet himself, also once rich but ruined by the wars. For a time the widow resided in the Isle of Man, but later returned to Archangel to join her own relatives. There the boys were educated, learning Russian and German before they learned English. She came back and settled in London in 1832.

Mark Collet had returned earlier, and was already in employment as a clerk. In that year he was taken to Liverpool by his employer, Henry Patry, who represented there one of the chief American banking houses in London, Thomas Wilson & Co. When Wilson's went into bankruptcy in the crisis of 1837, Patry continued in business in Liverpool, and in 1840 took young Collet with him to the United States in an attempt to collect claims outstanding against southern cotton firms. The mission, though continued over a second winter, was fruitless, and Collet persuaded his principal to turn to something else. Patry was taken in by an old friend, Joshua Bates, who represented Baring's in Liverpool, while young Collet himself found employment as a sub-manager in the Bank of Liverpool. After some years of valuable banking experience, he returned to London as the partner of a West Indian merchant, and a year later went out to New York to manage a firm there which his principal had taken over. Two years later, in July 1851, he came to Liverpool as a partner in Brown, Shipley & Co. His daughter, Montagu Collet Norman's mother, was born just before they left New York, and his wife, an Eyre of Beverley, died on arrival in Liverpool.

Brown, Shipley & Co. was the English side of a firm of merchants, founded by an Ulsterman, Alexander Brown, in Baltimore, Maryland, in 1800. Beginning as an importer of linens, a trade he knew well, the founder developed a general business in imported manufactures, which he invoiced in sterling. Sterling bills were plentiful, since they were drawn on English firms by American exporters of raw cotton and tobacco. It was a natural development for one of the sons to settle in Liverpool in 1810 and for the firm to combine with their merchanting business a wider business in handling sterling exchange. Thereafter the business grew rapidly on both sides of the Atlantic, the centre of gravity in America shifting from Baltimore to Philadelphia and New York, until by the middle of the century they were probably the largest dealers in either America or England in sterling exchange. The name of Shipley was brought into the English title of the firm, to mark the services of an American Quaker, Joseph Shipley, a partner in Liverpool from 1826 to 1850, who in addition to bearing a large part of the responsibility for the business throughout his partnership, successfully conducted the firm's negotiations with the Bank of England in the crisis of 1837.

Collet was admirably qualified to take Shipley's place. He had a wide experience of merchanting, both in England and America. The Liverpool house was still mainly engaged in handling commodities : it had extensive warehouses and warehousing staff; it received large imports of cotton on consignment and of manufactured exports for forwarding — one of the partners was more often called in to settle disputes over quality of cotton than anyone else in Liverpool. To this commercial experience Collet added a wide range of financial experience, including his seven years of deposit banking. In the firm he concentrated on credits and financial business. Local attachments and sentiment long deferred the transfer of Brown Shipley to London, but the interruption of Liverpool's trade with America by the Civil War precipitated the decision to open an office in London, and the subsequent change in the character of foreign trade, especially after the development of cable communications, led ultimately to the closing of the Liverpool house. When the office was opened in London in 1863 Collet was the natural person to take charge.

Thereafter his career was in the City of London. The mercantile business of the Liverpool office rapidly shrank after the American Civil War. The firm became purely merchant-bankers, financing trade by acceptance credits but not handling commodities, and this business could best be done in London. The Liverpool office was, for personal reasons, not closed until 1889, but from 1873 onwards London had been the centre of the English business. A firm operating in New York, Philadelphia and Boston on one side of the Atlantic, and London on the other, with old-established commercial connections in both continents, but confining themselves to finance, had great and expanding opportunities as America expanded and drew more and more imports from the rest of the world. Until 1914 this business was still mainly financed by sterling bills, and the American offices of the firm gave American importers access to these by arranging acceptance credits with the London office, in addition to which the London office originated similar business of its own. An incidental development was the provision of Letters of Credit for American visitors to Europe; this was provided by Brown Shipley to an extent which no other firm approached, and involved them in an immense volume of detail (for which a West End branch was opened specially), justified by a wide range of valuable personal connections. The organisation of the firm — a private partnership, operating in different countries but with all the partners partners of all the branches — and the intimate ties of kinship and friendship which united the different members of the firm, made such a widespread system of credit practicable and safe.

In 1866 Collet was elected to the Court of the Bank of England, just before the failure of Overend Gurney. Writing many years later, he said: 'I remember with gratitude that having taken a more or less active part in all the great commercial panics of the last sixty odd years (1837, 1848, 1857–58, 1866 and 1890–91), and in the business that led up to them, I have been preserved from any more serious consequences to myself than the anxiety involved and perhaps some money loss; but the remembrance of 1857, 1866 and 1890 remains too vivid ever to pass from my memory'. He was Deputy Governor of the Bank in 1885–87 and Governor in 1887–89. During his Governorship he was the chief adviser of Goschen (Chancellor of the Exchequer, 1887–92) and the executant of his great conversion of the National Debt; his services were recognised by a baronetcy. He, and his firm, took an active part in the great example of co-operation in a crisis, which his successor as Governor, Lidderdale, organised in the Baring crisis. Other bankers, his friends, sent their sons into Brown Shipley to be trained. He was typical of his class and time in his sincere evangelical Christianity; more than one of the American visitors to his home, sons and friends of his partners, have said that nothing impressed them more in England than the practice of family prayers and Collet's conduct of them.

He had made his home at St. Clere, an eighteenth-century house near Kemsing in the county of Kent, which was to become extremely familiar to his eldest Norman grandchild.

The family into which Montagu Collet Norman was born was thus typical of Victorian prosperity. Grown rich with the commercial expansion of Britain in the eighteenth century, it had moved into banking. With like families, predominantly bankers, it formed a pleasant community of neighbours in Kent and other districts within easy reach of the City of London. There were few great fortunes among them — banking by itself does not make for great fortunes quickly acquired; but equally there were few failures — evidence of caution and practical judgment, instilled in successive generations by experience and teaching. It was a comfortable community, enjoying great security. The stability of that life owed much to the religion by which it was permeated, an undemonstrative but sincere Christianity, little troubled as yet by doubts. Though this religion implied what seems to later generations a narrow outlook — one of the partners in Brown Shipley, as late as the 'nineties, rebuked a week-end visitor, who deplored the missed opportunity of getting in the hay on a dry Sunday in a stretch of wet weather, by asking, 'Would you then disobey the laws of Almighty God?' — it insisted on personal responsibility for the conduct of social relations. It was a society in which scandals were as rare as financial failures. Its interests owed as much to homes rich in books and pictures and lively social intercourse as to the schools and universities, usually Eton and Cambridge in the Norman household, at which it sought its formal education; cricket, hunting and shooting were interests common to both. While bankers predominated, the links with the Army and Navy, with the Church and the Law, were close. George Warde Norman's eldest son lost his life before Sebastopol; a nephew made a place for himself in Canadian history as Dean of Quebec, and another nephew, after holding a commission in the Scots Guards, became the head of Brompton Oratory. There is a curious and complete absence of politicians in the family record; and there was little direct association with industry. Collet brought in a new range of experience and connections; foreign banking based on foreign trade, and linked with American partners, offered a career which was to prove more attractive to Montagu Norman. But it was still banking, and socially its exponents mingled indistinguishably with the older line of bankers.

(ii)

Montagu Collet Norman was born on 6 September 1871 in his parents' London house. Later the family moved to Hayes Common in Kent, and his childhood was spent in the society of Normans and Norman relations and friends clustered round his grandfather's home on Bromley Common. He was the eldest of three children, two sons and a daughter. The family was brought up in the Christian faith and observances of their parents. The boys were initiated into the customary sports, cricket — the professional of the Bromley Club brought in to coach them was the father of H. G. Wells — shooting and hunting at an early age ; as a boy Montagu followed the hounds on his pony with the intensity that characterised all his activities, and would arrive home exhausted for his mother to massage him back to life. In 1887 his father, wanting a more adequate house for a permanent family home, and unable to find what he wanted in Kent, moved to Moor Place, Much Hadham, Hertfordshire.

Following the tradition of his family, Norman entered Eton in the Summer Half of 1884. Eton was a singularly happy home for his father, his brother and his nephews, but he was not happy there. There were many reasons. He was unlucky in his initial personal relations ; he entered Warre's house, but Warre left almost immediately to become Headmaster. He was attached to the tutor, Impey, to whom he was transferred ; but was taken from Impey by his Housemaster, Donaldson, a change he resented although it was the beginning of a lifelong friendship with Donaldson's family. To most boys of his age, these changes would not have mattered ; but Norman was extremely sensitive throughout his life to the personal relations involved in work. In any case he could not uphold the family tradition of pre-eminence in games. His father and one of his uncles, and subsequently his brother, were captains of the Eleven ; he himself, though not without aptitude for games, was never really fit and suffered from recurrent headaches. The work he found uninteresting and therefore distasteful. In later life in company with contemporaries he himself used to say that he was always at the bottom of the form; the records show that he was never bottom, once top, and normally in the undistinguished middle. He reached First Hundred without difficulty, but there is no evidence that any intellectual interest was ever kindled. He had not the kind of mind that excels in examinations; throughout life he tended to reach his conclusions intuitively, or, if he reached them after a long process of rumination, he never found it easy to explain and justify them.

Contemporaries say that he was a rebel, resenting the rules and restrictions inevitable in any community of boys. If it was so, it is curious that one who showed such zeal in imposing order and discipline in the field of his adult activities, should resent them in youth. For certain types the pressure of life in a close community may be torture; and a sensitive boy whose ability does not find ready expression, who cannot shine in the games on which popular esteem is most readily based, small and undistinguished in appearance (surprising as this will be to a later generation which knew Norman as physically one of the most impressive figures of his time), but conscious at the same time of great innate powers and perhaps ambitious already of influence, may well have been unhappy at school. Something may perhaps be attributed to the contrast with the stronger physique of his younger brother. His experience did not kill the loyalty which Eton inspires; he followed the fortunes of the school, so long as he had any interests outside his work. The annual dinners of his Housemaster's pupils and the Lord's Match were among the few regular social engagements he allowed himself in the years between his return from South Africa and the outbreak of the First World War.

Following the family tradition, in 1889 he went up to Cambridge. His father, realising perhaps more clearly than his son where his interests would lie, sent him, not to his own college Trinity, but to King's. The experiment was not a success; he had an interesting social life, but was not drawn into the intellectual life characteristic of King's — he resented, indeed, being separated from the friends at school who went to Trinity. In accordance with Cambridge practice, he lived in lodgings in his first year. No diary or letters survive from that time; the pages of a scrapbook may be taken perhaps as indicative of his interests — the programme of a performance of Gluck's *Orpheus* in the Opera House; the Rules of the King's College Musical Society; the printed menu of a dinner given by Mr. M. C. Norman at 26 Trinity Street; a newspaper cutting of 'fracas in the hunting field' at a meeting of the Essex and Puckeridge Hunt; a notice from the Dean requesting Mr. Norman to be more regular in his observation of the eight o'clock rule and three requests to call on the Dean; notice of election to the University Pitt Club; menu of a dinner of the Amateur Dramatic Club; notice of election to the M.C.C. At the end of the year the College and he parted friends by mutual consent. Years after, motoring to Cambridge to receive an honorary degree, he recalled a remark of his tutor, the historian Prothero, that it was no use his staying on, he was not the sort of person to get a degree. It was not a verdict he would have quarrelled with.

Norman's serious education began when he left Cambridge. It was decided that he should go abroad and improve his languages and he was transplanted from the society to which he had been so far confined to a Dresden boarding-house. There he proceeded to learn German, and there also his passion for music flared up. Forty years later, when his concentration on the Bank had for many years crowded music out of his life, his stepson was trying over some Wagner when he came in; he joined him and went through opera after opera with a knowledge that was still intimate and familiar. His forceful landlady, who led the conversation at the common table, also discovered for him another interest, philosophy, though it was some years before he found time for any extensive reading. After a most enjoyable winter in Dresden, his brother joined him and they went together to Prague, Vienna and Heidelberg, after which he visited Bayreuth. His next move was to Switzerland to perfect his French. Intellectually his year there was less stimulating; but it was extremely important physically. He lived with a pastor from whom he got little; but he spent long days in the forest with the forester, who became a great friend, and helped the villagers with their cows and harvesting. It was probably the first time since childhood that he learned the meaning of physical health; he was happy, in a new way, and came back a changed man. Although he did not retain this perfect physical health when he settled down to his profession, the memory of the new experience must have meant something to him.

After this two years of less formal education he came home, and in October 1892 went into Martin's Bank at 68 Lombard Street. It is interesting to speculate whether he ever contemplated any other career than banking. In later life he would sometimes object to the continual references to his 'long banking tradition': there was a long connection with banking on his father's side but on his mother's, with which he came to be identified, there was only one link in Collet. There seems little doubt that he was much attracted by the Army. Soldiers were almost as frequent among his own relations as bankers, and when accident made him a soldier in the South African War, he found it a life exactly to his mind. Moreover, he much admired a first cousin of his mother, General Sir Edward Hutton, with whom she had been brought up for some years as a child, and who was a familiar and intimate figure in his home. Although the General may never have urged Norman to follow him into the 60th Rifles and although his parents would probably not have favoured such a course, there was here a natural source of interest in the Army as a career. It may be an indication of this interest that in January 1894, almost as soon as he was settled in work in London, he took a commission in the Militia as 2nd Lieutenant in the 4th Battalion of the Bedfordshire and Hertfordshire Regiment.

Again, when he came to visit America a few years later, he found there a congenial society and outlook. But there is no evidence that he ever seriously thought of any career except the one that opened naturally before him as the eldest son of a partner in Martin's Bank, and the grandson of the leading English partner in an international banking house. The only question was whether he would choose deposit banking or international banking. After some months in the Lombard Street office of Martin's he was sent to Paine's branch of Martin's in Sittingbourne, and after a few months' experience there was brought back to the main office. But his choice, whether the experience in Martin's enabled him to make up his mind or was merely part of his training after he had made it up, was to go into Brown Shipley. He entered the office in Founders Court in 1894.

Brown Shipley was a natural choice : its field was international, and it offered prospects of travel. But although Norman was probably more attracted by international financing than by deposit banking, there were domestic influences at work which may have been decisive. Sir Mark Collet's only son had to leave England because of his wife's health, and could not succeed his father. Norman was devoted both to his grandfather and to his step-grandmother, and he slipped naturally into the position of being almost their son and his grandfather's successor. Their house, St. Clere, took precedence of his father's house, Moor Place, as his home.

For a person of Norman's eager and expansive energy, there were, as it turned out, two drawbacks in his new work. Since Brown Shipley in London were mainly engaged in giving acceptance credits to American customers of Brown Bros. in New York, most of the interesting and responsible work of examining applications and gauging credit-worthiness fell to the New York partners. Still, Brown Shipley were in no way limited to work originating in this way ; there was room for a partner with the necessary enterprise and a knowledge of languages to extend their connections to other countries ; while the American connection provided a solid basis and an assured income for expansion. The other drawback was the age of his new associates.

The firm was still a leading house in the great acceptance business carried on by London. It had been for years now completely divorced from the actual handling of merchandise in which it originated ; and it had not yet begun the transition to the general provision of capital, especially by the handling of new long-term issues, which the older and larger of the other merchant-bankers in London had made, and the New York house of Brown Bros. had begun. Its standing remained high, and Collet's position in the City lent it prestige. But at the moment of Norman's entry it was rather in the trough into which any institution falls when one generation is near its end and a new generation has not arisen. The partners in 1895 — that is to say, the London partners, though by the constitution of the firm the London and New York partners were all partners in both houses — were F. A. Hamilton, eighty-one years of age and not to retire for another eight years, a man of forceful character, who had brought to the firm in its commodity-handling days a vast experience of the raw cotton trade both in the Southern States of America and Liverpool; Collet, aged seventy-nine, who retained his partnership till his death in 1905; Frederick Chalmers, fifty-nine, who had left Cambridge, where he was preparing for Orders, for the Army at the outbreak of the Crimean War, served through that war and through the Indian Mutiny, and, returning to civilian life in 1861, joined Brown Shipley and became a partner in 1869, a brother-in-law of Collet's second wife, and a partner till his sudden death in 1898; and Alexander Hargreaves Brown, a great-grandson of the founder, fifty-one and a partner since 1875. Writing in 1909, the senior American partner, John Crosby Brown, gives as one reason for the harmony that characterised the relations between partners throughout the firm's history the fact that thirty-two of the forty-seven partners were either direct descendants or closely allied by marriage with descendants of the founder. The English branch of the family made but a small contribution to this impressive roll; although with one short interval it has always provided one of the partners, its interests have been divided between banking and public life. While the American Browns have staffed a business that extended from Baltimore to Philadelphia, Philadelphia to New York, and New York to Boston and Chicago, the English members of the family, contributing only five partners for the banking business, have provided Parliament with two Members and a Speaker, the Services with many officers, and the family with two baronetcies and a peerage. John Crosby Brown makes another comment:

As far as I have been able to ascertain, the two most important working partners of the Liverpool and London houses made but one brief visit to the United States after entering the firm. This was before 1862. . . . No international business can now be conducted with any degree of success without a constant interchange of partners.

When he began to work in London, Norman lived with his brother at 5 Sussex Square, their father's London house, and later in a large old rectory in Hackney; the rector, Lawley, afterwards Lord Wenlock, had married a sister of Norman's Eton tutor, and the Lawleys remained friends of Norman throughout their life. For a year he was being initiated into the routine of a banking house. It was necessarily dull; when he had spent some time in America and came back to presumably more responsible work he still found it unsatisfying. Even so, he did not wish the arrangement by which his place was in London altered; but he would be 'glad of something to do in London, besides keeping a high stool warm'.

In September 1895 he went to New York into the office of Brown Bros. Thatcher M. Brown, who came into the firm a year later, and after fifty years still remembered his kindness in showing him the way about his work, recalled that Norman, being an Englishman living away from home, began with a stipend of $500 a year, whereas he himself had only $250. The process of routine initiation was continued; it does not seem to have been any more congenial in New York than in London, but he could look forward now to some experience in the Philadelphia and Boston offices of the firm, and to an extensive tour of the whole country. He was homesick and unhappy after his arrival, living in hotels or clubs; but very soon — as he wrote years after — he was 'gathered in from a miserable existence and welcomed at No. 42'. The benefactor was Eugene Delano, one of the New York partners; No. 42 was in Park Avenue, and the household consisted of 'a stern father, a holy and quite delightful mother' and five children. The Delanos had visited the Collets at St. Clere and Norman's friendship, especially with one of the sons, William Adams Delano, the architect, and a neighbour who was in and out of No. 42, Ruth Draper, lasted as long as he lived. He had many introductions; one of his first invitations was from the President of Columbia University, and his mother's relations, the Eyres, were living in the neighbourhood of New York. But his closest friendships were with his new colleagues in Brown Bros. and their families. One of them, James Brown Markoe, a man of his own age, found Norman still unsettled when he was back in a hotel, and took him off to live in his own home with his widowed stepmother. Here his only complaint was of excess of comfort, and the kindness of Mrs. Markoe was to last as long as they both lived. James Markoe was killed in 1902, stopping a pair of horses that had bolted: Norman stepped unconsciously into the place which he had held in Mrs. Markoe's affections, and continued to use her house, in New York or Bar Harbor, as a second, American, home so long as it was possible for him to visit America. In his first summer in America he joined the Staten Island Cricket and Baseball Club, and kept reports of cricket matches in the neighbourhood, but there is no record of his playing. He was becoming interested in American politics; he went to hear Bryan [1] speak, and sent home articles on the Trusts and on Morgans' relations with the U.S. Treasury.

The purpose of his visit to America was, first, to continue his training and to familiarise him with the methods and business of the firm, and, second, to give him an opportunity of seeing something of America. The first of these tied him to New York through most of 1896, though he was able to get away to visit his father's cousin, the Dean of Quebec. At the beginning of 1897 he was lunching with the Delanos, and took the opportunity to ask when he could expect to leave New York. He writes to his mother:

18 January 1897

Mr. Delano did not seem to think it could be arranged for about a fortnight: which disgusts me altogether. As long ago as the end of October, I was told I might expect to go away 'shortly': and in the meantime I was put with the Bookkeepers. Ever since then I have been simply hanging on from week to week, and now I have half a mind to pack up and go right away on my own account. The fact of the matter is that both Mr. Brown and Mr. Delano are literally so rushed every day and all day that they do not realise how I stand, although always willing to talk any matter over with me.

However, a fortnight later, he writes:

2 February 1897

I have started on my travels. I left New York early last Thursday with Mr. and Mrs. J. C. Brown and travelled via the Baltimore & Ohio Railroad to Washington, where we arrived about 6.30 P.M. nearly an hour and a half late.

[1] William Jennings Bryan, Presidential Candidate, 1908; U.S. Secretary of State, 1913–15.

At Washington I stayed at the Arlington Hotel, while the J. C. B.s stayed with some friends of theirs (the Fosters, Mr. F. was Secretary of State some years ago). That evening I went with Mr. Brown and Mrs. Foster to a 'Reception' given by the President and Mrs. Cleveland to Congress and the House of Representatives, which was interesting as showing one what the leading men in this country have to undergo, and because I met a number of interesting people. . . .

In Congress I heard a debate on International Bimetalism, a well-worn subject, but the statements made by some of the western Senators were almost more absurd than one would have supposed could come from sane men. In the House there was a debate on what is called the Union Pacific Railroad Bill: the point being whether or not the government should foreclose certain mortgages it holds on that property. The more honest of the members were in favour of the government parting with its rights for the highest figure obtainable. . . .

One sees numbers of people about, all of whom appear to be engaged on some important business: but on listening to their conversation (as one cannot fail to do in a hotel) it is evident that they have all come there with a definite object and that is to grind their axes on the government grindstone. . . .

I am told that the Arlington is the best hotel in Washington, but it is a very bad one. None of the bedrooms is heated, and as the thermometer was not far off zero each night I was there my room was unbearably cold. I came away at midday on Sunday and travelled to Grafton via B. & O. where I slept the night. I did this for two reasons, first because I wanted to see the country and line on which I was, and secondly because I did not wish to reach this place (Cincinnati) in the small hours of the morning.

Ten days later he was in California:

12 February 1897

I wrote to Gertrude [his sister] from New Orleans, at which place I spent several days and saw much that was new to me. It was pleasant to leave behind one the frost and snow which has been more or less continual for many weeks in the more northern states, and to step as it were into springtime. But even greater than that change has been the one from the South Eastern corner of this country to the Pacific Coast, where I am writing this letter.

I left New Orleans on Monday morning by a train known as 'Sunset Limited' on the Southern Pacific Railroad which runs through to San Francisco (about 2500 miles) in 74 hours. . . . To Houston the land is all cultivated, mostly cotton, sugar and rice, also a great quantity of water and forest (mostly pine). Houston is a large cotton market and somewhat of a busy place. From there to San Antonio there is a certain amount of cotton land but more pasture, huge numbers of cattle and horses to be seen. After that the country gradually becomes more barren, and there is less life and water about. . . . From El Paso for several hundred miles there is scarcely any vegetation to be seen, nothing but a sandy desert followed by a huge salt plain 260 feet below the sea. This was the most unpleasant part of the whole journey : it was very hot with a strong wind so that in places the track was covered with sand, which came into the cars in quantities as well as into one's mouth. . . . Somewhere about fifty miles from Yuma the desert suddenly comes to an end, the hills grow into snow-capped mountains and we passed into the San Gabriel Valley, all cultivated and full of fruit trees of all kinds. . . .

I have picked up one B—— of New York, a dyspeptic Jew, whose plans are much the same as my own, and unless we quarrel we shall probably spend the next ten days together. To-day we spent at Pasadena — about 12 miles from here. It is as lovely a spot as you can possibly imagine. To the north are snow-capped mountains perhaps 10 or 11 thousand feet high and only a few miles distant. To the east is a valley of fruit trees. To the south and west the Pacific distant perhaps 20 miles or thereabouts. Fruit trees are everywhere in abundance, huge crops of oranges and lemons just ready to pick (one can buy a dozen elegant oranges for 10 cents, and a dozen rather inferior ones for 5). Roses in full bloom, hedges of fuchsia and geranium, rows of palms of all sizes, to say nothing of cypress and many other trees whose names I do not even know. To-morrow or Saturday I mean to go down to San Diego for a few days, but I shall be in San Francisco about the 22nd of this month. . . . It seems clear that I cannot get off next Training, so I shall leave New York towards the end of next month. . . .

From San Francisco he writes :

24 February 1897

I have managed to get a very good idea of this city as well as of some of the surrounding country and have been trying to get some sort of an understanding of the various large interests which practically control the Railroads and a considerable part of

c

the rest of the business. There are a certain number of very rich men, who have mostly made their fortunes in the mining districts and now control almost everything that exists here, in one way or another. . . .

The people I have met here have all been most hospitable and have done everything to show me all there is to be seen : notably Capt. Oliver Eldridge (formerly a captain of the Collins Line between N.Y. and Liverpool, where he remembers Gpapa 'many many years ago'). . . .

I had intended leaving here to-night for Portland, but the train is so crowded that I cannot get a berth, so that I have to wait till to-morrow. And even then I have only done so thro' Capt. Eldridge, who is able to 'pull the inside wires'. In this country the ordinary mortal has not much chance, and I should never have got on as well as I have, unless I had been able to bring some influence to bear on such occasions as this.

From Oregon he again writes to his mother :

1 March 1897

Even a journey of only 36 hours (which here is considered of no importance) is enough to make me heartily sick of the cars. Of course one can get no exercise worth mentioning — the shaking is too great to allow one to read in comfort for any length of time : and if it is merely for the sake of killing time, one is apt to take three meals of sorts per day, where one would be more than enough. . . .

On account of the letters I brought with me, I can do and see all that there is to be done and seen hereabouts. My plan had been to go to Salt Lake to-morrow and thence to Denver : but I have changed this, and instead am going to give up a week to going over the Oregon Ry. and Navigation Co.'s property. B. B. & Co. have had something to do with this, and the President (tho' absent now) is a friend of Mr. J. C. Brown. So it seems to me an opportunity of seeing something of the inside working of a railway, which ought not to be missed, and I am to start out to-morrow morning in a private car with one or two of the company's officials and travel slowly over 1000 or 1500 miles of road, besides, I hope, seeing some of the mines in the district south of Spokane : (they are mostly in the State of Idaho). . . .

I have spent to-day in going over the railway shops and ware-houses, a new sawmill and a meat packing concern, so I have not been idle.

You must excuse me for having written so much 'shop' to you in this letter, but for some reason I had it in my mind that I was writing to Father. . . .

His trip ended on March 17.

18 March 1897

My travels came to an end yesterday when I came in from St. Louis, and was quite glad to be at rest once again. . . . I am certain that it was my best plan to have made some such trip : rather than to remain in the office here, or elsewhere. If I have done no more, I have at any rate learnt some geography — a more necessary knowledge than most people imagine.

Mr. Brown has spoken to me at length on the subject of my going to work with B. S. & Co. and I am glad to find that the plan is quite approved of here. I shall to-day go and see about a state room on some steamer returning within the next week or so.

. . . As nothing definite has been settled about my coming back here, I shall bring over all my belongings. . . . It is difficult to realise that my long stay here is so nearly at an end, and tho' I shall be glad to be in England again I cannot help wishing that I was going to stay here a little longer and then to have done, once and for all, with this sort of wandering life. . . . There are very few people in this country whom I shall be sorry not to see again for the present, but these have been so kind to me right along that I cannot help being sorry at having to run away, after having — so to speak — got all the good out of them I can! . . . On looking over the notes I made during my travels I find that I was away (roughly speaking) 950 hours, of which 450 were spent on the trains. I travelled about 11,600 miles, and spent about $12 per day. . . .

April came before Norman left New York. It was necessary for him to return to England to fulfil his obligation to put in a period of training as a Militia officer. In June he took the necessary examination, and was gazetted Captain on July 21. His bank training was complete, and it was arranged before he left America that he should take his permanent place on the staff of the London house. On September 3 he was given a limited power of attorney, but at the beginning of October he was sent back to America, partly to work in other offices of the firm, partly to extend his travels in America. In the latter half of October he was living with the Markoes, finding the 'rush

and bustle' of New York very trying; he could not go his own
pace.   His first visit was to the Boston office, where he spent
three weeks, interrupted by a trip on a private railway car to
Bangor via Portland, Maine.   He was interested and picked
up a good deal of information; but he confessed to a great
desire to borrow a rifle and go off shooting the deer and
moose.

Before Christmas, which he spent with the Dean in Quebec,
he got in another trip to the south with one of the partners in
Brown Bros., Charles Dickey, as companion.   Their first day
they spent looking over Richmond, 'a picturesque town, with
many old English-looking houses, crooked streets and idle
inhabitants'; he found the memory of the Civil War a good
deal fresher there than in most places.   In the evening they
met the President of the Chesapeake and Ohio Railway, and
travelled with him to Newport News, Norfolk, back to Richmond and slowly to Cincinnati.   There the President left them;
Dickey and Norman went on to Louisville, and Norman with
the Manager of the Railway to Indianapolis — 'a regular
middle-western city, bustling and bitterly cold, being on the
edge of the prairie'.   Returning through Cincinnati to Hinton,
he spent some time going through the mines — entered by
lateral openings, not shafts, and free from gas, so that the miners
carried naked lights.   The working was easier than in England,
and the business a large and important one.   It was, he wrote,
a most interesting trip in which he saw a lot of new country;
moreover they made one very comfortable in a private car.
The New Year found him in Philadelphia.

3 January 1898

We are back at work again, with things going on as usual.
I am only too glad to have it so, for holidays and the like which
upset one's natural manner of living, and after taking away one's
usual occupation, give one nothing instead, are to my mind an
abomination.

On January 11 he writes:

On Saturday afternoon I went over to New York and spent
the night with Mrs. Markoe.   I had arranged that Adam Delano
should come here and spend the Sunday with me (this being his
old home), but Mrs. Markoe was so pressing.   She is always

wonderfully kind to me, and if I was her nearest relative she could scarcely try to make me more at home than she does. . . .

I like Phila. well enough, but so far have made no acquaintances. This is my own fault entirely, because there are some half dozen people I ought to go and see. But I find something to do at the Office, and generally stay there till rather late when I go to the Club and have dinner. Paying calls would mean going back to the hotel and changing clothes. I am a 'guest' at the Rittenhouse Club, very comfortable and with an excellent library where I always sit. It is not the *swell* club here, but I much prefer it. Next Monday I expect to go up to Cleveland for two or three days. . . .

On February 10 he was able to begin his new trip south. Beginning again with Norfolk, he travelled inland to Columbus, Ohio, and then by Roanoke to Charleston and on to the Florida coast. He found the continuous travelling really hard work, but very interesting, and necessary if he was to see all he wished to see. Though he was 'so busy cramming his head' that he could think of nothing but the journey, it was not only the business aspects that impressed him:

17 February 1898

It is curious to see the difference between the people in this part of the country and those farther North and East, where I have lately been living and travelling — almost everyone has time to spare here, and whether what they may be doing is finished to-night or to-morrow seems to make very little difference. This I suppose is due chiefly to two causes. First, the fact that until thirty years ago the blacks were the only people who ever did any work, and the idea that other people are not supposed to work has not yet died out. Second, the fact that comparatively speaking this is a warm — if not a hot climate. (For instance, when I was in Norfolk on Saturday, it was so warm that one was glad to take the shady side of the street.) There are I suppose other reasons than these two, but these are probably the chief ones: of course a long settled (and for the time being perhaps a 'played out') country is naturally less industrious than a new one. . . .

St. Augustine was the limit of his travels, though he thought of crossing to the Gulf of Mexico on his way north again. Life in a luxurious watering-place oppressed him.

For an individual travelling alone, and rather hurriedly, there is no pleasure to be got out of most places, and my only object in coming here is to get an idea of the country and its geography. The hotels are in their way magnificent. . . . The residents are all divided up into fashionable sets, having daily parties. . . . Personally I hate the life, and neither know nor want to know the people.

He was back in Philadelphia on March 11, after being away four weeks, sick of travelling, and disappointed at missing several of the people he wanted to see and the information they could have given him.

Just before he set out for the south he had heard from home that Collet was ill, and that he might be needed at St. Clere. His answer reveals how close his relations with his grandfather were :

I am sorry to hear how badly things have gone. The illness itself is of course painful, but I should not wonder if the rest it is causing did him good in a general way. (This sentiment is rather on the lines of 'every cloud has a silver lining', a platitude I detest. But what I mean is that Gpapa is such an unrestful man as a rule that *anything* to make him keep quiet for a time is an advantage.)

I agree with you that it seems as if I ought to be at St. Clere ; in fact I am willing to come back now if it is *really* necessary. But of course I could not live at St. Clere and attend to my work at the same time. In fact I do not expect to keep that up even in summer, another time.

You may or may not know that I have a standing promise made to Gmama, that in case of any mishap to herself, I will at once go and live with Gpapa, wherever he may be. . . .

I am gradually spending all my substance on this hotel life, and shall be glad when the time comes for one to make some change. . . .

It was not necessary for him to return ; but it appears that Collet took steps to assure or improve Norman's position. Some time in the following year, possibly in anticipation of his admission to partnership, Collet gave him £18,000 (later deducted from his share, one-twelfth, of Collet's residuary estate) ; but he was a long way from such responsibilities in February 1898. Writing from Charleston, 'a pretty old town, very quiet and sleepy and dilapidated, many fine old houses but few of them in good repair', he says :

24 February 1898

I am sorry to hear how gloomy things look at St. Clere, and it makes me half inclined to come back to England at once. . . .

I hear by this mail, too, that the Training will not take place until August. From my own point of view this is a great advantage, and my inclination is to remain in this country several months longer than I had expected. There is always work to be done either in Philadelphia or N.Y., and one can learn something and perhaps be of some use, which is almost more than is possible in Founders Court. . . .

Please tell Father that I am writing to-day to Grandpapa in reply to his letter. I am of course very grateful for what he has done, but there is no reason for supposing it alters my position for the present. In fact I don't in the least want it altered. . . .

As soon as he got back to Philadelphia he was brought over at short notice to New York, to take the place of James Brown whose father was very ill; there, he wrote, he was certain to be hard at work all the time, whereas in Philadelphia he could more or less choose his own work.

His obligation to attend camp as a Militia officer was not the only reason why Norman had to curtail his American travels and return to London in the summer of 1898. Collet's health was uncertain, and Norman's special relations with him made return advisable. With his return his apprenticeship may be taken to end. He did not go back to America until the autumn of 1899, and went then, not as a learner but as a responsible officer of the firm. He had settled down in Founders Court, and on 1 January 1899 was given a full power of attorney to sign for the firm. He could no longer complain that there was nothing for him to do. In after years he used to look back on his early life in America as the happiest part of his working life, and to speak as if he would have been happier if he had settled in that country. One remark has had wide currency — that he would never have left America but for the call of the South African War. In old age he doubted whether he ever made that remark, and explained it, if he did, as one of the irresponsible things said in youth which are not to be taken seriously. His own letters show that he encountered in America the same delay, frustration and tedium as ardent and ambitious youth encounters in entering any established and conservative organisation in any country, and that he never contemplated seriously anything except a career in Founders Court. His residence was not continuous; he returned each summer for military training; and he had to press, in New York as in London, for opportunities of escape from the routine of office training.

Nevertheless, it is evident that America made a great and lasting impression on him and did much to form his interests and character. Once he had got over his homesickness, he found American society congenial, and throughout his life as a private banker — and after — he grasped every opportunity of resuming and extending his American friendships. He met in America for the first time a rapidly expanding community, saw the development taking place over a whole continent, met the men who were responsible for that development, handled the financial documents which arise from the movement of commodities and visited the areas where the commodities were produced. There was more variety and a wider range of social background in the set of American friendships he formed, and he may well have felt that America was a country in which he could have sent down roots.

Most of all he learned by experience American ways of banking and doing business, American habits and ways of thinking, and met many of the men who were to shape American banking in the new century. He had already done much to safeguard himself from the greater criticism that John Crosby Brown had brought against his London seniors, and he was to make any such reproach impossible by the frequency and the importance of the visits he made to America when he became a partner in the firm. His training and experience may have had an influence outside his own firm. When he became Governor of the Bank it was still narrowly English in its organisation and outlook; one of the great changes he was to make was to link it with other Central Banks throughout the world, to encourage the promising members of the younger staff to travel, and to provide it with a permanent corps of officers who knew other countries, because they had lived and worked in them.

(iii)

On 22 September 1899 Norman wrote from his father's town house to his mother:

It has been decided today that I am to go out to America at the end of next month, to be back by Christmastime: I shall not do any work there (worth speaking of) but shall have to go for a few days both to St. Louis and Pittsburgh which will mean a certain amount of travelling. I am convinced that this is a wise use to make of my holiday (which will be longer than it would be if I were to stay in England).

He sailed from Liverpool on November 1. In the interval war had broken out in South Africa, and, even if he had not already arranged to do so, he would have found it necessary, as a Militia officer, to get back to England in December. A story which was current in the City when Norman was Governor of the Bank gives a picturesque account of his joining up. He was, it ran, visiting Montreal on business, when he saw a troop of volunteers for service in South Africa marching to the docks. This so excited him that he went straight back and finished his business, took the first steamer home and enlisted. But for this 'call' of his country, he would, it is added, never have returned. Evidence to the contrary has already been given: as a Militia officer he would realise that his battalion was likely to be embodied, and would welcome the opportunity of service overseas if it came.

His battalion was in fact embodied early in January 1900; the commanding officer was Lord Cranborne, later Marquess of Salisbury, who remained 'Colonel' to Norman for the rest of his life. The battalion unanimously volunteered for foreign service a few days later, and was moved to Beggars' Bush Barracks in Dublin to await embarkation. It illustrates the difference between the world in which he was brought up and that of to-day that he took his own (civilian) servant with him: he realised quickly that a barracks was no place for such a man and substituted one from his company. There was not enough to occupy him, and he was worried over his lack of experience. It was in fact greater than that of most of the officers: his own subaltern, Barton, with whom he kept in touch till he was killed

in the First World War, had just left school and joined only
the day before they left Dublin. 'Nothing could have been
more fortunate', he wrote, 'than these first few weeks of my
new career' : he was wonderfully well and, because they were
short-handed and his senior officer ill, he enjoyed an exceptional degree of responsibility. After a month in Dublin transport became available and the battalion sailed from Queens-
town on February 27. They coaled at Teneriffe and reached
Capetown on March 20. Even then they had to wait three
days before they could dock and entrain.

Before Norman's battalion sailed the news was known of
the British reverses with which the war opened — the defeat
and investment in Ladysmith of the main British force in the
east, the investment of Mafeking and Kimberley in the west
and the defeat at Colenso of Buller's attempt to relieve Ladysmith. On the other hand, they left just as Roberts's reorganisation and strategy began to show results. His plan was completely successful : Kimberley and Ladysmith were relieved,
the way to Bloemfontein opened and Cronje forced to surrender
at Paardeberg. The relief of Ladysmith came on February 28,
the day after the battalion sailed, Paardeberg on the 29th;
they would hear the news at Teneriffe. The organised Boer
forces were broken down : Mafeking was relieved on May 17,
Johannesburg occupied on May 31 and Pretoria on June 5.
But resistance did not cease, as had been hoped, when both
capitals were occupied : nor when the largest remaining
army under Botha was defeated at the end of August and, a
month later, the formal annexation of the Transvaal was proclaimed. The Boers turned to guerrilla action, which was not
crushed for another eighteen months. Even in the north
of Cape Colony it was necessary to guard communications,
while in the Transvaal and Free State a regular military
occupation of the whole country was needed. Opposition
continued to flare up, and raiding commandos attacked
isolated posts, recruited 'pacified' farmers and intercepted
supply columns.

The 4th Bedfords, as soon as they could be landed, were
sent straight up to Kimberley to join the 9th Brigade. On
arrival Norman found that the commanding officer was his
mother's cousin, General Hutton ('quite the General — asking

all sorts of questions we would rather have left unsaid. But
we all liked him'). The battalion was divided into four companies of which Norman was given one. The newly arrived
units were being moved up to replace more seasoned troops
needed nearer the active front, and Norman was sent to War-
renton on the Vaal River. It was a real initiation, because it
was the northernmost post towards Mafeking, and the Boers
still held the opposite bank. In a few days he was moved back
to Belmont, and thence detached to take charge of a township
called Richmond about fifteen miles west. Here, in addition
to his own company, he had under him 50 mounted infantry
of the Munster Fusiliers and two guns of the Cape Artillery.
Richmond was the Headquarters of a district through which
much of the traffic from the Cape to Kimberley and the
Western Transvaal had to pass.

For seven weeks Norman ruled his territory under martial
law. Most of the farmers in it had been in the field with the
invading Boers, and he suspected their sympathies still. Frequently there were incursions of Boer patrols, which he was
seldom quick enough to intercept. Rebels, who had been
released and returned to their farms, had to report periodically
and could not move about without a pass ; so he held a court
most mornings to administer the oath of loyalty and to hear
applications to move, which 'on the general principle that the
applicants would be safer at home' he generally refused. Occasionally he routed out a suspect, or sent out a patrol through
part of the district ; but the position was delicate, because the
farmers were more afraid of the Boers than of the British, and
anxious not to offend them. The natives were another problem
— for the same reason — and it was impossible to prevent
information leaking out through them.

His work must have been satisfactory, because first his
Colonel, and then Sir Charles Warren,[1] visited him and found
everything to their satisfaction. Increasingly he was occupied
with forwarding and contributing to the transport — mainly
ox-wagons — moving up into the Transvaal. It was not till
the end of May that he received orders to rejoin the rest of the
battalion at Fourteen Streams. With the advance of the
British forces to Johannesburg, his post was no longer important,

[1] Commanding 5th Division, South Africa Field Force.

while men were needed to occupy the Transvaal farther
north. He rejoined the battalion to find that two companies
were detached farther north and that out of 24 officers
originally there were left no major and only 3 captains and 6
subalterns. He gives his own reflections on his first independent command :

Richmond becomes a place of the past and . . . I am glad
of it. But I had an interesting time there and have had an insight
into this war as far as the rebels are concerned which I could have
had nowhere else. Moreover, I have been my own master in a
small way — 150 men and 2 guns — which has been a new experience. Happily I have kept out of scrapes with the authorities. . . .
A big toad in a small puddle is an entertaining position and teaches
one more than its reverse.

At Fourteen Streams he was in contact once more with
friends. His letters have more comments on the political than
the military situation. Apart from a couple of patrols he has
little to do. The dust is trying, but

I am so abominably well that nothing makes any difference to
me. I must have been made for some such life. Since I was in
Switzerland I have hardly ever *felt* what it was to be as well as I
was then and am now, and in spite of a mixed and curious diet and
lots of exercise, I fear I am getting fat. I have certainly a straggling
and unkempt beard — too long to be tidy.

On June 10 he was detached from the battalion again.
With his old company enlarged (100 men and 2 subalterns)
he was ordered up the line where there had been some disturbances. As far as Christiana he had a similar company of
King's Own Scottish Borderers with him ; they were to stay
in Christiana while he went on after a while to occupy Bloemhof. 'I feel I am extremely lucky', he said. 'There will be
lots to do and it will be satisfactory to be some 60 miles in the
Transvaal.' Norman reached Bloemhof on June 24 — at the
head of a caravan consisting of 101 men, 3 officers, 1 guide,
2 wagon-conductors, 14 natives, 4 telegraphists and part of a
repairing party ; also 7 ox-wagons, 1 ammunition cart, 1 mule-
wagon and 1 water-cart and 3 horses. It was only a large
village but was the market and administrative centre of a

district some 900 square miles in extent, lying well to the east of the railway line but on the road to Johannesburg and Pretoria. He found it completely severed from the rest of the country, so the telegraph was quickly restored and a post established. The farmers offered no resistance to being disarmed, turned in arms and made their declarations of neutrality very readily : they were sick of the war and reassured by the British treatment of them. Life 'in detachment' was more interesting and supplies better than at Headquarters. Some extracts from letters give the best description :

June 26

We made quite a discovery to-day, a dozen or so rifles etc. just behind the Magistrate's House, he having been yesterday (by way of) helping me to get together all arms, concealed or not, and having signed a declaration that he had no arms and knew of none concealed. What he now says is that his wife had hidden them, 'in case the English should find them'. Of course the information came through natives : it certainly seems that if you only frighten them they will tell all or more than they know. We also found 50 sacks of tobacco belonging to the Transvaal Govt. when we searched the same man's house. I have now on hand about 100 horses and cattle, part belonging to Transvaalers and part looted by them . . . in a short time I shall have enough decent horses to mount about 10 of our own men and do some patrolling.

June 27

I seldom go out, as I am busy as policeman, magistrate, postmaster, customs officer or something of the sort. The question of the future here does not appear to me so difficult and complicated as in the Colony, partly because the men are not all, or any of them, rebels, and therefore can be treated as a whole : and partly because complex questions of compensation etc. do not arise.

On the whole it really seems that, when once they see we mean them no harm, these Transvaalers dislike us less than our own colonists. Certainly in my small circle I am finding them easier to deal with. . . .

It seems to me the authorities are showing great wisdom in simply planting down people in the sort of position I am in, and leaving them to 'paddle their own canoes'. Beyond the very broadest instructions, one is left entirely alone. In fact the freedom, in some respects, is almost (if anything) too great, for, I imagine, one is liable to be called to account for any mistake or misdeeds.

Things were not, however, so easy as they seemed at first. If many rifles were given up, many were held back. The discovery and collection of arms was a continuous task, effective only when patrols could be organised. There was a stream of refugees, ordered north by the Boers and now returning, or making their way back from dispersed commandos in the Free State. Norman collected their horses and rifles and took away cattle or sheep that he had reason to believe they had seized elsewhere. The farmers did not wish to lose their horses, and he caught them turning in the same horse two or three times: after that he made his own brand and marked them all. Apart from arms and stolen property, he paid for everything and was quickly faced with the difficulty of finding money. British coinage was seeping in and there was some Boer coinage; but most holdings were in Dutch and Transvaal notes which were unacceptable. He sent one of his subalterns down to Kimberley with a few mounted men ('it seems rather swell to have our own mounted infantry, but it is just what we need') and succeeded in getting some money; but he had to use his own money to eke out official supplies. Once there was an adequate supply of currency, his government became 'a paying business — we fine evil-doers and pay salaries from the proceeds'. The reflux of natives was a problem; it was no use telling them to 'go home and keep quiet', because the farmers, their employers, could not pay them, and they had nothing to eat. He found a settler of French descent, who spoke their language and seemed reliable, and created an office of Assistant Commissioner for Natives for him.

Big as his district was, there was need of co-operation with the adjoining districts, and trouble if they dealt, whether with the white or the native residents, on different lines; accordingly he got hold of his neighbouring commissioner and agreed common principles with him. His neighbour, he thought, 'simply tyrannised over the inhabitants. He makes out that I am much too soft and lenient and I am afraid he is right; but to me it is almost impossible to treat men, well beaten, as if they were dogs.' The most difficult task was again dealing

with complaints of natives against farmers and farmers against
natives. The chief work of the daily 'court' was dealing with
the charge of concealing arms; the more substantial residents
were the chief offenders. A little later he writes:

July 20

I have told you before that I hate the Boers: but gradually I
believe they are getting to like me. At first they were mostly
afraid to come into the office: now they are beginning to troop
in: men, women and children at once, sometimes. And they
come a long way to ask the most absurd questions you can imagine:
most of which have *no* answers.

The duties of the post were not confined to disarming and
administering the neighbourhood. Headquarters had an insatiable hunger for remounts. Since to deprive a Boer of his
horse was as effective as depriving him of his rifle, Norman
could meet this demand with enthusiasm, only keeping back a
few horses for his own company. When the needs of the troops
round Pretoria led to demands for oxen as well, he obeyed
orders, but it went against the grain, because he saw they
would be needed to get the farms working again.

One of the attractions of a settled post was that occasionally
he could take out a gun. There was any amount of game —
buck, and korhaan and other birds — which he described for
his father's benefit, as he does, too, the plants. He had the
chance of turning some of his men into mounted infantry. At
first they cannot be so described: 'six of our men on horses —
I can't put it otherwise'; a fortnight later 'For the much
despised Militia, I think we are doing rather well — the men
now ride quite decently, and any sort of horse'. But it was the
work and the climate that made the life:

July 16

We have been soldiering exactly 6 months. It has done me
more good than anything and I wish it could last six years. The
difference in one's health, temper and spirit between this life and
England is beyond description.

He succeeded in getting up from Kimberley one 'store'
which gave him much satisfaction. He had commented on
the patience of his men; less well-clad for the climate, fed on
food they were not used to, living in tents in continuous wet

weather, they never complained; hardest of all, they were deprived of their accustomed comfort, beer, and given no substitute. Now he was able to get up for them a barrel of beer.

Even to Norman, remote from the main centres of activity, it seemed ridiculous to suggest that any troops could be withdrawn at this stage in the war, but he did not foresee how suddenly and quickly the Boers could come back. On July 25 he heard by telegraph that they had reoccupied Klerksdorp, the next station north of his on the road to Pretoria, and seized a mass of stores; he had himself despatched only that day 300 cattle thither. He put the town in such a state of defence as was possible, and communicated with Kimberley; but no troops were available there for his part of the Transvaal. On July 31, after several false alarms, more credible reports came in of five to eight hundred Boers nearer Bloemhof. He had made preparations to withdraw and acted on them as his orders were in case of necessity to withdraw without fighting. He gave out that he was going up to a post five miles north-east, and did not leave till dark. After marching five miles N.E., he turned south on the road to Christiana, and marched through the night. He had left his mounted men near Bloemhof; they joined him at 7.30 A.M. with the report that all was clear; after two hours' rest they completed the thirty-three miles to Christiana by 1 P.M. In addition to the men and wagons he had taken out five weeks earlier, he brought back the loyalists, some wagon-loads of suspects, the cattle which had turned back from Klerksdorp, several hundred sheep and some horses. The stores he could not bring he had dumped in the river. From Christiana he wrote:

Whether I was right to leave Bloemhof or not is of course still a question and always will be, however the authorities may decide it. The sapper major here says I ought to have left 3 days earlier: and the supply people say I ought to have brought the stores along (in my trouser pockets, I suppose). Certain it is that there were Boers enough and near enough to cut me off altogether at any moment: and had they made a determined attack they must have got in to Bloemhof. The place is too large and straggling for 100 men to hold: and we had hardly any tools for making entrenchments (we are not much better off here).

Whether our retiring did more harm to the district than the chance of our being cut off by the Boers, I can't say. Had we been taken, it would have been a greater blow: had we kept them out when they came, the effect would only have told on the village, for they could have overrun all the rest of the neighbourhood.

Eager as he was to be given service with a Division, he had hoped to be allowed to 'finish the job' at Bloemhof. He bitterly resented the breakdown — or the over-confidence — which had forced him to withdraw, but he had done a good deal. He had disarmed and dismounted a large area; it was some consolation to learn at Christiana that there were three hundred Boers assembled near who could not move for want of horses. He had organised a military government; and, if it was a one-man government, it was probably the better for that. He had got on good terms with his 'subjects', without any dereliction from a rigorous conception of his duties. He had met the demands of his Headquarters for horses and cattle, kept his men in health and order, and — what pleased him most — taken the opportunity of creating the nucleus of a company of mounted infantry. This second experience of an independent command had been more exacting, and he had risen to its opportunities promptly, and without strain. His own master, with a good deal of riding in a climate that suited him, it is no wonder that he enjoyed the life.

He was to be kept five weeks in Christiana. At first the problem facing them was whether they could hold the town against attack. They had no guns, and Kimberley at first could spare them no help. They had no cavalry and were confined to the defensive; they could not ascertain what was the risk of attack, though they knew there was a Boer laager twenty-five miles away, and Boer scouts were continually paying them visits. They wired the town against night attack and then dug trenches and dug-outs to resist artillery. After a week or two their numbers were brought up to four hundred, and first a pom-pom and then a couple of guns brought in. The weather was unkind, gales driving dust and sand into everything until a torrential storm of rain flooded them out of their tents. Boer sympathisers dammed the irrigation channels and diverted the water into the dug-outs. The difficulty was that they were 'opposed not by an army, but by the population'.

D

Meanwhile the Headquarters of his battalion was at Mafeking; drafts had been sent out to bring its strength up and Norman had let the colonel know how much he wished to rejoin. On September 5 orders reached him to join the battalion with his company and he arrived at Mafeking on September 11.

This second phase of his South African experience — 'the dull routine of battalion orders' — was to last six months. Mafeking was serving as a base for Methuen's force as he moved up and down the Western Transvaal, endeavouring to suppress the scattered resistance that had broken out again. So rapid and unpredictable were the Boer Commando movements that a garrison was necessary, outposts had to be manned, and the surrounding country patrolled. In addition there was a continual movement through the place of drafts coming up, sick and wounded sent back and supplies coming through. The Bedfords provided about half this garrison: the battalion was continuously short of officers, especially officers of any experience, so that the work if dull was exacting. In Mafeking the period he enjoyed most was a month when he was acting as adjutant and assistant to the commandant of the camp:

A good deal of writing to do, our own parades to attend (when we have any), outposts to arrange and visit, and the incoming and outgoing of drafts to arrange for. . . . I like the work immensely and have managed fairly well so far. . . . Busy all day, literally from 6 A.M. till mess at 6.35 P.M., and again for an hour afterwards. This just suits me, and I can't help wishing . . . I should get job of adjutant permanently. I was miserable here as long as I had only half enough to do; now I am as happy as a King with almost too much. It only shows to what an extent one's so-called happiness depends upon occupation irrespective of place and people.

The climate lent interest, and discomfort, to the life. In the hot weather in which he arrived, the high winds made dust a continuous irritation. Before the rains came the damp heat made life a continuous discomfort. The officers dealt with it characteristically. They cleared (with prisoners' labour) a pitch for cricket and polo, and later on hockey:

1 October 1900

I have been bold enough to play in a cricket match to-day. Garrison v. Mafeking: we got badly beaten though I'm not sure that we were really the worst side. I scored well in one way and another — a black eye, a cut knuckle, sore knee, several on the thigh and 45 runs.

The polo was not expert: he wishes he had learned the game years earlier. Few of the players and none of the ponies had played the game before, and accidents were numerous. Another resource was jackal-hunting: they had formed a pack of mongrels (which they fed better than they fed themselves) with which they hunted, but seldom caught, jackals and any other game that offered. Norman had quickly slipped into the colonial habit of using his pony for the shortest errands; the climate had cured him of his habit of walking. The wet weather interrupted all sport; it cleared the air, but caused continual trouble, flooding the camp, sometimes laying the tents flat and reducing the whole area to a swamp. Not knowing how long the battalion was to stay there, they could not incur the expense of permanent arrangements, and continued to live in tents. It was a great luxury when Norman got a tent to himself.

The influence of the General Election in the autumn of 1900 reached remote Mafeking. Cranborne, the colonel of the 4th Bedfords, was included in the new administration, and left them on November 3. It was a loss to Norman, who had a great respect for him and had worked happily with him. It also left the battalion even more undermanned than before; a few weeks later, with one captain acting as commanding officer, one with another unit and two away sick, Norman was the only captain still available for ordinary duties. The additional work suited him, and he continued to escape the illness to which so many succumbed, with the exception of toothache. He recurs to the idea of settling in South Africa. He could get now a quasi-military job, which might not come so easily later; for example he could get a £800-a-year post in the South African constabulary being formed, which some of his men were joining. But when challenged by his father, he had to reply as before:

October 28

I don't suppose I really am thinking of remaining out here permanently. I agree with Father that I am really not free to do so, having allowed myself to become 'attached' in England. My ties there of course I do not regret and I should have been a fool, at the time, had I not taken my opportunity. But it was taken more or less in ignorance, for I did not realise until quite lately how unwell one generally is in England and how well one can be elsewhere. I admit of course that my relative position in England is far far better than it would be (or could be for many years) in S.A. But in time I suppose one rises in S.A. as elsewhere. 'Let come what come may' I shall come home when the time arrives, just as if there had been no attraction in the veldt, and no doubt it will in many ways be a great pleasure to be back in England.

Even in this routine life, however, camp was not permanent. On 4 January 1901, while he was getting up, a most unexpected order arrived to get ready to go to Bulawayo and relieve the mounted men there. Headquarters remained in Mafeking; he was to take half the battalion, and as many officers as could be spared. He left Mafeking next day with 250 men and 5 officers. Arrived at Bulawayo he found that they would be, in a short time, the only troops left in Rhodesia, and what was left of the Rhodesian Field Force was being demobilised and dispersed. He regretted Mafeking and the life into which he had fitted himself; he resented being sent quite out of the sphere of any possible soldiering. However, he appreciated the promotion to an independent command again, and — his usual recipe for content — he was presently completely absorbed in work.

The camp was in great disorder and his tidy military mind could not tolerate it. He set himself to improve his force; managed to get hold of a couple of maxim guns after a lot of correspondence; set about raising a mounted infantry company, as he did at Bloemhof, 'but on a larger scale', and secured a promise of horses. It was cooler than in Mafeking; it was possible to get some polo and cricket, and the men, and he hoped the officers too, became entitled to an addition to their pay on January 16 when they had served a year. 'For me', he says, 'it has from the beginning been an *annus mirabilis*, for I have never before been so continuously well and so congenially employed.'

This episode ended as unexpectedly as it began. On January 28 orders came to return south. The rest left, but Norman was stranded in hospital with a mild attack of dysentery. He had escaped the disease hitherto, and could not understand what caused it. He was lucky in the care of a first-rate doctor in whom he had confidence. On February 10 he was able to leave and travel comfortably back by himself to Mafeking. There he found that Boers had recently penetrated the camp and got away with 80 head of cattle. The defence was reorganised ; the mounted men were put together, and the forts and outposts manned by the infantry were moved farther out and enlarged. A tedious and uncomfortable couple of months followed. It was a monotonous life, twenty hours of the twenty-four on outpost duty for four weeks on end, and wet more often than dry. At the end of it, early in April, he had a slight return of dysentery, but thought nothing of it, as such a return was usual. Possibly more serious was a severe chill, such as he had not had before, which 'got hold of him inside'. He expected to be well again as soon as the rains stopped. He mentioned a personal loss :

One of my ponies, Jock — you have probably heard of him — died yesterday of this *infernal* horse-sickness, a complaint which no one even pretends to understand, and for which there is no cure or adequate safeguard known. I'm sorry about him, for he was a good little pony, most friendly, nice to ride, especially at polo. In fact we were great friends, for ponies here become much more friendly and *personally* amiable than at home ; one 'lives' with them so much more and passes by them so many times a day, and they always have something to say.

Then, without notice — as usual — he was faced with another change.

April 10

I have rather fallen on my feet to-day. On Friday I am to come off outpost and take over the Mounted Infantry which are being somewhat increased. They will, I hope, include all the mounted men here, except Police and Yeomanry, possibly 170 or thereabouts, of whom upwards of 100 belong to this Battalion. This is certainly better than going on with humdrum existence, as one has had to do since coming back from Bulawayo. It means, too, a lot of new stuff to learn and something new to think about, besides endless patrolling, etc.

This change of duties was a just reward of foresight and persistent effort to make the necessary preparation. As soon as he was on his own responsibility, nearly a year earlier at Bloemhof, he had seen that Mounted Infantry were going to be the chief need in the type of war then opening, and he had formed a small troop there. When next he held a separate command, in Bulawayo, he set about forming a Mounted Infantry Company. It was only fair that he should be given the command, but he was still doubtful whether he would be given the opportunity of using his Mounted Infantry for its proper purpose. Large numbers of new Yeomanry were coming into Mafeking. They were quite inexperienced and untrained, and were left in the town for training. He feared that the Bedfords would be left to do this training in the intervals of their 'everlasting patrolling'. Already they had had to go down and detrain the new Yeomanry's horses, because the latter had shown themselves quite incapable of doing it for themselves. His fears were confirmed when orders came for all mounted men, except the new Yeomanry and the Bedfords, to join Methuen. Within a week, however, after an expedition towards Zeerust, he got back to find Methuen in Mafeking again, and to learn that his company was to go out with Methuen in two or three days. From the middle of April until he had to leave his unit through illness in October, he was to be moving continuously about with one or other of Methuen's columns.

Methuen's was one of four or five commands in central and western Transvaal. They were engaged in continual sweeps through the country between the garrisoned towns, picking up small parties of Boers, cutting off their supplies and destroying crops and farmhouses which might prolong resistance when winter came, and bringing the non-combatant population into refugee camps like Mafeking. Norman's new life began with a column, some 2000 strong, commanded by Colonel von Donop, which was trying to round up some Boers, and to collect their wagons and stock if, as was usually the case, it could not catch the Boers. They would set out as early as 4 A.M., march for six or seven hours, make a break for a meal and rest in the middle of the day, resume their march from 4 to 9 or 10 P.M. and then camp for part of the night. It was bitterly cold: Norman had never been so cold in his life; at night it was sometimes impossible to sleep, though the arrangements for camping and supplies were most effective. He enjoyed the life in spite of the cold. On one long march he surprised a party and took some twenty prisoners and the cattle they were moving. Von Donop, who was kind as well as efficient, must have mentioned this modest success to Methuen. Methuen was already interested in the Mounted Infantry, and had visited them and questioned the men in the course of their trek. Now, when they were waiting for another column, Norman writes:

May 25

I think we have managed to get into the General's good books, for he told me this morning he should keep us with him and if necessary send some Yeomanry to Mafeking to take our place; and I fancy he was quite pleased with our work the day before yesterday.

Norman did not mention in his letters at the time the incident which probably decided the General to keep them; but a report of it reached his parents, and he replied to their inquiries on August 8:

The story H. Ellis gave Father of this Mounted Infantry 'saving Methuen' is — like most yarns — rather exaggerated. The thing happened at Korannafontein at the end of May, if I remember right. The Yeomanry did run away and the Boers came up within 7 or 800 yards of Methuen on one side and of two guns on another, and I quite think my men helped to 'clear the air'. Anyhow the General appeared very pleased with us afterwards and had the Yeomanry before him next morning and gave them a piece of his mind. I think I told you this more or less at the time, but have no idea where Ellis got his news. Of course an episode is always liable to appear in a different light to different people: but I was pretty close when this one took place.

Thus at last he had achieved his ambition of 'active soldiering', in which his company's experience told, and they were more useful than the Yeomanry who had still their experience to get. Methuen, he guessed, was glad to have them, even if they were only eighty strong, and with the Australians, when there was anything to be done, they had to do it. They were, he thought, booked to trek with Methuen through the winter.

The broken country between the High and Low Veldt, now that the rain and warmer weather was bringing out the green, was the most beautiful he had seen. It was very difficult for a column to make its way through, particularly difficult for the Mounted Infantry out on the flank to keep in touch; and what constituted difficulty for the column was just what helped the Boers, who dogged them, sniping from the kopjes and ambushing fords and defiles. Methuen had Norman to dinner, asked after relatives of his and 'a lot of other questions'. 'I am no judge of Lord Methuen as a soldier,' he writes, 'but as a man he is kindness itself.' They were left in Zeerust for a few days when the division went on to the railway; it was a rest, and the weather was warmer, but Norman found that neither he nor his men could settle down after six weeks' continuous movement, while they could not ride outside the town without the risk of sniping. The proximity of Boers did not prevent a couple of games of football — soccer — the first he had played since preparatory school.

When his company rejoined the division, another difficulty came up with the Yeomanry. It was decided to merge all the mounted men — Yeomanry and Bedford M.I. — in a new regiment. The proposal was so unpopular with his men (his sergeants applied to be dismounted, and returned to the battalion) that he had to protest, and the scheme was dropped : the root of the trouble was the difference in pay. Back to Mafeking to collect stores and horses, to clear up his pay accounts, and to deal with a doctor who had, he thought, made a muddle of an injury to one of his men; back to Zeerust, and then back again with wagons and refugees to Mafeking.

July 16

I understand we shall lie here for a week and then start a long trek southwards. It's sure to be colder down there, so a week later will be an advantage. Moreover, it will give us a chance of 'getting square'. Everything — clothes, saddlery, horses and all we possess — get in such a mess and muddle on the move that a week off is a great blessing, if not an actual necessity. I hope also to be allowed to collect all my M.I. Coy together.

To-day if I am not mistaken finished 18 months during which I have done nothing but soldier. I feel a different person now to what I did at the beginning of that time, but tho' in many ways one enjoys the life one cannot help a sort of longing to be really comfortable again — or should I say luxurious? One looks ahead with something of dismay to the time when one will again have to 'settle down' to a civilised life again ! !

When the column moved again, he had collected his company.

July 26

I have quite a respectable little Company now — 3 Subalterns and 135 men all told with about 150 horses mostly very respectable animals. We are already on these abominable 'plains', just a little scrub here, but not a hill in sight of any size, clouds of dust and a cold wind. That's what it will be all the way down to S. Reneke, where rocks and kopjes begin again — and cold for certain: I like the country further north a great deal better.

Methuen was moving south, with von Donop to the west of him, towards Tamego. Boers were reported to be collecting on the west of the railway; but the chief object was to connect with General Featherstonehaugh for a sweep eastwards and north. It was very hard work for the Mounted Infantry.

July 27

This has been a miserable day. We started at 2 A.M. from Lichtenberg with the ox-convoy, nominally to do a short march. It was most horrid cold, so that I kept on cultivating icicles on my moustache, short as it is. We travelled easily enough for a few miles, then the road apparently crosses a 'vlei' or marsh. The first wagon was all but across when it must have got off the track. Anyhow it stuck. The next one tried to pass, but stuck too, and all the wagons behind, the longer they stood still the deeper they went. We all had to go and muddle about in the mud and water and to make a long story short (at least to us it seemed long) we didn't leave that place till 4 P.M. and then with many wagons in such a condition that they kept breaking down. Eventually between 8 and 9 P.M. we reached the camping ground.

. . . I'm almost too weary to write this evening: for really the way we are being worked is getting 'a bit thick'. Last night the Boers came and fired into camp and we had to get up and muddle about for an hour or two. Then we marched at 4 A.M. and surrounded a place called 'Damascus' by dawn, only to find that some 200 Boers had left while we were coming round. Then we came on some 16 miles (S) to Zoupan, camping at 3.30 P.M. We saw a certain number of Boers to-day who kept ahead of us and were all the time firing the veldt, thus making us wait once or more to get along.

The eastward and northward sweep took them forty miles north of Bloemhof past farms he had visited a year ago. There were Boers in front of them trying to take stock away for the winter; with four columns pursuing them, they had to sacrifice most of the stock and a few prisoners were taken, but the return seemed small for the effort and a small contribution to bringing the war to an end. Methuen's column collected 17,000 sheep, 2000 cattle, a few prisoners and wagons and the non-combatant inhabitants of farms. The greatest strain fell on the mounted men, sent out after every report of Boers — 'fifteen hours on the go, after four or five hours' sleep makes me feel a bit weary'.

They got a day's rest when the horses were knocked up; the General ordered a Church parade and explained to them the purpose and results of the trek, seemed very satisfied and was complimentary to Norman's company. They turned off to spend a week in Klerksdorp; all the columns had accumulated a mass of sheep, cattle, wagons and refugees, of which they wished to disembarrass themselves, and they needed remounts and clothes to replace the rags to which they were reduced. Norman took the opportunity to make up his pay-sheets; the men wanted money, and there was no paymaster, so that he had to draw £130 on a letter of credit of his own. While he dealt with the company's business he let his two subalterns take the opportunity of a daily train (eight hours) to visit Johannesburg.

From Klerksdorp the column moved west again, sniped at as it went along, and meeting parties of Boers when it got down again into the broken country of the Low Veldt. Once they succeeded for a change in ambushing a few Boers who were sniping at the column, by leaving behind a concealed force while the column went on. A few days later, for the first time, his letters admit the strain of the life: 'for the first time for several months I feel a rest is what one wants'. Instead of a rest he was confronted with a problem for which there was no satisfactory solution. The General sent for him and said he proposed to form a flying regiment of 500 mounted men to operate with the column but to be free to leave it in order to follow up the elusive Boer, and to put the Bedford mounted infantry in it; but there was a condition — they could not be released at a moment's notice if the battalion were ordered home. This was a great compliment, since the rest of the column were all picked men; but Norman felt bound to consult his men, who unanimously declared against anything that might interfere with their return. He had to report this to the General, who 'evidently thought us a pack of milksops' and might turn them off the column altogether. Norman himself, though he eagerly desired to form part of such a unit, felt he ought not to do anything to obstruct his return home; but apart from his personal inclinations, he feared that there would be trouble if his men were put into a unit in which all the other men were paid five times as much as they. His fears were justified.

On September 26 the General, at short notice, *ordered* them to join the flying column. Norman and his three subalterns of course accepted the change; but the men protested violently, burned the distinctive bands with which they were issued, got drunk and many of them disappeared. By dint of strenuous efforts all through the night, Norman collected them again and produced them when the column started; but his sympathies were with them, and his annoyance was not relieved when he was told that he would be held 'responsible' for any further trouble.

When he found the column was to spend a week or ten days in Mafeking he had applied for leave. There was nowhere to go, but he thoroughly enjoyed life as a sort of loafer, lying in his blankets till the sun was up and other luxuries. He was 'for the time being weary and sick of everything to do with men, horses, camps and treks'; 'perfectly well so far as health goes', but 'full-up and stale'.

On October 4 Norman admitted to himself, what he had only hinted at before, that he was ill.

October 4

It was a long day, and I confess that before we reached camp, I was quite knocked up. Indeed, for several weeks I haven't been really well, not half as well as all the rest of the time we have been out here — and tho' I have tried to take it easy, I haven't been able to do so. There has been one bother on the top of another all the while — immaterial in themselves perhaps, but none the less worrying.

So to-day I had to give myself over to the Field Hospital and that's where I am now. With luck 2 or 3 days' quiet will put me right. Don't think there's anything really the matter with me. I assure you there is not. Even the Doctor thinks I am a bit of a humbug, as I'm neither wounded, nor got Dysentery nor fever. It's just about two years this month since I felt like this — just before I went to the U.S. last time.

It seems to have been not dysentery this time but persistent gastritis. The open-air life and exhilarating climate of South Africa had swept away any remaining traces of his youthful delicacy for a year and a half; but the continuous strain of campaigning in heat and cold, dust and rain, with little sleep and indigestible food was too much even for the exuberant health he thought he had established. Though he did not realise it, this was the end of his military life.

The future of his company disturbed him. It was not the ordinary work of trekking and fighting — his juniors could deal with that as well as he : it was the possibility of a recurrence of the discontent he had had to deal with in Mafeking :

October 5–12

My M.I. Company has now been with Methuen for some 5 months and has, I am led to believe, done fairly well and earned a certain amount of credit. But questions — as I have already told you — have cropped up within the last three weeks which would or might have been serious had they spread further, and which were not stopped without some trouble and anxiety (on my part). . . . I do not wish to claim credit for managing these matters better than others. It's a question of experience and not of ability : besides that the men know me and that is to my advantage.

While he was in hospital he heard that, on September 4, he had been mentioned in despatches. He found it difficult to follow the principles on which the selection had been made. There should be no distinction, he thought, in having done one's ordinary duty, however arduous, but the number of names showed that this was not the principle followed. He concluded that he was mentioned because he was fortunate enough to be in a command which had been ready to delegate authority. He got more satisfaction from finding that of ten 'mentions' in the 4th Bedfords his company received five. A little later, November 1, he heard that he had been awarded the D.S.O., and this he found even harder to understand :

Wonders will never cease. I was a good deal shocked to find my name in Despatches : but this is still more surprising. So far as I know I have done nothing to merit such special reward. This much however I have done (tho' it was simply a part of my duty and what we all came out for). For 21 months I have done my best, as things came along — I have never shirked any work. I have at different times been more or less roasted, frozen or drowned : worried to death and almost tired to death : and for six months I have had the pleasure of being shot at almost every day, by some miserable Boer, sitting behind a rock. I'm sorry to have written all this now. . . .

He must have realised that his service in the last six months at any rate had been exceptional. Methuen's Farewell Order is clear enough :

The G.O.C. Western District cannot let the 4th Bedfordshire Regiment and the 3rd South Wales Borderers leave his command without expressing his admiration at their good conduct and gallantry in the field under his command. . . .

The 4th Bedfordshires, helped by the 3rd South Wales Borderers, supplied a company of Mounted Infantry, which for gallantry in the field and endurance of continuous hardship was second to nothing in the Division.

From Zeerust Norman was moved to Mafeking — the journey knocked him up — and, after a short stay, to a big hospital in Kimberley. The heat and the life there he found very trying — the rules 'must have been compiled by someone who once kept a private school' — but he was fortunate in finding a first-rate doctor. He was still weak, exhausted by a quarter-of-a-mile walk and unable to make any use of delicacies sent out to him. He still resisted the suggestion that he could not go back : but he was moved from Kimberley to Wynberg convalescent hospital near Capetown on November 20. He appeared before a Medical Board on the 26th :

They began by asking what I wanted to do, and I answered that I should like to go back to my Duty. This they said was impossible : so I asked for a fortnight's leave in this country — also impossible. Then I applied for 2 months' leave to England, as it was evident they didn't mean me to stay out here. . . . My Board seems to be final, so there is nothing for it but to make up one's mind to be sent home as a 'crock', a rather disappointing finish as no place in the world could possibly have suited me better than this country.

He sailed early in December, and was home in Moor Place on 4 January 1902. Arrived in England he was not recalled even for light duties, and was released from service on 22 July 1902. He retained his commission and attended yearly training again when his health permitted, but finally resigned his commission on 10 January 1907.

Norman's experience of active campaigning was limited to five months; but it followed on fifteen months of almost continuous hard work. All the time he showed the same unresting energy, improvising to cope with emergencies, attacking other people's arrears of work, planning ahead and pressing forward with his innovations. If he had, as he realised later, asked for a transfer to the regular forces as soon as he came out, he would, with his four years of militia training and experience and his obvious qualities of energy and initiative, almost certainly have secured it. His success, in spite of the handicap of remaining in the Militia, shows that he would have made his mark, and he would probably have been lost permanently by banking to the Army. But loyalty to his battalion and his personal relations with its commanding officer made any such move inconceivable. When, later, he was labouring under a sense of resentment at the neglect of the Militia, the shortage of experienced officers in the battalion made it equally impossible to think of moving. Moreover, in spite of the interest which soldiering had, and still more the persistent attraction which the country had for him, he always, in the last resort, felt that he was committed to the career and the associates he had chosen in England.

17 October 1901

At the end of this year I shall have been away from my proper business for two whole years, and it seems hardly fair that I should stop away any longer. Apart from the fact that others have to do my work all this time while I am doing no good, I am forgetting everything that I ever knew, and it will I expect be a struggle to settle down again when the time comes.

Part of the nervous strain of the last few months was due to the feeling that he was letting down his partners without really justifying his staying on in South Africa.

The climate, the open-air life and the change to continuous largely independent activity, together made his health better than it had ever been before, which enabled him to face, almost to welcome, the hardships of the life. Extremes of heat and cold, of rain and dust, long hours of work, everything indeed except lack of sleep, he accepted without complaint. But the conditions must have had an effect. He was not constitutionally robust, and, when an attack of dysentery had lowered his abounding vitality, and he had to put up with long hours in the saddle, shortage of sleep and the personal responsibilities of a mounted auxiliary in a continually moving column, it is not surprising that his constitution gave way and an old weakness recurred.

There is not a sign in his letters that responsibility ever caused him worry; he faced the problems of organisation and equipment, discipline and health of his men, relations with subordinate officers and his superiors, systematically and without apparent effort. In an emergency (like the evacuation of Bloemhof) he was clear what to do, and proceeded without hesitation to do it. He describes objectively but briefly the skirmishes and more serious actions in which he was involved; nothing he says suggests any consciousness of danger, but he deliberately spared his parents the more painful side of war. He wondered how he would ever settle down to civilian life again; he was to find it less stimulating and congenial, and for many years offering less scope for the habit of initiative and authority native in him and brought out by his experience of war.

CHAPTER II

THE PRIVATE BANKER

(i)

THE army doctors had been right in sending Norman home. He was quite unfit for work when he reached England; his convalescence was slow and set back by recurrence of his illness. Although at work in 1902, it was not until towards the end of the following year that he was able to resume regular and uninterrupted attendance at Founders Court. A new chapter in the history of the firm was opening; the senior partner, F. A. Hamilton, a partner since 1845, retired at the end of 1903. Collet, a partner since 1851 and the most influential member of the firm for many years, had withdrawn from active work and died in April 1905. The third partner of senior standing, Alexander Hargreaves Brown, who had been a partner since 1875, had also been a Member of Parliament since 1868; he was now one of the senior members of the House of Commons, and held an important position as chairman of Private Bill Committees, which was recognised by a baronetcy in 1902. The partners left in effective control of the business were L. E. Chalmers, the son of a former partner admitted to partnership in 1898, Edward Clifton Brown, a nephew of Sir Alexander Brown, admitted in 1899, and Norman, who was made a partner in 1900, just after he joined his regiment. There was no one as yet to give the firm the standing in the City which Collet had given them; but they were still a leading accepting house.

Norman had wondered in South Africa whether he would ever settle down again to his old civilian life and find the work congenial. When he was able to resume it, he attacked it with the energy he had shown in South Africa and accumulated in a year's enforced idleness. Some reorganisation of the firm's methods was probably overdue; it had been dominated

by partners brought up when its business was different. Next
he went on to overhauling the staff, in which it does not seem
that his changes were always justified by results. He did,
however, a little later reinforce the firm by bringing in another
experienced partner, in James Leigh-Wood. But his chief
energies were directed to increasing the business of the firm.

Brown Shipley gave acceptance credits to American customers jointly with Brown Bros. of New York. The initial,
and more interesting, negotiations would lie with New York;
but Brown Shipley were equally liable on the acceptances.
They were limited in what they could do by their available
resources. This limit may have been an occasional irritation;
the firm had made large profits for many years, but much of
these had been taken out by partners who left the business or
the families of former partners. Norman was able to increase
his personal stake when he inherited a share of Collet's estate,
but by much less than was taken out. Since it was difficult to
attract deposits in the face of the competition of the larger
banks, he urged that the partners should agree (without entering into any formal obligation), once they had paid up their
respective quotas of capital, to deposit from their share of
profits an amount equal to half their capital, and that the firm
should pay them $4\frac{1}{2}$ or 5 per cent interest. Nevertheless, the
business was expanded, Brown Shipley forming syndicates when
the credit required was larger than they could handle by
themselves.

In two directions his energy and imagination made his
influence felt. In the first place, he made sure that the London
house should not again expose itself to John Crosby Brown's
reproach that the London partners did not keep in touch with
American conditions by personal visits. He visited the United
States in the years 1906, 1907, 1908 and 1910, and Canada in
1911; and one year James Brown accompanied him on a visit
to the Scandinavian capitals. On his visits he would take part
in the current decisions of his American partners, visit the
Philadelphia and Boston offices, and usually contrive to see
something of the country's business outside these centres; more
than once he said he had been in every state of the Union
except one. Conversely he welcomed and entertained the
American partners in London and ensured their personal

E

participation in important London decisions. By this policy he strengthened the bonds between the partners on opposite sides of the Atlantic, increased his own share in the firm's activities, and therefore its interest for him, and satisfied the wish — one might almost say the longing — he continually felt for a share in American life. His American partners, on their side, could not have too much of his company; he was welcomed to their counsels and decisions, and, had he ever made up his mind to leave England, would have rejoiced at the opportunity of bringing him into their family.

In the second place the firm developed direct relations with countries other than the United States, building up a valuable business in financing trade with Europe and the Empire. Norman did something to satisfy his passion for concrete detail by learning the currents of commodity trade for which acceptance credits were required and the standing of the firms requiring them; and he became a master of the working of the bill and exchange markets. His accurate memory for persons was always useful. The West End Branch, opened in 1900, continued to serve the requirements of a large number of rich Americans travelling in Europe, cashing their letters of credit and handling their correspondence. It was not remunerative, but it was a convenience to customers whose commercial business was sought and it contributed to the firm's reputation. A related department handled foreign exchange, mainly for the New York house. This also was unremunerative, and Norman, though it also was a convenience to customers, was inclined to keep it down to a minimum because there was always a temptation to take a position and he wished to reserve the firm's resources for its primary business of giving acceptance credits and the supplementary business of wholesaling securities.

Norman schooled himself to the requirements of business. He had naturally the fundamental quality of untiring attention to detail : his ardent and impetuous temper was never allowed to hurry a decision, still less to dictate it. He was — so his most experienced contemporary, who was also an intimate friend, describes him — a first-rate business-man, with a 'sense of smell', an instinctive grasp of the possibilities and dangers in a document or proposition, a liking for 'a trade' — he would have made a good merchant — great energy and drive. He seemed

to the few friends who were in a position to judge to dominate
his firm, too much so perhaps; but he was known little outside.
Characteristically, he gave up one after another his outside
interests in order to concentrate on his business; after 1906
he gave up shooting, for example, because his partners liked to
take their leave in the autumn, and he was not averse to being
left in sole charge; but he took no part in the general affairs
and society of the City. His small circle of intimate friends
included other bankers, but his friendship was with their whole
families, the very opposite of a purely 'business' friendship.
One or two fellow-bachelors in the City used to dine with him
regularly, but again the attraction was personal, not professional. The few who knew him recognised his ability, force
and courage; to others he must have seemed, as one of these
friends describes him, 'a lonely queer man'.

Actually, recognition from the profession did come, and
come early. In October 1907 he was elected to the Court of
Directors of the Bank of England. It was natural that the
Court, in looking for recruits, should think of George Warde
Norman's family and Mark Collet's house; but they would not
have invited Norman if he had not already impressed himself
on his business associates. He himself was taken by surprise,
and sought the advice of his friend Vivian Hugh Smith [1] on
whether he should accept. The advice was clear enough: 'Of
course you will accept and, when you are on the Court, remember that you are as good as they are'. The Bank gave him a
new field of interest, and he tended to give more of himself to
the Bank, as he found less satisfaction in his own business. But
the position of an ordinary Director of the Bank was not at that
time very interesting or exacting; it was only when war broke
out that the Bank began to offer an alternative outlet for his
energies.

One early experience it did give him, which may not have
been without importance in his education. He joined the
Court just as the speculative boom on the New York Stock
Exchange broke, a week before the Knickerbocker Trust Company closed its doors and precipitated a panic. His American
colleagues were never in danger, even of serious embarrassment, and took an important part, under the leadership of

[1] Later Lord Bicester.

J. P. Morgan and Company, in stemming the panic and improvising measures to deal with it. But London was affected, and Norman had the opportunity of observing at close quarters a masterful Governor, in William Middleton Campbell (Governor 1907–9), handling a crisis. He was impressed; he always said that Campbell was 'a man'; in putting up Bank Rate on his own responsibility without waiting for the Court, 'he was dead right'; and the experience gave Norman one more thing in common with his future friend and collaborator, Ben Strong, who was also in business in banking and lived through the crisis.

In addition to expanding their basic business of acceptance credits, Brown Shipley began about this time to expand in a different field, that of providing long-term capital for overseas developments. They were well placed by their connections to undertake new public issues of bonds, and this they did, although not on a large scale. There were also opportunities of 'wholesaling' securities; but in this type of business they would be responsible to their clients for any amount of the issue which the public were unwilling to take, and this might make a demand on the firm's own capital, already engaged in the acceptance business. Some members of the firm were attracted by the opportunity which their position gave of financing entirely new projects. They were, for example, interested in Russia by Leslie Urquhart; they formed a syndicate to enable him to prospect for minerals and secure concessions, and then to finance the exploitation of these concessions. In this way they developed iron-ore deposits in the Urals, and iron and copper deposits in the Caucasus; and finally, during the First World War, a big mineral area in Central Asia near Irkutsk. The two former were profitable until war interrupted their development; the last was promising until it was killed by the Russian revolution. In projects of this type they would provide credits in the exploratory and developing stages, with the intention of issuing securities later. Another example was the formation of a trust company to conduct a land mortgage agency and general finance business in Canada in 1911.

It is likely that this innovation both attracted and repelled Norman. He was always attracted by any financial operation with a concrete constructive object, and he had the imagination

and courage to respond to opportunities of risking a large investment for a large, though deferred, return. He urged that they
should aim at representation on the boards of companies whose
securities the firm wished to handle. Other private bankers
were combining the business of long-term financing with acceptance credits : the greatest of them were also the chief sponsors
of foreign government issues on the London market. Moreover,
the New York house of Brown Bros., in spite of greater responsibilities as deposit bankers, were cautiously experimenting in
the same field, in the different conditions of their own market.
Nevertheless, it was this development which eventually led
Norman to a final break with his partners. His logical grasp of
principles made it difficult for him to accept the combination of
responsibilities which the new business entailed. As granters
of acceptance credits they were responsible for the bills they
accepted if their customers did not meet the bills at maturity.
The ultimate security for their ability to discharge this responsibility was the firm's capital. A modest amount of new issue
business was compatible with this, but not — as he thought —
the simultaneous employment of capital in other, and not
always liquid, directions. One of his junior colleagues suggests that Norman proposed to give up the firm's acceptance
business. He may have put to his partners the alternatives as
he saw them — either withdraw from the financing business
or cease to give acceptance credits : but it is improbable that
he would have been prepared to sacrifice what was the main
substance still of the firm's business and source of its profits.
Years later he described Brown Shipley as 'the finest acceptance business in London'. His friend and contemporary in the
American house, Thatcher M. Brown, is quite clear in his
recollection of events.

It is perhaps interesting to note here that in 1915 Mr. Montagu
Norman, then a partner in Brown, Shipley & Co. and Brown
Brothers & Co., retired as a member of the firm on that very issue.
He felt that Brown, Shipley & Co., known in London as an acceptance house, their chief business being the financing of exports and
imports from one place to another by acceptances, should not issue
securities or participate in underwriting the issues of other bankers.
The majority of his London partners did not agree with him, and
consequently he retired from the firm. We note further in passing

that the private banking houses in London still perform these functions without apparently raising any question of their wisdom among their clients or the public there.

An intimate friend of Norman's during this period would place the emphasis differently. The issuing business of Brown Shipley was small and they were unlikely to get the most important issues. What Norman objected to was extensive underwriting, or issues of the American type in which the issuing banker extensively engaged his own capital. In later years he still held to the view that the two functions were in principle incompatible, though commonly associated in practice : in private conversation he declared that the principle of the American Banking Act of June 1933 was sound in separating commercial banking from the making and underwriting of security issues. In terms of his own firm, what troubled him was the tying up of resources in new and unmarketable, even if promising, ventures, because in a crisis the firm might find itself illiquid. It must be added that Brown Shipley did not suffer from the course they actually pursued : but in after years Norman habitually criticised people who did not stick to their own business, and his experience as a private banker may well have helped to form this view.

This final difference was only the culmination of a long period of internal strain underlying the friendly relations of the London partners. At first sight it might have seemed that the team was admirably balanced, the conservatism of the two Browns against the more speculative tendency of Chalmers, and the combination of enterprise with caution that marked Norman. In fact, these differences in attitude arose from differences in character which gave rise to recurrent conflict and strain. Norman's restless energy led him to set a pace which his more conservative (and senior) partners did not wish to maintain. In spite of his concentration on his work and its expansion, the firm did not provide him with sufficient scope ; yet he resisted developments which might have absorbed his surplus energies. By his personality he tended to dominate the firm ; it was not surprising that he frequently met with opposition.

Then the unfortunate characteristic which handicapped him until much later in life, that his powers of explanation and advocacy always fell far short of his powers of insight and decision, must have made agreement difficult. He would see what ought to be done, and decide that it ought to be done; but he was miserably incapable of explaining *why* it should be done. In informal converse he was articulate enough, lively and interesting, and later in life he had a gift of economical, penetrating and striking expression; but he was slow to learn how to make a case in a committee of equals, and the shyness which had handicapped him at school hampered him still. He could not in business simply give orders (within the limits of his authority) as he had done in the army; that was one reason why army life was so congenial, and why business life had for him so much frustration. In the small partnership of a private banking-house above all others, the practice of full discussion and agreement among equals was the customary and proper procedure; it was not a procedure that suited his very individual gifts and limitations. He drifted away from the firm, however, only when his health gave way in 1911, a breakdown to which this strain of his work contributed. Moreover, it must not for a moment be thought that the firm was not continuously successful. Norman's private business career was virtually confined to the eleven years, 1903–14, in which he was an active partner; and even this was curtailed by a year's absence through illness. For the whole of his subsequent life he was debarred by his position, not merely from taking part in any private business, but even from seeking to improve his fortune by the skilful management of his investments. Years later he said, 'I think if I had been free I could have made a lot of money — I have a nose for it'. To understand his breakdown in health, however, it is necessary to turn to his life outside Founders Court and the Bank.

(ii)

As soon as he resumed work Norman began to look round for a house of his own. Temporarily, in March 1903, he took a furnished house, 1 Albert Place, Kensington, from a cousin, moving to 12, then 35 Victoria Road near by later in the year. Week-ends and bank holidays he spent at his father's house,

Moor Place, or with the Collets at St. Clere. During the winter
he had been on the Riviera, and in the spring had made a trip
to Jamaica with a cousin. He was in Scotland, shooting, just
before he returned to Brown Shipley in November. He found
what he wanted early in 1904 in Thorpe Lodge, Campden Hill,
an old house rebuilt early in the nineteenth century, on the
Phillimore estate. It was at the west end of a cul-de-sac,
Airlie Gardens, protected to the north by a reservoir, to the
west by Moray Lodge, beyond which lay Holland House and
its park, and, to the south, where the ground fell away, by its
own paddock. On March 25 he paid £5750 for the fifty-year
lease. The house had been unoccupied for three years. The
previous tenant, the artist, Wells — who painted the famous
picture of the Archbishop announcing her succession to the
young Queen Victoria — had constructed, or adapted, a large
room as a studio. Norman set to work to reconstruct the house
and the grounds drastically, and the carrying out of these plans
was his chief recreation for the next few years. 'I know how
fascinating a work it is to make a home', he wrote to a friend
in 1913 — 'and to make it fit, just as a snail makes his shell
to fit himself (and doesn't pick up some old shell and squeeze
himself into its unnatural corners !).'

Work began on July 22. His architect was Walter Shirley
(afterwards Earl Ferrers), a pupil of Basil Champneys, who
not only made plans for the structural alterations and interior
decorations, but helped to design furniture and other work.
They found among the contractor's men one, named J. H.
Wakelin, who was so much in sympathy with Norman's aims
that presently Norman helped to set him up in business on his
own account [1] and used him for much subsequent work on the
house. Norman himself designed much of the furniture, and
was continuously busy making sketches for his architect, or the
Guild of Handicrafts, to work out. All the metal work —
latches, lamps, fire-irons, scrapers — was designed specially.
Norman found a working craftsman, called A. J. Shirley (no
relation of his architect), who could carry out his ideas; for
years Shirley did work for Thorpe Lodge which still interests
other artists though his work is not known elsewhere. Sometimes, on his way home from the City, he would call in at

---

[1] The firm is still carried on by his son at Sunningdale.

Shirley's workshop and work himself at one of the lamps or latches Shirley was making for him. Norman was much interested in varieties of wood and imported special woods from Africa and Central America, to be sawn and planed and polished. The material for the covers of some of the furniture was woven to fit. In everything the aim was to make use of the individual characteristics of the material and to express the purpose which the thing was to serve, simplicity and the avoidance of over-elaboration, rest and the avoidance of everything merely pretty and fussy. A visitor might have been struck, when the house was completed and lived in, by the absence of pictures and extraneous ornament. A few water-colour drawings and etchings — gifts or scenes with some local sentimental association or, as he notes, bought at the request of some friend — were kept out of the way; there was one gift of fine Japanese pottery (described by Norman as 'a bribe'), but a more integral part of the decoration was a number of Chinese jars and white and blue plates. The walls of the entrance hall had a covering of unusual tiles; Norman was struck with the beauty of the fractured silicon compounds used in making crucibles for smelting, and had tiles made of the material. Almost wholly the house depended for decoration on the design of the rooms and furniture, the variety of woods used in floor, panelling, cupboards and furniture, the upholstery and carpets (a few Persian rugs and a South African kaross, but mainly plain carpets in colours selected for the rooms), the metal fittings and furnishings, and a very small number of decorations incorporated in the walls. One room, the study or library, was dominated by a magnificent panel of embroidery representing a peacock, which filled the centre of the end wall, and by a large overmantel of de Morgan's tiles above the open hearth at the other end. The studio, which was converted into a beautiful music-room with low platform and small gallery, had a seventeenth-century stone fireplace and mantel which had been found by a friend in Italy in 1905 and sent home. The dining-room had a barrel roof, a reminiscence of the tilt of a South African ox-wagon. Two other panels of de Morgan's tiles were used in other places; though de Morgan had given up making them before the transformation of Thorpe Lodge began, Norman must have been interested in the man, because he remarked once on the unfortunate management of the business side of his enterprise. Table-ware was got from Wedgwood and Copenhagen.

In all this the inspiration of William Morris, or rather an innate sympathy with him, is apparent. Norman admired Morris not only as an artist but as a rebel and a hater of shams. They never met; but the interest is shown in his collection of Morris's books and his employment of the firm Morris founded. Mackail's *Life of Morris* influenced him, as it did a whole generation, and Mackail was a friend. The Kelmscott Chaucer in his library was a gift from his father in the year it was published. Other Kelmscott volumes he began buying at auctions as soon as he had a house of his own. The remaking of Thorpe Lodge and its furnishings gave him an outlet for this element in his make-up; even in business his intellectual processes were more those of a creative artist than an economic man. He had an interest in colours which the house allowed him to satisfy. He was unfortunate that, unlike Morris, he had few opportunities to use his hands; his health might have been better had his profession offered them.

The garden offered almost as much scope as the house. The previous tenant had been content to leave it as a paddock in which he kept a cow. Norman began planning and planting it as soon as he was assured of the lease; he had already planted thousands of bulbs before he paid for it. He terraced the ground, and on the terrace in front of the house built a loggia, which was a favourite place for meals. He planted fruit trees and flowering shrubs, and his diary records his interest year after year, not only in lists of plants to order but in notes of the earliest appearance of aconites and crocuses. The stables were converted into rooms for the staff.[1]

One of the rooms of the house was clearly intended for use as a library. Unlike most libraries it does not proclaim its purpose in rows of open shelves on all the walls and books lying about on tables and desks. Only in the middle of each of the long walls a projecting bookcase with glass-fronted

[1] The land on which Thorpe Lodge and Moray Lodge stand has been acquired by the London County Council for a school, but Thorpe Lodge will be preserved as a building together with the wood panelling and some of the furniture. A plaque will commemorate that Norman lived there for nearly fifty years.

shelves above and cupboards below displays a small collection of books. The larger and more characteristic collection is hidden in shelves occupying most of the end of the room, hidden by solid or curtained doors in such a way as to suggest panelling, and in other cupboards with solid doors fitted in recesses in other places. There is no attempt to disguise the fact that these are cupboards; they are examples of Norman's orderly mind, which preferred books to be tidily disposed of and would not have tolerated them lying about. A curious result of this arrangement — and his room at the Bank was equally clear of books and papers — was that casual visitors, and even friends, were often unaware of the range and depth of the interests of which his books are evidence. He inscribed practically all his books with his monogram, usually with the date, the place where they were bought when bought away from home, and with the name of the donor when they were gifts. Often he marks passages and sometimes annotates and puts references on the fly-leaf sufficiently to indicate the extent to which he read and found them interesting. Lacking these indications, his oldest colleague describes him as widely read but with 'no books on his shelves'. According to his oldest and most intimate friend, confirmed by the books themselves, he read mainly poetry and philosophy, and was not interested in history. Though his reading was unsystematic, there is evidence enough that it was extensive and serious, at this time when he was creating a home and shaping his business career.

He came towards the end of a generation which had been forced by the challenge of natural science to re-examine and re-state the Christianity by which it lived. A mechanical and materialistic view of the universe was not tolerable to him; on the other hand, he does not seem to have found the settled and conventional dogmas in which he had been brought up satisfying. He seems to have sought to find a view of life in which he could rest, first, by reading the current more popular books on philosophy. Among his books, but without date or address to indicate when he acquired them, were Green's *Prolegomena to Ethics*, Renan's *Antichrist*, a popular summary of Herbert Spencer's philosophy, a work called *The Great Law: a Study of Religious Origins* by Williamson, and volumes of Jowett's translation of Plato. In 1905 and the following year or two there is evidence of more systematic reading. He bought Haldane's *Pathway to Reality*, in which he marks the explanation of philosophical terms; and read most of Hegel's *History of Philosophy* — he has queried the words 'rightly enough' in which Hegel comments on the execution of Socrates. About the same time he discovered Royce's *The World and the Individual*; and when *Philosophy of Loyalty* by the same author was published a few years later, he read that too. During the rest of this phase, which ended with the outbreak of war in 1914, he bought William James's philosophical essays, Eucken's *Problem of Human Life* and Bergson's *Laughter*. Like his contemporary, H. G. Wells, he seems to have been attracted by F. C. S. Schiller's *Humanism* and other essays of that school. He pursued the same intellectual problems in biographies: Leslie Stephen's *Agnostic's Apology* and Maitland's *Life of Stephen*; a life by McIntyre of *Giordano Bruno*; F. Harrison's *Creed of a Layman*, of which he did not think very much.

From philosophy he was drawn to theology. W. Adams Brown's *Christian Theology in Outline*, Farquhar's *Gospel of Divine Humanity*, Oman's translation of Schleiermacher's *On Religion* (with criticisms of 'cultured despisers' of Christianity and Oman's preface marked) and some of Hocking's writings. A year or two later he was apparently reading the publications of the Theosophical Society — G. R. S. Mead and Mrs. Besant — and translations of Lao Tse and other Eastern sages. There are a number of the books of James Hinton, apparently well read; a collection of Edward Carpenter's books; the works of mystics like St. John of the Cross and Swedenborg; and a volume of lectures by a friend, Adela Curtis, *The New Mysticism*. There are some curious excursions into science — Bose's *Comparative Electro-Physiology*, Boole's *Lectures on the Logic of Arithmetic*, which he bought in 1904, and Osler's *Science and Immortality*. He was becoming interested in the bearing of men's thoughts, and ways of thinking, on their health; there is a volume by a group of Boston doctors called *Religion and Medicine: The Moral Control of Nervous Disorders*; there is a copy, unmarked and not inscribed, of *Science and Health*. But the writer in this field, with whom he seems to have found himself most — and longest — in sympathy was an American doctor settled in England and practising (without an English medical qualification) in nervous cases, J. Porter Mills, whose *Health Abstract and Concrete* (1905) was a kind of manual for mystics. This interest was shared with two or three of his narrow circle of friends, the wives, as it happened, of his closest associates in his profession. He always found women easier to talk with than men.

A cupboard with some fine editions indicate his interests in pure literature : Kelmscott Morrises, one of the prose romances acquired in 1897, a copy of *Sigurd the Volsung*, bought in Sittingbourne in 1893 when he was learning branch-banking; and *Guinevere* in 1894; *The Romaunt of the Rose, Aucassin and Nicolette*, and other translations of medieval romances; a first edition of Browning's *Pacchiarotto* bought in 1899, and other books by and about Browning; Lafcadio Hearn's *Kokoro* and other works and his life, F. W. Bain's Indian romances, and W. Hastie's *Divan of Telaleddin*, a criticism of Fitzgerald's *Omar Khayyám* bought in 1903; and the poets of the time — Yeats's *Ideas of Good and Evil* bought in 1904, A. E. (George William Russell), Francis Thompson's two volumes, Housman and all Kipling's verse. Modern translations of the New Testament and of the Excluded Books, and the Report and three volumes of the evidence of the Royal Commission on the War in South Africa — Preparation and Organisation — recall other interests. But Norman's main preoccupation while he was living by himself from 1903 to the breakdown of his health at the end of 1911 was a serious, though amateur, and unassisted attack on philosophy, theology and psychology, in an endeavour to work out a coherent view of life which would allay the restlessness of his mind and meet a need which his work did not satisfy. He did not succeed, because his mind was the type that solves its problems in action, and only a change of work could provide a solution. Writing to an American friend after America came into the First World War, he says :

I can imagine the changes which you speak of as having grown up suddenly around you as the result of the War. In spite of its misery and troubles I am sure a sort of personal content comes out of it, and especially to those who hitherto have either not learned or not recognised the luxury of occupation. . . .

When we used to sit in your garden and talk of inward unrest, we were only accustomed to outward peace. Now *that* is all changed. I doubt if anyone now has or even wishes to have that peace which we then aimed at. It might be aloofness rather than peace ? There is, I doubt not, a peace and a serenity which can be and is now maintained amid the hardest work, but it is hardly the particular condition we used to discuss in your garden. Therefore I do not claim to have found *that* peace within myself. At the same time, and altho' like yourselves we here have all been worried and perhaps are strained, I have known no such unrest these last three years or so, as we used to discuss in your garden. That is an honest opinion or so far is certainly true. At the same time and perhaps for the same reason I have been much better in health.

It would have saved him trouble if any of his tutors at Eton or Cambridge had realised that the conventional and rather difficult schoolboy had an acute mind and a potential interest in speculation worth cultivating, and had done something to cultivate it.

(iii)

In the two years between recovery from the illness which brought him back from South Africa and moving into Thorpe Lodge Norman went out a good deal. Thorpe Lodge, though not a big house, was admirably adapted for entertaining : but, as it turned out, his social life became more and more restricted as the years went on. Once established there, preoccupation with the house, growing absorption in his business, and an increasing interest in his reading began to narrow his circle of visits. Music was an exception. The music-room was used for small concerts regularly : and, though Norman was never much attracted by formal or frequent entertaining, he was by no means a recluse. A member of a large family, he had a wide circle of cousins among whom he could always find intimates. It was convenient to entertain his partners for discussions more protracted or otherwise more suitable for an evening in his house than an office. Especially when an American partner was over would these dinners take place, and the American partners, and their families, furnished him with some of his closest and longest friendships. Apart from this, he did not let his numerous business connections overflow into his social life ; two or three other bankers, bachelors like himself, used to dine with him, but as personal friends, not professional

associates. His architect, Walter Shirley, S. C. Cockerell [1] and
C. R. Ashbee [2] were friends to whom he was drawn by the
work on the house — one evening in 1910 Ashbee brought
Lloyd Wright [3] to dinner. A few public occasions drew him
out: the Fourth of June at Eton, the Eton and Harrow match
and the Ramblers' dinner, the Bankers' dinner, the annual
dinner of the Society of Merchants, not least the Mounted
Infantry dinner where he renewed his memories of South Africa.

He did not make friends easily; writing from his South
African hospital in December 1901 he had said:

I well remember the last Christmas I spent at sea. It was
somewhere on the Gulf of Lyons on the way from Egypt to Mar-
seilles and home. That was seven years ago: and thro' those years
I have faithfully kept myself to myself. Since then, I have hardly
made a new friend, except in America, and more often than not,
those I have met have almost looked askance at me, a surly, disagreeable individual.

For the society which was indispensable to him he relied on his
relatives and on two or three married contemporaries at whose
table and house he was always welcome — his brother after he
married, the Vivian Hugh Smiths, the Robert Holland Martins.[4] As their families grew up they gave a new link; 'I am
learning the duties and requirements of a bachelor uncle', he
writes at the end of 1907, and he was equally devoted to his
godchildren in the other two households.

A private banker's life made possible frequent holidays:
Italy in the spring and Brittany in the summer of 1905; Switzerland and Venice in the summer of 1906 and the Riviera in the
late autumn; a motoring tour in the Cotswolds and the West
at Whitsuntide the following year; but the Riviera again in
January of the two following years; Italy again in 1910,
Switzerland in the winter of 1910–11 and Italy in April. Next
year he was sent to Egypt and the Sudan, on the first of a
number of long trips in pursuit of health.

The visits to the Riviera recurred for most of his working
life. His mother's half-brother, Mark Collet, the second

---

[1] Later Sir Sydney Cockerell, Director of the Fitzwilliam Museum, Cambridge.　　　　　　　　　　　　　　　[2] Architect and Designer.
[3] Frank Lloyd Wright, Architect.　　　[4] Chairman of Martins Bank Ltd.

baronet, lived there for many years because his wife was an invalid, unable to stand the English climate. This was one reason why the son did not succeed the father in Brown Shipley, and therefore left his place among the partners to be filled by Norman. The relations of the cousins who chose such independent lives — Collet devoted himself after his wife's death to local public affairs in Kent until he retired to an estate in the Isle of Man — was one of complete harmony. Through a lifelong friendship there was never the slightest feeling of rivalry; and Collet's Riviera residence, Le Bocage at Costebelle, was a frequent resort.

It should perhaps be mentioned — since the change contributed to the distinctive appearance which impressed the public in after life — that in 1906 Norman allowed his beard to grow. He had done so during his South African experience; but this time it was a matter of deliberate choice. He joined his brother who had been spending some months after an operation in Venice, and announced that he had thrown away his razor and never intended to use one again. His brother remonstrated, but without any effect.

His business visits to New York were more refreshing probably than his holiday journeys. Partly it was climate; partly it was the business atmosphere. Returning from a visit in 1906 he wrote:

I don't think you realise how much (in the way of work) New York can supply which London either cannot or does not. America is not much of a place for a holiday, nor perhaps for the so-called amenities of life as compared with Europe. But for Work, which to an individual may mean everything or nothing, and particularly for that kind of work we call business, no place in the world can match it.

Six months later, writing from the steamer again, he said:

I am rather filled with dismay by the feeling of, as it were, going back to gaol — of having left the more unfettered paths behind me, partly because, at home, I *do* live in a rut and am bound by many involuntary but seemingly enforced shackles — called generally by the vague name of appearances, and I lack the common basis of fundamentals, which, with yourself and the likes of you, enables so much to be taken for granted.

Shy as he was, he found Americans easier to talk to than his fellow-countrymen.

The first evidence of any illness was the recurrence of fits of depression which became more and more severe from 1909 or 1910 on. 'Times are not getting any easier here,' he writes to the wife of his closest American partner in November 1908, 'and outwardly the dark days seem to make them more difficult. . . . I am very well, but like most of us have really too much work — and I guess we are all a bit strained.' A growing feeling of frustration in the business to which he had sacrificed other interests, the failure to find any illumination in his reading, and a tendency to withdraw from social life into himself, are amply sufficient to explain depression. They help to explain but hardly to account for a definitely morbid condition, though it was not until the autumn of 1911 that he allowed the state of his health to interrupt his normal activities. His previous experience as a young man in the mountains and as a soldier in South Africa had shown that full occupation with the social relations which occupation brought with it — the forester and farmers whom he worked with in the Jura, his fellow-officers and men in South Africa — and an active physical life in the open air were the conditions under which he was well. He could still write a long letter in verse to amuse a godchild. It was only his most intimate associates who were aware of this cloud on his mind. When he realised he was ill, and refused to see anyone from outside except his closest relatives, he would still think of his domestic staff, having them in in turn, and asking them about their family. If he was late for dinner he would apologise and explain that he had 'met a friend'; his cook knew that the 'friend' was a neighbouring housemaid whom he had noticed once washing steps, and always afterwards stopped for a chat when he saw her, or a Breton onion-hawker, from whom he would buy a string and carry it on his stick over his shoulder, and perhaps give a few to the postman. In November 1910 he was discussing a trip to the Sudan or South America; but business called him to New York, after which he was able to spare time only for a week's skating in Switzerland. In March he made his tour of the Baltic capitals with two of his American partners, and in the summer was entertaining more extensively than usual.

F

But at the end of July he had to see a specialist about an attack of eczema, and on September 24 was taken ill at Moor Place. He could attend to no business (except one or two alterations in Thorpe Lodge) until the end of the year.

His illness, whatever it was, was definite and sudden. He writes to his American partner, Thatcher M. Brown, on December 24 :

I remember, tho' not very clearly, that I had a letter from you on the very day that my machine stopped working. That letter has vanished, and I don't know what it said, and from that time until now I have neither read nor written a letter. Indeed I have been a close prisoner and to me it seems that the Prison was constructed on the lines of Hell ! . . . . Anyhow I want no better imitation !

And even now, though I am out of prison, I am not free ; for the Fates now insist on my starting off in a few days for the Sudan ; and there is nothing for me to do but to obey.

I owe you and all of you an apology for such behaviour. How or why I was knocked out, is more than I know or can explain : certainly I was proud enough to think that I knew better and even had some (perhaps too much) confidence in my powers of keeping going.

He was advised to take a long voyage and left Southampton on December 29 for Port Sudan. With his disposition it was perhaps not the best way of ensuring a complete rest. He writes, a month later, to Thatcher Brown's wife :

KHARTUM.   28 January 1912

You see where we have got to — coming round by sea all the way from England to a new harbor in the Red Sea — called Port Sudan, and thence by Rail over the hills and down into the Nile Valley. Once you have had one look at this country, you have seen it all. . . . And so it will hardly surprise you if I say that I only want to go home and have some work to do. Loafing is a miserable occupation — and tho' we all know how a vacation is, when we take it of our own free will — it is *wretched* and unsatisfactory when we take it 'for our good'. . . .

I wrote a long grumble to Thatcher about a month ago and from it you may have guessed how miserable one can be for no particular reason. And I believe the chief reason why time hangs so heavily and why one is so odious to oneself is simply because all work is taken away. And without some sort of work it's hardly possible to get along. I used to think that perhaps all one's spare time could be filled up with reading, but I find that I, at any rate, can't go on reading beyond a limited time every day: if you do there comes on a sort of indigestion of what you have read and you can hardly remember what it was all about!! In point of fact *general* reading isn't work and is no good for taking the place of regular occupation. If I had known this, I should have tried to get up some special subject and brought out special Books — though it would only have been a sort of dodge to fool oneself and to pretend one was some good when really one was a useless loafer!! And it's hard work to fool oneself for long! . . .

Whether with the consent of his doctor or not, he was back at work in London ('Bank and Founders Court') on 4 April 1912. He was seeing his doctor every other month and was sent to be X-rayed in September, but he was not less active than before for most of the year. At Christmas at Moor Place, however, he was, he notes, 'mostly bad', and in the New Year he was sent off on another tour, this time to Central America (after considering Australia). He left on 7 January 1913 for Bordeaux to join the S.S. *Guadaloupe* for Trinidad.

Apart from his fits of depression he suffered from disabling attacks of pain in his head, but between these he was capable of work. On this journey to a part of the world new to him, he was as interested as usual in his fellow-passengers, and as usual took every opportunity of inquiring into the economic conditions and personalities of the places he visited. His partner, Thatcher Brown, recalls that as a young man, staying with James Brown, he unintentionally persuaded a visitor, a surgeon from Honolulu, by his searching questions that he had lived in Honolulu himself, when all his information was derived from the answers to his own questions; so throughout life, he would fasten on a visitor and extract from him whatever of interest to a banker he had to say. He had an introduction to the proprietor of a large coconut plantation in Trinidad; he visited others as well, and sent a report to his partners in London. He enjoyed the colours of the vegetation, and the Spanish architecture of Cartagena and Colon, and the Dutch aspect of Willemstad later; but in Panama, though he saw over the canal works, he was more interested in a bank with which the firm might do business, and in the conversation of the most experienced merchant of the place, and of the manager of the bank. The advice of the latter, whom he clearly respected as a business man, had a momentous influence on him entirely outside business. This acquaintance, either from personal experience or the experience of some friend, was familiar with the symptoms of Norman's illness and spoke of great benefit from treatment by certain Swiss physicians, of whom the best known was Carl Jung. Norman noted their addresses on February 25 and decided to seek their help. He did not turn back at once: on March 8 he had an interview with the President [1] ('a sound man and no politician; fears domination of United Fruit Co.'), and started home next day, reaching Southampton on the 31st. He was glad to be back.

The resort to Jung in Zürich was to prove a bitter — almost, it is not too much to say, a fatal — disappointment. He arrived in Lausanne on April 8, having telegraphed Jung from London for an appointment; his sister-in-law, Lady Florence Norman, accompanied him. They moved to Zürich on the 14th, and he saw Jung twice the next day. Jung sent him to colleagues to have his blood and spinal fluid tested ('bled and marrowed', as he put it). The process was painful and exhausting, and he was in bed for the next few days. On April 21 Jung saw him again and gave him his opinion. Norman had built great hopes on this visit. During his trip to Panama he had, he writes to a friend, been seedy and in pain nearly all the time. He got seedier, not better, until he gave up all his plans and came to Europe to see 'a leech who', he was assured, 'could perform wonders'. He found him 'a charmer, sensible and human — said I was fit to go everywhere except for a mechanical kink in the brain but too far down the ladder for him to tackle then'. His own note, April 21, of Jung's opinion, is as follows:

Perfectly sound throughout, including blood serum etc., but head entirely exhausted and therefore unresponsive. Consequently unable to undergo his or any other cure. After a complete rest, lasting a 'lot of months', may come back to him and if sufficiently recovered, shall go thro' his treatment which takes weeks or months, according to individual. Meanwhile lead quiet, easy, selfish life: no work at all: plenty of rest and amusement: travelling (and

[1] Dr. B. Porras.

tropics) : bed : massage and medicine useless : grub and air good. At home better than in any sanatorium, thereby avoiding cranks. Cannot predict time needed for recovery nor ultimate result.

Norman was prostrated. 'That verdict', he wrote, 'was the finishing touch, having been slowly going downhill ever since January; I collapsed and nursed a raging head at Zürich for more than a month.' Jung's report to Norman's friends was different; the tests of his blood and serum were negative, but his general condition was such that he would not live three months.

His brother came out to help in the care of him; when he and his wife had to return to London for a few days, Mark Collet took their place. A friend, hearing what had happened, wrote urging him to consult another specialist in nervous diseases in Lausanne, Dr. Roger Vittoz, whose methods were unconventional but in her experience successful. His brother, who had joined him, visited Vittoz and arranged a consultation. Norman was not very hopeful at first, though immediately attracted by the man. He writes to the same friend on June 4 :

Two or three weeks ago, I got up and came here — Lausanne — (rather than go back to England for the summer, where there would have been nothing to do) and have been under a Doctor since then. Outwardly I am now, as I have often been during the last year or two — perfectly well : but there is said to be a very erratic corner in my brain which makes all the trouble, and I shall not know for another month what this man can do for it. So far he hasn't committed himself at all ; but he is clever and *very* understanding — and although I don't expect to get back to where I used to be, I quite hope he will do a great deal towards setting me up. So think of me from now on as a lame duck ! !

And on June 16 :

I am much better : can go about anywhere and expect to leave here in a couple of weeks. . . . I don't know when — if ever — I shall get back to the old life. For a good many years I lived upon the mountain tops and now I have been in deep valleys. At one time I feared the change was from wrong thinking or wrong living : of course I worked hard — perhaps too hard — in more directions than one, and of course there was friction which seemed unavoidable and still seems so, but which hurt me a good deal.

But it seems my brain has always worked wrong in a mechanical way and *that* ought to have ditched me years ago. But only after long grief and pain would one believe it — even if one had been told so earlier — and then it's hard to alter the natural and lifelong working of one's rudder. But perhaps much remains that is worth having — I think so.

He was able to take an interest in some plans for altering Thorpe Lodge and could see visitors — Collet, Lady Ferrers; later in the month, Walter Cunliffe,[1] already Governor of the Bank.

He saw Vittoz first on May 9; thereafter he saw him alternate days until the end of June. After his return on July 2, he continued Vittoz's treatment, and reported regularly to him by letter. The treatment apparently consisted in helping him to concentrate his mind on exercises with no emotional quality, and to make him do this regularly. When he was treating the patient himself in Lausanne, Vittoz made him concentrate intently on following in his mind a complicated series of linear patterns; though whether this was devised to suit Norman's idiosyncrasies or was a general treatment is not known. Norman practised his exercises regularly, and not only when he was with Vittoz — when he was walking about, for example. His reports to Vittoz, after he returned home, make it possible to follow his recovery.

The first was on July 14; he had not written sooner because his condition had been normal except on two days when he suffered from pressure and pains in the head; he had continued the exercises without much difficulty, but ordinary life still seemed too difficult — he could only wait. A fortnight later he had had no recurrence of pain, but he could not yet face any work. Another fortnight of normal life followed, spoilt at the end by some headaches and a return (after two years) of eczema; these passed away but it was discouraging, especially since he had hoped to start work again on September 1. The next report, August 25, was that there had been no return of pain or trouble; health seemed to depend on a perfectly quiet life; however, he looked forward to work again in ten days. On September 8 he was able to report that all went well, and after two months' idleness in England he had begun a little work. On

[1] Director of the Bank of England, 1895–1920. Deputy Governor, 1911–13. Governor, 1913–18. Lord Cunliffe, 1914.

the 22nd he was working more and more without ill effects, and hoped soon to accustom himself to office work again. On October 6 he was not so cheerful ; he had been forced to realise he was not armed against strain, since he had been forced to bed two or three days by headaches. The next fortnight all went well and he worked four days a week without difficulty. He had a slight setback in November, which might have been due to the onset of winter, and at the end of the month he was troubled by excessive activity of the brain, preventing rest ; as a result he knew he was difficult with everybody, work bad and felt miserable. These symptoms, however, had disappeared by December 8, and his brain worked as it should ; he continued the exercises, and his mood was more hopeful — ' Mais en tout cas — me voici — je vis encore ! et tout va assez bien en attendant la prochaine chute — peutêtre ! ! ' Already he was working and seeing his friends again. He had made his first appearance at the Bank and at Founders Court on September 10, and he gave a dance for his god-daughter at Thorpe Lodge on October 20. So long as he took things easily he was not troubled ; but in March 1914, when he was back at work, he had a recurrence of the pain ; work, he reported to Vittoz in April, was always difficult, but it was not so much the work as his fellow-workers — it was against them that he needed to be armoured. However, that was the last report he sent.

Whatever the source of his illness, the remedy seemed to be a life of continuously exacting work, which would crowd out all worries except worries involved in the actual decisions of the business, and these were not worries to him ; but there was a limit to the nervous strain he could undergo ; he had to reserve himself strictly for his work, and he had to make sure of real holidays. The war was shortly to provide some of these conditions ; this he could not know, but before it came he had made up his mind to relieve himself of the strain of disagreement with partners. He visited his American partners in May and June. His decision to retire from the firm may have been made, and even made known to his partners, before war broke out. It did not take place simply because the war pushed such issues on one side ; before July 29 they had reached a point ' when agreement is impossible — in fact the break had come, the word of cleavage had been written '.

(iv)

War took the City by surprise. After the murder of the Arch-duke Francis Ferdinand at Sarajevo on 28 June 1914, individual firms proceeded to strengthen their position, it is true, by redu-cing new commitments and calling in such overseas credits as they could. The markets of the Continent, with a livelier sense of the danger, showed signs of alarm and panic before London. But the lines along which credit and payments ran all led to London, and the difficulties in which war would involve the Continent implicated London before war was declared on Tuesday, August 4. The Austrian ultimatum to Serbia on July 23 precipitated a panic on the Vienna Bourse; on the 27th the Bourses in Vienna, Budapest and Brussels closed, and there was serious pressure on the security markets of London, Paris and New York. Paris, which had been building up balances in London, drew on them, forcing up their exchange and requiring heavy gold movements; most centres, however, were in debt to London. Traders all over the world had drawn bills on London in anticipation of the movement of goods; they were liable for these bills on maturity and sought means to remit funds to London to meet their liability: even Austrian banks were reported to be attempting to remit to London through Switzerland weeks after war broke out. Dealers in securities had instructed London brokers to buy securities for them, and were liable for payment. In every crisis other centres relied on London, the one completely free gold market and source of credit, for assistance in exceptional needs. The first effect of war, therefore, was an intense pressure to remit to London.

New York, though no one thought of America yet as a possible belligerent, was affected as much as or more than European centres. Normally New York was drawing on Lon-don at this season in anticipation of the exports of wheat and cotton which would move in the autumn, and it happened that a New York City loan was due for repayment in London at the same time, payment of which, it was said, an important firm of New York bankers had guaranteed. Moreover, the atom-istic banking system of the United States made it difficult to mobilise the gold reserves of the country to meet a sudden external demand. Unable to secure new credits in London, other centres bid up the price of London bills, and the exchanges moved in favour of London. Gold could not readily be shipped to relieve the pressure ; but New York shipped more than any other centre. The obvious remaining resource was the sale of securities to raise sterling, and securities were thrown first on the bourses of the Continent, breaking prices there and causing panic, and then on the Stock Exchanges of London and New York. A Stock Exchange account closed in London on July 29. On the 31st the Exchange was closed, for the first time in its history, to give time to meet the difficulties the account brought to light. New York followed suit the same day. The London discount market had already ceased to function, London accepting houses having refused to grant new credits on July 27.

The working of the credit system of which London was the centre assumed and depended on peace. Its chief characteristics were its reliance on continuity of business and the interdependence of the different agencies constituting it.

Once this continuity was interrupted, everyone was involved in the consequences. If the foreigner could not remit, the firm which had accepted his bills could give no further credits, and would have difficulty in meeting its outstanding liabilities. Its difficulties were less immediate than those of bill-brokers and discount firms which carried bills on short-term loans, overnight in many cases, from the banks. If the foreign centres sought to raise money by selling securities, they produced a collapse of security prices, which undermined the solvency of dealers carrying securities on similar short-term bank loans. Thus the joint-stock banks found themselves threatened with an inability to recover the loans they had regarded as most liquid, and a possibility of demands from their depositors for cash far in excess of the reserve of cash.

Underlying all these strains and stresses was the certainty that war would check, reduce and dislocate the movement of goods and the provision of credits for other purposes, which the system had grown up to make possible and on which ultimately it depended for solvency. One large section of world trade, that between the two groups of belligerents, would become illegal ; trade with neutrals would be reduced by blockade ; the transport of gold in settlement of ultimate balances would be threatened by submarine warfare and might be impossible to insure; and the ability to meet past debts and future liabilities of all peaceful traders would be rendered uncertain by the distortion of peaceful trade by war. The markets characteristically anticipated and responded immediately to such future dangers.

In a temporary payments-crisis London relied on the Bank of England. The Governor, Cunliffe, in his second (which would normally have been his last) year of office, accepted his responsibility without hesitation, and acted with vigour. He met demands for credit by lending freely; in the two weeks ending August 5 the Bank's holding of 'Other Securities' increased by £31,700,000, representing chiefly loans to billbrokers to enable them to meet calls made on them by the joint-stock banks. Similarly, he made no attempt to evade the Bank's liability to pay gold on demand against its notes. Some of the joint-stock banks, in the endeavour to strengthen their own position, had cashed customers' cheques in Bank of England five-pound notes. It was the week before Bank Holiday, and most of the demands for gold were for holiday currency, which in those days meant sovereigns. At the last meeting before war, on July 30, the Court had put Bank Rate up from 3 to 4 per cent as a warning; the following day the Governor raised Bank Rate to 8 per cent and the very next day, Saturday, August 1, to 10 per cent.

That same day the Governor informed the Chancellor of the Exchequer (Lloyd George) that he would be unable to continue meeting the demands upon the Bank unless he obtained authority to issue notes against securities in excess of the amount authorised by law; whereupon he received a 'Chancellor's Letter', modelled on similar letters in the crises of 1847, 1857 and 1866, recommending him at his discretion to exceed the limit, on condition that the minimum rate of interest on any further advance should be 10 per cent, and promising to apply to Parliament for indemnity. In the event, this authority was not used [1]; and in the subsequent discussions of the bankers

---

[1] As was stated some time later (9 November 1915) by the Prime Minister in the House of Commons, the only occasion on which the Bank had had to exceed the fiduciary limit was on August 7 and 8, by which time the Chancellor's Letter had been superseded by an indemnifying clause in the Currency and Bank Notes Act, 1914, which had become law on August 6.

with the Chancellor the Governor maintained that he would and could have met the demands on him for gold. Furthermore, the Governor maintained, there had been no good reason for the joint-stock banks' refusal to part with their gold ; nor would there be good reason for a general suspension of specie payments.

No plan for meeting a credit crisis had been included in the Government's preparations for war. The measures adopted were worked out in discussion between Ministers and the bankers and traders affected. Even for such discussion the City was not well organised. There did not exist the practice of continuous and intimate contact, through the Bank, between Treasury and City, which has developed since. The Chancellor had therefore to listen to deputations or appeals from traders and bankers, from Discount houses as well as Clearing Bankers, in addition to 'a number of financial and business men' whom he had met at lunch on July 28, and to the Governor of the Bank himself. Fortunately the Chancellor was quick to grasp a new situation and prompt to act, and fortunately, too, he was assisted at the Treasury by Lord Reading, the Lord Chief Justice, who had an equally quick and penetrating mind and understood the work of the City.

The first need was to remove the immediate threat that the £300/350 million of bills outstanding would lose their value through inability of acceptors and endorsers to meet them. This was lifted by a proclamation on August 2 postponing for a month payment of bills accepted before August 4. The following day the Postponement of Payments Act was passed through Parliament, authorising the Government to suspend temporarily other payments. This also legalised retrospectively the proclamation of August 2 and it was followed by other proclamations on August 6 and 12, permitting the postponement for a month of payments due under contracts entered into before August 4, wages and certain other payments being excluded. The joint-stock banks, who had asked the Chancellor for this moratorium, had undertaken to cash cheques for wages, but they would ration the cash which customers took over the counter for other purposes ; and they asked the Bank for help in protecting their cash position. The Bank agreed to give the facilities asked ; for the Governor had

no intention of taking accounts from the clearing banks and
he had already refused some. But the immediate threat of a
rush for currency (if it ever existed, which the Governor denied)
was met by extending Bank Holiday over Tuesday, Wednesday
and Thursday, and the need of currency was met by the
provision of Treasury notes. The details of this issue to the
banks were left by the Chancellor to be worked out by Sir
John Bradbury [1] and the Governor in consultation with the
bankers.

These were temporary measures; they would not suffice to
restore a working system of making payments. To make this
possible, accepting houses must be in a position to resume the
giving of acceptance credits, and holders of bills to sell or
borrow on them. Accordingly, on August 13, it was announced
that the Bank of England, under Government guarantee against
loss, would discount at Bank Rate, without recourse to the
holders, all approved bills accepted before August 4, and that
acceptors of such bills discounted at the Bank might postpone
payment at maturity by paying interest at 2 per cent above
Bank Rate varying. Then on September 5 it was announced
that the Bank of England would provide acceptors with funds
to pay all pre-moratorium bills at maturity at 2 per cent above
Bank Rate, with an undertaking not to claim repayment of any
sums not recovered by acceptors from their clients until one
year after the end of the war. Provision was made for new bills
on similar terms, and for the much smaller needs of the Stock
Exchange for account-to-account loans. The general moratorium came to an end on November 4, and the Stock Exchange
reopened on 4 January 1915.

(v)

Norman had returned from New York on 1 July 1914. He was
feeling the strain of his return to work, and 'far from well'.
The problem of his future relations with his firm overhung his
mind, but he was seeing much of his friends and relatives,
spending the day at Lord's and dining with the old pupils of

[1] Joint Permanent Secretary, H.M. Treasury, 1913-19. Principal British
Delegate to Reparation Commission, 1919-25. Later Lord Bradbury.

his Eton tutor. The week-end before the crisis he was in the country; he came up on July 28, but went down to Gloucester-shire the following day. He was brought back by telegram but was too late for the meeting of the Court of the Bank on the 29th. When he did get back, it was the difficulties facing an accepting house like Brown Shipley that first absorbed him. A junior colleague in his own firm recollects calling on him on the Sunday morning at Thorpe Lodge and asking whether he could be of any help. Norman tossed him a telegraph form and said: 'Yes: finish this. I have been trying to for two hours.' It began, 'Europe prospects very gloomy'; it was sent without any addition. War was declared on Tuesday, August 4. In letters to his partner, James Brown, in New York he gives an account of the crisis as it appeared to him just after the event.

12 August 1914

. . . As one looks back the time has been one long maze of apparently impossible conditions necessitating innumerable prompt decisions on points never heard of before and certainly never con-sidered since the Napoleonic Wars.

. . . All of a sudden and without notice, financial transactions with Belgium, France, Germany, Austria and Russia — to say nothing of other countries had come to an end; the indebted-ness of these countries falling due from day to day being of course enormous. The immediate result must have been the failure of all Accepting Houses and Banks so soon as their cash should be exhausted, with the corresponding liability on those who were holders or endorsers of maturing Bills of Exchange.

The first actual result of war which alarmed those who were watching events was the sudden demand at every branch of every Bank for currency. This danger was met in the first instance by a Royal Proclamation making Monday to Thursday (inclusive) of last week Bank Holidays, so allowing time for emergency measures to be taken. These emergency measures took the form of the issue in large quantities of Government Notes for £1 and 10/- as legal tender. There was no serious run when the Joint Stock Banks re-opened; and there is no evidence of any general hoarding.

More or less simultaneously, three enactments came into force which had a vital effect upon business:

(1) The extension of maturing Acceptances for a month at a time, so temporarily saving the position of Acceptors.

(2) The closing of the Stock Exchange and deferment of all payments and deliveries due thereon; necessary, firstly, to avoid panicky sales and consequent shrinkage of values; and, secondly, to preserve fifty or a hundred firms who had dealt on foreign account and could not complete their bargains.

(3) A month's Moratorium as regards all debts due on demand, which has relieved the Discount Market and similar houses from having to repay any of their loans.

Needless to say, the work and confusion attendant on carrying out these various enactments have been very difficult and severe. Many mistakes must have been made, many details must have been overlooked : and while as regards persons (other than Enemies) domiciled in this country no great trouble may therefrom *inter se* arise, their position *vis-à-vis* foreigners is likely to present endless difficulties and, I should imagine, many lawsuits.

Let us now consider for a moment what is the present position; . . . London is owed money by practically all the world, and her present object is to collect her debts as quickly as possible. The Joint Stock Banks here, having already received the promise of such assistance from the Government as they seem likely to require, can continue so far as the domestic position is concerned. Loans and advances are being, and can be, made by the Bank of England to an almost unlimited extent on satisfactory security. There should be no necessity for the country to part with Gold, firstly because she has very little to spare, and secondly because for the time being remittances are universally due to London. The fact, however, remains that for the moment every channel of credit is practically closed. The Stock Exchange cannot open because buyers cannot pay, and because sellers by pressing securities for sale may so depreciate prices as to make all existing loans bad. The Discount Market cannot work because none of the Bills they hold are being paid, because their liability on Bills already held or endorsed is incalculable, and because nobody can lend them money with which to take new Bills even if they were willing to do so. The Accepting Banks and Houses are in greater or less degree insolvent : there certainly is hardly one among them whose cash in hand would permit of Acceptances already falling due being paid, while those whose main business has lain with the belligerent countries have debts due therefrom and gradually maturing which many times exceed their Capital. Nor must I forget to mention the sums due here on the Acceptances of the various foreign Banks with branches in London; those of the Enemy having already been closed by our Government.

. . . Perhaps the first thing is to deal with Acceptances, which would vastly relieve the Joint Stock Banks and the Discount Market, neither of whom for the reasons given can buy Bills at the present time and on both of whom an immeasurable liability seems to hang, due to the fact that if pressed very few of the Acceptances they hold could be met.

Norman was put on the Bank committees set up, one to deal with pre-moratorium bills brought to the Bank for discount, and the other to consider applications from accepting houses to the Bank for funds to pay approved pre-moratorium bills.

No reply from James Brown came through until September; but on August 16 his partner cabled the outline of a scheme for an emergency clearing of exchange which a group of bankers had, at the request of the Federal Reserve Board, discussed and recommended. Norman was already familiar with the proposal, and, while he could see the attractions, did not think the Bank of England would feel justified in recommending it. In a letter on August 29, after a further exchange of cables, he doubts whether the critical position of New York will last long enough to justify such an exceptional measure. He concludes:

. . . Lastly, I would have you remember that this country is at the beginning of perhaps a long war: that the outlook for the immediate future is anything but certain: that this country, though largely creditor, is being able to collect none of its debts from any European country, and scarcely from any country or colony in the world: that in addition to having to bear the brunt of supplying our Government with funds, it is supplying assistance on a very large scale to help our domestic trade and general business: that we have already begun, and shall have to continue, to finance Belgium and possibly other countries as well; and that whatever advance is thus made to the U.S. will surely be used as a lever for similar advances to Canada and other Colonies. So that with all these requirements and difficulties, we obviously must not extend our credit more than can possibly be helped in other than necessary directions, and the mere fact of the United States not being at war leads one to hope that every endeavour

will be made to meet her citizens' debts contracted in this
country.

Norman writes again on September 24, answering some of
his partner's arguments for the clearing scheme and giving
further news of the position in London :

. . . I agree that for the moment the United States was almost
put in the situation of a Bank perfectly solvent but asked suddenly
to pay 100 cents on the dollar on all deposits. But the position of
the United States has, in point of fact, been made comparatively
easy by the indirect advantage her traders have taken of our
Moratorium. And unwilling though every reasonable man must
be to put the U.S. in such a situation, there was during the crisis
no alternative consistent with the safety of our banking position
but to make every attempt to collect payment before lending or
re-lending any monies. Of course, the crux of our position was,
and is, the question of gold exports.

. . . In the meantime the question no longer affects our Firms
as acutely as it did a week or more ago, since you have lately been
able to remit in full on behalf of all credit customers, notwithstand-
ing the high rates of exchange which have prevailed right along.

. . . The General Moratorium will probably be prolonged
again, but as it embraces only ante-bellum conditions, it is gradually
becoming more precautionary than real. It is the trouble about
outstanding Loans and their margins (chiefly on the Stock Exchange) that really prevents its coming to an end, and we are now
working on various plans to make these Loans capable of being
treated as liquid and transferable during the continuance of the war.

As regards the Accepting Houses, their post-bellum business
is now extremely sound, as it ranks ahead of ante-bellum business
and I almost fear some of them may be tempted before long to go
too far afield in order to do any volume of business commensurate
with standing charges, since their usual business seems to have
been curtailed by perhaps 70%. But sooner or later — not more
than one year after peace is effected, to be precise — the day of
reckoning must come, and its effect would seem to depend on the
eventual position of their clients in enemy countries, and to less
extent on the power of resuscitation among their clients in allied
and neutral countries, and on the scope of and reserves behind
their general undertakings.

. . . But the direction in which prospects are most indefinite
and hopeless is in regard to the value of 'miscellaneous securities'.

These, being mostly born of 'promiscuous under-writings' in the comparative shelter of a passing whim or local craze, seem to need the glamour of good times before they can for the most part again achieve any liquid or actual value. Even our Stock Exchange List contains many such perpetrations and has in the past been thought to impart an actual value to many such as could not otherwise have possessed it . . . but I fear that a deal of water must flow under the bridge before — even to the most sanguine — it can be expected to do so a second time !! You cannot watch the spending or wasting of millions of pounds a week without the conviction that water is being squeezed out of something, and I submit to you that it is, *inter alia*, out of miscellaneous securities. So we must all expect to be poorer, and therewith must somehow be content.

James Brown, writing on October 4, emphasises how much of American difficulties was due to the atomistic character of American banking. 'Neither the Comptroller nor the Secretary of the Treasury having any power, who was to persuade a little bank with $25,000 capital in Waco, Texas, that it was its duty, for the benefit of the country at large, to ship to its New York correspondent ten per cent of its gold reserve?' By that time, however, he thought that the exchange situation was out of the way: the next problem was the opening of the Stock Exchange. He was apprehensive of the vast amounts of American securities which might be dumped on the New York market by British holders, and which would in turn react on the exchange market. His comment on London may be added:

With the multitude of things we have had to think and write about, I feel that I have failed to express to you the admiration which everyone here who knows anything about international finances feels for the way in which the English bank crisis has been handled. It has been a marvel of ability, judgment, and foresight, and, from this distance, it does not seem as if one single mistake had been made. The fact that such an emergency could be met without suspending specie payment seemed impossible.

Norman wrote again on October 22:

I am inclined to think that, if anything, more than was actually necessary was done in order to take care of the crisis; but when acting suddenly in order to restore confidence, it is better to go

G

too far than not far enough and so miss fire. I am glad to think that, looking at the whole matter in perspective from your disinterested standpoint, you approve the general plan.

On the whole, general business and the general position here are improving. Debts are gradually being liquidated by Neutrals, and commodities are being used up and paid for; but, while this improvement may continue so long as the War news is good, we might still be liable to a rude disturbance in the event — improbable as I think — of a decided success on the part of the Enemy.

At the same time, although arrangements are in hand which will help to liquefy outstanding loans on securities or at least to make them good, I can see no immediate prospect of a resumption of business on the Stock Exchange. In fact, I think that dealings in securities may have to grow up (so to speak) outside the Stock Exchange under conditions where the buyer seeks out the seller, and when, long hence, this process shall have gone far enough — and it is already showing signs of progressing — the opening of the Stock Exchange will be a comparatively simple matter. Nor can I see how your Stock Exchange can open with impunity yet awhile. Of course, it may be done at any time under considerable restrictions, but were it to be done so as to put dealings back at once on the old lines, I think that the sales from Europe might at any time be heavy and bring about demoralising results. . . .

Let me just add that, certain branches of business being evidently very active owing to war requirements, the outlook has correspondingly improved, so that openings will perhaps occur for those who are in a position to take them. In fact, I am convinced that had we ourselves been conducting business on proper lines, the present would soon yield a golden opportunity. For as regards Credit business, we, along with —— and ——, are the only people who ought not to have been hit at all: and, as regards Security business, we, along with ——, are the only people in that line who need not to have suffered severely. As it is, I beg you to tell me upon what basis you propose to conduct a credit business of large dimensions after the end of the year's changes. 'I told you so' is the only consolation that you will get from me!! for an agreement never completed in due time is no more solace than a sick headache. And you may soon watch the position which ought to be held here owing to the absence of Enemy accounts being frittered away, partly owing to idiotic credits and partly to promiscuous securities of uncertain value and still more remote worth.

(vi)

The crisis in which the outbreak of war involved firms like
Brown Shipley postponed Norman's personal problem of his
relation with the firm.   Actually the extent of the assistance
which it sought under the Government and Bank's scheme
was very small, not more than 2 or 3 per cent of its liability on
acceptances.   But until the measures taken had assured the
solvency of the London banking community generally and
then while the accepting houses were adjusting their relations
with customers and overseas partners to the new conditions of
business, there was more than enough to occupy him.   On top
of that he was already feeling the shock of war casualties ; for
two of his cousins and eleven or twelve more of his circle of
friends were killed or wounded or missing in September, Barton
his South African subaltern was killed, and he lost another
cousin in November.   But he still expected to withdraw from
the firm, and he was looking round for war work.   He began
to spend more time in the Bank of England in the New Year ;
apparently he had already told the Governor personally of his
intention to leave his firm.   His engagement book begins to
record conversations with other, senior, Directors on the questions with which the Bank found itself faced.   Especially does
he begin to discuss the country's growing problem of finding
dollars with Edward Grenfell,[1] who as senior partner in Morgan
Grenfell & Co., the London house associated with J. P. Morgan
& Co., the American bankers, was the main informal link
between the Bank and New York.   Morgans were to become
the agents first of the Bank and later of the British Government
in the measures taken to support the dollar value of the
pound.

On 20 April 1915 Norman began regular work in the War
Office as adviser on financial questions arising in the course of
the cable censorship.   For this his experience of international
credit business and his knowledge of firms and persons in
America and on the Continent fitted him.   An international
banker could help in detecting transactions with neutral countries, innocent enough on the surface, which originated or
terminated in enemy territory.   At first the work involved

[1] Director of the Bank of England, 1905–40.   Later Lord St. Just.

continuous attendance at the War Office, seven days a week, and then, when the first rush was over, a new task offered itself. This was to act as chairman of a committee, called the Aircraft Insurance Expert Committee, appointed in July 1915 to implement a scheme of insurance against damage from enemy aircraft and bombardment; and at the request of the President of the Board of Trade, Walter Runciman, Norman accepted the post. The scheme provided for insurance by the State, its agents being so far as possible the Fire Insurance companies. Once it was working, the scheme does not seem to have involved any difficult financial problems; but Norman was to find, even after he had come to the Bank full-time, that the routine work would take him an hour and a half a day. The scale of operations seems small in the light of experience in the Second World War — just under £3 million for claims up to the end of hostilities, with estimated liabilities still to be met of about £400,000.

A week after Runciman's invitation there came another, this time from Reginald McKenna,[1] who had succeeded Lloyd George as Chancellor of the Exchequer. The Chancellor wanted Norman to take the chairmanship of a small committee to deal with applications from contractors for variation of the original terms of their contracts to allow for the rise in their costs, and he said politely that he knew of no one on whose judgment on such matters he would sooner rely. But work at the War Office and on the administration of the Aircraft Insurance Scheme left Norman no time, and he was forced to decline. Even so, it was not long before Norman's special knowledge was drawn on by other departments : the Board of Trade, for other insurance problems; the Postal Censor, the War Trade Department, which was set up in February 1915 to take over the licensing work of the Trading with the Enemy Committee; and the Foreign Office. Not until he became Deputy Governor in March 1918 did he give up his daily visits to the War Office; and then he arranged for his place to be taken by a member of the Cornhill Committee, which was a friendly channel of liaison between the City and the Ministry of Blockade and the Postal Censorship. Nevertheless, he agreed to go every Friday

[1] Chancellor of the Exchequer, 1915–16. Later a Director, and from 1919 Chairman, of the Midland Bank Ltd.

and to go once a week also to the Postal Censorship. He finally gave up his visits to the War Office in April 1919.

In February 1916 he began to advise the Postal Censor regularly, and later another engagement developed. This was with the Ministry of Blockade, where the Controller of the Finance Section, Sir Adam Block, began to draw frequently on Norman's advice, especially on the use of censorship for intensifying economic pressure on the Central Powers. Germany was making efforts to get funds to America for propaganda, and to collect securities and claims on America and other overseas countries to provide the funds. These efforts were not always easy to identify, and the attempt to intercept them involved interfering with neutral bankers and agents. Norman's help was used to draw up rules for the operation of the blockade to catch such financial assets, to discriminate between legitimate neutral business and concealed aid to the enemy, and to devise measures to forward the Government's aims when they were not strictly within the scope of the blockade. They wanted, for example, to check shipments of gold from America, partly for exchange reasons, and partly on the general ground that the Allies wanted to borrow in America, and would find it easier if America were full of gold — as American bankers were telling them in their letters. When a Ministry suggested bringing pressure to bear on a London house which was — quite legally — facilitating this movement of gold, Norman suggested to the official concerned that they should confine themselves to holding up the firm's letters in the censorship, when the firm would complain, and the Controller could talk to them. Similarly, he dissuaded the Postal Censor from taking up formally with a Dutch bank its handling of German-owned securities, since the case was not watertight and in any case it was not certain that the traffic could be stopped. Norman suggested restricting cable facilities to neutral bankers suspected of aiding the enemy, but he warned the Ministry against bringing pressure generally on Holland. The problem was to prevent transfers to and from Germany, while allowing for the increase in neutral transactions because of the war.

At one point the financial blockade converged on another of Norman's interests: the dollar and other exchanges that were engaging his mind in the Bank. He helped the Ministry of

Blockade to draft a return for banks to fill in of exchange transactions, and later of sterling balances held by them for account
of overseas countries; but he was convinced before the end
of 1916 that a comprehensive control by the Government of
exchange transactions was necessary. He often urged on Block
that strict control was necessary not only for blockading the
enemy, but also to lighten the burden of maintaining the New
York exchange, which was under pressure through the dealings
of both the neutrals and the Allies. All gold, thought Norman,
should be notified to the Treasury, and exchange business
restricted to a few banks under tight rules. He found his
official friend 'obstinate'.

A recurrent difficulty was the lack of co-ordination between
different departments. On one subject, gold shipments from
America, he notes that the indecision and lack of unity of the
Treasury, the India Office (which was selling Council Bills on
terms which ensured an automatic profit on private imports of
gold from America), the Foreign Office and the Ministry of
Blockade made it impossible for the Censors to take an intelli-
gent line or know how to act. The Treasury seemed to be
trying to get the whole thing into their hands, to the exclusion
of the London Exchange Committee, which had hitherto
advised. When America came into the war (April 1917)
Benjamin Strong, the Governor of the Federal Reserve Bank
of New York, pressed Norman to visit America in order to
advise on the organisation of a censorship. He was unable to
go, but wrote that the essential thing was to entrust to a single
government department with technical advice the handling
of all censorship work.

In spite of the mediation of friends, W. W. Paine [1] and
R. M. Kindersley [2] in particular, to reconcile Norman and his
partners, it is clear that he had no expectation of returning to
Brown Shipley. He was prepared to agree to any arrangement
which would postpone a public break until the end of the war;
but he was telling his friends on the Court of the Bank of his
decision. A last attempt to find a working arrangement was
made through a friend in June 1915, but came to nothing. He

---

[1] Later General Manager of Lloyds Bank Ltd.
[2] Director of the Bank of England, 1914–46. Knighted, 1917. Lord Kindersley, 1941.

notified his partners in that month, and records in his engagement book, under December 24, 'Fetched "things" from Founders Court', and under December 31, 'A. H. B. and E. C. B. [his partners] hail and farewell'. The first entry in his engagement book for 1 January 1916 is 'Free man to-day'.

Norman made a note after his resignation was announced, which makes the sequence clear :

For several years before War I was not in Agreement with my Partners here.

In the spring of 1914 Senior gave formal notice of his intention to retire that year.

In consequence thereof and as no agreement concerning future business was possible, I too was willing to retire in 1914.

But the War came and all such questions were temporarily suspended.

In 1915 I offered the choice to my partners — either that I should retire at once or that I should stay on until after the War.

They chose the former.

The legal separation was 31 December 1915. War would in any case have drawn him away : a letter to him from an American partner six months later shows that it was inevitable.

. . . You know, I hope and think, what the separation last January meant to me personally, and although I have not written it is still as deep a regret and loss as ever it was. Up to the very end I hoped that some solution of your differences in London might be found which would mean your continuance, but the more I have thought of the situation there as it had existed for many years the more inevitable became the final break. I am glad for your sake, just as I am glad for my own, that you have been so busy mentally and physically since the 1st of the year that you have not had too much time to think about it. It would have done no good.

The pity of it all is that it should have come just at this time when we here in America would seem to be making some real ground and regaining in a measure our position.

CHAPTER III

FIRST YEARS IN THE BANK

(i)

WHEN Norman finally left Brown Shipley his colleagues on the Court of the Bank took steps, very cautiously, to provide him with an alternative office. On 6 January 1916 the Deputy Governor, Brien Cokayne,[1] wrote to him:

> Will you be so kind as to come, regularly, and 'devil' for me here? I think that pretty well expresses what the Court on the suggestion of the Treasury Committee have informally given me leave to ask you to do. It would be quite an informal arrangement between you and me except in so far as the Court will formally (if you are good enough to consent) add your name to all the Bank Committees of which I am Chairman, so that you may do the work while I take credit for all your wisdom! You would have no official status nor be put on the Treasury Committee, and the latter told me specially to tell you that my making this request to you would not in any way imply that you would be nominated as the next Deputy Governor.
>
> I think that sums up all the 'cons' that I can think of from your point of view, and I fear that the 'pros' are all on my side. I shall be most grateful if you will come and help me with my duties, of which I am compelled to neglect a good many in these days, and there is no one whom I would sooner have at hand to consult in all the problems which arise at every minute in the day.
>
> The dear old Governor has been ordered to give his mind an absolute rest and is not allowed even to open his letters or papers. I hope and believe that he will get well all the quicker so.
>
> It appears to be quite understood in the City that you have left your firm to devote yourself to public work, and if you come and help me here your action will be more 'intelligible' still.

[1] Director of the Bank of England, 1902–32. Deputy Governor, 1915–18. Governor, 1918–20. Knighted, September 1917. Lord Cullen, April 1920.

Norman replied next day:

The vagaries of the Post brought me your letter too late for it to be acted upon to-day — and I presume to-morrow may be ignored? But I shall be very glad to come on Monday and regularly thereafter, as soon as I get away from the W.O.

I quite understand and agree that for the present I am no more than your 'devil', without any position: and that for the future, I have no rights or expectations of any kind whatever.

But I shall try to be, or to become, your willing and cheerful fag, and I am only grateful for the kindly way in which you have chosen to make this suggestion to me.

I hope the old Governor can be persuaded to take enough care of himself to get well without delay.

He records in his engagement book on January 10, underneath the regular entry 'War Office and Insurance', 'Begin today as Deputy's devil'.

It was not long before his usefulness was recognised. On March 29 the Committee of Treasury recommended to the Court that Norman's signature be accepted in lieu of one of the Governors while he is assisting the Deputy Governor; and on May 4 he was added to this Committee. There was room for an executive director to assist the chief officials in the administrative work of the Bank, which had had thrust upon it a new and unprecedented burden of work for the Government in raising money, moderating the inflationary effects of such borrowing, and meeting the Government's urgent need for dollars. Evidence of this was seen in the expanding staff and in the purchase in October 1916 of a building in Old Street (an old asylum called St. Luke's Hospital) for conversion into a printing works for bank-notes.

In the new environment Norman's health improved. He was able to work through Easter without a break and, when he got three or four days away, to take long cross-country walks. In his new position he had the opportunity of meeting and entertaining at Thorpe Lodge Ben Strong, the Governor of the Federal Reserve Bank of New York, on his first visit to London in March. What struck Norman most, as a newcomer to the higher direction of the Bank, was the unsatisfactory state of relations of the Committee of Treasury with the Governor, and the difficulty it caused to the effective handling of the big issues of policy.

The Governor's handling of the crisis at the outbreak of war had been masterly. The Committee of Treasury, which normally provided continuity and guidance to administration by Governors who changed every two years, had been satisfied to leave the Governor to act with only such consultation as he thought fit, so long as prompt decision and forceful action were essential. Even when a basis for a war-time system of credit and currency had been established, his colleagues had been content to leave him to run the Bank, advise the Treasury, and conduct relations with the other banks and agencies in the City, with very little interference. But even before he joined the Committee of Treasury, Norman had come across evidence of doubt and concern among his fellow Directors. The Bank had been entering into large commitments, at home and abroad, and the Governor had not always troubled to keep his colleagues informed.

To explain Norman's part in affairs from the time that he came actively on the scene, it is necessary to trace the story of Britain's struggle during 1915 to find enough dollars to pay her way. It begins early in the year with the fall in the dollar-exchange rate, which the Bank countered on February 18 by asking Morgans (in association with two other New York banks) to take up all sterling bills coming on offer up to an amount of $10 million, raised a few days later to $25 million. This limit was overrun in May, but still Morgans went on buying sterling and the Bank began to sell gold to reduce the debt. On June 23 the Governor arranged with the Chancellor (McKenna) that the Government should take over forthwith the liability for these borrowings, but agreement was delayed by differences of opinion on points of detail. Eventually, at the end of August, the Bank accepted entire responsibility for the transactions up to date, but declared that they would give no further support to the sterling-dollar rate. They informed Morgans accordingly and shipped another £12 million of gold, making nearly £25 million in all, to extinguish the debt. While these negotiations between the Bank and the Treasury were going on, the Bank had received from Morgans a further advance of £10 million worth of dollars, which was liquidated soon afterwards by the sale of British holdings of American securities.

As a result of the Bank's withdrawal of support, the dollar

rate fell heavily. A recovery was then brought about by the Bank's mobilising on behalf of the Treasury large blocks of American securities, and by the issue in October of a loan for $500 million to the British and French Governments in equal parts. But these were only temporary reliefs. Anxiety in the City was mounting, and although the Bank's only corporate pronouncement throughout the year was a Resolution by the Court on November 18, warning the Chancellor of the Exchequer that the growing drain on gold 'might imperil the maintenance of the gold standard in this country', individual opinion was more specific. Grenfell told Norman as early as July that the expropriation by Act of Parliament of American securities in English hands was the only hope. At the beginning of November Norman notes a warning from the three most experienced international bankers on the Court, Grenfell, Lord Revelstoke [1] and Sir Everard Hambro,[2] that the dollar position was critical.

On the same day that the Court were passing their warning Resolution the Chancellor was engaged in giving formal effect to the advice that had been urged on him by the Governor with the support of other prominent bankers. This was to appoint a body, called the London Exchange Committee, 'to act as a Committee for the regulation of the foreign exchanges' with full authority to act for the Treasury and to have at its disposal all that the Government might possess in gold, foreign securities, and loans from abroad. These were wide powers — too wide, in the opinion of McKenna's successor, Bonar Law, when he took office in December 1916; but by that time the Committee had established itself as a valuable body, claiming in practice no more than reasonable powers, and Bonar Law acquiesced. The original membership of the Committee was the Governor and Deputy Governor and two clearing bankers, Sir Edward Holden and Sir Felix Schuster. Holden soon withdrew from active membership, his place being taken by a merchant banker, Gaspard Farrer of Barings. In 1917 there was added to the Committee the Financial Secretary of the Treasury, Stanley Baldwin, and a representative of the Foreign Office. Except that a Treasury official

[1] Director of the Bank of England, 1898–1929.
[2] Director of the Bank of England, 1879–1925.

took the Financial Secretary's place in 1918 there were no other changes in the composition of the Committee before its dissolution on 31 December 1919. The Committee's first act was to arrange a loan of $50 million between groups of bankers in New York and London. This was repaid in gold in June 1917. The British authorities continued to use Morgans as their New York agents.

In the summer of 1916 the Governor and Deputy Governor began to take Norman with them on their visits to the Treasury when they discussed foreign exchange. His comments reveal his fears. On May 30, after a discussion at the Treasury in which the danger of the position was explained and a loan proposed, he was left with the impression that they did not realise the true position. Norman also records of this occasion that McKenna considered himself limited to moral suasion as regards the sale of undertakings to America, and talked hopefully of the freedom of action which default would give him in dealing with the public and asking powers from Parliament; and that he could not have known what default would really mean. A similar note on June 6 records the same impression of a Treasury muddled and a Chancellor blind to the exchange position. Unless something turned up, as the Chancellor seemed to expect, default was inevitable. Another discussion at the Treasury later in the month, while the Governor was in Scotland, showed a slight change. The dollar position was at last admitted to be serious; but even yet no provision was being made for debts that were accruing in amounts of which neither we nor Morgans knew the size. The Chancellor 'walked up and down protesting that he wished to have balances in America irrespective of the cost of interest, but takes no steps to get them'. Norman went so far as to warn Lord Robert Cecil, whom he saw as Minister of Blockade, of the serious exchange position.

The Committee of Treasury were becoming restive. The Governor had come up on June 14 from his holiday and shown them the 'complete skeleton' of the gold and foreign exchange position. They had special meetings on August 9 and 10, when the Governor had returned, and another meeting on the 14th, from which the Governor took a letter for the Prime Minister (Asquith):

Following on our frequent interviews I have consulted my Committee of Treasury here, and I find they are in complete agreement with me in considering that, as the Chancellor's views regarding International Finance, Foreign Exchanges and other important Financial problems connected with the War are so frequently at variance with the views of myself and my Committee, we cannot associate ourselves with a policy of which we do not approve, a policy which, had it been carried out, would in our opinion on several occasions have seriously endangered the credit of the Country.

Hitherto you yourself with Lord Reading, Mr. Montagu [1] and Sir Robert Chalmers [2] giving their assistance at the Treasury, have been able to overcome the grave difficulties into which the Chancellor's methods have led us — as for instance the American Exchange fiasco in August, September and October of 1915 — but now that they have all left the Treasury I am very much afraid that matters cannot long go on as they are without a disastrous breakdown.

As I pointed out to you, I shall have to meet the Joint Stock Bankers early next week and I should like to be in a position to reassure them.

Whether this was necessary may be doubted. American securities in British hands, though there was no compulsion, were mobilised to provide collateral for a two-year secured loan of $250 million in New York, dated September 1, a direct obligation of the British Government. Norman would have preferred such a loan to be issued through a corporation formed *ad hoc*; but Morgans were alarmed at a partial failure of a French Corporation Loan, at the size of this British loan, which was barely secured, and at the shilly-shallying of the Treasury. Further evidence of official awareness of the position came on September 19, when Morgans were told to budget for payments on British account of $50 million a week for an indefinite period. This was the first time that any indication of future needs had been given to Morgans, who, though the Government agents, had been working in the dark. It was new, too, to Norman, who thereupon made his first attempt — without success — to persuade the Ministry of Blockade to control

---

[1] Hon. E. S. Montagu, formerly Financial Secretary to the Treasury.

[2] Joint Permanent Secretary, H.M. Treasury, 1916–19. Under-Secretary for Ireland, May–September 1916. Later Lord Chalmers.

exchange as a function of theirs outside the scope of the Exchange Committee.

A second loan based on British-owned securities, amounting to $300 million, was underwritten by a New York syndicate and issued on November 1. These loans had not been planned with the care that Norman thought necessary. The securities had not been prepared in advance, nor were they in hand at the time of issue. Nor, again, were adequate preparations being made for the future, whether by forcing the deposit of securities, by coercing municipalities and others to borrow in New York, or by purchasing large blocks. 'A strange way of maintaining British credit!' he commented. Moreover, these two issues did not meet the full need. By mid-November the position was already growing worse and in spite of urgings by Grenfell and Morgans, and various suggestions for issues in New York, there was no move to forestall a crisis by raising fresh money on something longer than the shortest term. The expedient adopted, at Morgans' suggestion, was an issue of Treasury Bills in dollars. It was not a novel one, but Norman recognised that it would tide over a critical period and he was prepared to support any measure recommended by Morgans.

Nevertheless the exchange position continued to deteriorate. Reconstruction of the Cabinet involved delay in Government decisions, and finance in New York had become a Cabinet question. On December 6, at the request and with the guarantee of the Treasury, the Bank had agreed to open a credit in London for £20 million in favour of an American financial group, the group to pay the equivalent in dollars to the Treasury account with J. P. Morgan & Co.; these, according to the London Exchange Committee, were the only terms on which it was possible to borrow in New York. The Committee of Treasury agreed reluctantly. Norman was away that week but he was back for the next meeting of the Committee on the 13th, when there was, he notes, a 'nasty discussion'. The Committee learned for the first time what he had learned two days previously, that the Bank was also (by a misunderstanding) borrower for the Treasury on short loans up to $100 million in connection with the second loan raised on American securities in British hands. This had, the Governor explained, been inevitable to enable the Government's financing in America to be continued, and the Government supplied the collateral. The Committee of Treasury did not like the Bank's name being used, but again approved the Governor's action. A week later the Committee learned that Dutch and Japanese bills had been guaranteed by the Bank, without discussion. The second collateral loan put the Government in funds in New York for a few weeks. Future needs had to be met by drawing on gold placed in Ottawa. There was talk of a commission to go to America in the New Year, and on January 26 an Order was published enabling the Government to conscript securities — 'better late than never'. But in the New Year it was also becoming clear that the whole situation might be changed. Diplomatic relations between the United States and Germany were broken off on February 3, and on 6 April 1917 the United States declared war.

(ii)

To have held the value of sterling within about 2 per cent of its parity in dollars for three years, without any preparation or plan beforehand, without any power to requisition exchange holdings, gold or securities and without any authority to prohibit transactions in exchange so long as they did not involve trading with the enemy, was a remarkable achievement, for which the chief credit must go to Cunliffe and to J. P. Morgan & Co. But improvisation inevitably leads to misunderstandings and friction. We have seen that Cunliffe, and those of his Bank colleagues whom he brought in, found the Treasury sometimes difficult to move, and it can be inferred that the Treasury found the Governor difficult to work with. The same difficulties arose in the Bank. While his colleagues were content in the early months of the war to leave to his unfettered initiative and willingness to take responsibility the handling of the tasks thrust on the Bank by war, they became uneasy as time went on and they found the Bank involved in liabilities which they had had no opportunity of discussing.

The ineffectiveness of the Committee of Treasury, as we have already observed, was the first thing that struck Norman when he was put on the Committee in May 1916. 'They seem', he says, 'to be content to receive no information and to give no advice or even approval, except implicitly. I certainly gain no information by being a member, and I already knew more than can be gathered from meeting.' His position was, however, exceptional. He was familiar with the New York market, which was the Governor's chief concern at the time, and he was in touch with exchange questions and the London Exchange Committee through his work for the Censorship; though it was the Deputy Governor he had been brought in to assist, he was drawn in to the Governor's activities and came to be taken into his confidence. He did not enjoy the visits he paid to the Treasury. It was 'a thankless job' and ineffective. Moreover, he thought that the Bank should restrict executive work to the Governors. It was the tradition of the Bank that visits to the Treasury were always made by the Governor and Deputy Governor together, but Cunliffe slipped into the practice of going alone. Early in October 1916 the Committee of Treasury strongly criticised an issue of 6 per cent Exchequer Bonds and wanted to know who was responsible. The Governor confided to Norman afterwards that he had virtually approved it, and was surprised at its effect on markets.

Norman was disturbed by the effect of internal differences on the external relations of the Bank, and prepared some notes to use if he had an opportunity of a talk with the Governor. He proposed to say that as most of the Committee had agreed to the Governor's re-election for another year, he should make a point of regular and full disclosure of Bank affairs and of his advice given as Governor. This was due to the Committee of Treasury by long custom, and was now essential in order to prepare for an inquiry after the war that Norman regarded as certain. He had the opportunity he was looking for when the Governor asked him down to Bath for the week-end of November 17. In the interval the Committee of Treasury had agreed formally to recommend re-election of the Governors, expressing the hope (but not making it a condition) that the pre-war advisory and consultative status of the Committee would be restored, and the Court had acted on their recommendation. There had been some recrimination, which, Norman thought, pointed to the need of fresh blood on the Committee, full disclosures, and then fresh (banking) blood on the Court. He had long talks at Bath with the Governor and found him entirely reasonable and aware of the future dangers to the Bank. Others also were moving. On November 1 Revelstoke had shown Norman in confidence a memorandum he had written on the internal organisation of the Bank's government, with which Norman generally agreed. Nearly a year elapsed, however, before any formal action was taken, and then it came only after the Governor had involved the Bank in a serious dispute with the Treasury.

In March 1917 the whole of the gold held on British behalf in Ottawa, whether for the Government or the Bank, was placed under the control of H.M. Treasury's representative in America, Sir Hardman Lever. This arrangement was still in force when Morgans on July 3 gave notice that they were obliged to call in two demand loans to the Treasury, one of which, for $85 million, was in the name of the Bank. The Governor immediately requested the Canadian Government (who were the custodians) to place at Morgans' disposal £17½ million of gold. Two days later, on learning that Lever also was continuing to draw gold from the Bank's stock, the Governor, without consulting the Treasury, had a telegram sent from the Bank to the Canadian Government instructing them to refuse any more gold until the whole of the Bank's debt had been repaid.

The confusion over the control of the gold, though regrettable and perhaps reprehensible, was not of itself sufficient cause for a quarrel; and even the maladroitness in sending the telegram without consulting the Treasury might have been smoothed by a quiet protest and apology. But personal relationships were already raw, in particular because the Governor had lately complained to the Chancellor (Bonar Law) of the Treasury's failure to keep him informed, as Chairman of the London Exchange Committee, on matters of exchange. The Chancellor, therefore, chose to see the telegram as a deliberate reprisal and to take it as a personal affront; and in those terms he complained to the Prime Minister (Lloyd George). He complained also that the telegram reflected on His Majesty's Government's credit.

The first the Committee of Treasury heard of these events was on 4 July 1917, when the Governor informed them that he had placed £17½ million gold at Morgans' disposal in discharge of the $85 million debt to them. Then, at a special

H

meeting of the Committee on July 9, the Governor informed them of the telegram and of the Chancellor's anger. He also informed them that three days earlier, on the 6th, he had had an interview with the Prime Minister, and that next day he had in consequence sent to the Chancellor this letter, a copy of which he showed them :

7 July 1917

DEAR MR. BONAR LAW,

I was extremely sorry to learn from the Prime Minister that, in telegraphing to the Canadian Authorities that after giving preference to the Gold so far ordered by Sir Hardman Lever they were to complete the Bank's order before doing more for Sir Hardman, you consider the Bank has damaged your credit in Canada.

I can absolutely assure you that nothing was further from my wishes or those of the Bank, and the instructions were purposely framed to imply that after the completion of the Bank's order Sir Hardman's further orders should be complied with ; thus giving the Treasury time to instruct him privately to pass his orders for Gold which has not been paid for by the Treasury (and is therefore still in our figures) through the Bank in future.

I have, of course, to admit that in my anxiety to assist the Exchange Committee at a very critical time, and with implicit faith in your good self and Sir Hardman Lever, I made an unpardonable mistake, for which there is no excuse, in allowing anyone to control Gold in the Bank's figure, and I am sure my Court will not only never permit it again, but censure me for having betrayed my trust in ever permitting it. But short of reverting to that system I will do anything you can suggest to remove any idea that the Bank's faith in you and Sir Hardman Lever is impaired, as such is not the case and never has been.

Believe me, yours sincerely,

CUNLIFFE

On July 11 the Governor reported to the Committee of Treasury a further interview with the Prime Minister, who had invited him to sign a memorandum to the effect that during the war the Bank must in all things act on the direction of the Chancellor whenever in his opinion the national interest was concerned, and must not take any action likely to affect credit without previous consultation with the Chancellor. The

Governor had replied that he could not sign such a document without consulting his colleagues, whose opinion he now sought. The Committee decided that it would be impossible for the Bank so to renounce their functions, and proposed that the Governor should again see the Prime Minister. This he did later the same day, but without progress. As he reported to the Committee of Treasury the following day (the 12th), the Prime Minister had spoken of 'taking over the Bank' if they would not submit. The Governor added that in order to remove any personal friction he proposed to take a holiday and leave the negotiations to the Deputy Governor. The Committee also desired to eliminate from the controversy both the personal question and the Treasury's relations with the London Exchange Committee, and to limit it to whether the Bank was or was not justified in tendering payment, by the only means in its power, of a debt which it had incurred and of which payment was demanded. But they suggested that the Governor should once more see the Prime Minister in an attempt at conciliation. Reporting on that to the Committee next day (the 13th), the Governor said that the Prime Minister had advised him to take his proposed holiday and later on to send through him a letter addressed to the Chancellor.

The Deputy Governor informed the Committee a few days later that he had seen the Chancellor, who assured him that he had no personal feeling in the matter and did not want the Governor to resign; and further, that the Government had agreed to take over the liability to Morgans for the Bank's debt of $85 million and also the Bank's undertaking to hold £17½ million against it. The Committee then agreed to the terms in which the Governor should write expressing regret at not consulting the Chancellor before the telegram was sent, and the Governor accordingly wrote [1] on July 16 (under a covering letter to the Prime Minister) :

[1] The account of this controversy is left as Sir Henry Clay had drafted it. In his biography of Bonar Law (*The Unknown Prime Minister*, p. 354) Mr. Robert Blake prints an extract from a letter which he says Cunliffe wrote to Bonar Law on July 13, offering to resign his office at any time at the request of the Chancellor. The letter 'was returned to him eventually but a copy was kept by Bonar Law'. The extract appears to be taken from a draft letter which the Prime Minister sent to Cunliffe on July 13, and of which Bonar Law may have had a copy. After consulting the Committee of Treasury, Cunliffe refused to sign the letter, and wrote instead the letter of July 16 here printed.

DEAR MR. CHANCELLOR,

    I much regret that I did not consult you before causing the recent telegrams to be sent to Canada about the Bank's Gold in Ottawa.

    I have laid the matter before my Committee of Treasury and am authorised to assure you that the Bank fully realise that their relationship with the Treasury must during the war be so intimate that complete and harmonious co-operation between them is of paramount importance.

    To this end the Bank will not fail to confer with the Chancellor of the Exchequer before taking any action during the war involving the general conditions of national credit or substantially affecting the Gold holding of the Bank.

Yours sincerely,

CUNLIFFE

    The Governor, while promising to consult the Chancellor on 'general conditions affecting credit', did not regard this as depriving the Bank of its ordinary initiative in controlling the market. He told the Committee of Treasury on August 29 that he would point out that it might be necessary to raise Bank Rate; but 'he did not propose now or at any time to obtain the Chancellor's special sanction in regard to such changes as might be contemplated in the Bank Rate'.

    Norman was on holiday in Scotland when the dispute arose, returning only after the meeting on July 4 at which the Governor had explained his action; but he was present at the crucial discussion on July 12. He noticed that relations with the Treasury were more strained — earlier he had commented on the improvement which followed Bonar Law's arrival at the Treasury — and that the Governor was intolerant of any action of the Treasury not at his instigation. There were rumours in the City that the Chancellor had demanded the Governor's resignation and that the Governor for his part had demanded the resignation of Chalmers, a Permanent Secretary to the Treasury and a consistent friend of the Bank. Of the first of these rumours Norman had evidence that it had at any rate been discussed, and the second he believed to be true. He noticed also that the telegram from Morgans, which started the train of events, was not, as had been thought at first, a notice to the Bank to repay, but only a message to the Chancellor that

Morgans had to ask for repayment, and strictly should have been seen by the Chancellor alone. Morgans, it is clear, had no option in the matter, for they had committed themselves to the other members of the syndicate which made the loan and could not carry out their own undertakings if the Bank defaulted.

Norman had a good deal of sympathy with the Treasury, for in his own experience he had thought the Governor unhelpful. On two long-standing questions, for example, the Governor would do nothing. One was the gold still in the joint-stock banks' possession, the collection of which, without compulsion, had been agreed to in July in response to a letter from the Chancellor; and the other was the maintenance of adequate public deposits, so that the Government should not be forced into hasty and ill-considered forms of borrowing, such as premium bonds. The Chancellor was consequently encouraged to look elsewhere for banking advice, while the Governor seemed to be looking outside the Bank for supporters. Towards the end of the year Norman notes that he himself had lost the Governor's confidence, and without that a No. 3, or even the Deputy Governor, could do no good.

Differences between the Governor and the Committee of Treasury had become more vocal, and Norman inevitably, in view of his knowledge of the Bank and the Government's business, was often the voice. He had long thought that the rates the Bank was giving on deposits, and approving on Government issues, were too high. In September 1916 he had urged on the Governor that it would be a mistake to issue higher Exchequer Bonds and that the rate on Treasury Bills should be lowered. Again, in January 1917 he asserted that the price of money was being kept up by the Bank's paying high for all deposits, and that there ought to be two rates, one domestic and one foreign, as there should also be for Government borrowing. As the volume of Treasury Bills and Ways and Means Advances climbed up in July and August, he urged a tap bond to be funded within, say, ten years instead of a market issue, which could not be handled at the time. He put this proposal to the Committee of Treasury in September, and to H.M. Treasury, and got general support for it: eventually the Governor came round to it.

Before the war the Bank had occasionally accepted deposits

from customers, not at interest but with a provision that they should be employed in the market, so that the depositor received some return on them; and at times the Bank had borrowed from the market itself, paying interest, when that was the most convenient way to make Bank Rate effective. As Government expenditure expanded in 1914 and 1915 large balances had accumulated to the credit of bankers. Intermittently at first, and from early in 1916 continuously, the Bank borrowed these balances from the Clearing Banks and re-lent them to the Government. The Government's disbursements were thus removed from the banking system before they had had their full potential effect in inflating credit. In January 1917 these borrowings were extended to other banks. This was one of the practices which Cunliffe initiated before informing the Committee of Treasury, which he did on this occasion about two months later. The Committee approved it on condition that it was not used to compete with the commercial bankers and was confined to customers who maintained adequate balances. When they learned of the payment to the Clearing Banks of a higher rate of interest than to other banks in respect of foreign balances redeposited with the Bank of England, they complained that they had not been consulted first. The Governor explained that the arrangement was made under pressure from the Government, and the Committee accepted it; but it was resented by other bankers, and the higher rate was later extended to them.

Another difference between the Committee and Governor showed itself when a proposal was made in October 1917 for a special committee on the reorganisation of the Bank. The Governor had agreed to it when Revelstoke had approached him, and though he accepted it now for the sake of peace, he saw no good in it, remarking characteristically that 'there are no Bankers' and 'no good Governor could be effective with any Committee of Treasury unless he could ignore them as I have done and should do again'. The proposal was the outcome of a great deal of thought on the relations of Governor and Committee, and of Bank and Public. Revelstoke was chairman, and the other members were Norman, who played the most active part after Revelstoke in its discussions, Huth Jackson,[1] Cecil

[1] Director of the Bank of England, 1892–1921.

Lubbock [1] and Kindersley. The internal discussions called
for such an inquiry: but outside the Bank also there was
criticism. Even if the personal methods of Cunliffe were
accepted as necessary in the emergency, the war had changed
the Bank's function and its relations with Government and
other banks. What, asked *The Economist* on 8 September 1917,
if Cunliffe had been weak or vacillating? Need the Governor
be an autocrat? And the Bank secretive? More use, it was
asserted, could be made of industrialists and bankers.

The Revelstoke Committee's recommendations, accepted in
February 1918, reflected the controversies of 1917. They were
anxious to relieve the Governors 'of any occasion for the exercise
of an autocratic control' and their first substantial recommendation was that the Governors 'should be under obligation to
inform the Committee of Treasury of the Bank's affairs'. The
Committee, which should be elected by free and secret ballot,
should be limited to not more than nine members, including
(not as hitherto in addition to) the Governors, and should
include at least three members who had not served as Governor
or Deputy. The field from which members of the Court should
be drawn should be widened by drawing on directors of British
Banks with branches in India, the Colonies or South America;
but the exclusion of Clearing Bankers should be maintained, and
also members of the Discount Market. Directors should retire
at seventy. Norman was disappointed at the first Committee of
Treasury elected under the new arrangement: the Court proceeded to choose by seniority, as if there had been no change.

It was necessary, by the end of October 1917, for the Committee of Treasury to decide whom to put forward for election
as Governor and Deputy Governor in the following March.
At meetings in September Cunliffe himself suggested resignation, but on October 10 he suggested that the selection for the
following year be postponed from November (the normal
month) until March. Norman replied that he did not think
this was the Committee's view, and the matter dropped. Afterwards the Governor said that Norman's remark was unfriendly;
it was in the interest of Bank and nation that he should continue, and he wished to go on to the end of the war. Norman

---

[1] Director of the Bank of England, 1909–42. Deputy Governor, 1923–25
and 1927–29.

denied any unfriendliness, and pointed out that a postponement of the usual notice in November would excite comment and scandal outside. The Committee of Treasury confirmed Norman's view the following week, as did the Court
when Cunliffe put his suggestion to them, after which he withdrew his motion with good grace. He seemed to Norman to be
seeking now only a peaceful departure; which only showed
that the Bank, as distinct from the Governor personally, could
at any time have asserted its implicit authority and prevented
the 'one-man-show which has brought us into disrepute'. On
November 6 the Committee of Treasury selected the Deputy
Governor, Brien Cokayne, for recommendation as Governor,
and Norman as Deputy Governor for the following year. The
Court accepted these recommendations on November 8, and
on 26 March 1918 they were elected. Cunliffe signalised his
departure by a speech at his last General Court, of which he
had told the Deputy Governor and the Committee of Treasury
nothing, eulogising the bankers and the Press and promising, as
chairman of the newly appointed Committee on Currency and
Foreign Exchanges, to secure amendments by statute in the
Bank Charter and the Act of 1844; 'an unfriendly finale',
Norman comments.

In December 1917, when the Committee of Treasury had
decided to recommend new Governors and the Court had
accepted their recommendation, they apparently made some
inquiries to discover how their decision had been received. Five
Clearing Bankers and others whom they consulted differed on
the advisability of retaining Cunliffe as Governor; on the
whole they preferred to leave the responsibility for choice where
it lay, with the Bank. Their references to the new Deputy
Governor indicate how little he was known outside the Bank.
One 'knew Cokayne personally, liked him, and thought him
a good man of business. He was not acquainted with Mr.
Norman.' Another said that 'the new Deputy Governor was
not sufficiently well known in Banking circles for him to be able
to express any opinion about him. He believed him to be
capable, but he had only met him personally on one occasion.'
A third said that 'he did not know Mr. Norman personally but
he was given to understand he was "very very good"'. The
other two did not mention him. He must have made some

THE DEPUTY GOVERNOR: 1919

From a portrait by Philip de László

impression during the past two years; for towards the end of
1916 he had been approached about joining the board of the
Anglo-Persian Oil Company, but had not felt free to consider
it. When he succeeded Cokayne as Governor, few realised
that he would be a very different choice from the long line of
merchants and merchant-bankers whom he followed.

(iii)

The new Governors, who took office in March 1918, were able
to look up from the immediate task of financing the war to the
problems that would face them when peace returned. The
hand-to-mouth struggle to find dollars for American supplies
had been ended by America's entry into the war and American
credits also did much to relieve the Treasury, and the Bank, of
the difficulty of meeting the rising cost of the war in Europe.
The new system of short-term bonds on tap made further spec-
tacular loans — at rising rates of interest — unnecessary. There
was, however, much to alarm the Governors and the Committee of Treasury in the further outlook. Already in June
1916 Norman had written to Strong:

I am sorry not to be able to tell you of a reduction in our unfunded debt; for you used to comment on its size even when you
were here. All I can say is that it must long since have passed any
danger point that exists. . . . The Government is selling securities
to run from 3 months to 5 years but I have no idea when it may
be possible to introduce any general funding scheme. . . . Both
for domestic and foreign expenditure we are living from hand to
mouth.

Cunliffe's successor, Cokayne, a more conservative financier,
faced with the actualities of a situation which Cunliffe had
only apprehended, began to press the Government for remedial
action as soon as he took office. His Deputy, Norman, supported
him, first with suggestions of policy and, as time went on, more
and more in interviews and negotiation.

Their difficulty was an inevitable result of war. For four
years, to be extended after hostilities ceased to a fifth, the
Government had been paying out sums far in excess of the

amount collected in taxes. Exchequer Receipts exclusive of
borrowing met little more than a quarter of the £9600 million
expended (including loans to Dominions and Allies) in the
financial years 1914–15 to 1918–19. Expenditure abroad was
met by the export of gold, issue of loans and sale of securities,
until America entered the war. At home the gap was filled by
borrowing, from the public some £4370 million in the form of
long-term War Loans and medium-term War Bonds, and from
the money market and the Bank nearly £1200 million in
Treasury Bills and Ways and Means Advances. To the Internal
Debt must be added also the £1365 million of external borrowing, more than four-fifths from the United States and Canada,
and more than four-fifths of this from the Governments of those
countries. Of all this borrowing it was the increase in the
Floating Debt that affected the Bank most directly, with the
demand obligation to repay the United States Government's
credits in the background. These confronted the Bank with a
problem with which it could not deal without the co-operation
of the Government, because they multiplied the potential
claims on the Bank's reserves, while rendering impracticable
the traditional weapons of defence — raising the Bank Rate
and taking redundant funds off the market.

During the war the Bank could do little. The Government's
needs were paramount, and these might have forced the Bank
and the Market away from the path which post-war considerations might dictate. In May 1918 the Chancellor (Bonar Law)
asked the banks, who agreed, to reduce the rate of interest they
paid on deposits, in order to force the depositors' money into
the new Treasury Bonds. The Committee of Treasury recognised that Bank Rate was quite out of touch with market rates,
but thought it better not to lower it. Norman was thinking out
ways of getting rid of the Special Deposits which the banks made
with the Bank of England out of their surplus — largely foreign
— funds : he wanted to take no more home money and to force
French and Italian money into War Bonds. These Special
Deposits were a potential weakness in the Bank's position ; for
they were withdrawable at three days' notice, whereas the Bank
could never be sure that the Government, to whom it handed
on these deposits in the form of Ways and Means Advances,
would repay the corresponding advances. Or, if one looked

forward, they were a threat to the country's exchange position, since, if they could not be dealt with betimes, any strain on London's exchange resources might precipitate their withdrawal when it was most inconvenient — as was to happen in 1920.

In August 1918 the Bank's private warnings had been reinforced by the Interim Report of the Committee on Currency and Foreign Exchanges after the war, of which Cunliffe was chairman. This Committee consisted of bankers of wide experience with the addition of Sir John Bradbury, then Secretary to the Treasury, and Professor Pigou of Cambridge. It confined this Interim Report (to which it added little in its Final Report sixteen months later) to 'the broad principles upon which the currency should be regulated'. It described the working of the pre-war Gold Standard and reviewed the changes affecting this system brought by war conditions. The Committee concluded :

It is imperative that after the war the conditions necessary to the maintenance of an effective gold standard should be restored without delay . . .

The pre-requisites for the restoration of an effective gold standard are

(a) The cessation of Government borrowing as soon as possible after the war. . . .

(b) The recognised machinery, namely, the raising and making effective of the Bank of England discount rate, which before the war operated to check a foreign drain of gold and the speculative expansion of credit in this country, must be kept in working order. This necessity cannot, and should not, be evaded by any attempt to continue differential rates for home and foreign money after the war.

(c) The issue of fiduciary notes should, as soon as practicable, once more be limited by law, and the present arrangements under which deposits at the Bank of England may be exchanged for legal tender currency without affecting the reserve of the Banking Department should be terminated at the earliest possible moment. . . .

They recommended also that the principle of the Bank Charter Act 1844, governing the Fiduciary Issue, should be maintained, subject to provision for issue in excess of the legal limit with the consent of the Treasury in an emergency ; and

that the gold reserves of the country should be concentrated
in the Bank of England.

Of their main finding, the restoration of conditions necessary to the maintenance of the Gold Standard, they say, 'We
are glad to find that there was no difference of opinion among
the witnesses who appeared before us as to the vital importance
of these matters'.   That their witnesses were not in this unrepresentative is shown by the Report of another official inquiry on
Financial Facilities, in the November following, by a committee
with a majority of industrial and commercial representatives.
While it recommended an improvement in the machinery for
new issues (and, for a time, Government supervision of them),
its conclusions on the Credit System were in complete harmony
with the Cunliffe Committee's :

To achieve the reconstitution of trade and industry on sound
financial and economic lines it will be necessary —
  (a) To re-establish a sound financial basis by means of an
      effective gold standard;
  (b) To check any undue expansion of credit, which can only be
      reflected by a further rise in prices;
  (c) To take steps to reduce to more normal proportions the
      inflation of credit due to the war.

The Committee of Treasury had settled the evidence to be
given to the Cunliffe Committee on behalf of the Bank by the
Governor on the basis of a memorandum provided by Norman
as Deputy Governor, and the recommendations were in line
with the policy they wished to pursue.   Norman would have
added further safeguards : to the answer on the restoration of
the exchange, which read — 'The first action should be the
arrangement of the debt which the Government has contracted
with foreign countries' — he would have added : 'accompanied by (i) the prohibition of all unnecessary imports ; (ii)
the encouragement of exports and (iii) the prevention of export
of capital and foreign loans'.   And he would have limited the
prohibition of the export of gold to the 'reconstruction period'.
The Bank, like the Cunliffe Committee and public opinion
generally in 1918, assumed without argument that the aim
of policy must be to restore the pre-war Gold Standard in
essentials.

A year later the Government was to give its approval to the principles and proposals of the Cunliffe Committee; but in September 1918 the Chancellor was still under the pressure of war necessities, and urging the Bank to ease money by lowering Bank Rate. The Bank refused, and Cokayne's reply to the Chancellor's suggestion opened a continuous pressure by the Bank for dearer money:

I have been thinking about what you said yesterday on the subject of cheaper money and do not feel any more reconciled to it. I still believe, although as you say I cannot prove it, that a further reduction would have little or no effect in increasing the subscriptions to War Bonds, and I am convinced that the temptation to employ money abroad is already too great. . . . I also feel strongly that it will be impossible to preserve our international credit unless we have comparatively dear money after the War and that the more we artificially cheapen it now, the more difficult it will be to revert to normal conditions. In fact, as you know, my own feeling is that money is too cheap here already.

This he followed up on October 17, expressing his alarm at the suggestion of a French loan by London, and protesting that the 'artificial lowering of money rates, of which we have already been so much afraid' (the Treasury had just reduced Treasury Bill rates) 'has not only encouraged the present fever of speculation but also made it impossible to apply the usual preventative to such dangers as I fear', and he urged a funding operation at once. If the foreign exchanges were to be brought under control, our position as a debtor instead of a creditor nation would require high money rates, and funding would become more expensive. Norman, writing on December 11 to Strong, gives the background of the Bank's policy:

Our domestic conditions give us more misgivings on the financial side than yours need give you, and for such reasons as the following:— Our business has been much more disorganised by the War than yours and will therefore come round more slowly; our floating and unfunded debt is large and may be difficult to handle; our need of raw materials is great and immediate; our foreign debtors (as a whole) are good only in the long run, if at all; our debts abroad are large and do not tend to ease the exchange position. Meanwhile the need for fresh money both at home and abroad for enterprise and imports is growing insistent and will

tend to compete with the Government's need, so that each is apt
to force the pace against the other and to hamper the other's legitimate requirements.

Over and above these domestic considerations, a cloud of
uncertain bulk is hovering in the shape of the Peace Conference. . . .

Towards the end of the year Cokayne and Norman were
hopeful that a funding loan would be issued; but these hopes
were disappointed. On December 17 the Chancellor invited
representatives of the Bank and the Clearing Banks to a small
conference at the Treasury, and asked for their advice. There
were differences as to the form the loan should take, and the
Chancellor said that, if there was not unanimity, he must wait
and see. A month later (January 1919) Bonar Law left the
Treasury to lead the House in the new Parliament, and Austen
Chamberlain took his place.

In the first few months of his office as Deputy Governor,
Norman had been occupied mainly with the internal affairs
and organisation of the Bank. The staff luncheon club needed
reorganising and new arrangements had to be made for the
large number of women clerks who had been recruited temporarily during the war but were recognised now as an important element in the Bank's permanent organisation. In March
of the following year (1919) he was chairman of a committee
to hear and consider complaints from the staff, the 'Grumblers
Committee' in his appointments diary. This held frequent
meetings and presented ten reports to the Court in the next
five months.

Externally, Norman took on more of the Governor's work
in assisting and advising other banks and agencies in the City,
and by the end of the year was taking almost an equal part
with the Governor in discussions with the Treasury. He took
over the regular meeting with the Discount Market, and the
occasional meeting with the Overseas Banks. He also had to
handle the negotiations over the future of an important private
banking firm of German origin. The Bank had earlier protested against the sale of the London premises of the Deutsche
Bank, and had resisted the tendency in some quarters to
alter the international character of London by prohibiting or

narrowly restricting foreign banks. Then there were endless
negotiations over the repayment of the war-time loan to the
Bank of France.

An inconvenient incident of the general rise in prices was
the rise in the price of silver until the value of silver coins as
bullion threatened to exceed their face value and offer a temptation to melt or export them. Norman was continually watching
this possibility, discussing with the Treasury the prohibition of
exports of silver and its melting, and taking steps to provide a
supply of notes if the silver coinage did begin to disappear. He
was to be faced with the same problem in the 'thirties in another
connection. A difficult negotiation, which continued for over
a year, was the revision of the terms on which South African
gold was bought for the Government. The producers grew
more and more restive under the arrangement by which they
were paid only the pre-war sterling price and in addition had
to meet the cost of refining in London. The Bank endeavoured
to meet the latter grievance by establishing a refinery of its
own; but by then the industry could not be deterred from
setting up a refinery on the Rand. With the war over, the
Bank, in March 1919, pressed the Government to pay the world
price for gold, and the Government finally assented. The
essential thing in the Bank's view was that South African gold
should normally come to London.

(iv)

On the opening page of Norman's desk diary for 1919 there
is a list of memoranda which indicate his preoccupations. Internal and technical Bank questions predominate: 'the refinery, branch policy and rebuilding, selections for vacancies on
Court and Committee of Treasury; arrange for the Advances
and Discounts Committee to grade acceptors; discount for
banks invariably below market rates; increase margins on Chief
Cashier and Branch loans'. Bank interests overlap the Treasury's; 'turn out French and Italian moneys, get bankers' gold
into Issue, settle the Banque de France credit, invent a "Registered" Bond for the next loan'. Finally pure policy appears:
'allow unrestricted money rates at once, issue no more War

Bonds under ten years, announce the issue of a Funding Loan next summer (these two suggestions, it is noted, were turned down), make Treasury consent for New Issues legally necessary, maintain the prohibition against the export of capital'.

With hostilities at an end and a new Chancellor (Austen Chamberlain) at the Treasury, the Governors renewed their efforts to free rates. At the meeting of the Court on January 30 the Governor forecast the freeing of bankers' deposit rates and gradual rise of interest and discount rates, in order to bring exchange rates up to parity before the signing of any peace treaty. The same day he wrote to the Chancellor asking for the co-operation of the Government in achieving these ends, which would necessarily include a funding operation.

He followed this up on February 12 by pointing out that the Bank's advances to the Government were rising again, though revenue collection was near its seasonal peak, and deploring such 'pure creation of credit'. A more formal letter on February 28, protesting that Ways and Means Advances were being increased so as to reduce the volume of Treasury Bills, was withdrawn after a talk with Bradbury: Norman comments, 'No good crying for the moon'. But after another discussion in Committee of Treasury and interviews with the two leading representatives of the Clearing Banks, who had now come into line with them, the Governors sent to the Chancellor another formal plea for restoring the Bank's power to control the market.

The Chancellor replied in general terms of reassurance, and suggested that the Governor was unduly alarmed by the amount of Ways and Means Advances. The Governor at once responded that he sympathised with the Government's need of borrowing, but that the cost of a somewhat higher rate on money was of relative insignificance to the country as a whole compared with the evils produced by maintaining rates below other centres, evils which would be increased as war restrictions were removed. The support which had pegged the sterling-dollar rate since the beginning of 1916 was removed on 20 March 1919, and Cokayne took the occasion to press his advice on the Chancellor to allow freedom of deposit rates and an increase in the discount on Treasury Bills. On April 1 the export of gold except under licence was prohibited by Order in

Council [1] against the wishes of Cokayne personally, who would have welcomed the pressure of gold losses, but in accordance with the unanimous wish of the other bankers.

The Bank sought to reduce the inflationary pressure in its market by its own action. Though the prohibition of foreign lending was not lifted till August, the chief accepting houses, and one of the big clearing banks, had been arranging credits for France, Italy, Belgium and others since February. The Bank refused to discount at the finest rate any bills drawn against these credits, and used all its powers of persuasion to check such lending, even threatening to raise Bank Rate if it went on. It had not been helped by a promise, given by the Chancellor in Paris in March without consulting the Bank, of a two months' commercial credit to France without any exchange guarantee. Norman doubted even his closest associates, writing of one, who came with a proposal for a big drawing credit to Belgium: 'I said we were opposed to such borrowings, long or short, as having more of our own debts than we could manage. He agreed; but it will be done.' At the same time the Bank warned the Discount Market and banks that it would discriminate against finance bills: it would give all the help it could to financing the movement of goods, but the help would depend on the actual movement of goods, and not be extended to bills continually renewed. It sought to stop the attraction of foreign money to London by preferential deposit rates. First French and Italian deposits were deprived of the special rate, and finally any foreign money. The special rate of 3 per cent was terminated in July, and in October the entire scheme for borrowing foreign funds was brought to an end. These measures, however, could have little effect so long as the Bank could not impose its policy on the market, and this it could not do so long as there was a Floating Debt of over £1000 million. Norman had used a short absence through illness to set down his own ideas for dealing with this:

15 April 1919

All Floating debt was incurred as War expenditure, and should be treated as such without delay.

Its existence paralyses the money-policy of the Treasury. The

---

[1] This gave express legal force to what had been general practice throughout the war.

I

ordinary method of a public invitation to subscribe to a loan with or without the big drum will not produce the desired result. . . . Nor can we contemplate loading the Banks again.

Therefore the Government must, as it were, underwrite an issue.

The scale is, of course, too great to admit of any voluntary scheme. So the Income Tax-payers must stand by and take firm the requisite total, *pro rata* to their Tax returns. They will not like it, but they (and the community) will thus suffer less than by any other method of raising (or failing to raise) such a Loan at this stage.

They will be entitled to ask for —

a. Payment spread over 12 or 18 months.
b. Temporary advances to actual subscribers from the Banks.
c. A free market upon which to unload.
d. A stock acceptable for death duties, etc., of subscribers.
e. The temporary right to charge any depreciation on their holdings against interest or profits before taxation.
f. No levy on their capital.

On the other hand the Treasury will obtain —

a. A perpetual stock.
b. A full price (as things go).
c. A clean sheet on the basis of which to deal separately hereafter with (i) Fresh needs and (ii) Maturities 1921 and onwards.

He carried his colleagues at the Bank with him, and urged on the Chancellor early in May the principles of his proposal, namely, compulsion because no voluntary scheme could ensure funding of the Floating Debt under present conditions, and assessment on the same basis as Income Tax. But the Chancellor was not convinced. He decided on a voluntary loan, and proceeded to call on the Governors for advice on terms and for help in organising support among the bankers. The latter joined the Governors in pressing for funding without further delay.

The loans accordingly issued, by announcement on 12 June 1919, were 4 per cent Funding Loan 1960–90, at a price of 80, and 4 per cent Victory Bonds at 85. Both had sinking funds attached, and could be tendered at a named price in payment of Death Duties: and for the Victory Bonds there were to be annual

drawings and repayments at par. Some £575 million nominal
was subscribed in cash, in addition to £193 million in conver-
sions. It was less than had been hoped, and Norman once more
pressed on the Chancellor his proposal for a compulsory loan,
in vain. Treasury Bills, which had averaged £1019 million in
May, were brought down to an average of £671 million in
July, but their issue had been suspended in order to assist the
new loans at the beginning of June. Their reduction was, in
large part, offset by increases during June and July in Ways and
Means Advances, which were not brought down again to the
level of May until August, by which time the rise in Treasury
Bills, and in the Floating Debt as a whole, had been resumed.

Now that the funding issue had been made and brought in
more than the amount of the Government's debt to the Bank
in Ways and Means Advances, the Governor pressed for the
extinction of those Advances and for future borrowing by the
Government to be restricted to loans from the public. The
Chancellor met him by reducing the debt to the Bank, and by
taking the 'first step necessary' to freedom of interest rates by
releasing the banks after July 31 from their pledge to pay no
more than 3 per cent on deposits ; but he would not yet allow
Treasury Bill rates to be put up. Strong, the Governor of the
Federal Reserve Bank of New York, lunched at the Bank on
July 22 and found the feeling among the Directors 'very blue'.
What oppressed them was the huge Government expenditure
in excess of revenue, the large maturities looming up — nine
or ten thousand million dollars in the following eighteen months,
the large foreign debt, especially the American debt which they
wanted to see reduced to more definite terms, and also the
general unrest of labour and the policy of paying 'unemployment wages'.

In their advice to the Chancellor, however, the Governors
confined themselves to their own business — the money market.
Even in this field the Chancellor did not find it easy to follow
them. External events, however, now began to reinforce the
monetary arguments which the Governors urged. Prices, which
had fallen after the Armistice, rose sharply from April 1919 onwards. Wages followed suit. Security prices rose throughout
the year, and the rise was accompanied by a flood of new
issues, released from control in April, and by intense activity

on the Stock Exchange. Meanwhile exports and services to
other countries did not recover rapidly enough to cover the
cost of imports, and the adverse balance on current account was
intensified by a continuation of loans to Allies, with the result
that the exchange rate on the dollar fell rapidly after the middle
of the year.

A technical change brought out the influence of the inflationary condition on the monetary position. Until the end of
July the expansion in Currency Notes called forth by rising
prices and expanding activity involved no fall in the Bank's
Reserve Proportion. Then, however, as a result of a proposal
made to the Bank by Sir John Bradbury at a special meeting,
the Committee of Treasury agreed that any increase in the
Currency Note issue should be matched by the setting aside of
Bank Notes to the Currency Note Reserve. The subsequent
rise in the combined note circulation was thus reflected in a fall
in the Proportion. In its Interim Report in August, and again
in its Final Report, the Cunliffe Committee made the same
recommendation, which the Government adopted.

The Bank could therefore renew its appeals to the Chancellor
with additional evidence of need, and the Chancellor was now
sympathetic. The Governors proposed that when he made his
next routine application for Advances during the ensuing
quarter, their reply — which would be published — should
point out that Ways and Means Advances were acquiring the
character of a permanent loan: and this the Chancellor
accepted. To the further request for higher Treasury Bill rates,
he replied that he could not carry certain of his colleagues in
the Cabinet, particularly the previous Chancellor (Bonar Law)
and Lord Milner; but he invited the Governor to make his
reply to the routine request for Advances brief and formal, and
then to address to him a reasoned statement on home and
foreign finance, 'in the nature of a State paper', which (after
agreement) he would willingly circulate to the Cabinet with
his recommendation of its proposals. The formal letter was
sent on September 22, the reasoned Statement on September
25. On October 6 the rate for 3-months Bills was raised from
3½ per cent to 4½ and on 6-months Bills from 4 per cent to 5.

The raising of Treasury Bill rates failed to check the signs
of inflation which alarmed the Bank. Prices continued to rise,

stock market activity to develop, note circulation to increase, sterling to depreciate and the Bank's reserves to fall. But the principle had been admitted of using monetary discipline. The Committee of Treasury at the beginning of November approved of another approach to the Chancellor; the increase in the Note circulation and the fall in the Bank's reserves called for a rise in Bank Rate, and this should be recommended, provided the Chancellor would agree to a general advance in Rates. The Chancellor agreed and Treasury Bills were raised by a ½ per cent on November 7, a day after Bank Rate was put up to 6 per cent.

The change of policy was marked by a statement by the Chancellor in Parliament on December 15. Subject to the obligations on the Government arising out of economic conditions in Europe, he accepted the chief recommendations of the Cunliffe Committee, including the automatic restriction on the issue of Currency Notes. He may have been influenced by a long talk with Ben Strong. Strong had pointed out that, so long as London kept down its rates, any attempt by New York to bring about liquidation and lower prices by putting up rates would make London's position worse, and he would much prefer to work out a friendly policy of co-operation. Now, on his return from a tour of Western Europe, he reminded the Chancellor of the 'historic' dangers of inflation which he feared — default of Governments and collapse of Government credit on the Continent, collapse of private credit, stopping trade, and ultimately distress and disorder. The Chancellor shared his fears.

The Bank's view of the change is given in a letter from Norman to Strong on the day Bank Rate was raised:

Since you left here our general position has not altered to any great extent. There was, as you will have seen, an increase in the rates for Treasury Bills about a month ago and about the same time the special rate of 4½ on foreign money deposited here was discontinued. The result has been sufficient to absorb slowly the Ways and Means Advances, but not enough to contract expansion. We have long been, as you know, anxious to move gradually towards considerably higher rates and the step above mentioned was in the right direction. To-day we have been able, with a very good reason, to raise the Bank Rate to 6% and the rate on Treasury Bills will follow at once to 5½%. The reason for the former, which with the concurrence of the Treasury has led to the latter, was the steady increase in the circulation of Bank Notes and Currency Notes, caused to some extent by covering part of the Currency Note expansion by a deposit of Bank Notes. The result of this has been to bring our Banking Reserve down to very little over £20 million and it is really the decrease to that figure which has been the ostensible reason for the rise in the Bank Rate.

At the same time I cannot regard the certainty of sound money as definitely settled. On this subject the community, in so far as definite views are taken, may be divided into three groups: (1) the advocates of unadulterated sound money; (2) the advocates of expansion and the printing press, which to a considerable extent is the view held by many political leaders; and (3) the advocates of confiscation euphoniously called 'Levy on Capital'.

Politically, I cannot think the situation has improved in spite of apparent triumphs of the Government. For one thing and perhaps to some extent because the truth of the financial position as disclosed by the Chancellor in August was too strong and unpalatable, a 'lump of toffee' was administered last week in the House of Commons. The upshot of this is that, given a normal year and no fresh expenditure, all will be well; but a normal year is as remote as a 'blue moon' and meanwhile, with extraordinary expenditure, both ends cannot meet.

Further, a fresh demand for an issue of Premium Bonds has also grown up. . . . On similar lines the Stock Exchange, who have already more business than they can easily deal with, are bestirring themselves to get rid of cash dealings. . . . From a domestic standpoint I can see some advantage in such a change because the position would be steadied by 'bear' accounts whereas as things are every operator has been a potential 'bull' for the last few years and (with the rise in values) has forgotten what it is to make a loss; but from the international position, and especially with the uncertainty which still hangs over European markets, I think we ought to go slow and give as little leeway as possible to the foreign operator.

This letter crossed a letter of the same date, November 6, from Strong, enclosing a notice of a change in Federal Reserve rates, designed to check excessive loans under the fifteen-day rate but leaving unchanged the rates on commercial bills and

loans on Government securities, which were pretty well divorced
from the speculative call-market rate. 'We are determined',
he added, 'to stop this mad march of speculation and expansion, whether it be in securities, real estate, commodities or
what not', and 'at last the first step has been taken towards
freeing Federal Reserve rate-policy from the overshadowing
influence of the Government's borrowing.'

The Bank's anxiety to make a more drastic use of its restored
authority in its market sprang from similar fears of speculative
excesses leading to a subsequent break of confidence. Contemporary comment shows that its anxiety was widely shared. *The
Economist*, which was a critic of the rise in Bank Rate on the
grounds that, off gold, it could only increase the cost of
Government borrowing, nevertheless on January 3 explained
clearly the danger in which the currency stood in the New
Year:

> Trade is clamorous in its demands for credit in banks which
> have been obliged during the War to expand credit, against
> Treasury Bills, etc., for the Government, which has made no
> successful attempt to reduce these liabilities to the banks, the out-
> standing amount of Treasury Bills, being actually higher than a
> year ago. By their holding of these bills the banks can, if they
> choose to do so, force the Government to give them fresh currency,
> whatever may be said by Treasury minutes.

The only way to use credit to check speculation was for the
banks by joint action to reserve credit for producers and restrict
it for those who were holding up commodities.

Writing to Strong on January 15, Norman was more hopeful. The recent rate increase in New York by the Federal
Reserve Bank had tended to soften the effect of the Bank and
Treasury increases in London, but 'we forgive you for the
sake of the enormous benefit to both sides from close and
personal co-operation'. Moreover, the increase in London
rates was now becoming effective. Hitherto the banks had
been preaching cheap money as well as practising it in their
rates; now the demand for commercial advances had so
grown that they were loaned up to the hilt and in self-defence
were almost bound to put up their rates and scale down
their customers' requirements. Government indebtedness had

probably reached its apex, and next year extraordinary receipts from the sale of stores would more than cover extraordinary expenditure, while increased receipts from taxation would cover ordinary expenditure and provide for some reduction of debt. The American Exchange, though it had fallen, was not demoralised; the cost of living had stopped rising; and the Currency Note circulation was contracting. Strong replied on February 6 that the rate changes were not at all what he would have recommended; they were a compromise between different views in the Federal Reserve System and the U.S. Treasury. But, were they to permit such developments as they had witnessed during the last few months to proceed to their logical conclusion, they would put it beyond their own power to render any sort of aid to Europe by their extravagance and waste.

Nevertheless, the conditions which had called for dearer money ever since the Armistice remained; for the raising of rates in October and November had come too late to check them. Moreover, while the Treasury was under pressure from the Bank to carry further the policy instituted then, it was now under pressure from other quarters to reverse it. Norman was at the Treasury on February 4 discussing monetary policy, and learned that the Prime Minister and Bonar Law were pressing the Chancellor to lower rates so as to facilitate the issue of Housing Bonds, to reduce the cost of borrowing to the Government, and, by putting up the price of securities, to allow bankers to liquidate their position. The Chancellor was resisting, but he felt the need of support and asked the Governors to let him have another reasoned statement on the effects of Dear Money. The Governor sent this on February 25 with a covering note in which he said that the Bank could not add much more to the large accommodation already given to the market without applying the corrective of higher rates, which the market was in fact expecting. Market rates were already higher in America — the Federal Reserve Bank of New York had extended its higher rate to loans against Government certificates of indebtedness, which were mainly loans to industry — and the situation there looked difficult.

The memorandum claimed that the rise in rates so far had inflicted no hardship or restraint on the development of legitimate industry, which was still profitable, but had encouraged a reduction of stocks and an increase of sales, and so checked the rise in prices. It had discouraged borrowing to finance speculation in securities as well as commodities; and, by discouraging the tendency of foreigners to finance themselves in London and the attempts by London to lend abroad, had strengthened the sterling exchanges. In fact it had had the effects which experience led one to expect.

The memorandum went on to emphasise the importance of ending the current inflation in order to improve the export trade and stabilise internal conditions. The appropriate instrument for this was the rate of interest, and a high rate was natural in face of the high demand for capital caused by economic reconstruction. The process of deflation of prices which would follow a check to the expansion of credit must necessarily be painful to some classes, but people with fixed incomes and the great body of the working classes would be greatly relieved by a decrease in the cost of living. 'The Government will have to pay more for their loans but the increased cost to the Nation is as dust in the balance compared with the restoration of free trade and the removal of social unrest and political discontent.'

The Bank was not without difficulties in its own special field. Gold had to be found for the repayment of the 1916 Anglo-French Loan raised in New York, and Paris, so far from contributing towards it, was seeking to borrow funds in London; in fact the Bank had already had to take up part of an issue of French Treasury Bills (with no exchange guarantee) issued in January. The houses whose business was the issuing of foreign loans were assailed by former clients and they sought to meet their needs; loans the Bank had turned down in 1919 were all turning up again in 1920. Speculators were taking advantage of the lower rates on borrowing in London to buy speculative securities in other markets and hold them for appreciation. All through the year Norman was pressing Clearing Banks (with McKenna's support), Accepting Houses and the Discount Market to restrict bills to commodity transactions, and stop the use of them to provide blank credits, finance without commodity backing, excessive terms (as for shipbuilding) and repeated renewals. The pressure on the new issue market — for housing loans, industrial expansion, the raising of additional capital to finance the higher cost of stocks — made for higher rates, and more pressure on the banks, and in the background was the spreading cloud of economic disorder on the Continent. The Chancellor's reply to a memorial addressed to him by a group of bankers, published on February 12, showed that the Government was conscious of the dangers in Europe but unable as yet to do more than deal with the inflationary situation in the United Kingdom and promise to co-operate in any concerted measures for European reconstruction.

The necessity of drawing on the Bank's gold to contribute to the repayment of the Anglo-French dollar loan provided an opportunity for pressing the need for further monetary action, and the Committee of Treasury agreed that the Governors should ask H.M. Treasury to consent to higher rates. The Chancellor replied that he must consult the bankers and consider alternatives, the Committee of Treasury accepting his decision 'in view of the importance of co-operation'. At a meeting called by the Chancellor on March 9 the majority of the bankers were against any raising of rates, whereat he warned them that in default of some alternative, *e.g.* the rationing of credit or some other way of limiting advances, rates must go up. 'A financial failure but a social success', Norman notes on this. 'Low rates will some day ruin us.'

Two days later (March 11) they met again. The bankers remained opposed to higher rates, because 'ineffectual', but they could suggest no alternative except to limit (not reduce) their advances. The Chancellor hesitated: but the situation was getting beyond control by such expedients. In the first quarter of 1920 the Government's revenue collection exceeded its expenditure. The banks could no longer replenish their cash from an expanding issue of Currency Notes. Their advances in the twelve months to March had risen from £507 million to £862 million, while their Cash had fallen since December from £125 million to £96 million. They had reached a point at which they were forced to let their Treasury Bills run off, and could not help the market to take up new Bills to replace those maturing; while the Bank of England, in its turn, could not safely help the market unless it were allowed to apply the corrective of higher rates.

(v)

On 31 March 1920 Norman was elected Governor of the Bank, for the first of twenty-four successive years. He at once put the Bank's position to the Treasury in these terms :

12 April 1920

DEAR MR. BLACKETT,[1]

Will you be good enough to read this in connection with your letter of the 16th March.

Since the Wednesday of that week, the following changes have taken place :

The Total of Treasury Bills outstanding has fallen by	£16 million to £1043 million
The Total of Ways & Means Advances outstanding has increased by	£88 million to £264 million
The Total of Currency Notes outstanding has increased by	£15 million to £341 million
The Bank's Ways & Means Advances have increased by	£40 million to £55 million
The Bank's Reserve has been reduced by	£11 million to £24 million
The Bank's Proportion has fallen from	23·5% to 14·9%

Each of these movements is evidence of either a definite tendency to further expansion or a further serious worsening of the Bank's position. Although I am aware that before making a change in Treasury Bill rates the Chancellor wished to see the effect over a few weeks of the Bankers' policy of rationing credit, the Bank's position, already very unsatisfactory, is so rapidly deteriorating as to make it an urgent question whether further delay before making a change will not be fraught with serious danger.

I beg you to bring this position to the Chancellor's attention with a view to my seeing him at his early convenience. At the same time, please direct his special attention to the fact that the Bank's active circulation and the Currency Note circulation have each risen by about £2 million since Easter, the fiduciary issue of the latter being now less than £15 million below the maximum and

[1] Controller of Finance, H.M. Treasury, 1919–22. Finance Member of Viceroy's Council, 1922–28. Director of the Bank of England, 1929–35. Knighted, 1921.

remind him that even the Bank of France has at last raised its rates for discounts and advances to 6% and 6½% respectively.

Yours sincerely,

M. NORMAN

The following day he met the Chancellor with his Treasury advisers, with the result that he was able to report to the Committee of Treasury on April 14 that the Chancellor had raised the Treasury Bill rate to 6½ per cent; whereupon the Committee recommended the Court to raise Bank Rate the next day to 7 per cent.

For a time it looked as if the bankers were right when they opposed dearer money on the ground that it was 'ineffectual'. The Bank's cable to the Federal Reserve Bank of New York on May 4 reported:

Demand for accommodation continues beyond the amount bankers are able or willing to grant. But as demand for higher wages continues circulation tends to increase and our position to worsen. We note indications that certain commodities are less saleable at recent or somewhat lower prices which may perhaps be attributed to continuing pressure of high rate.

The Bank hoped to avoid any further increase in rates; but on June 1 rates were again raised in New York. The Federal Reserve Bank explained the rise as necessary to reflect existing credit conditions and to impress borrowers with the necessity of postponing less urgent business and assisting bankers to control credit now, in preparation for the autumn requirements. In London, Currency Notes were pressing against their limit. At the end of May the Governor urged the Treasury either to raise the limit or allow it to have its intended effect in restrictive action by the Bank. He still thought that a 7 per cent Bank Rate was enough for internal conditions; but there was danger in keeping London rates below the rates in the two creditor countries, America and Japan. The immediate danger of exceeding the Currency Notes limit was circumvented by the Treasury's withdrawing from circulation the first two issues, amounting to some seven million pounds, which were printed on poor paper and by this time dirty and hardly circulating at all. 'If', Norman wrote to a correspondent, 'you say this is rather tricky, I shall not quarrel with you. Perhaps it was a political means of getting out of a hole without facing the music.' His view of the position is illuminated by notes he made for his first speech as Governor at the Bankers' Dinner at the Mansion House on July 15:

We are striving to return to the normal, which ultimately means a gold standard. To this end we have for months been following a consistent policy; first by the repayment of foreign debt, and secondly by the first steps towards a slow contraction of credit. This policy has worked well. It has generally been accepted by the public here and by those abroad, and, if followed out, will go as far as anything to reinstate the finances of this Country. . . .

. . . It is precisely what was advocated in the Report of the (Cunliffe) Committee on Currency and Foreign Exchanges after the War, and adopted by the Government. The Chancellor has had the thankless task of administering this policy, and we owe him a debt of gratitude for his consistency — which history will confirm. Anyone who now reversed his policy would be assuming grave responsibility. A debtor nation cannot expect lower rates than those of a creditor nation, and our rates are now below those in America.

Three weeks later Norman felt bound to urge on the Chancellor a further rise in short-term interest rates on the ground that the dollar-sterling rate was falling, that prices were rising and that both the note circulation and Ways and Means Advances were increasing. He reported to the Committee of Treasury that he had the support of the Treasury officials, but could not move the Chancellor. Privately, he was probably aware of the Chancellor's difficulties. With rates left as they were, Norman found much to do. He was still uneasy over the volume of the Floating Debt. Earlier in the year (April) he had urged on the Chancellor a proposal of a group of bankers to impose a special addition to Income and Super Tax for three years to repay debt; this was rejected as unlikely to raise an effective sum (though the Chancellor had not realised how low in the scale of incomes the sponsors would have gone), and Norman returned to his old proposal of a compulsory loan on the basis of Income Tax assessments. But the Chancellor objected to the principle of compulsion, and preferred a new issue of Treasury Bonds; moreover, he was now assured of a surplus on revenue account. There remained the Governor's routine but fundamental work of guiding and regulating the money and capital market; and this, in the conditions of transition from war to peace, was more than enough to occupy him.

The pressure on London for loans continued; and in addition there was the financial strain of concessions to war-time Allies and of the first steps in aid to Central Europe, which the Bank was anxious to assist. Certain forms of borrowing, an issue in London of Treasury Bills by a foreign Government for example, the Governor would not allow; but some funding of foreign Governments' short-term debt he encouraged. The chief domestic pressure on the capital market came from the demand of Local Authorities for Housing Loans. The Governor thought their demands wasteful, but, to help them, induced both the Local Authorities and the issuing banks to group themselves so as to reduce the number of separate issues, and then arranged an informal queue. Dominion and Colonial borrowers were similarly induced to take their turn.

The resumption of normal relations with the enemy powers raised problems. At what point could German bills, frozen in the Bank's hands, be liquidated? How could British assets, such as holdings in Continental banks, be salvaged? How were pre-war claims to be related to Reparations? Financial relations with Russia were not resumed; and though Russia was selling gold (which the London dealers were anxious to handle) and any addition to the Bank's holding would have been welcome, dealings had to wait for an agreement between the two Governments. Should London banks resume business with German firms in South America? There seemed no reason why not, since the business was not complicated by an Allied Control or a claim to Reparations. At home, the first effects of war expansion and peace contraction began to appear. Armstrong Whitworth, an old customer of the Bank, needed finance to convert its capacity to peace-time purposes, and another steel firm in the same process of transition relied on a small issuing house that was not able to implement its undertaking, and might involve others in its difficulties. The process of purchase and merger by which deposit banking was being concentrated in a few great concerns was proceeding, watched on behalf of the Treasury, and helped, where the Treasury approved, by the Bank. Norman had already had the satisfaction (when he was Deputy Governor) of learning of the project for merging his family bank, Martin's, with the Bank of Liverpool, and ensuring that it should, after an interval, take the name of Martin's Bank. All these problems and projects were brought to the Governor, and all received his concentrated study. He was helped by the confidential information which came to him from the stream of visitors through his room: visitors who came for advice and helped to pay for it in part with the information they brought. Thus, a difficulty in selling exported woollens, a fall in metal prices, the difficulties of the motor industry, the excessive commitments of individual concerns reached him long before they reached the papers or influenced index numbers.

By the end of the summer of 1920 it was becoming clear that the post-war boom was over, but the situation facing Treasury and Bank was still far from easy. Though wholesale prices were no longer rising but showing signs of a fall, in retail prices the rise continued, drawing wages up with it or leading in the alternative to industrial stoppages. The profits of stock market speculation had given place to losses. Industry was pressing on the market new issues of debentures and shares either to finance the high cost of materials or to avoid loss in liquidating stocks at falling prices; and some large undertakings, in the search for capital, were turning from the Clearing Banks to the Bank itself. Overseas governments, Empire and foreign, were all eager to borrow. The Treasury, although the Budget was more than balanced and tax receipts exceeded expenditure, was faced with the persistent problem of renewing short-term debt, and was looking forward to the problem of meeting in two years' time the maturities of successive series of National War Bonds.

The latest issue of Treasury Bonds in October brought a most unsatisfactory response, and a Conversion Loan the following April, in spite of extraordinarily generous terms, was to be little more successful. The Bank was therefore more inclined to raise Bank Rate than to reduce it, but deferred any action until the Treasury should move. The Chancellor, for his part, met the bankers on September 15 and scolded them for increasing their advances and for co-operating in the proposed issue of securities in London by certain ex-neutrals. Moreover, he warned them that an increase in the Treasury Bill rate, quite apart from any change in Bank Rate, was largely dependent on their own action. The Governor continued to resist the pressure on the market by discouraging overseas lending — hard up as he knew Australia to be for sterling, he refused to help with a loan — and by discounting freely for customers.

In December Strong paid another visit to the Bank, and reviewed the position with Norman. They agreed that the policy of making money dearer had been successful, though it would have been better six months earlier. They agreed, too, that deflation must be gradual ; it was becoming now too rapid, and they favoured a small reduction in rates in both London and New York. Strong, who had been for some months past under treatment in a sanatorium and was not yet back at work, cabled to his colleagues in the Federal Reserve Bank in New York as follows :

The Bank of England perplexed by outlook over next few months. They consider general rate policy has so far been wonderfully successful although the position here might be better to-day had they been more drastic six months earlier. The fact remains that world deflation has been started and while this bound to continue they as we wish it to operate slowly rather than quickly. They do not believe such deflation can now be stopped but think possibly its rate of progress might with advantage be slowed. If you share these views I would be glad to learn your intentions as to rate policy for discussion here. Your letters September 17 November 26 indicate no intention to change present policy but rather possible increase of rates. Are you still of this view ?

The Reserve Bank replied that the deflation of commodity prices was near completion but was not yet reflected in manufactured goods and retail prices. Nor was credit deflated : while prices had fallen by 25 to 35 per cent since May, commercial bank loans had decreased by only 5 per cent and currency not at all ; call loans had been reduced more, bringing down prices of industrials ; but in spite of high money rates credit had been kept elastic. New York's view was that they should not consider reducing their own rates until market rates were below them ; for though a reduction might give the stimulus needed when underlying trading conditions were ready, at present it would be premature and ineffective.

Norman reluctantly acquiesced, in the interest of maintaining a co-ordinated policy. He had been pressed by some commercial bankers to tighten credit, in order to force stocks into the market. On the other hand, McKenna had called on December 23 and asked whether it would be agreeable for him to force the Bank's hand for rate reduction the following week. Norman replied that it would not, because although it *might* improve the domestic position he felt strongly that the American position made reduction unwise, if not dangerous — the Federal Reserve System wished first to get some of its re-discounts paid off, and there were demands for repayment of Government debt. He began, however, to canvass opinion among commercial bankers. It was divided, and he doubted whether the advocates of lower rates were as much concerned with the needs of the country as with their need to liquidate their own position. He reported to the Committee of Treasury on February 2 that H.M. Treasury might be forced for political reasons to lower its Bill rate. A few days later McKenna called to give his opinion that the financial position, especially the psychology of the market, had so improved that he had no fears for the banks, but he still thought lower rates were wanted to stimulate trade and employment. On March 10 the Treasury Bill Rate was reduced to 6 per cent. The Bank did not at once follow suit. Strong wrote that, though under pressure to reduce rates in New York, he now thought it inadvisable. Norman was still waiting for the cost of living to come down: at its present level he thought the miners were being asked to accept an unreasonable reduction in wages. He wanted to keep in line with the Treasury, but also to keep his rate a little higher than New York. Meanwhile he had been pressing for the restoration of the tender system for the issue of Treasury Bills. Except for a short break in 1917 the tender system had been supplanted since 1915 by issues at advertised rates. On 21 April 1921 tendering was restored, though not to the exclusion of the other system. A week later, Bank Rate was reduced to 6½ per cent. Two months later, when it was clear that the national stoppage in the coal industry was approaching its end, it was further reduced to 6 per cent.

K

CHAPTER IV

THE RETURN TO THE GOLD STANDARD

(i)

THE ending of the boom in the summer of 1920 was followed by depression as sudden and steep as the preceding expansion. In the United Kingdom prices fell from 325 per cent of the pre-war level in April 1920 to 205 in April 1921, and continued their fall for another year and a quarter, when they steadied around 155. Employment did not fall off seriously until the autumn; in December 1920, when the extension of unemployment insurance to the whole industrial population gave for the first time a reliable indication of unemployment (including short-time), the percentage of recorded unemployed in Great Britain was 7·8, but thereafter it rose rapidly (even if the three months of the great coal stoppage are ignored) to 17·7 in December 1921, and continued above 10 per cent throughout the following years. The index number of the cost of living did not rise so far or so soon as wholesale prices, but fell more slowly and not so far, as also did wage-rates; neither reached 280 per cent of the pre-war level or fell below 170 per cent. Retained imports fell from the unprecedented figure of £1710 million in 1920 to £979 million in 1921 and £899 million in 1922, exports of British produce from £1334 million in 1920 to £703 million in 1921 and £720 million in 1922; but in both cases the fall was accounted for by the fall in prices.

While the extent and suddenness of the change were without recent parallel, the distress caused was not in proportion; the extension of unemployment insurance provided a safeguard which had not existed before, the large losses succeeded corresponding profits and large business savings, and the fall in prices was a benefit to large classes with regular money incomes, who had suffered from the rise in prices. These social compensations may explain the recovery of trade as early as 1922 from the depths of depression, intensified by a national coal stoppage, in 1921, though unemployment remained a problem throughout the inter-war years.

The New York exchange, which had fallen to 4·50 in March 1919, when support was removed, and to 3·21 by February 1920, fluctuated during the rest of 1920 with no marked trend, and then moved up nearly to 4·00 before the coal stoppage in 1921, and to 4·24 by the end of the year. In December 1922 it was 4·61.

Depression at home, which quickly diverted political and commercial interest from Europe and concentrated it on domestic conditions, did not figure prominently at this time in the correspondence and notes in his diary which indicate Norman's preoccupations. He was concerned, of course, with his own market and the effects on British trade of the policy he was trying to carry out in co-operation with successive Chancellors. But the stream of visitors through his room were much more concerned with conditions on the Continent and relations with New York. The City remained international in its outlook when the rest of the country relapsed into its normal insularity, and Norman's primary interest was already in the restoration of the international economy of which London had been the centre. He could not fail to notice the fortunes of other countries ; his attention was drawn to them every other week by a visit from some London banker who was pressed by former Continental clients to make some loan, short or long, to meet an emergency, or whose own position was jeopardised by the inability of Central European customers to meet their obligations on pre-war acceptance credits. Whereas German prices by the beginning of 1919 had risen little more than English, they rose threefold in the course of 1919 and then, in the two years after May 1920, while British prices fell by a half, rose twelvefold ; even then they had still to exhibit the complete loss of value of the currency which followed the loss of all control of the monetary situation. In Austria the movement of events was similar. In France and Belgium prices had risen more by 1920 than in England, but fell as in England to 1922, and then resumed their upward movement.

The Cunliffe Committee's Report continued to state the policy of the British Government. There had been little criticism in Parliament, the Press or the City. It was supported in its chief recommendations by the spectacle of the Continent's difficulties and by the consideration of these in international conferences. Already in the spring of 1920 a concerted approach was being made by leading bankers and business men, who asked their respective Governments to convene an international financial conference. In spite of a refusal by the American Treasury to co-operate, a Conference was held at Brussels in September. The Governor, though he felt it would be improper to act as a British delegate himself, encouraged other bankers, Kindersley and Brand,[1] to attend, and persuaded his predecessor in office (now Lord Cullen) to go as British Government delegate. Its report attributed the inflationary rise in prices and weakening of exchanges in Europe to government expenditure. Its most urgent recommendation was that government expenditure should be brought within the limits of government revenue; to this end expenditure should be reduced, borrowing stopped, a beginning made of the funding and repayment of past borrowings. Countries which had lapsed from an effective Gold Standard should return to it, and to ensure this Central Banks should be freed from any political pressure and should conduct their operations on a basis solely of considerations of prudent finance. Countries without Central Banks should establish them; impediments to international trade should be removed, and attempts at exchange control terminated. Looking to the future, the report recommended that deflation, if and when undertaken, be carried out gradually and with great caution, and expressed disbelief in any policy of attempting to stabilise the value of gold. The Conference's recommendations were based largely on a report of an expert committee which also offered a reminder to countries in difficulties that credits to them should be conditional on their own policy co-operating in the task of restoration and should enjoy priority over domestic claims until the credits had had time to exercise their influence on production — a principle which was to acquire importance in subsequent efforts to assist such countries.

French opposition had excluded any discussion of German Reparations from the Brussels Conference; it was similarly

[1] Later Lord Brand.

excluded from another international conference to discuss economic and financial problems which the Supreme Council of
the Allies called at Genoa in April 1922. At this conference
for the first time German official representatives were admitted
on terms of equality, though the unfortunate coincidence of the
signing of the German-Russian treaty of Rapallo destroyed the
nascent feeling of confidence and set back attempts to work out
a tolerable scheme of Reparations payments. The experts
who formed its Financial Committee, however, carried forward
the attempt to formulate the principles of economic policy
affirmed at Brussels. The first condition of European reconstruction was stability of currencies. The only practical common standard was gold. All European governments should
declare that the re-establishment of the Gold Standard was their
objective, and agree on a programme by which to achieve it.
They went further than Brussels in specific proposals for early
action. Parities should be established; gold should be eco-
nomised by extending the gold exchange standard on a basis of
guarantees for the free movement of deposits with Central
Banks. Central Banks should be the agencies of international
monetary co-operation, and to this end the importance of their
freedom from political pressure was emphasised afresh. A new
objective was proclaimed, which had been specifically rejected
by the Brussels Conference, the attempt to prevent fluctuations
in the value of gold itself (which a simultaneous attempt to
return to a Gold Standard might intensify) by co-ordinating
demands for gold and stabilising credit policies to keep currencies at the parities established. Finally, these aims should all
be embodied in a Monetary Convention, to be worked out by
a conference of Central Banks, which the Bank of England
should convene.

Norman had more hope of results from this conference than
from any of the previous conferences of Allied Governments.
It gave prominence to the return to gold and to co-operation
among Central Banks in preparing and administering an international Gold Standard, objects on which his mind had been
set since his first discussions with Strong at the end of the war.
He had had long talks before the conference with R. G. Haw-
trey,[1] whose ideas gave their distinctive form to the resolutions

[1] Director of Financial Enquiries, H.M. Treasury, 1919–45.

of the Financial Committee. Sir Charles Addis,[1] the Bank
Director on whose advice Norman relied and whom he used
most in his discussions on international co-operation with other
centres, brought back the Committee's Resolutions without
waiting for the end of the Conference, and Norman had a long
talk with the Chancellor (Sir Robert Horne) as soon as he
returned to London. Yet the conference of Central Banks, in
the form in which it was proposed at Genoa, was never held.

The reason is not clear. Norman was leaving for a visit to
America just after Genoa ended; the State Department had
approved Federal Reserve Board participation, and he used
the opportunity of his visit to agree on a draft invitation and
agenda with Strong, which he discussed also with the Central
Bank Governors of the Netherlands and Sweden on his return.
The Committee of Treasury approved the draft on May 30. The
Report of the Genoa Conference was enclosed with the invitation, and attention drawn to the Resolution which invited the
Bank of England to convene a conference of Central Banks.
The agenda would be the resolutions in the Report, and the
relation of inter-State indebtedness arising out of the war to the
re-establishment of the Gold Standard and of stable exchanges.
Proceedings would be 'non-political and confidential', though
it might be convenient to publish any formal conclusions
reached. The invitation was personal to the Governor addressed, or his substitute; and the date not before September.

Further discussions with European Governors took place
during the summer. In later correspondence Strong doubted
the advisability of putting detailed policy proposals on the
agenda; he thought the fears of competition for gold reserves
forcing up the value of gold an illusion, the rates of exchange
would take care of this without any agreements. The Swiss,
surprisingly, felt unable to assume an obligation to maintain
their exchange, or to commit themselves to the Gold Standard.
There were differences of opinion as to what constituted a
Central Bank and as to who should be invited. The true
explanation, however, seems to be that the conference was
crowded out by other claims on Central Bank Governors. The
British Government decided in the autumn to send a delegation
to Washington to discuss the funding of the British war debt

----

[1] Director of the Bank of England, 1918–32.

and to attach to it the Governor of the Bank; this, both the Committee of Treasury and Strong agreed, postponed any invitation to a conference till the debt negotiations were over. In the following year the difficulties of Austria, Hungary and Germany demanded more immediate and specific measures by the chief money markets than the discussion of general principles in conference. The return of the United Kingdom to the Gold Standard was delayed. Informal discussion and co-operation between Central Banks grew in frequency and effectiveness over the next two years, and Strong in 1925 was writing to Norman, who was still looking for an opportunity of carrying out his instruction to convene the conference, that what it was important to achieve had been done without any formal conference. The chief practical effect of Genoa, like Brussels, was to reaffirm the importance of a general return to an international Gold Standard as a safeguard against inflation and a basis for international trade.

The official policy, which the Governor of the Bank of England had to carry out, remained then the same. It was seldom challenged; when it was, as it was implicitly by a plea for a little inflation by a former Junior Minister in the summer of 1923, it was reaffirmed by the Prime Minister (Baldwin). When fears of a Socialist Government led to some flight from sterling, the new Chancellor, Snowden, stated in Parliament in June 1924 that it was still the intention of the Government to carry out the policy of the Cunliffe Committee. Criticism came not from Parliament or industry and trade, and hardly at all from the City; but economists whose special studies lay in the field of monetary economics began to have doubts, and presently to oppose the accepted policy. These criticisms centred on two issues — the delay in reversing the deflationary pressure of a high Bank Rate, and the determination to restore the Gold Standard at the old parity with gold and the dollar. No one seems to have opposed returning to the Gold Standard as such, until years after the return had been made.

As we have seen, Bank Rate was maintained at 7 per cent until April 1921, though Strong and the Governor had hesitated over maintaining it in the previous December. It was reduced from $6\frac{1}{2}$ to 6 per cent in June and to $5\frac{1}{2}$ per cent on July 21. On November 3 the Court accepted a recommendation of the Committee of Treasury that 'following on the projected change in the Federal Reserve Bank Discount Rate', Bank Rate be reduced to 5 per cent. The following February it was reduced to 4½ per cent, and on April 12 the Committee of Treasury agreed, 'failing the likelihood of any reduction in New York, and owing to domestic conditions', that it should be reduced to 4 per cent, the Court taking action on the following day. Six weeks later, the Governor reported to the Committee of Treasury on his talks during a visit to America, and after reading to the Committee extracts from the Report of the Agricultural Committee of Inquiry in Washington, which criticised the rate policy followed by the Federal Reserve Board, said that under present conditions in Washington it would not be wise to count on co-operation from New York in any further policy of rate reductions. There were further discussions on Bank Rate policy in the Committee in the following two weeks, after which the rate was reduced to 3½ per cent on 15 June 1922. A month later it was brought down to 3 per cent, where it rested for twelve months.

The references by the Committee to conditions in New York are significant. Strong had welcomed Norman's election as Governor with the promise that, if at any time he could personally or officially or in any way be of service to Norman as Governor, he wanted the opportunity. Norman found him a more sympathetic and congenial associate than any other, an American with an international outlook, a banker who shared Norman's hopes of Central Bank co-operation, and an equally convinced believer in traditional orthodoxy in monetary policy who was always ready to subject his theories to the test of current experience. They regularly discussed their respective rate policy; they deprecated suggestions in the press of 'joint action', an alleged 'money trust', but, Norman pointed out, London looked at rates as international, not national, factors, and London and New York rates could not be kept apart. Strong replied that there were only three alternatives — complete independence and ignorance of what the other was doing, a wholly selfish policy disregarding each other's interests, and a policy of mutual exchange of information, mutual understanding and co-operation whenever their respective interests made it possible. He could not see that there was any choice, and

there would be no ground of complaint 'so long as we are right
and not afraid of our critics'. In an early discussion they had
agreed that rates should usually be higher in London than in
New York.

In common with most observers they had canvassed stabilisation of exchanges much earlier than proved to be possible.
Already in November 1921 Strong was throwing out suggestions
for a provisional scheme. Recognising the principal causes of
current exchange disturbances — unbalanced budget, excessive
currency issues, the unsolved problems of reparations and war
debts — nevertheless there were certain countries whose affairs
were sound enough to present a reasonable possibility of stabilising their exchanges on the dollar, within some agreed limits.
He mentioned Holland, Switzerland, the three Scandinavian
countries and Japan : but added that no scheme would produce
the results desired without including sterling. He wondered
whether some organisation could be set up between these
countries for dealing in exchanges in the interests of stability,
the dollars required being perhaps advanced by the Federal
Reserve Banks and risks being limited by a willingness to settle
the ultimate net balance in gold.

Replying in February 1922 the Governor said .

Generally speaking, I do not believe that any artificial means
for the stabilisation of Exchange would, if ever, be practicable
until the debts have been settled, the Reparations adjusted, and
free Gold Markets have again become much more general than
they are now. And is it not true that when these things shall have
happened stability in the Exchanges will be looking after itself in
the old-fashioned way and artificial stabilisation will hardly be
necessary.

Other countries were expecting some such move. On 24
November 1921 the Governor sent Strong a confidential memorandum of a conference between the three Scandinavian Central
Banks. They were unanimous on the desirability of returning
to a Gold Standard at a fixed though not necessarily the pre-
war parity. No move was possible until there was agreement
between Great Britain and the United States. This was the
first step towards restoring an effective Gold Standard. Once
taken, other countries with favourable exchanges would follow

suit. It was the first condition for success in dealing with the problem of exchanges, and a step towards the ultimate purpose — a general economic restoration of Europe. Until the United Kingdom fixed its parity on the dollar, no Scandinavian country could stabilise the dollar value of its currency; and none should try. Bank Rate had lost its efficacy; it was effective only after stabilisation. In February he enclosed a letter from Moll (the President of the Sveriges Riksbank) asking Great Britain to return to a free gold market. Moll said: 'A return to the Gold Standard is the first and most indispensable condition of the establishment of regulated economic conditions in Europe. The clearer this becomes the more pressing does it appear that England, by taking the above measure, would break the ice and re-establish the Gold Standard in Europe. . . . Genoa was an opportunity; it would be the best possible starting point for the Conference. . . . An English return to gold would cut the Gordian knot.' Strong replied on 21 February 1922 that there was an attractive innocence in Moll's method of expressing the hope 'that you would be the kindhearted gentleman to bell the cat'. He sympathised with Moll's point of view; he had long believed that restoring sterling to parity with the dollar on a gold basis would affect so large a part of the trading world that it would be beneficial, that re-establishment of parity would require very small credits provided certain abnormal influences were eliminated, viz. reparations payments and inter-Allied debts. Other countries would follow sterling, but the first decision rested with the United Kingdom.

It did not, however, turn out to be easy to regulate credit in America in such a way as to meet both London's requirements and domestic needs. The London Bank Rate, after following the New York rate down till February 1922, moved downwards independently. Strong wrote in February that there was no chance of lowering the New York rate; credit was still strained in the South, commercial paper was above his rate and the Government was borrowing at a higher rate. Norman recognised his 'social and political difficulties'. Strong was worried in March over the loss of control over his market; the indebtedness of member banks had been reduced after the fall in prices, and the flood of gold pouring in confronted him with inevitable inflation; already a stock market boom was under

way, and they were in for a merry dance if they did not look out.
In June he was questioning the justification for the low London
rate and it was in fact raised to 4 per cent again in July in face
of an acute bull position on the Stock Exchange, and the need
of steadying the dollar-sterling rate well in advance of making
provision for the American debt service.   In January 1924
Strong was again writing that Coolidge's return in the Presidential election and European recovery might start a speculative
outbreak difficult to control ; rates could not be put up, but
they were putting in hand operations which would influence
the market without change of rate.   He thought the London
Bank Rate was too much influenced by sterling exchange and
the hope of influencing the dollar rate ; he leaned rather to
open-market operations.   In June New York had put its rate
below London with the deliberate intention of helping London
back to the Gold Standard, but he still thought higher rates
would be needed to check inflation in the New Year.

When American credits for war and relief ceased, the flow
of gold to America expanded.   This influx softened the impact
of the Federal Reserve Banks' deflationary policy in 1921, and
subsequently, when member banks had reduced their indebtedness to the Reserve Banks, threatened to remove them from
control by the Reserve Banks, should they be tempted to expand
credit.   The Reserve Banks countered this influence by selling
a large part of their holdings of Government securities, and
further by substituting gold certificates for Reserve Bank notes
as currency.   The circulation of gold certificates absorbed the
incoming gold without allowing it to increase bank reserves
and so make credit conditions easier.   It did not prevent some
increase in the country's monetary resources ; but it did prevent
the international movements of gold from having the compensating effect in the receiving country which would have eased
the exchange difficulties of the exporting countries.   The
United Kingdom had to maintain higher interest rates from
the middle of 1923 to the return to the Gold Standard than it
would have done if the New York rate had not been held
above London's from April 1922 to May 1924, and if American
prices had not tended downwards in 1923 and 1924 while
English prices rose.

Norman had criticised a Swedish policy with a similar

object; they bought pounds and dollars, he complained, and carried them in London at 2 per cent interest instead of pursuing the 'orthodox course' of letting gold in freely so that their reserves rose, and then making foreign loans freely; but he did not in his letters criticise American policy on gold. At one point he was clearly handicapped in his own policy by American conditions. His greatest problem between 1920 and 1925 was to control the tendency of London to lend too much abroad. The country had recovered its normal surplus on current foreign account, but the surplus was not large enough to provide both for the reconstruction of Europe, to which he thought it both the duty and the interest of the country to contribute, and the demands of other overseas borrowers. Among the latter he was usually anxious to facilitate loans to Empire Governments; but the greatest pressure came from the capital-starved countries of Europe. Even if they could borrow more cheaply in New York, London was nearer and more familiar, and in fact New York was dearer. Norman's only weapon in resisting such claims in the last resort was an interest rate, preferably higher and certainly not lower than New York's; but domestic needs, and the resultant political pressure, compelled him to keep down his rate. There was no hope of securing any legislative or other Government prohibition of overseas issues. Short-term credits he could fight by his influence over the market; but long-term loans he could prevent only by personal appeal and influence. Each year he armed himself with a letter from the Chancellor requesting banks to restrict such lending. The houses that handled it always informed him, as was the custom and as he insisted. Sometimes he made a note of the reply he made to his visitors:

Loan on German industries to provide Reparation payments: I say now impossible — Reparation payment in general — I say political not financial — Short loan for coffee valorisation. I say no. [28 October 1921.]
I protest against the £1 mn. Polish credit he has issued with right of renewal up to total of 12 months. [29 March 1922.]
M. asked to lend £2500 m. to France to repay us in May. I protest at length. He will consider but I fear he will agree. [26 Feb. 1924.]
I strongly disapprove of acceptance credit to L. H. on gold in B. de F. He will try to cancel entirely. I also ask him to arrange

no renewals of coal credit.   He agrees.   [One of four on 13 March 1924.]

Possible issue of £6 mil.   Dutch loan instead of further issues of D. East Indies : I say foreign loans too frequent, too cheap, and poor reasons.   [2 April 1924.]

McKenna : Foreign Loans — he agrees we have overspent : our only remedy a 5% rate, which must be used if such loans continue on a large scale.   [16 April 1924.]

Issue of Japanese Electric etc. Bonds in addition to those guaranteed by Trade Facilities.   I say impossible : explain position at length : prospects quite indefinite : depend on $ exchange.   He seems to accept the position.   [31 October 1924.]

In his evidence before the Macmillan Committee [1] some five years later Norman doubted the effectiveness of the unofficial 'embargo' on foreign loans which, with the Chancellor's backing, he had tried to impose.   Recorded public issues on overseas account in the four years 1921–24 averaged £130 million a year, sufficient to absorb the country's estimated surplus on current account and require some export of gold in addition.

The hopes of an early return to gold led by London, which had been entertained when the Genoa Conference was convened, were not realised.   In 1921 the effects of deflation after the post-war boom were still too much present in the minds of governments, and the dollar-sterling rate was still too low, to permit even a provisional arrangement.   Hope was renewed as the dollar-sterling rate rose in 1922 ; but there was still no debt settlement, and the condition of Germany was deteriorating.   The settlement of the British debt in February 1923 was followed by a rise in the dollar-sterling rate ; but in June 1923 the Treasury was warning Norman that a rise in Bank Rate might have serious effects on employment.   Norman, in a manuscript note on stabilisation, set out the pros and cons ; the Trade Balance could not be unfavourable, the Dominion gold-producers would gain, it would stop the inflationists, the Continent was waiting, foreign balances would come to London ; *but* unemployment might increase, trade might fall off ;

[1] Committee on Finance and Industry under the Chairmanship of Lord Macmillan appointed 5 November 1929.   Norman gave evidence in March 1930 and again in February 1931.

the debt to the U.S. was a burden, there were still two note-
issues and no unified control of them, a high Bank Rate would
be needed and the effect on industry must be considered. However, Bank Rate was raised in July; but by now the French had
occupied the Ruhr, and credit policy in London and New
York was diverging. The dollar-sterling rate fell from 4·69
in February 1923 to 4·26 in January 1924, and projects of
stabilisation were deferred.

One problem which the return to gold would raise was
considered early in 1923. Norman was concerned over the
Government's lack of concern over the means of making the
payments it had undertaken under the American debt settlement. He wished to accumulate in New York a reserve which
would always be available. This ought to be done before the
additional obligation of meeting demands for gold under a
restored Gold Standard were assumed; whether it was or not,
the obvious resort of the Government in face of a sudden large
need of dollars or gold was the gold reserves of the two note-
issues. Such a raid would relieve an external strain only at the
expense of a domestic crisis; either the Bank's gold reserve
would be so depleted that a sharp rise in Bank Rate would be
necessary, or the gold in the Currency Notes account would be
drawn on, the issue against gold reduced, and a demand excited
for a compensatory expansion of the Fiduciary Issue in spite of
the limit imposed by the Treasury Minute of 1919. The procedure finally adopted, on the recommendation of the Cunliffe
and Chamberlain Committees, and embodied in the Currency
and Bank Notes Act of 1928 had its origins in a correspondence
with Bradbury in the spring of 1923. Norman invited a small
group of his advisers to discuss his proposal. In reply to
Norman's inquiry, Baldwin said that he was 'most willing that
I should consult Asquith on financial questions'. In addition
to Asquith the group consisted of Addis, Bradbury, Gaspard
Farrer, Inchcape and Felix Schuster. It met twice, and agreed
on the following memorandum:

We are of opinion —

  1. That it is desirable to take steps to place a considerable sum
     (say, £100 million) in America within the next couple of
     years which should be invested in U.S. Bonds and should
     be available for contingencies.

2. That should it be necessary to draw upon our Gold Reserves here to make this transfer, the Gold Reserves should not be reduced at any time below 25% of the outstanding Legal Tender Notes.

3. That, in order to facilitate the above arrangements, it is desirable forthwith to amalgamate the Currency Note issue with the Bank issue.

4. That statutory authority be obtained to continue the Export Control Act until not later than 1930 — or until an amalgamated Gold Reserve of at least £150 million shall have been held under favourable Exchange conditions for two consecutive years.

Commenting on the memorandum in May 1923 Bradbury wrote :

While I am disposed to agree in principle that it is not safe — whether an American reserve is created or not — to commit ourselves to the re-establishment of a full-blown gold standard in 1925, I am strongly of opinion that if we get through the present autumn without a serious break in sterling, the time will have arrived for setting up arrangements which will lead automatically to such re-establishment within a definite period. . . .

All practical purposes will be served if a statutory obligation is imposed on the Bank of England both to buy and to sell bar gold at a fixed price.

An effective gold standard will be re-established as soon as this has been done and the buying and selling prices are sufficiently near together — say about 3d. per standard ounce apart.

There is, however, in present circumstances a good deal to be said for an intermediate period with a wider margin.

If the pound does not fall this autumn below $4·50, I believe it would be safe to fix a maximum selling price of say 85/- per standard ounce falling by say 1/- annually until the margin between buying and selling price is reduced to 3d.

The actual selling price could be fixed by the Bank from time to time at its discretion, subject to the statutory maximum and the return to parity thus accelerated if conditions proved favourable.

I am convinced that either the time is ripe for the adoption of an automatic arrangement on some such lines, or it is not ripe for amalgamating the issues. If we are to have a recrudescence of the doubtful blessings of an 'elastic' currency, it had much better be on the basis with which we are familiar.

The marriage of the Bank and Treasury issues is a somewhat risky experiment at best, regard being had to the lady's past, and the best hope for a virtuous menage is to postpone the ceremony until it is quite clear that she has weaned herself of her bohemian habits.

The Governor replied on May 26:

I agree of course that all practical purposes as regards the full-blown gold standard would be served by a statutory obligation on the Bank of England to buy and to sell bar gold at fixed prices. But I cannot see that the time has come to make this a question of practical politics, nor, personally, should I jump at such a sliding-scale arrangement as you mention.

The main points with which I am and have throughout been concerned are these:

(1) The need for the best part of $100 million by next winter towards which we have not got a cent in hand.

(2) The prospect that next year the fiduciary maximum of the Currency Note Issue will, under the Treasury Minute, very likely leave no elasticity except through the Bank Reserve.

I have had no help towards meeting these two points. I think there may be a great hullabaloo at the imposition of a high Bank Rate merely (as would be said) to prevent the re-writing of a Treasury Minute: I think there might be domestic trouble about imposing a high Bank Rate either to protect the Treasury Minute from being re-written or merely to restrict a circulation in which the Bank, as such, may be held to have no concern.

I want these two questions to be faced early so that there may be a settled policy for dealing with them if and when either or both should land us in a tight place. . . .

P.S. I wish we could have somebody's blood to atone for the way the Hungarians have been treated.

However, conditions were unfavourable to any move. Norman raised the question with the Committee of Treasury on October 10, whether it was possible or desirable to make a definite attempt to get back to the Gold Standard in 1924; after two discussions the Committee decided that the policy of waiting and controlling the market should be continued and 'any attempt to reconsider the Report of the Cunliffe Committee, at any rate until after a complete settlement of Reparations and inter-allied debts, should be resisted'.

(ii)

With the British war debt settled and the interest on it being regularly met, with a serious and concerted attack on the problem of German Reparations achieving at least a provisional settlement on the basis of the Dawes Report, with Central Europe recovering by the aid of League reconstruction loans, and with the domestic trade situation improving in both the United Kingdom and America, the effort could be renewed in 1924. The Governor drew the Committee's attention on March 19 to two answers by the Prime Minister and the Chancellor (Snowden) to questions in Parliament; first, that the Government was still guided by the conclusions of the Cunliffe Committee on questions of Currency and Foreign Exchange; and, second, that he (the Chancellor) saw advantages in the amalgamation of the two note-issues, but was unable to make a statement yet. At the same time the Governor invited the Committee's opinion on the expediency of appointing a committee to consider the amalgamation of the note-issues well before the freeing of gold movements. He must have done this by agreement with the Chancellor, because such a committee was appointed on June 10. Austen Chamberlain was Chairman, the other members being Bradbury, Sir Otto Niemeyer,[1] Gaspard Farrer and Professor Pigou — three of them members of the Cunliffe Committee. On May 28 the Governor discussed with the Committee of Treasury the recommendations he should make — amalgamation of the two issues, deferment of any attempt to settle now the amount of the Fiduciary Issue, no extension of the prohibition of gold exports — and the Committee once more recorded its unanimous support of the restoration of the Gold Standard. These objectives were reaffirmed by the Committee on June 23, with the addition that other bankers should pay any gold they held into the Bank of England.

A decision before the end of 1925 was crucial, because the Gold (Export Control) Act, prohibiting the export of gold without licence, expired with it; renewal of the law would be an admission of failure. Norman was assured of a Cabinet decision on the essential issues — the gold embargo and the

[1] Controller of Finance, H.M. Treasury, 1922–27. Joined the Bank of England, August 1927, a Director 1938–52.

L

note-issues — by October; but, again, political developments intervened. Writing to Strong on the 16th after the fall of the Labour Government he said :

   . . . Our sudden and unexpected political upheaval has come at the very moment when we had planned and expected to obtain an official decision about future gold policy, including of course the immediate or ultimate amalgamation of the Bank and Currency Note Issues. . . . I can only suppose that the decision will be to declare a free market here either at the end of 1925 or at the end of a somewhat later year, say, 1927. The former is the end of the period fixed by the present Law; any other date, such as the latter, would need fresh legislation. Undoubtedly an announcement ought to be made at an early date, and not less, one would suppose, than twelve months before the termination of the period fixed by the present law.

   I rather imagine that the course of the Dollar Exchange is halting by reason of the uncertainty of our policy and will eventually be helped by the announcement of an official decision. I think, too, that it would be neither necessary nor wise for us to take any strong measures in the meantime.

   I agree with what you write about the price levels in our two countries, though frankly I do not understand their course : it would not be sufficient to wait for exchange parity to be reached merely through the price levels coming together. Indeed, if while we were waiting your prices were to rise (especially wheat, cotton and the like) I do not believe we could ever prevent ours from following. I agree, too, that consideration of this subject by means of a chart needs more than the usual lines based on prices and facts : it needs, as you say, a line to represent the psychology of people generally, which means people in China and Peru as well as in New York and London. Perhaps, looking backward, you think that we have been remiss in not stimulating that psychology in our favour, as could have been done by showing publicly that we had confidence in the Exchange and in the return to gold. But it would have been difficult, and perhaps dangerous, to have proclaimed such confidence at any particular moment. There have always been some here to whom the idea of gold was repugnant. . . .

   Lastly, there has been the position of Germany — uncertain until the Dawes Plan was an accomplished fact and now possibly liable to be as much a danger as a help to sterling, though on balance I do not think so. Therefore, on the whole, my feeling is

that however wearisome the pace has been, we have been wise so
far to hurry slowly.

I agree entirely that we shall need some sort of an understanding between us as to the future gold policy. I think you are helping
to this end if you keep your rates as low as possible and lend freely
to the rest of the world as your Market is now doing. At the
moment, I do not think that we can do anything more than hold
our rates where they are and reduce our loans to the rest of the
world to a minimum. . . .

Preparations went on. Norman reported to the Committee
of Treasury on November 5 :

With reference to the American Exchange the Governor suggested that in the event of the Rate approaching parity it might
be advisable to obtain a large credit in America to steady the
position, and he asked the Committee to consider the suggestion.

And again on November 12 :

The Governor expressed his opinion that the Bank's account
with the Federal Reserve Bank of New York could properly be
utilised for purchases and sales in the Dollar Exchange Market
which would probably become necessary in the course of the
re-establishment of the Gold Market In London.

Norman told the Committee on 26 January 1925 that he
proposed to give evidence to the Chamberlain committee on
the following lines :

1. A credit of $500 million should be obtained in accord-
   ance with proposals in cables from New York ;
2. No extension of embargo on gold beyond 31 December
   1925 ;
3. Announcement in spring that embargo would not be
   prolonged ;
4. Meanwhile the credit should be arranged, and general
   licence given for export of gold : the Bank to take necessary steps to support the exchange.

The Chamberlain Committee reported on February 5. They
reviewed the Cunliffe Committee proposals and rejected two
alternative policies — return to gold on the basis of a devalued
pound, as unnecessary now that sterling was so near the old

parity on the dollar and, in their opinion, never a policy which the United Kingdom could have adopted ; and the substitution of 'the price level of commodities in general for gold as the regulating principle of the currency'. They concluded that, 'as a practical present-day policy' for the United Kingdom there was 'no alternative comparable with a return to the former gold parity of the sovereign', being supported in this conclusion 'by the overwhelming majority of opinion, both financial and industrial, represented in evidence before us'.[1]

When the Committee had first considered its report in September 1924, the New York rate was 10 to 12 per cent below gold parity, and the autumn drain on sterling had still to be faced. Even then they were satisfied that the country's current balance of payments made restoration of the old parity possible and a free gold market practicable, if the internal purchasing power of the pound were adjusted to its external parity by credit control. By February, when exchange rates and prices had altered the situation, this policy was possible without danger either of depletion of gold reserves or recourse to special measures of credit restriction. They recommended, therefore, a statement by the Government that an early return to gold was its irrevocable policy and that the restrictions on the export of gold would not be renewed. The two note-issues should be amalgamated as soon as practicable ; but the use of gold for domestic circulation was a luxury which could be dispensed with ; an obligation upon the Bank of Issue to buy and sell gold at a fixed price was all that was necessary. If gold credits were thought necessary, they should not be drawn on until there had been substantial gold exports. Two such credits were arranged — a credit with the Federal Reserve Bank of New York in favour of the Bank of England and a credit with J. P. Morgan & Co. in favour of the British Government, — the second being necessary because the Bank was not prepared to commit itself for the whole amount judged necessary, and because the Federal Reserve Bank was debarred by its statutes from making loans to foreign Governments.

[1] The Committee heard thirteen witnesses, including the Governor of the Bank, McKenna, Sir Robert Horne, Professor Cannan, Sir George Paish, Keynes and representatives of the Clearing Banks, the Association of British Chambers of Commerce and the Federation of British Industries.

The change assumed a concentration in the Bank of the country's gold. The Clearing Banks were reluctant to part with the right to hold and deal in gold. Norman attempted to induce them to surrender their gold voluntarily, but met with opposition. He reported to the Committee of Treasury on 8 April 1925 that he had attended a meeting of Clearing Bankers on the question of earmarking gold. No agreement was reached, but they thought they would probably agree for a time not to hold or earmark for themselves or customers in this country, but reserve the right to earmark for customers abroad. Certain bankers, he said, showed clearly their opposition to the Bank's policy and action in regard to Central Banks, with which they were in total disagreement; they were forced to admit that the policy they condemned had led to the reconstruction of several European countries which might otherwise have collapsed, but their opposition was in no way lessened. Since they could not be relied on to use their gold in case of an internal drain, it became necessary to relieve the Bank of the danger of having to deal with such a drain without having control of the country's whole gold reserve; this would be done by making notes convertible only at the option of the Bank.

Norman had, however, independently reasons for supporting the 'gold bullion' standard and not attempting to bring back a gold currency. They are given in an answer he sent some years later to a private inquiry from the Governor of the Bank of Norway; they are evidence also of the influence of the Genoa discussions:

May I thank you most sincerely for the compliment you have paid me in asking for my opinion about the kind of gold standard to which it would be well that Norway should return.

It must surely be the concern of all to avoid, so far as possible, disturbing fluctuations in the value of gold. I doubt whether at present the means exist for doing so in all circumstances, and I therefore think that every opportunity should be taken of improving the efficacy of such means as we have. The occasions where there is any liberty of action are relatively few, and every deliberate choice is apt to become a precedent for future occasions. I would therefore suggest that your decision should be taken on these broad grounds of principle.

In some other countries the question is complicated by the

habits and psychology of the public, but I understand that in Norway the convenience of paper currency is appreciated, and confidence in the value of money does not depend upon the existence of gold coin. You are therefore free to adapt your policy to circumstances. Such liberty, to my mind, is valuable, because the future gold supplies of the world are a matter of uncertainty. Demand is rendered more inelastic wherever the principle of gold circulation, for currency or for hoarding, is accepted, and any inelasticity may be dangerous when there are such unknown quantities as India and Russia. I do not believe that gold in circulation can safely be regarded as a reserve that can be made available in case of need, and I think that even in times of abundance hoarding is bad, because it weakens the command of the Central Bank over the monetary circulation and hence over the purchasing power of the monetary unit.

For these reasons I suggest that your best course would be to establish convertibility of notes into gold bars only and in amounts which will ensure that the use of monetary gold can be limited, in case of need, to the settlement of international balances.

In his Budget speech on 28 April 1925 the new Chancellor (Winston Churchill) announced that the embargo on gold would not be renewed at the end of the year, and that in the meantime licences to export gold would be given. Norman was present; his diary has the entry:

Budget — H. of C. (3–6)

GOLD STANDARD (about 4.5 P.M.)

The change was embodied in the Gold Standard Act, 1925, which became law on May 13. It had two sections: the second merely authorised credits raised for supporting the exchange within the two following years; the first relieved the Bank of the obligation to convert notes into legal tender coin and repealed the provision in the 1914 Currency and Bank Notes Act making Currency Notes convertible, but imposed on the Bank the obligation to sell gold at the statutory price on demand in four-hundred-ounce bars. The Bank remained under the obligation of section 4 of the Bank Charter Act of 1844 to buy gold at the statutory price.

Sterling rose to par at once, and there was no need to draw

on the two credits ; balances, as was expected, were transferred
to London. The danger which close observers feared was that
this movement of funds would give a false idea of permanent
balance in the country's external relations and undermine the
sense of the persistent need for effort and caution.

Norman, though he had arranged the dollar credits and
had put Bank Rate up to 5 per cent in March, was not reassured by the ease with which the return to the Gold Standard
was effected. He told Strong on March 26 that the Market's
expectations of a reduction in Bank Rate were not justified.
The gold attracted to London had not been attracted by the
high Bank Rate ; it came for special (not exchange) reasons in
every case, and was likely to be withdrawn in the autumn.
The City, he added, was optimistic, as opposed to industry,
taking the short as opposed to the long view.

Contemporary criticism of the return to gold in 1925 turned
mainly on the rate or parity at which the return was made.
The Cunliffe Committee did not consider any alternative to
the pre-war parity, and it does not appear that any alternative
was ever seriously considered in official discussions of policy
subsequently. Dr. W. A. Brown was told that the decision
to return to pre-war parity was taken the first day the exchange
diverged from it.[1] In a long series of discussions with the Committee of Treasury on the return to gold the Governor never
raised any proposal for devaluation ; the Bank and the City
would naturally attach great importance to the loss of prestige
which devaluation would have involved, and the Treasury
officials do not seem to have differed. The Brussels and Genoa
Conferences recommended devaluation, but only in the case of
currencies which had fallen so far from their pre-war gold
parity that it would have involved prolonged deflation and long
delays before a stable exchange rate was restored ; their expert
advisers took the same view, and one of them pointed the
moral: 'For the United Kingdom, where the exchange is
only depreciated some 20 per cent, the balance of argument is
clearly in favour of a return to pre-war parity'.

An official policy, once adopted on an important issue
involving continuous effort over years, is not easy to alter,
especially a policy which affects so many plans, domestic and

[1] W. A. Brown, *The International Gold Standard Reinterpreted*, p. 221.

international. Unofficial discussion was slow to suggest any change. *The Economist* in April 1922, it is true, and Keynes about the same time,[1] writing to urge on the Genoa Conference the importance of early stabilisation of exchanges, considered stabilisation at a rate below the pre-war parity. Keynes recognised the prestige of the pre-war rate as a reason for giving the Bank of England at least a year's grace in which to try the policy of restoration of the old parity ; but if success were not attained within a year the alternative policy should, he urged, be considered. Much as Norman desired return, however, it is abundantly clear from repeated references in the Committee of Treasury and in his correspondence with Strong, that while he never considered any rate except the pre-war rate, he was not prepared to take the risk of returning to the Gold Standard *at all* until the two great uncertainties in the international economic situation had been removed, War Debts and German Reparations. To this he always came back ; and Strong agreed. Given these views on policy, the explanation of his policy is obvious ; when sterling approached its pre-war parity, that would be taken as a reason for returning at that rate ; when it fell more, say, than 20 per cent below that parity, it would be a reason for deferring return at *any* rate.

The criticism that did most to form the adverse opinion which attached to the restoration was Keynes's pamphlet, *The Economic Consequences of Mr. Churchill*. The criticism was directed not at the Gold Standard as such but 'against having restored gold in conditions which required a substantial readjustment of all our money values. . . . Mr. Churchill's policy of improving the exchange by 10 per cent was, sooner or later, a policy of reducing everyone's wages by 2s. in the £.' In the event, money wages varied little from 1924 to 1929 ; real wages, thanks to the fall in the cost of living from the beginning of 1925, rose substantially. Employment as a whole expanded every year except 1926 until 1929, though bankers' cash contracted ; the *percentage* of insured persons unemployed rose in 1925, fell in 1926 till the coal strike, fell after the strike to its lowest point in 1927, and, after rising in 1928, fell again in 1929. Exports fell in value, but were 8 per cent higher in volume in 1929 than in 1924. American prices did

[1] *Manchester Guardian Commercial*, 6 April 1922.

not rise after 1925, but fell, though hourly earnings rose; British wholesale prices fell more than American to 1929. Keynes's fears were not realised except in the case of coal; and a judgment on the immediate effects of the return to gold will be much influenced by the assessment of its influence in creating the difficulties of the coal industry, and so causing the troubles of 1926. It is not possible, certainly, to attribute the whole to monetary policy; to do so would be to ignore the effects of the French occupation of the Ruhr and the German miners' passive resistance. The number of miners attached to the British industry was inflated to 1,230,000 in 1924; after the Ruhr had resumed production, coal-mining had been expanded in Poland and Holland and the French mines had been restored, inevitably it fell. At no time between the wars were the coalfields of Europe all fully employed at once.

In endless discussions subsequent to (though little if at all before) the return to gold, criticism concentrated on the effects on British export trade. The pre-war rate over-valued sterling and made it difficult for exporters to secure prices abroad which covered their costs at home. Norman's answer to this criticism would be that he could not take account of the difficulties of exporters when other circumstances made it desirable to restore the Gold Standard, because he could not know *then* that our exporters' chief competitors would subsequently fix the value of *their* currency at a level which gave them a lasting advantage in competition. These competitors were primarily the countries of Western Europe. Their economy was much like that of the United Kingdom, and their chief exports — textiles, iron and steel, coal, machinery — were the same as the chief exports of the United Kingdom. By adopting a low value in sterling for their currencies when they returned to gold — Belgium in 1926, Poland in 1927, France in 1928 — they gave their own industries new protection at home against British exports and an advantage over British exports in other countries' markets. The relation between British and American trade in 1925 on the other hand was complementary, not competitive. It was an advantage to the United Kingdom to have its currency over-valued, if anything, in terms of dollars, because such a value cheapened its imports from America, which were usually three or four times its exports to America.

The competition of France, Belgium and Italy on the basis of under-valued currencies did accentuate the difficulties of the depressed British export industries : but to have waited, either for them to lead the way back to the Gold Standard, or for a simultaneous return by international agreement at agreed parities, would have meant no return. Some country had to take the lead, and Britain was the natural country to take it, as the chief centre both of international trade and finance. Strong told Norman that the success of the Dawes scheme, by making it possible for Germany to put its currency back on a gold basis, would compel England to act. The smaller countries had been waiting — and pressing England — for a lead for years. South Africa 'stole a march' by taking steps to return before Britain did.

(iii)

The issue before the Treasury and Norman in 1924 was not the rate at which sterling should return to gold, but whether to return to gold at all. The immediate question was whether to maintain the embargo on gold exports; but behind this lay the choice between two policies — that of requiring of finance and industry a continual adjustment to external conditions at *some* rate, an adjustment that would remain a necessity under *any* rate; and that of taking *all* strains on the economy in its external relations by letting the exchange slip. What the critics objected to was the resumption of gold exports, just because that would compel finance and industry to adjust themselves to external conditions; if the rate were allowed to float there need never be any tightening of credit. But their alternative to the old parity was not a floating rate but a different fixed parity; and any fixed parity would at some time require to be supported by credit restrictions.[1]

---

[1] The controversy over the rate at which to return was confused by differences over the indices of prices to be compared. Indices of commodities entering into world trade would not serve, since trade would bring their prices in different currencies into accord with the exchange rates between these currencies; what was needed was an index for each country of internal costs. On the whole, opinion came to accept wage-rates — the price of labour — as the best index of such costs. On this basis a rate of 4·40 to the £ in 1924 would seem to have under-valued sterling, though 4·86 would over-value it.

There was an unstated assumption in the argument against the stabilising at the old rate — the assumption that the then existing (lower) rate, which would have to be forced up to 4·86 by credit restriction, represented a stable balance of prices or costs in Britain and the external world, a balance which would either maintain itself thereafter or could be maintained by credit policy without any difficulty or strain on the economy of the United Kingdom.   There was no justification for any such assumption.   The rate of July 1924, 4·40, the 10 per cent below the old par which it would be necessary to eliminate by forcing down British prices, was not a stable rate. It had been 4·30 two months before and was to be 4·50 a month later; it had varied between 3·21 and 4·72, since the war-time peg had been removed.   At a lower rate, no immediate credit restriction might have been necessary; but any subsequent (relative) fall in prices outside the United Kingdom would have called for credit restriction.   Any subsequent *competitive* de-valuation of Continental currencies would have confronted the United Kingdom with exactly the same problem as it found itself faced with at the parity adopted.   The choice was whether to hold *any* exchange rate or not; it was not to choose — in the absence of exchange control, import licensing, restrictions of capital transfers, inter-governmental loans and American Aid, which transformed the problem after 1939 — between the traditional rate and another.

Norman tended to look at exchange problems, so far as he related them to trade, from the traditional English point of view of imports.   Most of the country's raw materials and food-stuffs were imported; and altogether imports for home consumption tended to exceed exports of British produce by some-thing between one-third and three-fifths.   The increased cost of essential imports, due to reducing the value of sterling in other currencies, would quickly cancel the temporary relief from foreign competition given by devaluation, and result in fresh inflation.   Moreover, in paying for these imports the United Kingdom relied largely on income derived from overseas investment, shipping freights and financial services; all these were denominated in sterling and were not easy to raise if the value of sterling were reduced; in the three years 1922–24 they were estimated at £1083 million (net) as compared with £2288

million for exports. To these obvious advantages in working
for the pre-war rate, Norman would add the less definable but
not less real advantages of restoring and maintaining the
country's international position — the advantages of possessing
a world currency, which made payments to other countries
easy because they were always willing to hold balances in it,
and facilitated the entrepôt trade and international services
which contributed a large part of the country's overseas earnings. The immediate justification was seen in the expansion
of the volume of British exports in each of the four succeeding
years, of employment except in 1926, and of world trade to a
higher point by 1929 than ever reached before.

His evidence before the Macmillan Committee was one of
the very few occasions on which Norman attempted a public
explanation of his policy. It throws a good deal of light on his
practice when he was preparing for the restoration of the Gold
Standard. He was a bad witness, because he was answering
interrogations by critics who had a clear theoretical view of
events, while he deliberately refused to generalise, and explained
his action as a series of responses to particular market situations
which were never quite the same. He began by referring to
the background against which all his judgments were made —
'the troublesome question of perpetual maturities of debt' in
the domestic situation, and the urgent need of restoring stability
to the economies of European countries which had been disrupted by war and, with this object, of organising co-operation
among Central Banks, in external relations. Beyond this he
was not able to satisfy the curiosity of his questioners. Asked
whether in moving Bank Rate he had in view the consequences
to the industrial position of the country, he replied : 'We have
them in view, yes, but the main consideration is the international
consideration'. Asked how far he was a free agent, he replied :
'So far as the legislative position goes, we are, but so far as the
international position goes, not at all a free agent : the whole
of the international machinery is bound together and . . .
necessarily works as a whole as, indeed, it should do'. Sometimes international considerations were not predominant ; he
had to look 'inwards' as well as 'outwards' ; but the advantage
at home to industry and commerce of maintaining the country's
international position was paramount. He recognised the

difficulties of industry but did not think they were caused by financial policy.

Pressed by Keynes, who explained that the Bank Rate was 'effective', as Norman said it was, in correcting an adverse international position only by causing domestic unemployment, he at first demurred, and then admitted that the external and domestic effects were necessarily linked. But he thought, first, that the effect of Bank Rate was largely exhausted in the short money market; it was effective frequently without the necessity of any open market operations on the volume of money to enforce it; he judged the position mainly by the situation in the short money market, and did not wait for an outflow of gold. The untoward effects on British industry of returning to gold he attributed to the *subsequent* stabilisation of the currencies of foreign competitors, particularly France and Belgium, at much lower rates than ruled when we stabilised. To Keynes's suggestion that it would have been better to defer our return to gold until these other countries had done so first, his adviser Dr. Sprague [1] gave the reply which Norman would have given — that London led in these matters.

McKenna and Keynes pressed him to define his policy in relation to the volume of bank deposits. McKenna took a recent restriction of credit by the Bank's sale of securities; Norman questioned the fact of restriction. McKenna replied that the total amount of credit at the end of February 1930, compared with February 1929, represented 'a reduction in purchasing power of the public of £63,000,000'. Norman did not accept this identification of bank deposits with the purchasing power of the public, and pointed out that the volume of securities and deposits at the date from which McKenna measured the fall was abnormally inflated by the failure of the public to take up a Government loan issued to meet maturities; the subsequent reduction in the Bank's securities merely corrected this. When McKenna pressed him to say whether deposits as a whole ought to be increased, decreased or kept stable by his action, he refused to express an opinion, and merely pointed out that the fall of deposits in the first quarter of the year was due to taxation. Keynes pointed out that deposits, apart from such

[1] Professor of Banking, Harvard University, from 1908. An Adviser to the Governors, Bank of England, 1930–33.

accidental events, had been kept at a stationary level ; Norman
agreed that this was 'to some extent by design'. Keynes then
asked :

At least 10 per cent of the productive forces of this country,
both men and plant, are out of work and the existing volume of
banking accommodation appears to be fully occupied in keeping
the other nine-tenths going. Is it not absolutely impossible that
that other one-tenth should be employed as long as you pursue
what you call the policy of parity ? — No, I do not think that is
necessarily so.

How could they be ? — Perhaps I did not make my meaning
clear. It must be remembered that during the last few years there
has been no period when we have not had continuously to face
difficulties due to the international position, that is, up to a few
weeks ago. I do not myself believe that the mere provision of
more money to the bankers is all that is needed to meet the difficulties of industry. . . .

The nearest he came to a definition of his practice was in
answer to question 3450 :

I look — the Bank looks — to keep the market supplied in
normal circumstances with adequate funds. One of the criteria
by which we judge the matter is the amount of funds which the
Discount Market may have or may need. One of the unique facts
about the London market and its position is the existence of the
Discount Market. I should never think that there was real pressure
for money unless I saw indications that, in the absence of action
by the Bank, the Discount Market might find it necessary to apply
to the Bank for advances.

The price level and state of industry and employment were
'constantly in his mind', a fall would have 'a great effect on
his mind' ; but

. . . the state of the money market is largely the factor by which the
position must be judged and generally speaking I should not say
that the volume was inadequate in the absence of some indication
from the money market that money was in short supply, because
they after all are the source from which any bank can replenish
its needs.

But he refused to commit himself to any simple criterion or
formula ; even the state of the money market was only 'one of

the indications; I cannot say that there are hard and fast facts which would guide me in all circumstances': he did nothing 'automatically'.

His questioners and he were at cross purposes. Their questions were all based on the unstated, and possibly unconscious, assumption that monetary policy was the sole and sufficient explanation of the difficulties of British industry. Norman clearly did not accept this assumption, but did not bring it into the open. This fundamental misunderstanding apart, the questioners were looking for rules, principles, criteria, while he always had in mind an actual situation and would not commit himself further. His explanations, therefore, contributed little to the theory of credit which the members of the committee were trying to apply; but his practice saved him from neglect of the continual change and variety in the actual situations with which he had to deal.

The preliminary reference to 'the troublesome question of maturities' is important, though it was not taken up. He had the Central Banker's distrust of any redundancy in the supply of money. He entered the difficult decade of post-war reconstruction with the Government and the Bank at the mercy of the market, because the market held a vast amount of short-term Government obligations maturing continually and requiring replacement.

As he wrote to Strong in May 1921:

So long as a Government has directly or indirectly a large floating debt, I wonder if any system can leave the Central Bank of that country really free to manage affairs from a purely financial standpoint. Indeed it was the desire to make some step towards this freedom that made me glad that our Government should have made an attempt by means of a Conversion Loan to prevent our actual floating debt increasing in size even at some cost of interest.

This debt lay at the root of the expansion of business in disregard of physical volume of output, which had forced up prices and destroyed the balance between the import demands and external resources of most of the countries of Europe. So long as the Floating Debt remained substantial, the bankers could meet any demands on them for expanded credit for their customers and force the Bank and Government to supply the necessary basis of cash; under these circumstances the levels of prices and exchange rates were liable to incalculable disturbance from speculative movements. Although, therefore, prices had been brought down from the 1920 peak, some control of exchanges restored and the reduction and funding of the Floating Debt carried some way, the Governor was never at ease. The justification for his disquiet was shown by recurrent outbursts of speculation, now in commodities like rubber, at another time in securities as in 1923 or new issues as in 1922 and 1928, and all the time in foreign currencies. Quite apart from other centres, though he always had his eye on them, he would be disinclined to relax his hold on the reins by making money easy and cheap, until a stable relation between credit supplies, prices and Government needs had been reached.

There is no evidence that the criticisms of the Government's policy and the Bank's measures to implement it raised any doubts in Norman's mind. Economists had not then the authority with governments which they have acquired since; Norman listened to them — Cassel and Wicksell [1] were among his callers; he would no doubt have been satisfied with the consistent support for the policy of the Cunliffe Committee given by the holders of the leading Chairs, Pigou and Cannan.[2] But he was not doctrinaire, and adjusted his plans to changing circumstances.

Norman always refused to commit himself to any date for return to gold; he proposed in 1923 maintaining the restriction on the export of gold until 1930; and he was quite definite, with the support of the Committee of Treasury, that no return to gold was possible until a debt settlement and some practical rearrangement of Reparations had been achieved. Even with this condition satisfied, he was still waiting on events in 1924, 'hurrying slowly', and doubtful whether return would be possible. He no doubt agreed with Strong, who wrote that it was useless to wait for prices to come into equilibrium without help, an act of *force majeure* was needed; he should copy Sherman, the Secretary of the Treasury who had to decide on the resumption of cash payments after the Civil War, and enunciated the principle 'The way to resume is to resume'.

[1] Both well-known Swedish professors of economics.
[2] Professors of Political Economy at Cambridge and London respectively.

He had confidence in the importance and the efficacy of the instruments of financial policy with which as Governor of the Bank of England he was entrusted; but in contrast to his critics, he recognised their limits. Within the limits of his 'market', the Money Market and the other activities centred on the City which were connected with it, and for the purposes for which he used them, they were, in his opinion, effective; buttheir usefulness was limited to, and their effect usually exhausted in, that field. By varying Bank Rate and supporting it by the Bank's own lending practice and by open market operations (the sale and purchase by the Bank of securities on its own initiative), he could make 'money' plentiful or scarce, cheap or dear. He made it dear or scarce, when he wished to check 'speculation' and 'over-trading' or a weakening of the sterling exchanges. By speculation he obviously did not mean undertaking business which would mature only in the future, since most business enterprise necessarily has that speculative element. He meant undertaking business in excess of the physical requirements and possibilities of industry and commerce, in excess of the resources available in a crisis to the undertakers, which led only to the forcing up of prices; and he feared this, because in experience it resulted in profits representing no social service, prices that could not be sustained, the wasteful application of resources and loss of capital, and an inevitable reaction in business collapse. His instruments checked such speculation, not only by increasing the cost of carrying a speculative position in securities, commodities or currencies, but also by instilling in the operator the fear that prices would move against him and his expected profit would not mature. It was the *change* in interest rates and the credit base, rather than the actual rate and amount established, that had the effect sought.

In addition to checking speculation in the markets for securities and commodities, credit policy had an associated aim — to regulate the influx and efflux of funds to and from London. Directly, the change in the rate of interest influenced this movement, particularly of short money, but also, by raising or lowering the cost of borrowing, of long-term capital; indirectly, it checked fluctuations in the external value of sterling and, if successful, maintained the confidence of bankers and

M

business men in sterling, and consequently their willingness to hold sterling balances.

These were all effects within the limits of the Central Banker's own field. Outside his market, his action had an effect; but it was indirect and deferred, and only one influence among many others. As we have seen, the Governor demurred to the suggestion that a curtailment of credit in the Money Market had necessarily an immediate and important effect on industry, and that raising Bank Rate restored equilibrium in the exchanges 'only . . . through the chain of depressed enterprise at home and unemployment'. His pre-war experience was that the attraction (or repulsion) of short-term funds was sufficient, usually before any actual movement of gold took place, to correct the exchanges, and industry was seriously affected only by a large and prolonged restriction (or expansion) of credit in the Money Market. Since 1914 he had found that the volume of Government expenditure, at home and abroad, and the extent to which it was financed by inflation of bank credit, was a more important influence both on the volume of money available for investment or speculation and on business activity than any action of the Bank.

While he would not accept the monetary explanation of British unemployment, his own views have to be inferred from such occasional references and from his actions. The two influences he stressed before the Macmillan Committee were the dislocation of international economic relations, affecting a country so dependent on international trade as the United Kingdom, and the need of a reorganisation of the country's basic export industries to repair the 'coincidence' of ' misfortunes' which handicapped them. His pre-war experience of business, when industry had expanded on exports, and credit policy had affected industry only momentarily in times of crisis, may have influenced him; and increasingly his mind was occupied with the threat of a breakdown in economic life on the Continent, as the result of the breakdown of normal international economic relations, which led him to subordinate every other aim to the restoration of stable international relations.

Because Norman pursued a credit policy which he considered necessary in the interest both of controlling a potential inflationary situation at home and assisting the restoration of economic order abroad, he was regarded as indifferent to the most pressing domestic problem, unemployment. Actually he was not indifferent to it, but did not regard it as falling within his field of responsibility or power of control. Hence he did not express himself upon it, either in public or in his private discussions with colleagues. The question whether his attitude was reasonable requires some examination, however brief, of the problem of unemployment between the wars itself.

There were in it two elements. There was, first, the unemployment caused by depression following boom in 1920–22 and 1930–33. War accounted for the post-war boom, and monetary policy played its part in ending the boom. But the brake of credit-restriction was not applied until a situation had been built up which was bound to collapse and to involve depression as its sequel. Similarly, the excesses of the American boom of 1927–29, communicated to other countries by large purchases and by lavish and undiscriminating lending, led to the succeeding depression. In both periods monetary policy was crucial, though long-run effects of war accentuated the boom and prolonged the depression ; accentuated the boom by deferring the normal expansion of building, new technological developments and new markets until they combined with boom conditions to press excessively on capital resources, and prolonged the depression by leaving a necessary redirection and reorganisation of industry to be achieved in the face of trade depression. But the recovery from these depressions, of a type familiar from a century's experience, left still to be dealt with a second element, the element of more permanent change left by war. War upset established relations between prices, especially between selling prices and the price of labour, between accustomed markets and traditional sources of supply, between different countries and industries. Tariffs and subsidies were used to maintain war-time industries established, or extended, to supply the place of imports interrupted by war ; new sources of supply were developed, which remained to create over-production when former sources were once more available ; long-continued pre-war trends of capital exports and migration of labour, to which both exporting and receiving countries were adjusted, were checked or diverted. Inflation distracted and

deferred attention from the more persistent and deep-seated
effects of the war, especially the permanent effects of the intensi-
fication of nationalist feeling and policy throughout the world.

The criticism of the monetary policy pursued in restoring
the Gold Standard paid less attention to this second element in
unemployment; it was forced on the Governor's attention by
his routine intercourse. The difficulties of accepting houses
with clients in Central Europe began to concern him as soon as
their bills were taken out of cold storage after the war. The
troubles of the shipbuilding industry, traditionally subject to
exceptional fluctuations but between the wars also steadily contracting, were brought home to him by the needs of Armstrong
Whitworth and Beardmores, deeply in debt to the Bank and the
Treasury. The gradual closing by protection, after India
received fiscal autonomy in 1921, of the Indian market which
had absorbed two-fifths of the output of the English cotton
industry, was reflected in difficulties for Lancashire, reported
to him by banks doing business there. He was unlikely to
attribute the difficulties of the coal-mining industry in 1925
wholly to the restoration of the old parity of sterling with the
dollar, when he had been labouring for a year and a half to
bring to an end the French occupation of the Ruhr, which first
paralysed the British industry's chief competitor, and then,
having stimulated a further increase in coal-mining in all other
fields, released its production for export.

The regular publication of the percentage of insured workers
unemployed confused rather than clarified public opinion —
Professor Cannan advised an old pupil who was included in
the Labour Government of 1929 to get rid of the publication of
this figure or it would get rid of his Government. It diverted
attention from two significant conclusions to be derived from
the statistics. The first was that the volume of employment, as
distinct from the percentage unemployed, grew steadily; the
second that unemployment was never distributed evenly over
industry. By 1928–29 the concentration was found in three
groups — industries like engineering over-expanded by war
and not yet adjusted to normal peace-time demand; certain
industries, of which building and docks were the most important, in which unemployment was associated with a defective
system of engaging and using labour, so that any growth of

employment in them was accompanied by a proportionate increase in unemployed; and, largest and most important, the old-established industries, which had expanded on exports before the war and were still dependent to an exceptional degree on export trade — coal, cotton, woollens, engineering, steel, shipbuilding, shipping, docks and certain smaller manufacturing industries.

This persistent depression of the older export industries was not peculiar to Britain; had the industries of coal-mining, shipbuilding, the older textile industries, and (in this case) wheat-growing been concentrated in a single State of the American Union, it would have presented a picture of depression equal to that of the Clyde, Lancashire or South Wales. What was peculiar to Britain was the extent of its dependence on industries depressed throughout Europe and North America. Just because Britain had led in the development of great industries in the nineteenth century and maintained its lead in the generation before the war, its workers and resources were concentrated in the older industries and suffered most from the reversal of their fortunes. Their difficulties were evidence rather of a disordered world than of an inept domestic credit policy; they pointed to specific and peculiar influences apart from any general financial policy; and they were likely to react on the economy as a whole by depressing demand from the areas in which the depressed industries were localised.

While Norman did not formulate any theory of employment, everything he said and did declared his belief in the dependence of the United Kingdom on the restoration of the world economy of which it had been the centre before the war. Hence his insistence on restoring stable exchanges and confidence in currencies, the obligation which he felt as Governor of the Bank of England to co-operate in restoring the finances and currencies of Central Europe, his insistence on the observance of debt obligations, and his attack on the obstacles to international trade offered by war debts and Reparations. The interest of the United Kingdom lay in the restoration of this world economy, because so much of its wealth depended on exports and the associated services of shipping, banking, export of capital and insurance, and because the standard of life of its people was founded on imports. Devaluation could afford

only transient relief to a country which imported three-fifths
of its food and four-fifths of its raw materials : devaluation was
indeed, as Germany, Italy and France were to show, the surest
method of raising the cost of living, provoking demands for
higher wages, and starting an inflation of the Continental type.
A currency in which the world had confidence was essential to
Britain for a more fundamental reason ; unless overseas suppliers would accept sterling in payment, and hold sterling without uneasiness, the country would run the risk of slipping into
the plight of one Continental country after another, of being
unable to secure any imports without special measures in every
case to provide means of payment. Confidence in sterling was,
in Norman's eyes, the test of any policy. The restoration of the
Gold Standard at its old parity, though it was maintained for
only six and a half years, did so far restore confidence in sterling
that most of the world continued to accept and hold sterling
when Britain went off gold in 1931. It was still possible to pay
in sterling for most of the imports the country needed.

Fundamentally Norman's difference with his critics turned
less on monetary policy than on general economic policy, and,
indeed, political policy. By training and experience he was
international in outlook. He saw British economic problems in
an international setting, and used such powers as he had to
repair the weaknesses left by war in the country's international
position. In the specialised field of his direct responsibility,
credit policy and the money market, this meant restoring confidence in the value of the currency, internally and, even more,
externally. In the wider field of external relations, it involved
him in his long-sustained effort to remove the obstacles to
stability — debts and Reparations — and to secure a resumption of normal international business relations, with a co-
operative attempt to relieve the worst dislocation left by war in
Central Europe. With this effort we shall be concerned in the
following chapter ; but the restoration of the traditional safeguard against inflation and fluctuating exchanges, the Gold
Standard, with which this chapter has been concerned, was
necessary to the policy, as that policy was necessary to a
restoration of Britain's economic position. Inflation was the
contradiction of any such policy ; and any policy which overlooked the country's dependence on imports — large-scale

Government expenditure, deficit financing by short-term borrowing, meeting any loss of external balance by resort to devaluation — would lead to inflation. The relief of unemployment was essential; but relief at the cost of a progressive inability to pay for imports by exports involved dangers from which he instinctively shrank. Having met with little opposition before the restoration of the Gold Standard, he came more and more under criticism after. But his standpoint had not changed; it was still fixed on the external needs of the country, though the pressure of unemployment concentrated political interest more and more on domestic issues, and he preferred the discipline of an international Gold Standard to the exhortations of — or to — Chancellors, as security for a policy which respected the country's external needs.

CHAPTER V

WAR DEBTS, LEAGUE LOANS
AND REPARATIONS

(i)

NEITHER the new Governor, Cokayne, nor any official of the Bank was associated with the British delegation to the Peace Conference. Nor did the preoccupations of a dangerous inflationary situation at home leave Norman much incentive to look abroad, although a visit of Ben Strong, who arrived on 21 July 1919, began a long series of personal discussions on the condition of Europe. Even before Strong's visit Norman had said in a letter on 5 June 1919 that he did not think that private enterprise and credits could do much for the war-worn countries of Europe; short of some heroic scheme concocted in Paris, their needs, including currency and finance, must be treated by political measures. States which wished to stimulate exports would have to make loans to purchasing countries on longer terms than any exporter or banker could afford.

When the threat of inflation at home had been met, Norman became involved in three external problems — the United Kingdom's responsibility for its own debt to America, the danger of economic collapse in Austria and Hungary and the necessity of adjusting Reparations to Germany's capacity to pay, so that Germany could resume its part in the economic life of Europe. The three overlapped, in time and in the negotiations between countries to which they led. It will be convenient to take them in the order stated and to begin with the American debt.

American policy on Allies' war debts was determined by Congress in Washington, not by American financial representatives in touch with the actualities of the situation in Europe.

The debts were regarded as assimilable in practice with commercial obligations — $450 million of the British debt was in fact in respect of food purchases after the Armistice. They might be adjusted to the capacity of the debtor to pay, but this should be judged by his resources, and not made dependent on his claims on other debtors or on Reparation receipts. The British Government was required after the end of the war to give 5 per cent bonds for the credits received; subsequently, in February 1922, Congress enacted that debts could be funded but the capital amount must not be reduced and repayment must be completed within sixty-two years.

Strong had reported to the Governor on 8 February 1921 that the Chancellor's statement in Parliament that the British Government had approached the United States Administration with a suggestion of all-round debt cancellation had been unfortunate. When, on 1 August 1922, the British Government set out (in the Balfour Note) its proposals for offsetting inter-allied debts and restricting its claims on Reparations and its own debtors to the net amount required to meet its obligations in America, Strong sent cuttings from American papers. All were hostile, refused to accept any connection between the United Kingdom debt to America and the other Allies' debt to the United Kingdom, and stressed the provision in the Act creating a Funding Commission which prohibited any cancellation of debt.

Months before the Balfour Note, Norman had been forced to the conclusion that, however reasonable and equitable, the policy it set out had not a chance. Up to December 1921 he had hoped to keep some link between Reparations and debt; in that month he wrote to Strong:

It is for the sake of [a resumption of] international business that I am so anxious to see the Reparations somehow tacked on to the Inter-Allied Debts and settled as a whole. We are, as it were, in jeopardy to-day of making a temporary European adjustment of the Reparations payments which adjustment may last long enough to allow the Inter-Allied Debts to be settled next spring or summer as a totally different and separate question. Such a possibility is too ridiculous. Having, let us suppose, steadied the Exchanges by some Reparations adjustment, we are immediately to see them unsteadied by Inter-Allied Debt payments.

But writing in February 1922 he implied that he had given up this hope; they could approach the American Funding Commission from two angles:

(1) Europe is directly or indirectly in debt to the United States, and all the debtors, including Great Britain, want to negotiate for funding, etc. more or less simultaneously and on similar if not equal lines. The trouble is that it might seem to leave out the question of Reparations;

(2) if it be true that the United States is determined to treat Great Britain separately from her other debtors, then let Great Britain face the music and arrange to fund her debt as quickly as possible. That being done, at least in principle, let the United States and Great Britain, on terms of equality as it were, call a meeting of their debtors, in whom would be included most of the European countries (as well as the Colonies in some cases) and of course Germany.

He added that the German position was deteriorating: and in coming to this conclusion he was not alone. The Court of the Bank on June 22, referring to the Government's intention to draw on Bank gold to pay interest on this 'demand obligation' to the United States, wrote to the Chancellor of the Exchequer (Sir Robert Horne):

They understand, however, that it was an original condition of these obligations that, if the United States Government so requested, they should be funded. They further understand that in effect such a request has been put forward by the Foreign Debt Commission of the United States. They trust that His Majesty's Government will comply with this request.

The Court view with concern the gradual worsening of the economic position of Central Europe and the consequent instability of the exchanges. . . . They are of opinion that the funding of the obligations of this country to the United States Government (in general accordance with the Act of Congress signed on the 9th February, 1922) would facilitate the settlement of other Inter-State War Debts and pave the way towards greater stability of the exchanges and the re-establishment of general trade.

Norman makes a note of a call from McKenna, a few days before the Balfour Note was despatched, upset by reports he had received as to the intention of the Government not to fund in the

United States and to send a strong despatch to France, and begging that the opinion of the City be communicated to the Cabinet. Norman called at the Treasury the same day and made sure that the Prime Minister (Lloyd George) was informed; but the reply he got was that City opinion was fully known to the Cabinet, it was useless to do more and the despatch would go at once. A week after the Note was sent, J. P. Morgan was at lunch in the Bank, and Norman discussed debts and Reparations with him. Norman stated his conviction that prompt funding, or offer to fund, the British debt was the important thing, and feared the tendency to defer action and merely talk in Washington; Morgan agreed, unless the schedule of Reparations payments could be altered first, to which Norman replied, 'It can't: Poincaré won't'. He had reason to expect delay; as long ago as March 1921 he had been under notice from the Treasury to hold himself in readiness to go to Washington and, after waiting three months, had asked to be released.

The Government did not in the event adhere to the policy of the Balfour Note. America would not admit any connection between British obligations to America and British claims on their Allies; the Allies would not admit that their payments to Britain must depend on what Great Britain had to pay America, in disregard of their capacity to make such payments. The French could complain of a *volte-face* in the British attitude to the interdependent problems of Reparations and debts. Hitherto Britain had resisted the French claim to defer the fixing of Reparations until Allied debts were determined — 'moins on nous demandera, plus l'Allemagne sera déchargée' — insisting instead that Reparations should be based on German capacity to pay. Now Britain asserted a legal claim which, though limited to American claims on Britain, ignored the Allies' capacity to pay, ignored the bearing of Reparations on that capacity and left the Allies who did pay to cover the deficit of Russia and other Allies who defaulted. Almost as soon as the Balfour Note was sent, Norman was explaining to the Committee of Treasury that discussions on the debt in Washington would make it impossible to send out invitations before the autumn to the Central Banks' conference proposed at Genoa. On September 27, on return from his holiday, he was at the

Treasury, discussing the debt with the Chancellor : he told the Committee of Treasury that he would be leaving for Washington on October 18. The change of Government (with Bonar Law as Prime Minister) and General Election postponed departure until December 27, and substituted Baldwin for Sir Robert Horne as negotiator. It was the beginning of a long and close friendship.

The negotiators were fourteen days in Washington. The members of the Funding Commission — Andrew Mellon, Secretary of the Treasury ; Hughes, Secretary of State ; Hoover ; and two Republican politicians, Senator Smoot and Representative Burton — were as well informed of conditions in Europe and as sympathetic with Europe's difficulties as the debtors could hope. They proposed an annuity for sixty-one years on a $3\frac{1}{2}$ per cent basis ; Baldwin offered one of fifty years on a 3 per cent basis. The Commission offered to defer half the interest for five years, but would not go further, and the British Cabinet rejected their proposal. The Commission then offered a reduction in the rate of interest for the first ten years to 3 per cent ; they warned the negotiators that the terms would be likely to be worse if deferred, especially until a Presidential election, whereas a settlement would open the way for collaboration between America and Britain over European reconstruction and Reparations. The negotiators were satisfied that they should settle, and that the terms were the best they could get. Baldwin urged acceptance on the Prime Minister, who refused and instructed him to return. The Cabinet, however, did not support Bonar Law, and the settlement went through. A provision for which the negotiators had pressed, that if any other debtor should receive more favourable terms these should automatically be applied to the British debt, was refused by Congress.

The American Debt Settlement was a political decision ; but Norman was the Chancellor's technical adviser and properly — if obloquy is deserved — shares the obloquy which has attended it. His motives are obvious ; as in his attitude to the whole complex of external problems, he was concerned to lessen the uncertainty which handicapped the revival of international finance and trade, and he was not willing that England should set an example of default. In the case of the British debt, unlike the other problems of Reparations and the reconstruction of Central Europe which were absorbing as much of his energy as domestic routine affairs could spare, it was within the competence of the British Government to decide, and carry out its decision, on its sole responsibility. A settlement, if possible at all, was the condition also of American co-operation — co-operation which, in spite of the insularity of outlook of both Washington and New York of which his American friends warned him, was to prove invaluable in dealing with Reparations and Austrian reconstruction. The United Kingdom suffered, as she did in leading Europe back to stable exchanges, by acting as leader; but she would have suffered more in prestige and in opportunities of using her knowledge and other advantages in international affairs, had she rejected the opportunity of settlement and, continuing to ignore the 5 per cent interest due on the bonds given to America in 1919, had given a lead in default. Granted America's insistence on recognition of war debts, the terms of the settlement were reasonable.

There was little serious opposition to Baldwin's settlement at the time. The chief opponent, the Prime Minister's friend Lord Beaverbrook, writing in 1933 when default did take place, said :

The *Express* newspapers were the only opponents of the settlement in journalism. Bonar Law and McKenna and Keynes were its only opponents in public life. Later McKenna gave way and brought his influence on Bonar Law to sign the agreement.[1]

McKenna's attitude is explicable. When Bonar Law introduced the last War Budget on 22 April 1918, McKenna had pressed for an arrangement by which American advances to the other Allies, for purchases in countries other than the United States, should be made direct to those Allies and not to the United Kingdom, which then made them advances. Unfortunately the United States preferred the United Kingdom as its debtor. He might well, therefore, object to the terms of the settlement. But this did not weaken his support of the policy of effecting an early settlement, and, when faced with the practical alternative of the Baldwin settlement or no settlement, he

[1] Quoted by Sir James Grigg in *Prejudice and Judgment*, p. 103, to whose account of the Debt Settlement I gratefully acknowledge my obvious obligation.

threw his influence on to the side of acceptance. Keynes was
not faced with the responsibility for decision; when years later,
as head of the British Delegation to Washington in 1945, he
found himself like Baldwin faced with the responsibility of
choosing between a settlement on terms he thought oppressive
and no settlement at all, he used his influence to induce his
Government to accept the terms available.

Norman's own account of the debt negotiations was given
in a letter on 26 February 1923 to Blackett who was then
Finance member of the Viceroy of India's Council:

I don't know what your view now is of the U.S. Debt Settlement, but I should like to know. I feel sure you are well content.
Once admit the Debt was binding and the result *is* good and will
soon begin to bear fruit in Europe generally. But I think it might
have been better: that's a long story which I can only touch upon.
The Chancellor caught on in Washington from the very beginning.
The Commission behaved like gentlemen, never mentioning our
'scraps of paper' at 5%, or their limits under the 1922 Refunding
Act, but taking the line that the Debt question *had* to be settled
and that they would be prepared to recommend the terms most
lenient to Great Britain which at the last moment they thought
Congress would accept.

Thus to begin with we argued daily on principles and details
and reached a number of vague understandings without putting
a word on paper, a course they thought essential lest Congress
should demand papers or ask questions and so convert a fluid into
a concrete position. After a week or ten days of this it was time
to come to writing, in order to draft a provisional agreement which
was already in all our minds: to do this it was necessary to settle
a provisional period and rate of interest for repayment (as they
called it) or annuity (as we called it): they proposed $3\frac{1}{2}$ and we
would eventually have agreed to the basis of 3 for 10 years and $3\frac{1}{2}$
thereafter plus sinking fund — merely as a basis for a provisional
agreement, all points still remaining fluid. For this purpose the
Chancellor needed and strongly urged the consent of the Cabinet:
it was refused; * he came home at once to discuss the whole matter
and two or three weeks later the then merely provisional basis was
accepted here, a basis which in that period had crystallised and
become, so to speak, a take it or leave it offer — not a fluid basis
in the course of discussions.

That ended the affair. Had the Chancellor been allowed a

freer hand on the spot, helped as he was by a rising tide throughout the United States and by the French madness on the Ruhr, I believe he might have obtained from the Commission a recommendation on terms somewhat more favourable to this Country : for I am convinced that up to the last moment every member of the Commission wished to let us down as lightly as he could, without running the risk of a refusal from Congress. That's my view : I have discussed it with no one nor have I written it down till now.

As it was the Settlement was *most* strongly urged upon the Chancellor as being to the advantage of Great Britain by B. Strong and J. P. Morgan and such Democrats as Cravath, Polk, Leffingwell [1] and John Davis.

I think everyone at the Treasury and at the Bank is really pleased and satisfied : I certainly am and I now seem to see a light at the end of the tunnel !

* P.S. This refusal was almost entirely due to three persons : the Prime Minister, Beaverbrook and McKenna !

(ii)

The British debt to America was tied up with consideration of inter-allied debts and these with Reparations. Reparations in practice meant payments by Germany : Austria compelled Norman's attention by other claims. The Bank found itself with a private interest in Austrian affairs. Among the pre-moratorium bills for which it had accepted liability under Treasury guarantee in 1914 were some millions of pounds of acceptances by foreign and colonial firms, banks and agencies, established in Britain, among which were the acceptances of the London offices of two Austrian banks, the Anglo-Austrian and the Laenderbank. Both were in difficulties owing, among other things, to the severance of branches following on the break-up of the Austrian Empire. French capital was interested in the Laenderbank ; the Anglo-Austrian, it was decided on an accountant's investigation, could be dealt with best by reorganisation as an English bank. The Bank was willing to assist by accepting deferred stock instead of its prior claims and putting up some new money, and with the aid of a London

[1] Russell C. Leffingwell, Assistant Secretary, U.S. Treasury, 1917–20. Of J. P. Morgan & Co. from 1923.

board and a Central European expert, Peter Bark,[1] the re-organisation was effected. Subsequently, the difficulties of Central Europe led to its merging with other overseas banks in which the Bank was interested ; at this time it seemed to offer an opportunity of salving not only a guarantee but an important connection with old customers of London. The difficulties of other accepting houses caused by the collapse of Central Europe would in any case have compelled the Governor of the Bank to interest himself in Austria and Germany.

Drained like Germany of its economic reserves by four years of war and blockade, Austria was left with the govern-mental establishment and banking and commercial organisation adapted to a population of fifty million with only six million to support them. True, Austria participated in the relief, mainly American supplies, organised on behalf of the Allies by Hoover ; but, as an ex-enemy country, it was not eligible for gifts. To provide supplies, it was necessary for the other Allies to buy (on credit) from America and resell on credit to Austria ; even so, a third of the relief received was paid for in cash. After the Peace Treaty was signed, the inter-allied organisation came to an end : Hoover's activities as Director-General terminated in August 1919 ; and there was an interval until April 1920, when an endeavour was made at the instance of the British Government to provide machinery for credits to Central and Eastern Europe. American private relief also continued after governmental relief ceased. It was not, however, until 1921 that the Allied powers recognised that an Austrian collapse was imminent and would endanger the whole of Central Europe.

The obstacles to prompt help were that Austrian resources were depleted, and such as remained already pledged as security for the relief credits received in 1919, and that no international agency had existed to arrange for a release of assets to provide security for new credits. In March 1921 Great Britain, France, Italy and Japan agreed to release the assets pledged to them by Austria for Reparation and Relief loans, in favour of a Reconstruction loan ; asked the other creditor countries to do the same, and asked the League of Nations to prepare a reconstruction scheme. The Financial

[1] Formerly Vice-Governor of the Imperial Bank of Russia and Finance Minister, 1914–17. Knighted, 1935.

Committee of the League, with Sir Henry Strakosch [1] and Niemeyer of the Treasury and the Secretary, Arthur Salter,[2] as its most active members, provided the international agency needed, and from this time on was the organising centre of a large programme of reconstruction.   Norman was virtually an important though unofficial member ;   the Committee's schemes needed foreign credits, which he alone could find or provide ; he was the most intimate associate and adviser of the English (and other countries' Central Bank) members ;   and he shared and infected others with his passionate enthusiasm for an immediate and practical attack on the problems of Central Europe. The Committee stated the conditions of reconstruction at a meeting on April 4, and a delegation of the committee investigated conditions on the spot and formulated recommendations, which were approved by the Council of the League and forwarded to the Supreme Council of the Allies on June 3.   The cardinal feature of the recommendations — which, though they were not acted on on this occasion, reappeared in the successful scheme carried through in 1923 — was that only a *comprehensive* scheme could be of any avail ;   internal financial reform, adequate credits, and central control of the proceeds to ensure that they supported the internal reforms, were each and all essential.

Norman was brought in on the discussion of credits.   He wrote to Strong on May 23 that the French wanted an advance to Austria, and were possibly discussing it with New York ;   there was to be a meeting in London in a couple of days ;   the immediate need was a temporary advance, not the long-term loan that would become necessary.   He warned the Committee of Treasury on May 25 that France might be making an advance, in anticipation of a long-term loan under League auspices, and the United Kingdom should do the same ;   and, since the Government could not make such an advance without Parliament's authority, the Bank should consider making it ;   to which the Committee agreed a week later.   On May 27 he had a long talk with Avenol [3] and Gluckstadt, the Danish banker ; and on Sunday, the 29th, took part in a long conference on

---

[1] Member of the Financial Committee, 1920–37.

[2] Director, Economic and Finance Section, League of Nations and General Secretary, Reparation Commission, 1919–31.   Knighted, 1922.   Lord Salter, 1953.

[3] Of the Financial Committee of the League of Nations and a Member of the French Financial Delegation in London.

N

Austria at the Treasury with Blackett, two Frenchmen
(Monnet [1] and Avenol), Gluckstadt and Strakosch. Already
he had written to prepare Ben Strong for an appeal:

I want to say a word in your private ear about Austria. You
know the position of Austria is desperate and in my opinion nothing
could be done to improve it until the Allies should have come to
terms with Germany. But some weeks ago the Austrian Prime
Minister and Finance Minister came to London and various meetings were held with the allied parties. The result of these was that
the plight and the needs of Austria were somehow turned over to
a Committee of the League of Nations and for the last month or
so a Commission appointed by this Committee has been studying
matters in Vienna. I understand that in a couple of weeks meetings
will be held in London to consider the reports of this Commission,
and the possible outcome is as follows: The Austrian Government,
with the consent of all political parties in the Austrian Parliament,
will agree to the appointment by the League of Nations of a Controller or of a Committee of Control of Austrian Finance, Taxation,
Customs and Note Issue for a term of years. Subsequently it is
thought that the indiscriminate issue of Notes will be stopped;
that an internal loan will be issued to absorb some of the redundant
currency and that the Government importation of foodstuffs etc.
will be ended, thus leaving the feeding of Austria to private enterprise.

In order that this shall have any chance of success some improvement and stability of the Austrian Exchange is necessary. For
that purpose an external loan seems to me to be also necessary.
The Security that could be offered should be a charge on all
exports and imports (to be levied in gold?), and a first charge on
all Austrian assets ranking even ahead of reparations and of the
credits already granted for food, etc., by the allied and associated
Powers; both to be levied and collected by the Controller or
Commission of Control above-mentioned. (The Controller would
probably be a Dane or a Swiss — alternatively the Commission of
Control would be Representatives of the Allies and a neutral.)

Now under some such conditions as these could the Government
of Austria raise an external loan? Could they for instance raise
the equivalent of £2 million in Paris, perhaps in Switzerland or
Denmark and in London, and if they could do so what could be
done in New York? That is the question I wish to put for your
personal consideration.

[1] French Under-Secretary-General, League of Nations.

You will understand that I am only thinking aloud and basing my thoughts on surmises and not on facts. You will also understand that I raise the question because an agreement with Germany has now been reached and because the next step should be an attempt to rehabilitate Austria as a step towards the rehabilitation of distressed Europe. It seems to me that unless something definite is done the whole position in those parts must go from bad to worse.

At the same time he began canvassing the possibilities of a loan. He used his influence to try and arrange advances in Holland, Switzerland and Denmark : participation by neutrals was essential. He explained the position fully to McKenna and mentioned it to other Clearing Bankers. He had a visit from a French commercial banker with whom he went through the scheme. On June 27 Strong wrote him that J. P. Morgan had called to say that he would be interested in handling an Austrian loan in New York for the League. But on June 22 Norman had written that the whole Austrian scheme was in the melting-pot. Balfour, the British representative on the League Council, lunched at the Bank and Norman had a long talk with him on Austria at the Privy Council office on July 18. A week later he went over the whole question again with Monnet, and noted that the position seemed to him to be that either the whole scheme must be dropped permanently or it must be deferred till October at the earliest and altered to suit conditions then.

The primary obstacle was the reluctance of other creditors to waive their existing claims in favour of a credit or loan to Austria. Norman, writing on July 13, did not think the postponement of liens was the real difficulty. The irreconcilable clash was over the control to be exercised over Austrian finance. The French and Italians wanted a neutral administration in Vienna under the direction of a committee in Paris, representing in theory the League but in practice the Entente, as the Entente would apply any necessary political pressure on Austria. The alternative was a genuinely independent administration in Vienna, perhaps with an advisory committee to which it could refer, but such a committee must have a majority of neutrals ; under such a scheme, Norman told the French, the money could be raised from the public in the United States, Britain, Holland and Scandinavia, and similarly, he hoped, in

France, Switzerland and Italy. It would not be reasonable to ask the public in neutral countries to put up money for a scheme under Entente control; it would have to be British and French money, which made it a Cabinet not a financial matter. In Norman's opinion the main lines of the League Committee's scheme were sound and desirable, and he was working for neutral participation, not merely for the sake of neutral financial assistance, but in order to lift the problem of Austria's needs out of its political atmosphere and treat it as an economic problem.

There was no further official action until February 1922. There were still in July 1921 assets to provide security for a loan if they could be released. Austria's credit was still worth something, and an opportunity was lost in not acting before it was dissipated. Norman was out of England, visiting America, from August 6 to September 17. When he returned he was taken up with discussions with McKenna, the Chancellor (Horne) and the Prime Minister (Lloyd George) on credits for relief at home; but one of his first callers was the Austrian Ambassador, and he was in touch with the Financial Committee of the League, which was still concerned over Austria. His direct Austrian interests, the Anglo-Austrian and Laenderbank banks, also required his attention; the Austrian Parliament was considering the Bill needed to make possible their reorganisation. Austria's difficulties were increasing. He wrote to Strong on November 7:

After some lingering the British Government has now placed at the disposal of the Austrian Government (through the Anglo-Austrian Bank in Vienna) £250,000 which, though it does not take the form of a relief credit, is intended solely for that purpose. I think the French Government is making arrangements to do the same.

The conversion of the old Anglo-Austrian Bank into a British Company and of the old Austrian Laenderbank into a French Company are both nearly completed. I think I told you that in both cases the operation is made easier by the funding of the very heavy debts which both of these Banks owe in sterling to us, but at the same time it ought to be a help towards the opening up of Austria. The quarrels in Austria between the protagonists of the French on the one side and of the British on the other have been very unfortunate and of course all spring from the fundamentally different standpoints of the two Countries. Our basis is economic, the French basis is political, and nowhere is the distinction more clearly seen than in Austria.

In February 1922, to meet a crisis which could no longer be ignored, the Governments of Great Britain, France, Czechoslovakia and Italy granted Austria limited and temporary credits, and agreed to postpone their claim on account of earlier loans for twenty years, while in April Congress passed legislation authorising the release of assets pledged to America. By August enough assets had been released to provide security for a loan; but the bankers, who a year before had been ready to lend, were now unwilling — they feared depreciation and social upheaval. Norman had been approached in February and March by the Austrians, but refused to discuss a loan in isolation from a general scheme of reconstruction, and he pressed the same approach on American bankers. On his return from America at the end of May he was still doubtful. A month later the situation of Austria was worse, and he spent a long morning on it with the Chancellor and Balfour. The former he was seeing at the House of Commons on Austrian debts and clearings. J. P. Morgan & Co. found themselves unable to issue an Austrian loan, and the Austrian Ambassador told him on July 24 that he had no hope of credits this summer anywhere. Norman had sent the Austrian Government, through the Anglo-Austrian Bank, the advice that the new Bank of Issue they were organising could by itself provide no solution, and they should put themselves in the hands of the Conference of Allied Prime Ministers meeting in London and, if necessary, resign. When his Austrian contact, Bark, came to him in real fear over Austria, Norman could only tell him that the British Government were determined to 'sit tight and watch' (they were preparing to publish the Balfour Note on Inter-Allied Debts). As he told J. P. Morgan, the most practical step was to get the British debt settlement out of the way.

He was ill, and then on holiday in Holland, from August 22 to September 25. The Austrian situation had been changed in his absence by a public appeal to the Council of Allied Ministers by the Austrian Chancellor, Seipel, on September 6, who said that Austria was willing to accept a system of control as a

corollary of assistance. The Council referred the matter to the
League's Financial Committee, to which was added a special
political committee representing Britain, France, Italy, Czechoslovakia and Austria itself. The League Committee was, thanks
to its previous work, in a position to formulate a scheme of
reconstruction without delay, and the critical situation of
Austria secured the unreserved assent of the five Governments
represented on the special Committee. On 4 October 1922
three Protocols were signed, the first containing an undertaking
of the other States to respect Austria's political independence
and territorial integrity and Austria's undertaking to maintain
that independence; the second containing the reconstruction
scheme; and the third Austria's obligations and the functions
of the Commissioner-General under the scheme. The cardinal
feature of this new reconstruction scheme was, as before, its
comprehensiveness: the committee insisted that the whole
scheme depended on achieving a fundamental economic balance, internal and external. The Budget was to be balanced
by the end of 1924, by drastic curtailment of expenditure and
increase of taxation, the temporary deficit being met by loans.
Loans were to be guaranteed by the sponsoring Governments,
but to be secured on specific revenues and other assets. The
issue of paper money by the Government was to be stopped,
and an independent Bank of Issue established. A Commissioner-General was to be appointed to ensure, in collaboration
with the Austrian Government, that the programme was carried
out through his control of the disposal of the proceeds of the
loan: he was to be appointed by and responsible to the League,
with a committee representing the guaranteeing powers as link.
The object and test of success was the achievement of independence of further help.

Norman, though oppressed with the difficulty of raising
money for Austria while the general Reparations problem was
still unsettled, and regretting Balfour's retirement from the
League Council, had got to work at once on the loans. A long
discussion with Sir Arthur Salter on October 12 was followed
by talks with Avenol the next day and a partner in Morgans
the following week. On the 17th he had called on Balfour and
had gone over the whole subject. It was necessary to find a
neutral Commissioner-General and a neutral adviser for the

new Central Bank; a form for the loan satisfactory in detail
to neutral bankers had to be drafted. The problem of German
Reparations was approaching a new crisis, and a change of
Government in England was another diversion. The new
Chancellor (Baldwin) decided to proceed with negotiations for
funding the American debt and to take Norman with him.
One of the guaranteeing powers was seeking a loan in London
to support its own exchange. Between October 17 and his
sailing for New York on December 27 Norman was engaged in
continuous interviews with the Chancellor and Blackett at the
Treasury, Salter, Balfour and Sir Eric Drummond [1] in the
League, Strakosch and Niemeyer in the Financial Committee,
Avenol and Monnet on French co-operation and the bankers
— McKenna, ter Meulen [2] and J. P. Morgan who was in
England. By November 29 he had agreed with Salter, ter
Meulen and Monnet that Zimmerman was the man for the
office of Commissioner-General: he secured his appointment
and discussed the terms of the loan with J. P. Morgan for the
following spring.

Zimmerman arrived in Vienna on 15 December 1922, when
the scheme of reconstruction had already been worked out in
practical detail. Its success depended on finding some financial
assistance to carry the costs of government until the reformed
budget and currency provided a surplus of revenue over expenditure. Norman advised the League and Treasury officials
that no money, not even short, could be obtained on Austrian
Treasury bonds without a British guarantee, and that he himself
(as Governor of the Bank) would lend on Austrian gold, which
must be sent to London. He had raised with the Committee
of Treasury the question of the Bank's acting as issuer and trustee of the proposed loan in October, but it was then too early to
settle anything, and he had refused a credit secured on Austrian
customs at the end of November. On his return from America,
on 7 February 1923, he informed the Committee of Treasury
that at the request of the League he was endeavouring to
arrange the issue of a guaranteed short-term loan for Austria,
and had approached the other European Central Banks; he

[1] Secretary-General, League of Nations.   Later Lord Perth.
[2] C. E. ter Meulen, the Dutch banker, Member of the Financial Committee
of the League of Nations.

had spent the previous afternoon working out details with the Austrian Ambassador and representatives of the Austrian Treasury and Bank. The loan was successfully placed a week later; the Reparation Commission, as long ago as October 1922, had released the security pledged to it, and now released the security for a long-term loan also. By March 9 Norman was working with Niemeyer, Strakosch and the lawyers on the General Bond and choice of trustees for the long-term loan. The change in the atmosphere was shown by a call the next day from the representative of an important American banking house which wished to participate in its issue. The Bank had to help the Austrians to support their exchange, but on April 23 Norman was able to give them assurances as to the price of the issue in London. He had to press his Dutch friends, and he could influence Switzerland and Sweden indirectly. Thomas W. Lamont, a partner in Morgans, came over to deal with the New York *tranche* in May. The final details were settled in the Bank on June 6; Lamont (with Zimmerman) had already prepared the American press; underwriting for the £9 million London issue was completed on June 7, and the issue made on June 11.

The Austrian Government's pledge, which it had carried out, was to draw up a scheme for balancing the budget within two years, and to lay before Parliament a draft law authorising the Government to act by decree if necessary to carry out the programme. The Finance Ministry's control over expenditure was restored by the practice of estimating each month's expenditure in advance and closing each month's accounts before authorising next month's expenditure. The number and size of ministries was reduced; nearly 50,000 (the planned number) redundant officials were dismissed within six months. The railways, an important contributor to the deficit, were investigated by foreign experts, and their deficit eliminated in two years. So successful was the budget reform that the Commissioner-General was able to use 42 million gold kroner to complete schemes of electrification and secure large economies. Revenue increased much faster than expenditure was reduced; the loan releases necessary were substantially less than had been planned. Exports increased and the number of unemployed receiving assistance fell rapidly. The cost of living was stabilised. That this was possible, and confidence restored so quickly, was due to the stop to currency inflation. The inflationary note-issue was stopped in November 1922, and the Government provided itself with resources over the transition by an internal gold loan for 50 million kroner. The new Bank of Issue, with the exclusive right of note-issue, was organised, and its capital subscribed internally, in December 1922. No representative of commerce or government official was on the board, and a foreign adviser was appointed to contribute an independent judgment and help to create confidence in financial circles. At the end of the first year, foreign exchange reserves had trebled.

This success had not been achieved without constant pressure from Niemeyer and the Governor. The latter thought it a mistake that the head of the reconstituted Bank of Issue was an Austrian, and not a neutral expert brought in from outside. The programme had a set-back in 1924, when a stock exchange boom collapsed in a panic and unemployment rapidly increased. But the cause was an unreasonable growth of confidence and speculation, reports of which had reached Norman and induced him to send a warning; a League inspection reported that inadequate allowance had been made for the time needed for adjustment to financial equilibrium. The forecast was justified; conditions improved by the end of 1925, and in 1926 the control of the budget was withdrawn and the Commissioner-General's office terminated.

The Deputy Governor (H. A. Trotter) [1] had written to Strong on 6 March 1923 that the Governor had been working day and night on debt settlement and the preliminaries of the Austrian loan. There was a much better atmosphere here and in Europe. 'Without Norman behind them the Austrians would not have achieved much.' Norman revealed his hopes in a letter he himself wrote on April 9:

At the end of next month I hope there will be an issue of a Long Term Loan for Austria throughout Europe. . . . I am anxious Morgans do the same in New York. If we can thus set up Austria, we must tackle Hungary so as to establish one by one the

[1] Director of the Bank of England, 1909–34. Deputy Governor, 1920–23 and 1926–27.

new parts of *old* Austria . . . and then perhaps the Balkan countries. Only by thus making the various parts economically sound and independent shall we reach what I believe to be the ultimate solution for Eastern Europe, viz. an economic federation to include half a dozen countries in or near the Danube free of Customs Barriers etc. Roumania presents difficulties because she despises all the ex-enemy countries and is too proud (or insolvent) to make any sacrifice for the general good. Italy too claims a special position in those parts.

With the Austrian precedent justified, the League could encourage other countries to seek its help. In the spring of 1923 the Hungarian Government, finding itself for the second time since the war in financial difficulty, asked the Reparation Commission to release its charges, so that Hungary could raise a foreign loan. The Reparation Commission's conditions were not such as to make the raising of a loan possible, and in September the Hungarian Government approached the League, and the League Council, after consulting the other countries concerned, agreed to accept responsibility for a scheme. This depended on the agreement of the Reparation Commission, which was given on October 17, and the Financial Committee submitted a scheme to the League Council in December.

Norman had been approached about a loan already in June; he would have supported it only if recommended by a League inquiry, and this was impossible when the Reparation Commission refused release from its charges. He was approached directly by the Hungarians at the end of November; he told them that as soon as a Commissioner-General was installed and the plan fully adopted they should send a competent delegation to London, privately, and then elsewhere, and he would direct them to the proper backers. But, when the League scheme was completed and he saw it, he refused to have anything to do with it; as he explained to the Committee of Treasury on 9 January 1924, it provided for Reparation charges under the Treaty of Trianon which, even though limited in amount, would be payable during the currency of the Reconstruction Loan, and he could neither approve nor support. This was a shock to the League officials and Hungary's friends; a blow to the League, they said, and might

upset the Hungarian Government; but Norman persisted in
his refusal when the Hungarians approached him officially.
He had recently scolded Romanian visitors for withholding
their assent to the lifting of Reparations charges in the spring,
and provoked the obvious retort that the English were more
interested in the fortunes of their late enemies than of their late
Allies. The matter was one of principle. He recognised that
Reparations, debts and reconstruction were all political questions, and that he in his field could do nothing until government, directly or through the League, had removed the political
complications in the way; but, this condition satisfied, they
were all economic questions and should be treated as such, the
marketability of a loan, on which he had to pronounce, being
the test of respect for economic considerations. His opinion had
the more weight in that the League scheme, while proposing
that the reconstruction should be under the League's auspices,
did not provide, as in the case of Austria, for a guarantee by
any government except Hungary's own. It was not possible,
for this among other reasons, to place any part of the proposed
loan in New York, and the scheme was dependent on London
for two-thirds of the money required. However, in May, when
the League scheme had been adopted and a Commissioner-
General appointed, he was persuaded by Niemeyer and the
Chancellor (Snowden) to forgo his objection. He put the
Hungarian Government in touch with issuing houses in London
who would handle a market loan, and, when it was proved that
no more than £4 million could be raised in that quarter, provided the remaining £4 million required to make up the £12
million of the Foreign Loan by means of an advance from the
Bank of England to the Hungarian National Bank.

Although the claim to Reparations payments was not suspended, the amount was limited, and it was not to be made in
any year unless it could be made without destroying the equilibrium of the Budget, and not remitted unless the Central Bank
agreed to provide the necessary foreign exchange. This separation between the payment of Reparations in local currency
and its remittance abroad only if exchange was available,
provided a precedent for the Dawes Committee on German
Reparations.

In other respects the Hungarian scheme followed the general

lines of the Austrian scheme. It was as successful as its predecessor. Revenue exceeded expectations; the Budget was
balanced within a year; exports increased in spite of an unfavourable harvest; the currency was stabilised. Hungary had
not, however, the same resources as Austria; the redundant
officials displaced were not readily absorbed; there was not the
same volume of financial business to support a Central Bank.
On the other hand, there was no set-back caused by speculation — until both countries were involved in the breakdown of
the speculative boom in America, transmitted to them by
excessive foreign lending, in 1930.

The Austrian experiment was the first successful attempt
to deal by international co-operation with the economic difficulties caused by the war. It served as a model, not only for
the Hungarian scheme, and for assistance through League
Loans to Greece, Bulgaria and elsewhere, but also for the
solution — so far as any solution was possible — of the problem of Germany's relations with the Allied powers by the
Dawes and Young Committees. To these the rest of this chapter
will be devoted; but a word may be permitted on the reasons
for the Austrian success.

The attempt to relieve Austria's difficulties was deferred
until, quite apart from the intense internal suffering and
external dislocation caused, Austria's reserves and ability to
meet its external needs had been run down by expenditure on
relief. It was then deferred for another eighteen months by
the difficulty in securing release from all the prior liens in
favour of Reparations and earlier loans. When a scheme was
finally formulated, Austria's economic situation had so far
deteriorated that interim credits had to be provided: yet the
scheme in essentials was a concrete application of principles
expounded and generally accepted at the Brussels Conference
in October of 1920. Success needed two things; the pressure
of events to convince the rest of the world that they had a
real interest in Austria's difficulties; and the development of
an agency which could handle them. Nothing was done until
the continuous association of the League Financial Committee,
the senior officers of the League, British Treasury officials,
and bankers of the chief centres of international banking provided an agency for giving effect to the hitherto ineffective

proposals of planners.   Of the bankers Norman was leader
and chief. He provided wide experience and business insight
and his own dynamic personal drive, but also a centre through
which co-operation between different capital markets, between
private banking and government departments, between the
League and the capital markets, could be organised and made
effective.   A plan had no effect without an agency to carry it
out, while the financiers could not act without a plan.   The
dependence in the last resort of the succession of schemes on
the issue of loans for voluntary subscription in the world's
markets was an advantage; it compelled the submission of
every scheme to the hard test of the market.   In this way it
enabled Norman and his associates to insist on the treatment of
problems which were fundamentally economic by economic
means.   The economic difficulties of Central Europe were, it
is true, due largely to political causes; but the resolutions of
political authorities could not remove them except by setting
free the use of economic remedies.

The Austrian scheme came in a sequence of essays in international co-operation — the Brussels Conference which proclaimed its need in 1920, Genoa which carried further the
study of methods in April 1922, Austria which combined action
with diagnosis and exhortation for the first time in 1922,
Hungary in 1923, and the Dawes scheme in 1924.   It demonstrated the need for and the efficacy of a comprehensive plan,
and the dependence of this plan on aid in the form of foreign
loans, coupled with effective control by a neutral expert of the
expenditure of the funds loaned and, through that, of the
execution of the plan as a whole.   The establishment of Banks
of Issue, independent of the domestic government's immediate
control, was the means in every case of checking the over-issue
of currency : and the device of Bank Advisers, which gave the
banks independent foreign advice without foreign control or
interference, survived the restoration of internal balance and
the office of Commissioner-General.   When first confronted
with the complicated credit problems left by the war, Norman
had doubted the capacity of democracies to deal with them ;
certainly the governments of Central Europe came to feel that
some external compulsion was needed to enable them to carry
out policies which they themselves realised were necessary.

(iii)

The obstacle to effective international co-operation, which delayed and confused the attack on every other problem, was Reparations. The provisions in the Treaty settlement on which the American President and the British Prime Minister relied to adjust Allied claims to German possibilities — the League of Nations on the political and the Reparation Commission on the economic side — were disabled by the refusal of the United States to ratify the Treaty and co-operate in its execution. Reparations had been left to be determined in amount by the Commission; it was required to draw up a schedule of payments; it valued payments in kind; it could investigate Germany's resources and capacity, hear Germany's representatives, and then modify the form and date of the payments. All this implied an expert body, operating on a realistic study of conditions which could not be known when the Treaty was signed, and the presence on this body of an American representative who stood apart from European differences and was able to exercise a conciliatory influence. As it was, there was no American representative. With the exception of Sir John Bradbury and (for a time) the Belgian representative Theunis, the members of the Commission were not financial experts but politicians, who took their instructions from their Governments. The Chairman was elected annually and had a casting vote; so that the British representative would require to carry two of the three other members with him to secure his point in case of a division — Sir John Bradbury was in an almost permanent minority of one. It was easy for the Allied Governments to supersede the Commission, in defiance of the Treaty, and to settle, direct, questions committed to it by the Treaty, or to impose their decisions on the Commission. The Commission's own staff, with a judgment formed by continual contact with the Germans and their difficulties, found too little scope for the work of adjustment normally performed by professional diplomats and administrators.

The Treaty itself deferred the final settlement of the amount of Reparations and the schedule of payments until 1 May 1921, but laid down a minimum of 100,000 million gold marks, bonds for which were required at once, and required the payment of 20,000 million as an instalment on 1 May 1921. In addition the Treaty required certain payments in kind, of which the chief were the transfer of German shipping to the British Government and large deliveries of coal to France, Belgium and Italy. Outside the Reparations claim, the Treaty also required the payment of all the costs of the occupying forces.

Germany, like the other European belligerents, had suffered the exhaustion of four years' war. In addition, its supplies of imported foodstuffs and raw materials had been depleted by the blockade, continued for some months after the Armistice. It has been argued that Reparations cannot be blamed for Germany's post-war difficulties, because in fact payment of Reparations amounted to little before the Dawes Committee, and were offset by foreign loans subsequently. It is true that Reparations were not the sole cause ; the inability of post-war German Governments to cover their expenditure by taxation or loans from the public and the reckless emission of paper money to cover all deficits were no doubt the primary cause. But the Allied claims contributed materially to the financial difficulty which defeated these Governments. They had the same problem of relief to meet as other European countries, with virtually no gifts or credits in the heaviest period of need, the eight months or so after the end of hostilities. The internal cost of Reparation deliveries, the compensation of owners whose ships, overseas debts, livestock and other assets had to be handed over, and the payment for coal, timber and other supplies in kind which were being delivered for years, were a sensible element in the burden to be financed. Especially, the pressure fell on resources available for foreign payments. A country with an extensive dependence on imports for raw materials and foodstuffs must always have a reserve of foreign currencies or gold to cover seasonal and other temporary needs ; after five years' blockade this need was intensified. Germany had to pay 282 million dollars in cash for essential foods alone in 1919 — more than double the American *tranche* of the Dawes Loan in 1924 ; raw material stocks had to be reconstituted ; the charges for the occupying forces, civilian debts, and other claims outside Reparations, swallowed up the whole of the 20,000 million gold marks payable on 1 May 1921.

It was years before Germany's export trade recovered. The strain on inadequate exchange reserves — the Reichsbank gold reserve fell from the equivalent of $539 million to $266 million in the first half of 1919 — aggravated the difficulty of maintaining the value of the mark; exchange depreciation, as other countries were to learn, is a powerful stimulant to internal inflation in countries dependent on imports; and inflation in turn aggravated the difficulty of making external payments.

Norman was not brought into the negotiations over Reparations until the total amount had been determined and the schedule of payments [1] prescribed, in May 1921; by which time the problem had been given a form in which literal execution was probably not practicable. French and Belgian claims had been recognised to payments which no German Government was likely, or indeed able, to make. He was called in to the Treasury on May 21 to advise on difficulties that had arisen in the mechanics of payment; he sent Addis to Paris to assist the Reparation Commission and arranged with McKenna to go if wanted. He was aware of the underlying difficulties; writing to Strong on May 3 he had said :

I do not defend the proposed schedule of German reparation payments and I am happy to think I have not got to do so. This question of reparations is not as it should be, and as Mr. Keynes assumes it to be, a purely economic question. It is almost entirely a political question over which the French Government is forced to tug in one direction and the German Government in another. I doubt if the German Government could stand if they were to agree to any of the amounts which have been suggested, even if they could pay them; and I am afraid that if M. Briand were not to stand out for more he would quickly be succeeded by a fire-eater, probably M. Poincaré, whose main object would be to reach Berlin : and I believe our Prime Minister is having a moderating influence on both sides and going perhaps as far as possible without breaking up the Entente.

However, Germany did accept the Schedule, and Norman wrote to Strong later that he had been 'chuckling over being spared the chairmanship of the guarantee committee' (set up

---

[1] The London Schedule of Payments, prepared by the Allied Reparation Commission.

to supervise the execution of the Schedule of Payments) 'as being too orthodox !'

In June Norman asked the Committee of Treasury to agree to the opening of an account for the Reichsbank; this was merely in pursuance of his policy of establishing links with all Central Banks, but it brought him in touch with Havenstein, the President of the Reichsbank, and through him with Germany's difficulties. The Reichsbank did not, however, approach him for some months; in June he learned that some of the commercial banks had been approached, without result, but it was only towards the end of October that Havenstein visited him and explained his troubles. Norman wrote on October 28 to Strong:

The President is a quiet, modest, convincing and very attractive man : but so sad. I was much impressed by his attitude of almost hopelessness and by the pleasure which it evidently gave him to be treated in an open and friendly manner. But really he has nothing to say. . . . Banking as such does not exist in Germany ; his mind is preoccupied by rising prices and falling Exchange : by the payment for needful imports and by fears as to each succeeding Reparations payment. There is no position in Germany, whether of a Bank or a business or an individual, but that of the State, and at the present moment all are dominated by a bitter disappointment over the unfairness and futility of the Silesian decision and over the future Reparations payments.

He did not complain of the physical conditions of his people — he thought that there were comparatively few who were not employed one way or another — but it was perfectly obvious from beginning to end that to his mind the present state of affairs could not continue much longer ; that he was absolutely dismayed at the prospect of the occupation of further territory by France ; that he was bitterly disappointed about Upper Silesia (as to which the decision seemed to him to be due more to stupidity and lack of business knowledge than to wicked politics) ; and that he wanted above all things some help and some advice and indeed some consolation from your Bank and from ours. We gave it him to the best of our ability and I advised him of his own motion to get into touch with you, knowing you to be well-disposed towards Germany and towards Central Banks and to be as anxious as any of us for the rehabilitation of Europe.

As to the Reparations payments, I had to make it perfectly clear to the President that the provision of funds to make these

o

payments (without any definite prospect of their repayment) was not a banking matter which could be undertaken by either of us.

It was indeed becoming clear that the 'settlement' of May 1921 was no settlement. The effort of raising the 1000 million gold marks required as a first instalment by the end of August had driven down the exchange value of the mark, which had been steady from the beginning of the year until the end of June (and other European rates on New York with it), and a further precipitous fall followed in September. In October Germany was approaching London bankers for a loan on the security of German private industry. Norman said it was impossible; the difficulty was political, not financial. J. P. Morgan called with a cable from New York about a \$250 million loan to pay Reparations; Norman said that the Commission could not give the prior lien required, even if a loan was otherwise possible. Already on October 27 he had come to the conclusion that Germany would not be able to make the payments scheduled and drafted the following suggestion:

In the event of Germany being definitely unable to provide the moneys required for these payments and therefore forced to make actual default to the Reparation Commission at one date or another, the following plan should be considered.

H.M.G. to hand to the German Government an amount of French (and/or Italian) Sterling Treasury Bills equal to the amount of the Reparations payment upon which she would otherwise default, in exchange for a similar amount of German Sterling Treasury Bills or other approved Securities.

Germany to hand to the Reparation Commission in full settlement of the amount of her Reparations payment thus due the French (and/or Italian) Sterling Treasury Bills (which would become *pro rata* the property of whichever of the Allies is entitled to receive payment according to the agreed proportions).

From the point of view of H.M.G., this would entail an exchange of French for German Treasury Bills of like amount.

From the point of view of Germany, this would entail the issue of Sterling Treasury Bills or other Securities (which would rank behind the Reparation and similar claims) in lieu of cash payments.

From the point of view of France and other Allies, this would entail the receipt of French Sterling Treasury Bills in lieu of cash or approved foreign currencies, which she is entitled to receive. But could she refuse her own Bills?

He sent it to Strong with the following note :

The failure to make payment of sums as and when due for Reparations in future is a question of politics and must be decided by Governments.   But in seeking for some suggestion which we here may make to our own Government in this connection, we have hit upon an idea.   What I want to know from you is your opinion of the idea, what the attitude of your Administration would be, and of course any better idea that may occur to you.   (The British Government have as you know any number of French and Italian Sterling Treasury Bills representing part of the inter-allied debt.)

His reply to Strong's comments hints at its reception :

I am not surprised that you thought that the plan has various objections.   Had it not been at least drastic, and perhaps outrageous, it would have been of no use.   As it is, the effect of having this concrete — even if outrageous — plan to put before our Government and Sir John Bradbury (Reparation Commission) has done a great deal to make me hopeful of a moratorium.

In November the Reparation Commission itself, alarmed at the situation which was developing, visited Berlin to make an inquiry on the spot for itself.   On November 21 the Chancellor (Horne) and Blackett lunched at the Bank and stayed late discussing Reparations, Kindersley (the English member of the Committee on Guarantees) joining them.   This evidently moved Norman to another attempt.   He had already received Havenstein as a visitor and given him an opportunity of meeting a few people.   He now drafted a short general statement on Reparations, which he showed individually to his chief advisers in the world of banking — McKenna, Sir Harry Goschen, Baron Bruno Schröder.   They approved it, as did J. P. Morgan, who was in London :

Under present conditions Germany—
  (a) Cannot meet the Reparation payments without borrowing.
  (b) Cannot borrow — for a short or long period — for the purpose of meeting such payments.

Hence increasing loss of confidence and general disorganisation of business and Exchanges owing to impending dates of payment.

Therefore it is essential, above all things, that without a day's delay she be granted Time, and that the occupation of further territory be avoided.

In order to obtain settlement of the World's uncertainties and eventual stability, it is advisable that :

(*a*) Germany be granted at once a 6 or 12 months' moratorium in respect of Reparation payments, and that

(*b*) During that period a comprehensive readjustment or postponement of Reparation payments be agreed upon as part of a general and simultaneous settlement of all international indebtedness arising out of the War, and that

(*c*) Germany be required at the same time to readjust her own economic and financial position.

The whole of November 27, a Sunday, he spent at the Treasury in conference on Reparations. The purpose was to work on a detailed draft for the Cabinet, which started from the critical financial situation of Germany and the certainty of default on the 750 million gold marks due in January and February 1922, and then went on to discuss the conditions on which a moratorium should be granted : it would be necessary to secure the support of Italy and Belgium, and to make concessions to France ; but the situation would become worse if nothing were done until actual default. Bradbury was in the Bank on the 29th, discussing a moratorium ; Rathenau came over on the 30th on behalf of the German Government and saw Norman, by himself and with the Chancellor. Writing to Strong, Norman said that what was wanted was a long moratorium, with six or twelve months' notice of termination : some indefinite period terminable by the Reparation Commission at much shorter notice would prove fatal to building up business with Germany or by Germany. Rathenau, he said, had not been helpful : he was panic-stricken at the threatened occupation of the Ruhr and would advise anything to obviate this. The British Government and Norman were most anxious to prevent the occupation, but they were also looking for the means of assisting a revival or expansion of European trade.

One further step he was able to take. Evidently the Germans were being pressed to borrow in order to make the scheduled payments. He had arranged with Havenstein to write to him, stating Germany's position and asking formally for help in obtaining advances, at short or long term, in order

to avoid default. The answer, which he explained beforehand
to Havenstein was the only possible answer, and which he
agreed with McKenna, Schröder, Kindersley, Lionel Roths-
child and Blackett, was as follows :

I have consulted with those best competent to form an opinion
and I have to say, in reply to your request, that under the conditions
which at the present time govern the payments due during the next
few years by the German Government to the Reparation Commission, such advances cannot be obtained in this Country. I beg you
so to inform your Chancellor.

In December he had long interviews on Reparations with
the Chancellor every week, and discussions with Blackett at
the Bank and the Treasury in the intervals. J. P. Morgan was
consulted and kept informed. Blackett was still trying to work
out an arrangement by which Germany should accept a
liability for all inter-allied debts, contingent upon the extent
to which creditor Governments called on their debtors for
payment, and in return have her liability for Reparations
reduced by a corresponding amount; Germany would also be
required to undertake to deal drastically with her internal
inflation. On December 29 Germany formally applied for a
moratorium, and was invited to meet the Supreme Council
of the Allies in Cannes. Norman, in a personal note to Havenstein, said that he hoped Havenstein's visit would be a turning-
point in the discussions, but their object could not be achieved
by banking, even though the politicians did not know enough
about the financial implications to handle them. He hoped
the outcome would be a strengthening of the Reichsbank's position (a condition included in the British proposals for a moratorium) ; a Central Bank dominated by its Government was
not in a position to play its part in the country. To Strong he
stated his opinion more definitely ; an 'understanding' feeling
about Reparations dated from Havenstein's visit; in fact the
Chancellor had become as much anti-French as pro-German.
'He realises that the large question is the civilisation of Europe,
which includes the industrial machine — and no mere argument of pounds or dollars.'
Norman's hopes of a moratorium at Cannes were to be disappointed. A moratorium was the most he had hoped for, but

a conference would provide an opportunity of bringing together
the Prime Minister and the French Premier. Writing to
Strong on December 23, he had enclosed a confidential
note of a scheme for which there was some French support.
He wrote :

> Our people are anxious that German representatives should be
> invited to come and discuss the contents of the Agreement. The
> French will not have it at any price. I suppose it will end in
> Rathenau or some other well-informed German being unexpectedly
> found in a hotel at Cannes at the critical moment and in there
> being an unofficial meeting with Loucheur and some of the
> Britishers. That is the way the French prefer to carry on their
> negotiations.

The 'agreement' proposed to recommend to the Supreme
Council a postponement of the January and February scheduled payments on conditions which would settle the question
of Reparations for some time to come — Germany was to make
a total payment of 500 million gold marks for the year, using
Reichsbank gold for the purpose; the Wiesbaden agreement
on deliveries in kind was to be extended; the cost of the Occupation forces was to be met in marks; and the German internal
finances were to be reformed by restricting Reichsbank loans
to the Government and note-issue to the December 1921
amount, and introducing a foreign adviser to an autonomous
Reichsbank. In the event Rathenau argued officially and at
length with the Supreme Council, alienated them, and prevented any decision until the Briand Government fell: the
replacement of Briand by Poincaré postponed agreement once
more.

Writing to Strong again, on 6 February 1922, Norman said
that Cannes would do little more than recognise that some
modification of Reparations was necessary, and, incidentally,
demand complete autonomy of the Reichsbank. He added :

> Only one morning at Cannes, when everyone looked hopeful
> and happy; rumour was going round that your Colonel H.[1] had
> been damaged in a motor accident and people hurried out of the
> town to look at his corpse; but in a couple of days he was about
> again, and everybody was again looking hopeless and dejected !

[1] Colonel House, earlier Ambassador at large for President Wilson.

He wrote at the same time to Havenstein, urging him to resist the inflationary demands of his Government:

It matters not whether such policy may seem unavoidable or not. The important point is that the Reichsbank, once independent, should be known to adopt towards the Government the habit of making excessive note issues difficult, of recommending to the utmost limit contraction in respect of Treasury Certificates and other short forms of Government borrowing, and of insisting on a sound financial policy.

The Supreme Council returned the question of a moratorium to the Reparation Commission, to which constitutionally it belonged. The Commission substituted for the Schedule of Payments a provisional payment every ten days of 31 million gold marks, at the same time demanding within a fortnight a complete programme of internal financial reform. Further 'sanctions' were avoided for the moment; but the adjustment of payments to Germany's capacity was left untouched. A Committee of Allied experts then fixed the total amount to be paid in 1922, and detailed the financial reforms to be carried through.

One outcome of the Cannes discussions was the Genoa Conference. This was to be a general economic conference, including Germans and Americans as well as the Allied countries. This necessarily altered the character of the discussions, since, as Norman wrote to Strong:

The French will not permit any discussion of the German Reparation payments and your representatives — even if they should go to Genoa — will not permit any discussion of Inter-Allied Debts. Indeed I think it becomes increasingly clear that the French will not permanently readjust the amounts they hope to receive from Germany until they are satisfied on what basis their indebtedness to the United States is to be settled.

However, Reparations were discussed at Genoa, not formally but without objection being raised. The occasion was the summoning by the Reparation Commission of a committee to advise it on the conditions under which it would be possible for Germany to raise foreign loans to be applied to part-payment of the Reparations debt. Discussions were progressing favourably, when the announcement of the German treaty with Russia broke up the conference, and once more postponed any agreement.

One hope remained. The committee summoned by the Reparation Commission was a committee of bankers : Kindersley represented the London market, J. P. Morgan, New York, and Vissering, the President of the Netherlands Bank, was also included. It could not begin until it was assured of some agreement between Germany and the Reparation Commission; there was unanimity as to the desirability of a loan and the favourable condition of markets, but Morgan insisted that New York was so disgusted with European quarrels that an issue would be hopeless unless it was assured that the Allies were behind the loan and Germany determined to meet her obligations under it. An exchange of Notes between the Commission and the German Government at the end of May made it possible to proceed. Again, although there was unanimity on technical questions, political difficulties arose; the French member argued that the fixed Reparations debt could not be questioned, whereas the others held that they must take account of the burden Germany could bear. Poincaré took occasion to state in public in provocative language that the French Government would reject any suggestion to make a loan contingent on a reduction of French claims. The majority of the Committee resented this, and considered that further study on their part would be wasted. They were induced to agree to an adjournment, instead of a dissolution; but in a parting report they stated — for the first time in any public official statement — the fundamental need of external aid in solving Reparations differences.

Norman had had a long talk with J. P. Morgan in August on the whole subject. He himself was out of England visiting America from April 26 to the end of May, and on his return was occupied with the American debt negotiations and Austria's difficulties. Just before seeing Morgan he had written to Strong that the Central Banks' meeting was unlikely as there was a debt conference. Poincaré was visiting London and the immediate future of Central Europe, he thought, never looked blacker. He could not conceive how a break-up of Austria and conditions very near to civil war in Germany were to be avoided.

It seemed utterly impossible for the British Government to see eye to eye, or even come to terms, with the French Government in respect of methods to be adopted in dealing with ex-enemy countries.   In July Germany had applied for relief from further payments in 1922 without response.   In August, while Norman was writing, the Allied Prime Ministers were meeting in London, and Poincaré was pressing for 'productive pledges', by which he meant the occupation of the Ruhr coalfield.   This neither the Germans nor the British would agree to.

The German application for a moratorium was formally heard by the Reparation Commission.   Their representative argued that the failure to obtain a foreign loan had neutralised the great improvement in Germany's internal finances, and the further fall of the mark threatened the reform achieved.   A concession by Belgium made it possible to defer further payments in 1922 ; but the Commission deferred its answer to the application for a moratorium — Bradbury alone voting for it — until it had completed plans for the reform of Germany's internal finance, the reduction of the burden of Reparations, in so far as might be considered necessary in this connection, and for the issue of loans to consolidate Germany's financial situation.   Thus as Germany's actual situation became worse, some progress was made in recognising the practical exigencies of her situation.   Her Government endeavoured to accelerate the recognition by calling in the advice of a committee of experts — including Cassel, Keynes and Brand — on the stabilisation of the mark.   The majority were emphatic that the stabilisation would have to start with Germany's own efforts, not with external help, while the minority held that a foreign credit was essential ; but all agreed that Germany would have to be released from all payments under the Treaty of Versailles for several years.   Keynes had called on Norman while the Committee was at work and explained the position fully to him. After the Germans had put forward their proposals, with the experts' advice attached, Norman had Bradbury, J. P. Morgan and Kindersley for a long meeting at the Bank ; they were in entire agreement that any loan for Germany was impossible until the final Reparations debt was fixed by consent.   A week earlier Morgan had told him emphatically that there would be no advances for Germany on the basis of a two years' moratorium, and no meeting of the adjourned Bankers' Committee to consider anything of the sort.

The British and American view of Reparations was taking a practical shape. Germany must deal with her internal inflation by her own action; the total of Reparations must be fixed in relation to Germany's capacity to pay; temporary relief was necessary from Reparation payments; given these conditions a foreign loan was possible — very much the programme on which Austria's financial reorganisation was based. In a letter to Strong on November 27, Norman enclosed the following memorandum, 'drawn up a few days ago, so that the present Prime Minister (Bonar Law) and Chancellor (Baldwin) coming new to the question, should know where they stood *vis-à-vis* the French proposal for an early conference'.

M. Poincaré's idea is apparently to propose an arbitrary reduction of the reparation liability on condition that

(*a*) the French share of reparation is increased by the recognition of a priority for material damages,

(*b*) inter-allied debts are written down or written off,

(*c*) material security is given by Germany and close allied control established over German finances.

Gossip credits him with being prepared for a reduction to 40,000 million gold marks provided Great Britain will forgo her share of reparation altogether and cancel the inter-allied debts owing to her.

The objections to this policy are—

(*a*) The arbitrary fixation of the German liability at any figure which the French would be willing to accept would not now advance a settlement.

Germany would default in respect of the reduced obligation at a very early date and Great Britain would be then committed to coercive action with as little prospect as ever of such action producing financial results of any value.

(*b*) We should have sacrificed our share of whatever it may prove possible to extract from Germany and abandoned our claims in respect of inter-allied debts for no advantage whatever.

(c) We should waste a good deal of time in wrangling with Germany over securities which if we obtained them would prove useless and obtaining controls which would not work in practice and for the financial unproductiveness of which the Allies themselves would be responsible.

Until the market has been stabilised, budget equilibrium established and German internal credit restored, it is no good trying to fix a reparation total.

Until we know how much can be recovered from Germany it would be premature to decide how it is to be divided.

Until we know how much France will recover it is impossible to say what concessions are required in regard to Inter-allied debts.

It is suggested that either the Reparation Commission or the Allied Governments should appoint a Committee of Bankers to formulate a plan for stabilising the mark indicating clearly the concessions on the part of Germany's reparation creditors which are necessary to its success, and that the proposed conference should not be held until this report has been received and considered.

The last paragraph of this memorandum foreshadowed the Dawes Committee; but another year of wrangling and waste was to intervene. The Allies in conference did not agree, and on 11 January 1923 French and Belgian troops occupied the Ruhr. Germany retaliated by passive resistance. Havenstein called the attention of the Governor of the Bank of England 'as concerning the interests of all Central Banks' to the fact that French troops in the Ruhr had seized German bank-notes in the hands of manufacturers, finished them and put them into circulation; which the Governor duly reported to the Committee of Treasury. The Committee authorised further loans on the security of gold to the Reichsbank provided they did not disturb the London market. But the decision being sought on the Continent by methods of force could not be influenced by banking. 'The black spot of Europe', he wrote to Strong on April 9, 'and the world continues to be on the Rhine; there you have *all* the conditions of war except that one side is unarmed. How long can Germany continue thus? If Poincaré is to continue another year (till the next Election in France) where will German industry go? Her export trade and her necessary imports?' The German passive resistance, while it reduced French receipts from the occupation to less than they had been before it, was also strangling the economic life of Germany, and reducing its public and external finances to chaos. Germans came to London seeking private loans for coal to run their railways, but got little encouragement. The Chancellor consulted the Governor on the political *impasse* on the Continent. When one of the bankers who had advised Germany in the previous year called on him at the end of May, Norman gave it as his opinion that Germany should refer all questions to a bankers' committee; and, failing acceptance and withdrawal from the Ruhr, Great Britain should withdraw Bradbury from the Reparation Commission and its troops from the Rhine. McKenna agreed with him that Great Britain should break openly with France.

An inadequate and inept offer by Germany in May 1923 had been rejected. The British Government induced them to supplement it by a more conciliatory note; Norman was consulted on this note in draft, and on the British reply to it. It made no impression on the French Government. In July and again in August Curzon, the Foreign Secretary, addressed conciliatory proposals to the Allies, again without result. In September the Germans realised that passive resistance was futile and withdrew it; with its withdrawal the Stresemann Government fell. On October 30 the British Government made a final attempt to break the deadlock, this time in response to a suggestion by the U.S. Secretary of State, Charles Hughes. Their proposal was that the economic capacity of Germany to pay Reparations should be examined by a committee of experts. The United States Government agreed in principle, departing from its consistent refusal in the past to take any responsibility for Europe's difficulties. Poincaré refused to agree to terms of reference which, in Hughes' opinion, were the minimum needed to justify the inquiry. But the Reparation Commission saved the proposal; in response to an application from Germany to investigate German resources and capacity to pay, which Article 234 of the Treaty permitted, the Commission itself decided to appoint two Committees, with terms of reference that avoided political issues but allowed effective inquiry. One was to consider the means of balancing the German budget and stabilising German currency, the other to estimate the amount of capital exported from Germany and the means of bringing it back. The assessment of the Reparation debt was at last to be related to German capacity to pay.

Bradbury had been urging on Norman the importance of a decision on French action while the Dominion Premiers were in London in October. On November 28 he was consulting Norman on names for the committees; for the first they agreed on Austen Chamberlain and Kindersley, for the second McKenna, and Norman secured McKenna's agreement the same afternoon. The next day Morgan promised to think of Americans to serve. Chamberlain was not available, and on December 19 the Prime Minister (Baldwin) sent for Norman and urged his name for the larger committee. He protested; he was an official and not a free agent, Central Banks should be left out of international quarrels, others could do the work better or as well, politics were going to make the work at the Bank very difficult for the next few months. The next day he reported the matter to the Committee of Treasury. They took the view that they could not authorise a prolonged absence of the Governor from his post in London, and that it was their duty to insist that he devote himself exclusively to the affairs of the Bank. They persisted in their decision in the face of a personal appeal, on behalf of the Prime Minister, by Warren Fisher [1] later in the day. The Governor, writing to Strong, confessed that he would not have been averse to serving on the committee, but he could not be in two places at once. Eventually Stamp [2] was the second British member.

The condition attached to every concession and to every loan contemplated in the last two years had been an effective internal reform of German finances to stop inflation. The state to which Germany was reduced by the occupation of the Ruhr and passive resistance made it possible for the Government at last to force through such a reform. In the middle of June 1923 the mark was quoted at 100,000 to the dollar, but was still in use as a currency; by the middle of September the quotation was 100 million marks to the dollar, by the middle of October 4000 million. The virtual destruction of the nominal currency compelled the provision of a new currency. On November 15

[1] Sir Warren Fisher, Permanent Secretary, H.M. Treasury, 1919–39.
[2] Sir Josiah Stamp, later Lord Stamp. Director of the Bank of England, 1928–41.

a new mark was created, the Rentenmark, issued by a new
bank, the Rentenbank, created for the purpose, and endowed
with a charge on the whole of German industry and agriculture,
a charge reckoned in gold marks. The Rentenbank took over
the Reich's debt from the Reichsbank, and would finance the
Government until revenue balanced expenditure, but only up
to a maximum fixed at the outset of the reform. The Reichsbank was given independence, and prohibited from discounting
Reich Treasury Bills. At the same time taxes were converted
into gold taxes, and new taxes imposed; and the Finance
Ministry given power to control effectively expenditure by
other departments. The railways and Post Office were put on
an independent footing without subsidies. As soon as it appeared that the rentenmark would be accepted, the paper mark
was stabilised around 4·2 million million marks to the dollar,
and then a legal ratio of one rentenmark to 1 million million
paper marks established. That such a ruthless conversion of
a paper currency should succeed, and the budget be brought
into balance in spite of the disorganisation of industry and the
resulting expense of relieving the unemployed, is astonishing
enough; yet it survived even an additional burden in the
renewal on a heavier scale of deliveries of reparations in kind.
France refused to negotiate with the German Government over
the resumption of work in the occupied territory, and negotiated agreement direct with the industrial concerns affected,
who insisted on their deliveries and payments being credited
to Reparations account. Whether the rentenmark would have
survived, or been undermined like its predecessor by the inability of the Reich Government both to meet its internal
expenditure and make possible the payment for essential
imports, without the aid of an external loan, may be doubted.
But in fact a surplus of revenue over expenditure was achieved
by January 1924, and by restriction of credit and a Reichsbank
monopoly of foreign exchange the internal and external value
of the rentenmark was maintained until an external loan was
assured. As Bergmann the German historian of Reparations
says, the experiment 'succeeded because dire necessity had at
last taught the German people that their primary need was a
stable currency if they were to continue to live'.

The two committees, under the chairmanship of General

Dawes and McKenna respectively, assembled in Paris in January. The Governor was in touch with them and went over to Paris when they had drafted their reports. These were published on April 9. The next day the Governor was summoned, with the Chancellor (Snowden), Bradbury, Niemeyer, Sir Eyre Crowe [1] and others, to two conferences on them with the Prime Minister (Ramsay MacDonald). Bradbury was anxious to secure the Reparation Commission's immediate approval of the reports without alteration. Ben Strong had just arrived from New York, and the Governor discussed the reports with him, Owen D. Young and Kindersley. Already they were considering procedure and conditions of a loan, and the Chancellor and he agreed that if the Report was adopted the Bank should 'run the loan'. He also saw Baldwin and Neville Chamberlain to explain the reports, and stress the importance of prompt acceptance, and on April 17 went over to Paris again for ten days.

The Reparation Commission notified the German Government on April 11 that it regarded the Dawes plan of the experts as providing a practical basis for a solution of Reparations and that it was prepared to recommend it to the Allied Governments. The German Government accepted the report on the 16th. In reply to the Reparation Commission's note the Governments of the United Kingdom, Belgium and Italy accepted the recommendations of the experts. Poincaré made difficulties; but on May 11 an election for the Chamber of Deputies deprived Poincaré of his majority, and his administration was succeeded by a Government of the Left under Herriot. The Reparation Commission was now able to work without continual external pressure from the French Government, and the three committees provided for in the Plan were able to work out the details with little delay. These were committees of practical experts, German and Allied or Neutral in each case, Schacht and Kindersley being responsible for the organisation of the new Reichsbank.

Schacht, first as Controller of Currency and then as successor to Havenstein as President of the Reichsbank, had played an important part in arresting the progress of inflation and restoring German finances. He was consulted for his expert

[1] Permanent Under-Secretary of State for Foreign Affairs, 1920–25.

knowledge by the Dawes and McKenna Committees, and he
quickly established himself as the most effective agent in Germany with whom, on financial questions, the Allies could deal.
The Governor had recognised his quality at once; he had
invited him to London on 31 December 1923 and introduced
him to the Chancellor, to McKenna and the other leading
Clearing Bankers and to the merchant-bankers most concerned with the Continent. Schacht had devised a scheme for
a Gold Discount Bank, to replace the Rentenbank ultimately
and immediately to provide an agency for international business.
Its success depended on support from Central Banks in other
centres in the way of loans and willingness to take its paper.
The Governor approved of the scheme, and commended it
to other Central Bankers, by letter to Strong and by interview
as opportunity occurred in Europe. He reported Schacht's
visit and explained his plan to the Committee of Treasury
on January 9, and the Committee approved an advance of
£5 million to the Reichsbank to assist the establishment of the
Gold Discount Bank. The Committee also approved the
Governor's reply to a French proposal for the establishment of
a new Central Bank for the Rhenish Provinces of Germany,
that it would be in opposition to the wishes and interests of the
Reichsbank and would not be supported by English banks.
This help was valuable in tiding Germany over the long interval
between the report of the Dawes Committee and the final
provision of external resources by the Dawes Loan.

In July the new French Premier received Ramsay Mac-
Donald in Paris, and on the 9th the two Governments published a memorandum approving the Plan and convening a
conference in London on July 16 to consider measures for
carrying it out. On most of the agenda the work proceeded
smoothly and rapidly, but on two essential issues even a Radical
Premier was not prepared to give up safeguards the French had
regarded as essential. First, in case of German default, the
French insisted on the right of independent action by any of
the Allied powers; second, on the correlative question of the
authority which should establish default, the French held fast
to the Reparation Commission. The British delegation was
opposed to their position on both questions, and they received
support from an interested party, which was not represented

on the Conference — the bankers who would have to issue the 800 million gold mark loan, on which the Plan hinged. Their spokesman was Thomas W. Lamont; he was in touch with the Governor (whose own views were made known to the Conference) and wrote personally to Ramsay MacDonald, explaining the difficulty the bankers would be in if the final settlement reached by the Conference did not offer conditions on which the investing public in the world's capital markets would support a German loan. By the mediation of the Belgian delegation and the unofficial American participants in the Conference, the French were induced to modify their claims. The Reparation Commission should establish default, but only by a unanimous vote in which an American member added to the Commission would take part; and the question of guarantees in case of German default was withdrawn from the Conference for settlement by special discussion between the Reparation Commission, the German Government and the bankers. The bankers were not satisfied — they thought that an early evacuation of the Ruhr was essential from their point of view; but the compromise was accepted, and the final agreement embodied in Protocols signed on August 9. The Governor's special task — to raise the Loan which the new settlement of Reparations was to make possible and on which it depended — now faced him and his associates in the Reparation Commission, the Treasury and the other banking centres.

It is not easy to recall, after the experience of Government credits and gifts after the Second World War, the responsibility and the influence which bankers carried in the 'twenties. To-day the reconstruction of a devastated country, the restoration of the finances and currency of a disordered economy, the development of a poverty-stricken region are financed by large grants or loans from the governments of rich countries, most of all the United States, or they are not financed at all. In the 'twenties none of these resources was available. It was only with the greatest difficulty that the minority of internationally minded Americans were able to interest their countrymen in Europe's difficulties, and the British and other European Governments were all oppressed with the sense of their own financial difficulties. Finance for relief and reconstruction, and for the payment of Reparations through the reconstruction

P

of German finances and the substitution of German Government obligations to the capital market for obligations under Treaty to Allied governments, all depended on money raised in the markets of countries able to provide foreign loans.

The bankers who had to provide the 800 million gold mark loan included in the Dawes Plan were faced with two difficulties. The first was purely technical. In order to raise a large sum of money by loan in free markets, it was necessary to present it to potential subscribers in a form which they could study and understand; a prospectus giving all the information possible to judge the security, a bond specifying the security and binding the borrower to it, arrangements for underwriting and marketing the issue were all needed. As late as October Norman was corresponding with Bradbury on the problem of providing security by ensuring, roughly, a general as well as a specific charge. Neither the Reparation Commission nor the London Conference had attempted or was qualified to do anything of this sort; it was a task for specialised issuing houses who were familiar with the technique of issuing such a loan and knew the markets in which it would be offered.

The second difficulty with which the bankers were faced was to make sure that the underlying security for any loan they might issue was adequate to support it. Their intervention during the Conference had, by the temporary deadlock it caused, stiffened resistance to the French terms, which would have made a loan impossible, and thereby probably prevented a compromise which sacrificed some of the principles on which the scheme was based. The Dawes Report had based its recommendations on the assumption that the fiscal and economic unity of the Reich would be restored; that foreign interference, so far as it hampered the economic activities of Germany, must be withdrawn; that the Plan was 'an indivisible whole'. But the Conference left the French and Belgian forces in occupation of the Ruhr and Cologne, with no term agreed for their withdrawal. The Governor had raised with the Committee of Treasury the question of issuing the loan before he was officially approached by the Government on August 20; and told the Committee how unsatisfactory was the position in which things were left. He had written on August 16 to Lamont to the same effect:

. . . I had a long talk with the Chancellor [Snowden] yesterday; he was a good deal distressed at the way things had shaped
themselves. He seemed to think that the conclusions of the Conference were based too much on politics and too little on facts and
economics. Hence, trouble and misunderstanding might well arise
later on. He asked if, under the conclusions now contemplated,
the money required by the Dawes Report would be forthcoming,
but I could give him no definite answer whatever, nor did I pretend
to do so. He said, too, that so much pressure had been brought to
bear on the Germans in order to obtain their agreement that they
were almost acting under compulsion and, indeed, they might
represent that they had done so. I found myself in agreement with
his standpoint as I think you would have been and I continue to
wish that more attention had been paid to the requirements, so
far as they can be anticipated, for carrying out that part of the
Dawes Report which relates to the German Loan.

I also had a talk with the Prime Minister [MacDonald] and
found that he had no definite ideas about the Loan and not much
interest in it. He wanted a political agreement without delay,
however it might have to be reached. Too much, he said, had
been heard of the Bankers' needs which continually antagonised
the French and some of his own friends (the Socialists). He was
sure that no one in his position could reach a better settlement
than was being reached and even if not perfect or so good as had
been hoped, it would produce a new spirit in Europe.

I am writing to let you know how things look this morning as
I hope to leave them alone for the next month. In other words, I
mean to go away in a couple of days, partly because I must have a
holiday and partly because I am sure I can do no good by staying
here.

There was no doubt that he needed a holiday; on July 10
at a conference with the Prime Minister in the House of Commons he had collapsed and been carried to bed, where he had
to stay for five days.

On his return from his holiday he found little progress
achieved. He saw Lamont and J. P. Morgan the following
day, September 17. They told him that they had not yet
decided the *principle* of issuing the German Loan, let alone
details. They were waiting for reports from New York. The
Governor reported to the Committee of Treasury the same day
that he intended (in conjunction with Morgans) to conclude

negotiations for the Dawes Loan only after a satisfactory statement had been made in respect of (*a*) the Ruhr and (*b*) the
Cologne area. The Committee supported him in insisting on
these conditions. But a week later he had heard from Morgans
that, having consulted Washington, they were prepared to
negotiate with the Germans if they received satisfactory letters
from the Allied governments. He reported also that he had
put his difficulties in a letter to the Prime Minister, and received
a reply; and the Committee decided, in the face of the danger
to Central Europe if the Loan was not issued, that they should
ignore the remaining uncertainty still attaching to the conditions they had required, and the Bank should proceed to
issue the Loan; if necessary the Bank should commit itself to
a considerable subscription on its own account.

The Prime Minister's remark that 'too much had been
heard of the bankers' needs which continually antagonised the
French and some of his own friends (the Socialists)' crystallises
a misunderstanding of the bankers' functions and powers which
continually beset the Governor's attempts to further the reconstruction of Europe. The bankers were technicians, expert in
judging the forms in which potential lenders and investors
would take up new issues and the purposes for which any money
would be put up. Many of these investors were themselves
professional operators, managers of insurance and trust companies in a fiduciary relation to their stockholders and policy-
holders, and limited in their choice of investments by considerations of safety and return. When, therefore, the bankers
had been consulted in 1922, and now when they were asked to
raise the £40 million of the Dawes Loan, their primary duty
was to interpret the demands of the markets in which they
would have to raise it. Their view, while the London Conference was sitting, was that few lenders would be prepared to
entrust their savings to the government of a country which had
its richest industrial region occupied by and directed to the purposes of an alien power; and, further, that the Ruhr occupation
was only the most glaring example of a state of discord which
made any European loan unattractive to American investors.
Unless they performed their function of interpreting the market's
capacity and wants honestly and to the best of their ability,
they would sacrifice what trust the market placed in their

judgment and integrity and be quickly forced out of business.

It was perhaps fortunate that the Dawes Plan, by its dependence on the Loan, did in this way depend on an expert judgment of the reception in foreign markets of the scheme as a whole. There had been already too many 'settlements' of Reparations, which broke down because they were compromises between incompatible positions, and especially because they conceded political claims which depended on impossible economic concessions.

The dependence of the Dawes Plan on a foreign loan ensured that the economic proposals would be judged by economic criteria and not by the requirements of political bargains. The Plan might fail after all — when J. P. Morgan was under cross-examination in a Congressional Inquiry into the business of making public issues in 1933 he stated in answer to a question that the only foreign issues made by his firm then in default were the two, the Dawes and the Young loans, which they had issued in New York at the request of the American Government — but no settlement which did not provide for the assessment of economic possibilities by some independent objective examination stood any chance of success.

In spite of their disappointment over an early evacuation of the Ruhr, the bankers agreed to issue the Loan : the Governor agreed terms with J. P. Morgan and Lamont on September 29, and the same day communicated them to Schacht. The first ten days of October were occupied in continuous work with the lawyers in drawing up the detailed terms, but all necessary signatures were secured on October 10. The issue was made on October 15.

The Dawes Plan was not a final settlement — it left still to be determined the total charge for Reparations which Germany had to meet. It encountered the unforeseen difficulties in administration which arise on any large plan : but it removed the great obstacle to international confidence and trade which Reparations had constituted. With the early removal of the obstacle to Anglo-American co-operation offered by the British Debt to America, and with the restoration of stable monetary conditions under the lead of the United Kingdom, it led to four years of recovery in Europe and an expansion of international trade to an unprecedented height.

CHAPTER VI

THE GOLD STANDARD IN A POST-WAR WORLD

(i)

ENGLAND's return to the Gold Standard excited high hopes. Congratulations on his part in the achievement flowed in to the Governor from all over the world — from Ben Strong in New York, Schacht in Berlin, Bradbury in Paris, Blackett in Delhi, Salter in Geneva. The Federal Reserve Board in its Report for 1925 put the general banking view:

> In the international field the event of greatest importance during 1925 was the restoration of the Gold Standard . . . and the most distinctive achievement of the year in Federal Reserve policy was the arrangement of a credit by the Federal Reserve Banks for the Bank of England in connection with the re-establishment of a free gold market in London. . . . The return of Great Britain to the Gold Standard was accompanied and followed by similar action in other countries, with the result that over a wide area gold once more has become the basis of values and the major part of the world's commerce and finance has been relieved of the risks and uncertainties that arise from widely fluctuating exchange rates. . . .

Already, when this was written early in 1926, over thirty countries had stabilised their currencies, *de jure* or *de facto*, on gold, including Germany, the Netherlands, Switzerland, Austria and Hungary, Denmark and Sweden in Europe, the British Dominions and India overseas, Canada and, of course, the United States of America. The act of formal stabilisation by the United Kingdom did not, however, assure stability or end the struggle for the Gold Standard. The forces making for instability of the exchanges had still to be controlled : what the restoration of the Gold Standard did was to compel such control on penalty of loss of monetary reserves. Norman had been

218

aware of the difficulties he faced; only six months before Britain returned to gold he was warning Blackett in India of the dangers of premature stabilisation of the rupee, even while he affirmed his belief that the £ must be stabilised.

27 October 1924

What I cannot see is that the moment has come to stabilise at 1/6 sterling, leading as it would to 1/6 gold. My trouble arises from the uncertainty at the moment both of prices and exchanges. America has just taken to European loans. Will she continue? The Dawes Plan has been effective for a week. Sterling is 8% below parity, so is the Australian £, while the South African £ is about half way. The South Africans at the moment are disposed to go back to free gold at the end of June next; the Australians have no plan at all, except to stick with us. Our prohibition of export [of gold] expires at the end of next year, but beyond that we have no declared policy. If we had a policy and announced that the expiry of the present Act would stand, sterling would now be far above 4·50. Holland and Switzerland are waiting on this country. All of these points I mention because of their uncertainty and to them is, of course, attached the uncertainty of prices. It may be hazardous for us to attempt an early return to the old parity, though, personally, I do not for a moment think so. But for you to attempt to fix a new parity, whether with sterling or with gold seems to me fraught with difficulties.

For six years he was to be engaged in a continuous struggle to maintain sterling on gold, at the parity adopted, against recurrent strains which he could not prevent, with reserves which in the end proved inadequate.

At first the confidence inspired by the return to gold attracted funds to London, and gold came from Holland and Russia. South Africa, which had been accumulating its gold for currency purposes, resumed its normal shipments to London. On 6 August 1925 Bank Rate was reduced to 4½ per cent; the Governor explained the reduction to Schacht as 'simply following traditional lines of pre-war policy — which may or may not be a good reason at the present time'. But he had no alternative and reduced it further to 4 per cent on October 1. It was hoped that other countries would follow suit, as they did, and that New York would be able to maintain its 3½ per cent. Unfortunately this ease could not be continued;

two influences, which were to recur again and again, forced
the Bank on December 3 to put its rate back to 5 per cent.

The return to gold did nothing to check the pressure on
London for loans or repress the eagerness of the bankers and
brokers who handled such loans to meet the demand. The
Governor resisted them, relying on the informal embargo
which the Government still maintained, but he could do no
more than put a brake on the movement. Reconstruction
loans were permitted; acceptance credits for the movement of
goods (and not subject to renewal) he encouraged, and he could
not control private banking credits. He had to recognise that
the embargo was inconsistent with restoring a free gold market:
and as in October he wrote to Blackett:

By degrees . . . it became evident that the real benefits of the
embargo were being seized for themselves by the Dominions whose
appetites for new loans threatened to become insatiable. As we
were only just feeling our way through the early days of the revived
Gold Standard we asked the Dominions to go slow, or to raise some
of their requirements in New York, and, although the Commonwealth Government were very obliging and did as they were asked,
others were not so obliging — they even secured the support of
the Colonial Office — and we were therefore gradually forced as it
were to extend the Embargo to cover Dominion Loans. As you can
imagine, from being a mere matter of City policy the embargo thus
suddenly became a question of high imperial politics. . . . I hope the
Embargo will be removed without notice in the course of a few weeks.

The Chancellor (Churchill) announced the lifting of the
embargo at a public dinner in Sheffield on November 3.
Norman warned the Clearing Bankers to go slow, especially in
dealing with applications from the European countries which
had not succeeded in stabilising their currencies (or settling
their war debts to Britain), and repeated the warning to the
chief issuing brokers. He was engaged at the time in negotiations for a short-term credit to assist Belgium to carry through
a scheme for stabilising its currency. Experience showed the
danger that credits, and still more loans, would be used to
postpone facing the necessity of balancing the budget and
dealing with government debt as a prime condition of stabilisation, and London was being approached by France and Italy
who had not faced this necessity.

The other factor which explains the Governor's action was the beginnings of speculation on the New York Stock Exchange. Strong warned him on November 7 that 'the speculative temper of the American people is not going to be satisfied by a fling in the stock market, and may turn its attention to commodities'. He hoped that credit might be tightened gradually, by putting up rates first in Boston and then, say, in Philadelphia, and then perhaps elsewhere, to alarm the speculator; and London, open to foreign loans, might be forced to advance its rate. But Norman did not need the warning; he had already, in his letter to Blackett on October 27, said that his calculations had been upset by the boom on the New York Stock Exchange which put Call Money there up to $5\frac{1}{2}$ per cent, and attracted money (and therefore gold) from London, not for seasonal commodity needs, but for short-term investment.

In another respect this first year was typical of the new régime. The Committee of Treasury was alarmed by the growth in the amount of Treasury Bills with the public and the tendency to ignore the growth in the Floating Debt. The Governor had wished to apply the brake of gradual credit restriction, by setting aside Bank Notes as reserve for additional Currency Notes, the effect of which would have been to reduce the Bank's own Banking Reserve and deplete the market's liquid resources. 'But this', he wrote, 'is a highly controversial matter at the present time, held to savour of deflation and therefore to be against the interests of trade and industry which need all the encouragement possible.'

The rise in Bank Rate on December 3 was, however, effective; sterling was strong in the New Year, trade and employment were expanding, and the adjustment of British to American prices, which the Chamberlain Committee had looked for, was effected. Writing to Strong in November from Harrogate (he had been driven there by an attack of lumbago), Norman said:

On the whole, and in spite of various changes of plan and chances, (looking back) I realise that the fall has been very success-ful. No one here believed we could carry a 4% rate so long at that time of year; few believed that we were brave enough to try it; but nothing else could have done more to silence criticism of the Gold Standard. Add to this the position of France — so long held up to us as an example of the advantages of not being tied to the tail of the Federal Reserve System or indeed to gold.

This is no place for a white man who has nothing to do!

When 1926 opened Norman was in New York. Apart from the constant need he felt of intimate contact with the New York market and a continuous exchange of views with Strong, the purpose of his visit was to discuss a stabilisation loan for Belgium. Throughout the year, as is shown later, the largest claim on his time and thought was made by Europe for the maintenance and extension of stable monetary conditions. It was not that his own market was in enjoyment of untroubled peace; but his troubles were what might have been expected. In the early months increasing activity led to a demand for Currency Notes threatening the limit established by the Cunliffe Committee, which was saved only by co-operation between the banks who restrained the demand. In the later months, the economic condition of the country was dominated by the seven months' stoppage in the coal industry, about which he could do nothing — an approach to the bankers to intervene in conciliation he refused to consider. The stoppage was reflected in the increase in the Government's short-term borrowing which the Committee of Treasury deplored. More serious was the momentum which foreign lending acquired once the embargo was lifted.

Freedom for foreign lending and borrowing was a principal object of the policy of European Reconstruction, formulated at the Brussels and Genoa Conferences and carried out so successfully. Norman and Strong had relied on American participation in meeting the demand, and the rise in foreign issues in New York from 1924 to the second quarter of 1928 justified their hopes. But borrowers, especially Empire and European borrowers, thought first of London; and comparison between estimates of the country's balance of payments on current account and the volume of issues on overseas account, after all allowances points to a strain which must have been serious and might become critical. Britain was no longer the cheapest market in which to expend the proceeds of loans, and sterling was acceptable in any other market in which the borrower might use it. In 1926 the balance was restored by a flight into sterling from the franc. M. Caillaux, the Minister of Finance, put out feelers for a loan to France which would have reversed the flow; but the Governor would not in any case support a credit to a country as unsettled financially as France still was, and London was thus helped to tide over the difficulties caused by the coal strike. The underlying strain persisted.

The practical difficulties of working the international Gold Standard in the post-war world were showing themselves. One after another they appear in the Governor's correspondence with Schacht. Already on 6 December 1924 he perceived the danger of a stock market boom in New York:

Have you had time to notice the great activity on the New York Stock Exchange? I don't think anyone can have expected so quickly a turnover of 2-2½ million shares a day. For us, I think such activity means speculation and speculation means credit and needs money, and so in a word their period of ease is passing.

Just before the British return, on 28 March 1925, Norman was writing to Schacht:

You and we are indeed suffering — and are likely to suffer on the commercial and industrial side. For neither of us, as you say, is the home market adequate, and not only is the habit of Protection growing but the purchasing power of several countries in the world continues seriously depleted. You and your countrymen ought to worship Great Britain as being the one surviving — though I fear expiring — instance of Free Trade!! As such, we are worth much to you, both for purposes of trade and for purposes of example.

He went on to say that 'Central Banks must be prepared among themselves freely to extend credit abroad, especially during this period of reconstruction; it is often as necessary to extend credit abroad as to contract it at home'. He acted on this principle, and found himself faced with movements he could not control. Writing at the end of 1926 (December 28), he referred to some of his difficulties:

We are being rather inconvenienced by the continuous drain of gold from this market to Berlin. It was somewhat disturbing during the first week in November but then disappeared, only to reappear within the last week or two. The latest shipments (as for different reasons were the earlier shipments) must, I think, be due in particular to the American Loans to the Berlin Electric Railway and the State of Bavaria. These operations only show

how greatly the international machine is out of gear. Your German concerns borrow money in America (of which I do not think they have need, but that is another question) and Dutch or German Bankers, seeing the strength of the Mark-Pound Exchange, withdrew the proceeds of these Loans from London in gold. There is nothing within reason which I could do to protect this market : it is not a question of interest rates against which a Central Bank may need to be defended but is rather a question of $\frac{1}{2}\%$ or thereabouts on the charges for the shipment of gold from New York.

I am not complaining but merely thinking aloud of the difficulties which nowadays arise owing to our international machine being so greatly out of gear, and owing, in particular, to the fact that we are all slowly coming back to the gold standard (as we like to believe it existed before the War). But as a matter of fact the Americans are on a different gold standard, for having put into use a certain amount of gold the remainder they sterilise ; and no matter how much gold Europe may send to New York no results are thereby produced on their market conditions. The gold standard, therefore, only works one way, and we in Europe will perhaps need to concoct a method of sterilising gold for our future use rather than allow the Americans to do it to our general disadvantage ?

Replying on December 31, Schacht refers to his own difficulties and adds :

. . . Of course, the Dawes situation is closely connected with the problem of the whole European indebtedness to America and there is much truth in what you say about the American gold situation. But how can it be altered if for years and years to come Europe will have to pay such enormous amounts to America. I quite see the difficulties you have for keeping up the sterling exchange under these conditions.

Norman reverts on 5 January 1927 to his hopes of imposing some control on these extraneous movements by Central Bank co-operation :

I wish you would give further consideration, without special reference to the Dawes situation or to the question of European indebtedness to America, to the suggestion which I made a little vaguely about gold. In present circumstances, it seems to me that there is here a purely monetary problem about which we ought to be thinking and with which we might perhaps make some progress without waiting for the solution of other questions. Gold movements, it seems to me, are nowadays often fortuitous and irrelevant to the monetary situation in one country or another. Have we not to devise some means of making these fortuitous movements irrelevant in their results as well as in their origins?

Such far-reaching questions had to be postponed by the need to deal with more immediate problems. The Committee of Treasury had wished to follow the New York rate down in April 1926, but was deterred by the imminence of a coal strike. In the autumn a revival of speculation in New York was accompanied by a renewed outflow of gold to America. German borrowing involved further losses for London, and any reduction in Bank Rate was deferred till the the following spring.

(ii)

The year 1927 marked a turning-point in the struggle for order and stability in monetary relations. A World Economic Conference, convened by the League of Nations in Geneva in May, formulated the change. Summarising the Conference's deliberations its President, M. Theunis, pointed to 'the outstanding fact that except in the actual fields of conflict, the *dislocation* caused by war was immensely more serious than the actual destruction'. Evidence of this was that, while populations in Europe had increased by 1 per cent and production of food and raw materials by 5 per cent, the volume of international trade had diminished by 11 per cent. So the Conference sought to compel the world's attention to removing obstacles to the free movement of goods, labour and capital, to put an end to the increase in tariff barriers and to move in the opposite direction. Its report was an attempt to turn the minds of governments, not indeed away from their budgetary and exchange difficulties, but to the underlying trade relations on which finance ultimately depends.

The year was marked also by the stabilisation of French finances and the franc, and the apparent restoration to a normal economy of Germany. It was marked by growing difficulties for the London market, but also by an organised attempt to relieve these by Central Bank co-operation. Before turning to these, it will be convenient to glance at the course of events in New York and Paris. The hope that Norman and Strong had

shared, that a settlement of war debts and stabilisation of
currencies would attract American capital to the assistance of
Europe, was amply fulfilled. Increased lending checked the
influx of gold, and in 1925 and 1928 led to an efflux ; but over
the 'twenties as a whole the United States was drawing gold
from the rest of the world.

The banks were able to expand their deposits on this gold
later when the Reserve Banks were resisting expansion ; and
the caution of the Federal Reserve authorities in treating the
gold imports of 1920–24 as received, as it were, in trust, to be
returned when Europe was in a position to use them again, and
offsetting them by drawing funds from the member banks by
open-market operations, did not prevent, but only deferred,
an inflationary expansion of credit. Assured of ample reserves
in one form or another, the banks expanded credit to their
customers, and, finding industry and trade amply supplied,
passed the surplus on to the stock market to feed the growth of
speculation on securities.

In spite of a dramatic recovery in the spring of 1924 the
French franc had not shared in the progress towards stability
of the £ and German mark. Not only was taxation still insufficient to cover expenditure ; a more serious weakness was
the difficulty of renewing 50,000 million of notes and short-
term bonds, issued to finance reconstruction, as recurrently
they matured. In April 1925 an attempt to end the difficulty
involved the Bank of France in concealed advances to the
Government in excess of the limit imposed by its constitution,
and in exceeding also the legal limit on its note-issue. The
Government responsible fell, but for fifteen months afterwards
no State Administration could be formed that proved able to
deal with the difficulties of the situation. At the beginning of
1926 the franc was worth 3·72 American cents ; by June it had
fallen below 3, and on one day in July dropped almost to 2.

The very intensity of the danger made effective action
possible, as it had done in Germany in 1924, and the franc
changed — almost overnight, though this was not realised for
months — from the weakest of the great currencies to the
strongest in Europe. The weakness of the currency was a
reflection of the weakness of the Government. The crisis made
possible the formation of a Ministry of National Union under

Poincaré.   There was an expert plan available, the work not of foreign experts but of a French committee presided over by a Treasury official, M. Sargent.   That its policy succeeded was due to Poincaré's prestige and resolution, which dispelled the distrust of the Government's finances, and therefore of the franc.   Under the new régime the flight of capital was first stayed and then reversed and the capital which had been exported became a source of strength.   By December 1926 it became possible to stabilise the franc *de facto* at 4 American cents or 122 francs to the £.

The Sargent Committee had recommended that the Bank of France be given power to buy securities and foreign exchange in the open market, and that notes issued for this purpose should be permitted in excess of the legal maximum.   Using these powers, the Bank was able in the period of *de facto* stabilisation to prevent the franc from rising as the demand for francs rose.   The rate adopted under-valued the franc on a comparison of its purchasing power with other currencies, and helped to create a favourable balance of payments, fortified by the strong reflux of French capital.   Until 1928 the Bank of France bought mainly foreign exchange and accumulated enormous holdings of sterling and dollar bills, bonds and deposits.   When on 25 June 1928 legal stabilisation was substituted for the *de facto* control, the new legislation did not continue the temporary power to buy and sell exchange and gave only a very limited power to deal in securities on the open market; thenceforward the only practicable way of increasing the supply of money in France was by bringing in gold.   The beginnings of this movement, in 1927, and the threat involved in the conversion of French holdings of sterling into gold, constituted perhaps the chief problem of the British monetary authorities from that year until the suspension of the Gold Standard in 1931.

M. Moreau, the new Governor of the Bank of France who advised Poincaré in 1926, approached Norman towards the end of February 1927, to settle an outstanding problem in the relations between the two Banks.   In 1923 the Bank had, under pressure from the Government, extended a credit to the Bank of France.   It originated in a war-time credit of £72 million, on which the French Government found itself unable in 1923 to continue the repayments to which it was pledged.   The Bank was reluctant to give the credit, and insisted, first, that any credit it gave should be a credit to the Bank of France and not to the French Treasury, and, secondly, that it should be secured by the deposit, until repayment, of the £18 million of French gold left against the original credit. The outstanding amount of the credit was £33 million. In February 1927 M. Moreau raised the question of modifying the terms of the credit which he regarded as excessive. The Governor was handicapped in any negotiation by a promise, which the Chancellor (Churchill) had made without consulting the Bank, when negotiating the French debt settlement with Caillaux the previous summer, to press the Bank to modify the terms. The Governor was ready to modify the terms for the Bank of France ; he objected to the benefit going to the French Treasury. M. Moreau insisted that it must, in spite of written assurances in 1923 that it would not ; and offered, if the terms were not modified, to repay the whole of the debt at once. The Governor was surprised but accepted the offer. The pledged gold was not in the Bank's figures and could be returned without affecting the London market.

The general discussion, for which these negotiations pro- vided an opportunity, was renewed on a visit by Norman to Paris in May. The discussion in May is of more interest than the particular occasion of it. M. Moreau published a lively account of it ten years later in the *Revue des Deux Mondes*[1] — a publication of confidential exchanges against which the Bank of England protested, but which was more embarrassing to M. Moreau's successors in the Bank of France than to Norman. As a full and independent account of one of Norman's critical interviews it is worth quoting at length. Norman was anxious to cultivate friendly relations with the new Governor. Moreau, on his side, welcomed an opportunity of explaining the change in French finances which had taken place. They had earlier discussed Germany and America, and now Norman explained fully the position of London and Paris as he saw it.

'You complain', Mr. Norman says, 'that the capital attracted to Paris is too large. . . . I wonder how it could be otherwise, having regard to the ensemble of circumstances which appear to have been expressly evoked to precipitate this avalanche. . . . I

---

[1] See also Émile Moreau : *Souvenirs d'un Gouverneur de la Banque de France* (Paris, 1954).

quite understand your concern, and I share it, my dear Governor. But before trying to dry up the sources of credit abroad, personally I would have examined the position of the demand. All European floating capital is already in Paris. It cannot be stopped from this side. The movement has worn itself out upon reaching the maximum point. As to the influx of American capital, this is inexhaustible, like the water of a well. No external action will stop it. There remains internal action. I have thought about it and here are my conclusions.'

Our position, according to Mr. Norman, may be summarised as follows : a currency secured against any fall and which it can be foreseen may possibly rise : a long-term rate of interest higher than anywhere else in the world in a great country inspiring confidence, with the State too frequently undertaking not to convert its loans for several years : the refusal to borrow abroad or to allow French institutions to borrow abroad, another obstacle to a reduction of the rate of interest : private companies desiring to prevent an inevitable rise in their shares so as not to have to increase their dividends, keeping the price of their shares low, without appearing to take heed of previous experience, whereas abroad people are convinced that there will ultimately be a rise in the price of French securities.

'Is it surprising that in these circumstances you have an influx of capital!' exclaims Mr. Norman. 'Never before have such favourable conditions existed. $6\frac{1}{2}\%$ for life with, in addition, the hope of a premium on the revalorisation of the currency which may be considerable! In these circumstances it is a hopeless task to check the influx of foreign exchange whatever you do. . . .

'If you buy gold in order to cut short the credits for speculation, people will say: "The franc has more gold behind it, it is therefore worth more". If you abolish the law on the export of capital, many Frenchmen will conclude that there is no longer any risk in repatriating and they will bring their money back. If you go so far as to stabilise legally, you will attract nervous capital which has been hesitating up to now, belonging, for example, to many English people. . . .

'In the present circumstances any action becomes an attraction. At all costs let the necessary rise on the Stock Exchange take place as soon as possible. This will stop foreign purchases. At all costs reduce the price of money.'

As immediate measures, Mr. Norman contemplates *a reduction in the discount rate of the Bank of France*, which will act psychologically as a warning: the *modification* — not the repeal — of the law relating to the export of capital, so that the French banks may

Q

return at least foreign exchange abroad, taking advantage for their short-term funds of higher foreign rates than the market rate in Paris : a *declaration*, if not of stabilisation, at least of the firm intention of the Government and the Bank not to abandon at present the franc rate under pressure of the speculative bull movement.

Mr. Norman finally goes on to examine the position of the London market. He explains to us that the London money market is a machine of great precision : the volume of credit is calculated exactly to satisfy the requirements of British economy. It is thus difficult, even dangerous, to reduce the credit at the disposal of the market. Moreover he denies that the speculative operations which we deplore have led to the creation of any fresh funds. Actually, Paris has become so attractive to capital that that deposited in London has been temporarily transferred to France, as it was to Berlin or Brussels when these markets were being put on a sound basis. The Bank of France has thus become the holder of foreign funds in London, for which it is in fact the trustee. There is a concentration of foreign balances in London in the hands of the Bank of France. But nothing has changed in the position of London itself. It is even impossible for the Bank of England to detect the change of holder, the funds of the Bank being invested in the same excellent bills as were the funds of foreigners who have sold their sterling assets. Paris has acquired a power over London, but London has no power over the third parties.

Nevertheless, as soon as Mr. Norman was aware of my worries, he hastened to try and help us. He began to sell paper which he had in his security portfolio in the open market at the rate of $3\frac{13}{16}$ and later of $4\frac{1}{8}$.

As soon as this was noticed the market, which was already anticipating a reduction in the Bank Rate from $4\frac{1}{2}$ to 4%, turned about. It applied the rate desired by the Bank of England. Some people were ruined, but money became tighter, as M. Moreau wished. Mr. Norman does not think that Paris was relieved to any great extent. As he has already said, if the purchases of sterling at the Bank of France have fallen, it is in his view because the tendency to transfer European capital has spent itself.

Nevertheless he is inclined to maintain the market rate at $4\frac{1}{8}\%$. He had even thought of going to $4\frac{1}{4}$ or $4\frac{3}{8}\%$ but he cannot do so without endangering the Treasury, which has a good deal of trouble each Friday in finding subscribers to its Treasury Bills, if the spread between the market and the Bank Rate becomes too narrow.

Should he then raise his official discount rate ? The Governor of the Bank of England indeed thinks seriously that he could not do so at present without provoking a riot.   Paris can force him to do so and take the responsibility, but, however, without this being any relief to the Bank of France.   For himself he does not feel able to take this decision.

It is the condition of British industry which is in fact the tragic feature of the English situation.   Every bank in the Kingdom is heavily committed in the cause of industry.   The percentage of funds immobilised has reached a maximum.   54% of available bank funds have been lent to industry, which cannot do without them even if the rate for money is raised to 10%.   If it were reduced to 2% on the other hand, the banks could not immobilise their funds any further by granting fresh credits.

In these circumstances, it is for the Governor of the Bank of England an imperative duty to take advantage of every opportunity to reduce the burdens of industry : a reduction in the rate cannot increase the volume of credit placed at the disposal of industry, but makes things easier for it.   Inversely, any rise in the rate increases its burden without inducing it to free itself from debt. When one thinks of the suffering, the unemployment and the social repercussions which that means, one is bound to hesitate.

Mr. Norman tells us what is at the back of his mind : perhaps in a few weeks if the position and the psychology of the market have developed, he will be able without exciting the country, the politicians and the Government to go from $4\frac{1}{2}$ to $5\frac{1}{2}\%$, a move upwards as usual by a full point.   But will that offset in the eyes of international capitalists the advantages offered by investments in France ?   He doubts it.

Mr. Norman goes on : at the present time the Bank of France possesses tremendous power over London : it has tried to restrict credit there by having £5·5 million of its balances in the market transferred to the Bank of England.   A letter from M. Moreau has even spoken of raising the amount of these transfers to £20·5 million, but against these transfers £320,000 has been returned to the market by the purchase of gold in the open market.   Has the balance really been taken from the money market ? . . .

Any transfers to the Bank of England designed to convert sterling into gold results not so much in a reduction of credit in the London market as in a fall in the cover for the English note issue, since the Bank of England must put sterling back on the market.   But the Bank of France has enough sterling to enable it to create a situation at any given moment which would endanger the *maintenance of sterling on gold* and delight the enemies of the gold standard. . . .

In a word, Mr. Norman does not wish to raise his discount
rate nor does he appear any more disposed to bring pressure to
bear upon Schacht to cause him to raise the rate of interest in
Berlin, but he is fully conscious that our withdrawals of gold place
sterling in danger.

By way of supplement a couple of remarks, quoted by
Quesnay, an official of the Bank of France present at the first
conversation, indicate the line of the Governor's thoughts.
America, from which he had just returned, was prospering
while Europe was going downhill.   He went on to mention
weaknesses in the American position — the depression in
agriculture, instalment selling, the volume of credit outstanding
— and to state his opinion that its prosperity would come to a
stop before long; and then reverted to 'his favourite theme',
an *entente* of the European peoples, without which Europe's
decline was certain.   His dream was the economic and financial
unification of Europe, for which reason he wishes to bind the
Bank of England closely with the Bank of France, which, with
the assistance of the Reichsbank, could restore Europe without
having recourse to the United States.

The pressure on London culminated in the early months
of 1927.   New York was maintaining a high rate to discourage
stock market speculation.   France was drawing gold to reconstitute its circulation, Germany and other Continental centres
to reconstitute their monetary reserves.   Overseas borrowers,
who traditionally relied on London, such as the Empire Governments, were pressing claims which London bankers and issuing
houses were only too anxious to meet.   The rise of New York
to parity with London as a source of external loans and credits
had proved a great relief and aid to a world in need ; but the
sharing of the burden was not an unmixed relief to London.
Countries that wanted gold for monetary reserves might borrow
in New York but, finding it cheaper to draw gold from London,
could sell the dollars for sterling and take the gold from London.
More important was the compensating attraction which New
York now offered for other countries' balances.   A main source
of the strength of London before 1914 had been that sterling
was the only currency that every other country was ready to
hold, and London the sole centre in which other countries'
reserves and balances were pooled.

Now, unless London and New York functioned as a single interdependent market, the scope for offsetting claims and liabilities and for pooling and distributing the world's savings to meet the world's capital needs was limited. Such an integrated policy had been Norman's and Strong's hope; but neither could ignore domestic claims on his market when they clashed with external demands: and neither could exercise the control over his market — Strong even less than Norman — that such a policy required.

Thus Norman had to watch funds being drawn to New York, by the intrinsic attractions of the dollar and the opportunities of profitable employment of liquid funds, which formerly would have stayed in London. Some of these funds were British funds. Underlying this weakness of London was another domestic but equally fundamental change. Before 1914 sterling's usefulness had been due to the position Britain held as the world's greatest exporter. Other countries now offered alternative sources of supply and the almost automatic connection between British foreign loans and British exports had been weakened. Sterling might be sought to make purchases in other countries, and the final outcome of a series of multilateral exchanges might take the form, not of the purchase of a British export, or even of an increase in a sterling balance held by an overseas bank, but of a demand for gold. The Governor of the Bank of England, therefore, was not in the same position as his predecessors. He retained the instrument of credit policy, and could still protect his currency, if holders showed a tendency to get out of it into other currencies, by making it scarce and dear: but his currency no longer had the unique attractions it formerly possessed.

He was handicapped in another way. He was not even free to use the instrument of monetary policy to correct such a movement. The depressed condition of much British industry and of employment (although due mainly to the long-term effects of the war) would be aggravated by credit restriction, and Ministers could be relied on to draw the Governor's attention to this effect, if he had not been aware of it himself. As his explanation of the British situation to Moreau shows, and frequent references in his letters to Ben Strong and other correspondents confirm, he was fully aware of this effect.

In his difficulties Norman was able to draw on the fund of good-will created by his efforts, ever since he became Governor, to develop co-operation among Central Banks. Their help was limited to technical arrangements in their markets, but these might avail to tide over a temporary strain, seasonal or due to other influences. The year 1927 provided the best example of this co-operation. At the end of the previous year sterling was under pressure; New York was attracting short-term funds which went far to offset America's long-term loans; Germany had ceased to peg the mark on the dollar in August, and now found it cheaper, when the sterling-dollar rate declined, to draw any gold it needed from London rather than New York. Its needs were large since industry was expanding and securing short-term credits and longer loans from America and France. France was now in a position to draw on London, though for the time being she preferred to buy and hold sterling. India was attracting the funds of speculators who hoped for a one-and-fourpenny rupee. Britain was still paying for the long stoppage of the coal industry. Norman visited New York in January, Paris and Berlin at the end of February, and wrote to Strong on March 12:

Generally speaking, 1927 is going to be a barren and disappointing year for Europe. The plans we had vaguely made or thought about a couple of years ago are receding towards the horizon. Stabilisation and reconstruction, which have been the vogue since the League first dealt with Austria, have for the time being passed out of fashion. In greater or less degree this is true as regards Poland, Serbia, Greece, Roumania, Italy and France, and the effect on the Anti-Tariff Conference, planned more or less deliberately by the League for this summer, will I fear be adverse; you cannot of course expect Anti-Tariff changes without exchange stability having been assured. And just as Paris sets the fashion for silk stockings and hats, so has she now set the fashion against stabilisation (and indeed ratification) and in favour of wait and see. This is the third time M. Poincaré has seemed to hold Europe at bay — Cannes, Ruhr and now. If, therefore, we are to continue to enjoy the authority of M. Poincaré, we must wait in patience for stabilisation for perhaps a year. This is the story, though told in less graphic and more impersonal fashion, that I heard in the Bank of France. I repeat it to you as such.

He was doing nothing, he wrote a fortnight later, to hamper foreign loans, except when debts had not been settled; if borrowers were few, it was because they were not up to the standard which bankers required.   Meanwhile, he had been resolutely following a firm rate policy for the last six or eight weeks, which was having an effect on the exchange; but it had not pleased everybody, 'especially those who have no book to keep and a pot of ink for weapon'.   Strong tried to encourage him; it had been a fine thing to get through two years without drawing on New York, and in addition to accumulate huge reserves against the future.   He did not agree with the critics who felt that resumption of gold payments *per se* had restricted British trade, but thought that the imposition of strict control in foreign lending might have had a withering effect on British exports.

Norman had advised the Committee of Treasury in January and again in February that the exchange position made it unwise to lower Bank Rate — though he wished on domestic grounds he could have lowered it.   After his visit to the Continent in March he had the promise of Schacht to give any help in his power to ease London's position, while Moreau's repayment of the Bank of France war-time credit not only brought to an end the 'last important question between the Treasury and Bank arising out of the Reconstruction period', but introduced a habit for friendly co-operation with Paris.   These relations were confirmed by a meeting of the three in Calais on April 3, the immediate purpose of which was to discuss a Central Bank credit for the Bank of Poland.   He reported to the Committee of Treasury on April 20 that foreign purchases of gold had declined; the exchanges were favourable except the dollar, 'which could not easily be affected now by rates in London', and the easing of conditions in London by loans to the market during the French repayment made it impossible to maintain a 5 per cent Bank Rate.   It was reduced to $4\frac{1}{2}$ per cent next day.   These influences were transient and it is doubtful whether the lower rate could have been maintained over the seasonal weakness of sterling in the autumn if no other help had been forthcoming.   Such help did arrive.

The Bank of France was embarrassed by an influx of funds for a very different reason.   Moreau told Norman in May that

he was obliged to buy enormous amounts of foreign exchange
to keep the franc down to 124 to the £ ; his stock of foreign
exchange was already £100 million.   There was a campaign
in the Press and Chamber to let the franc find its own level ;
but stabilisation was not practicable before the new legislative
election in May 1928.

Schacht, though anxious to co-operate, had his own difficulties — as Norman explained to Moreau who criticised Schacht
for not raising his discount rate.   Schacht wrote on 21 May
1927 that, owing to the long-term loans pouring into Germany,
the Reichsbank had to buy devisen and so reduce its security
holdings virtually to nothing.   He had no control of the market ;
the money from loans was largely used in stock exchange
speculation, and the large cash holdings of government departments (the Railway Administration for example) were also
outside his control.   He was driven to reduce his rate to 5 per
cent ; this led first to withdrawal of foreign short money, but
it also stimulated stock exchange speculation in which foreigners
then joined.   He could not raise his rate, so he adopted direct
methods.   He called the bankers together and told them that
their business was dangerous, not only to the mark exchange
but to their own liquidity, and must be cut down.   They published his warning, which gave the market a shock.   Germany
was no longer getting the benefit of the English coal strike and
her exports were down ; but she had to remit foreigners' stock
market profits as well as Dawes annuities ; this she did out of
fresh long-term borrowings.   He would not raise his rate till
the banks' speculative advances were reduced ;   only then
would it have any effect.   Norman accepted his argument but
hoped he could raise his rate soon.   His own position was
difficult because French sales of dollars over London were
depressing the sterling-dollar rate.

The tangle of interlocking difficulties needed more concentrated consultation than Norman's correspondence and
visits to Paris, Brussels and Berlin provided.   Strong relieved
the tension by inviting Norman, Schacht and Moreau to New
York in July.   Moreau could not attend but sent his deputy,
Professor Rist.   The results were seen in a series of effective
measures.   The Reichsbank for the next year took what gold
it bought from New York and not London, lowering its buying

price to the minimum permitted by law when this was necessary
to offset the saving of securing it by buying depreciated sterling
with dollars, and converting this into gold.   The Bank of
France similarly switched its buying of gold to New York for
the time being ; or, when it converted sterling into gold, did
so by transferring it first to the Bank of England and leaving
there, earmarked, the gold into which it was converted.   At
the same time London was relieved of the strain on its dollar
exchange, due to the sale by France of sterling, by the action
of the Federal Reserve Bank of New York, which took over
from the Bank of England the balance of the sterling provided by the Bank of France in settlement of its debt, paying
$60 million for it.

The greatest relief was, however, the lowering of the New
York discount and associated rates at the end of July and beginning of August.   The Governor, in reporting his American
conversations to the Committee of Treasury, had hoped for
this, and for similar action in other centres, so that it would
not be necessary to raise Bank Rate against the autumn drain.
In the event, the autumn was uneventful.   The flow of liquid
funds to New York was reversed ; sterling rose to its highest
point since 1914, and the first substantial shipment of gold from
New York to London since the war was made in December.
The Federal Reserve Bank of New York gave further support
by investing in sterling bills.   Unfortunately Strong's policy of
friendship involved him in domestic controversy ; the Federal
Reserve Bank of Chicago refused to follow New York down in
its rate, and there was some danger of a Congressional inquiry
— the Governor reported this with deep regret to the Committee of Treasury.   London was helped by an agreement
with the Commonwealth Bank of Australia to take over most
of the proceeds of dollar loans they were issuing for their
Government, in exchange for sterling which suited their needs
better.   It would be possible to sell the dollars to the Federal
Reserve Bank if London did not require them, and the
Committee of Treasury gave authority to pay up to $77/10\frac{1}{2}$
for gold. Meanwhile the Bank's dollar holdings expanded,
and had reached nearly $200 million by the end of the
year.

(iii)

The years 1928 and 1929 were dominated by the rising flood
of stock market speculation in New York. In London, however, the full effects were not felt until the second half of 1928.
British trade and employment were better than in any year
since 1920; there was great activity on the Stock Exchange,
and in the new-issue market. The sterling-dollar exchange was
strong until June, and the Bank was able to build up its gold
holdings until the seasonal autumn drain began. In May it
even offered to lend the Federal Reserve Bank of New York
$50 million to assist it in controlling its market, though the offer
was not accepted. There was no embargo on foreign issues,
nor objection even to subscriptions to French funding loans
(though these may have suited London better than French
holdings of sterling deposits and bills). Bank Rate, which had
been reduced from 5 to $4\frac{1}{2}$ per cent in April 1927, was not
changed until 7 February 1929. The Bank was anxious to
assist industry, and therefore in addition to keeping rates lower
than it would have liked, helped to keep the Clearing Banks
liquid. At the same time, current propaganda for 'easy money'
was ignored: when gold reserves rose, their effect was offset
by reducing Banking Securities, so that the volume of credit
varied little over the period.

The current turned in July, when the third rise of the year
in the New York discount rate lifted New York money rates
above London again. The sterling-dollar exchange rate tended
to follow changes in relative money rates and from July onwards
the authorities in London were continually fighting against the
current. The Governor persisted, however, in a policy appropriate to a free gold market. While he neither restricted credit
(which would have embarrassed industry) nor relaxed it (which
would have stimulated stock market speculation) he accepted
the obligations of the Gold Standard. He told Rothschilds in
September that *all* demands for gold for export must be met,
though they should be taken first from gold coming into the
London market and only as a last resort from the Bank of
England, and should be directed to Europe rather than to
New York. He imposed no ban on foreign lending; but he
did use his position to make sure that bankers realised the risks

they were taking.   A few illustrations from his diary may be given.   He had received E. F. Wise [1] and discussed sympathetically his attempts to restore financial relations with Russia, and had seen Krassin [2] when he visited London.   But they could find no way over the obstacle offered by the Russian refusal to recognise the claims of holders of pre-Revolution Russian issues.   He told the head of one of the petroleum companies in November 1927, who reported 'attractive suggestions from the Soviet' :

I say no impediment by H.M. Government to legitimate trade, but wonder if time opportune and if he would be at ease with interests at risk in Russia.

And again, knowing that negotiations between the two Governments over debt recognition had just broken down :

I say too dangerous for any credit risk.

In January, 1928 to the leader of an unofficial trade mission, who called to explain the opportunities for British exporters :

I point out difficulties — Debt position (Stock Exchange, International Committee of Bankers, etc.) — with no advice or promise.

He had to insist on the need of an agreed settlement of outstanding claims before new lending in other cases, for example Romania and Bulgaria ; and insist not only in London but, as we shall see, in Paris.   Even when there was not this obstacle, he felt entitled to draw attention to conditions in borrowing countries which called for caution.   In May 1928 he notes his reply to a financier with large interests in Germany, who had raised the question of prospects there :

I repeat (without names) prophecy made by Stamp and Young separately that there will be no real settlement without a crisis — real, and *sufficiently* real to frighten politicians and public. . . .

Similarly to the London representative of a New York banker, tempted by approaches from Turkey in 1927 :

I give him general position as known to me, and advise him not to waste time and money on seeking such business now.

---

[1] Representing in London the Russian Co-operative Movement.
[2] Representative of the Russian Government.

And on a different project, to the New York banker himself:

> I tell him many facts, of which he was ignorant, and he leaves saying he wants nothing and will do nothing but is satisfied.

He was anxious to secure the co-operation of this banker with his policy of confining loans to Europe so far as possible to issues sponsored and safeguarded by the League of Nations Financial Committee; it was important to have the support of other bankers as well as Morgans. On the other hand, he would not countenance conditions on loans which he regarded as unreasonable; when negotiations had begun over a 'League' loan to Portugal, and he was approached twice by representatives of South African mining houses, who wanted conditions included to safeguard their supply of labour from Mozambique:

> I say loan uncertain, remote and international, therefore impossible include special conditions.

He encouraged a banking house with an old connection with Serbia, while a loan agreement was in abeyance, to send someone to Belgrade:

> As a warming pan . . . to remind them that London still exists, and to prevent the French from having a free field there . . . as a concern of London not merely of the groups concerned.

On the other hand, he was critical of attempts to use short-term credits for long-term purposes: he reported on 31 August 1927 to the Committee of Treasury:

> A credit of £5 million was being arranged to carry or valorise the Brazilian coffee crop for a year. He had opposed the original proposal that the operation should be carried on 90-day bills renewed 3 times; now on a cash basis and he could not oppose. He noted, however,
>
> (1) That banks participating were going outside their proper sphere of operations — after repeated complaints of insufficient funds to meet the legitimate needs of industry:
> (2) That restrictions might come to be necessary to control operations such as those which were an inconvenient strain on the Exchanges, which would not freely be allowed in any other European country and from which this country under post-war conditions seemed to derive no adequate benefit.

In 1928 and 1929, however, long-term overseas issues were not in excess of the United Kingdom surplus on current account with other countries. The real strain came from the attractions of New York for short money. Years earlier Strong had expected this, but had hoped that the accumulations of capital in New York would be turned for the benefit of the whole world. The outpouring of long-term loans from New York had seemed to realise this hope, but the attraction in 1928 was the profits of speculation, not investment. Advances to brokers and on securities reached a record level — for account of out-of-town banks and by non-bank lenders as well as New York banks. The policy of making money easy, adopted in 1927 to help Europe, was gradually discarded. As gold flowed out it was allowed to affect reserves without being fully offset; discount rates were raised in February, May and July, and supported by sales of securities. The result, in addition to reversing the flow of funds and gold to Europe, was some reduction in loans on securities; but loans reported by the Stock Exchange continued to rise, and the call rate on renewals of such credits rose from an average of 4·24 in January to 6·32 in June and 8·60 in December.

Norman's health had been unsatisfactory and he was out of England on a trip to South Africa from the middle of June 1928 for nearly three months. In his absence his Deputy (Cecil Lubbock) reported to New York in August that he was anxious to avoid raising Bank Rate; he would be followed by other countries and there was no revival in trade. He was supporting the sterling exchange by selling dollars; but there were limits to this and he would let gold go rather than raise Bank Rate.

Strong was also away trying to restore his health. In his absence, G. L. Harrison cabled that he would have preferred not to receive gold but did not wish to divert the Bank of England from its policy. The New York discount rate was 'effectively and vigorously' encouraging the banks to reduce borrowings; the Federal Reserve System might ease things in preparation for autumn requirements by buying some securities.

Norman on his return at the beginning of September at once cabled that he assumed that neither wanted to change the rate, but while continuing to sell dollars he would also let gold go to impress the public; he added that his proposals were, however, 'spitting against the wind' if call money in New York continued round 8 per cent. The same day, writing to Schacht to suggest a personal meeting, he said:

6 September 1928

I find that a strange and almost unnecessary position has arisen in New York, which may well threaten the gold holdings of Europe and which may for some time close the New York market to the sale of Foreign Bonds. If the Federal Reserve Bank maintains its official rate at 5% while call money in New York continues 2% or 3% higher, gold must be expected to leave London. We should not at all object to losing gold under these circumstances but I doubt if Strong would be glad to receive it. At the same time, owing to the exchange, gold may flow from London to Germany.

Two letters to Harrison (who had succeeded Strong as Governor) indicate Norman's growing apprehensions:

2 November 1928

First of all, I am willing and anxious to come to New York if I am needed but the particular reason for my coming does not seem to exist now as it did when I wrote to you on the 15th September. Secondly, therefore, let me say that if in accord with Gilbert [1] and in accord with the Geneva Agreement this Reparation Committee is to be set up in the near future, I would like to be here as long as it is sitting. Thirdly, we are trying at this moment to bring about some rationalisation in our textile industry and as this is a difficult and yet important opportunity, I would rather like to stay on this side until the present scheme has been adopted or rejected.

All the same, I mean to come whenever I am particularly wanted and in any case before very long: in fact I have made up a party to come with me.

I hope this long weakness in the dollar-sterling exchange is not going to continue indefinitely: sooner or later it will suck our vitals and though its continuance during this fall, and perhaps for another month or so, may be attributed to the usual harvest and currency requirements, yet if it should continue over the New Year I shall feel it has some real connection with your stock market situation. In this I would include the comparatively small totals of the loans recently issued in New York for Europe.

[1] Parker Gilbert, Agent-General for Reparations.

Europe has to pay large sums to America: a small part of those sums she may still borrow; part she may obtain from a trade balance or other such undefined channel. But she will, I fear, find it more difficult to continue the service of her Loans if your Bond market is dead and all her money is being attracted by the high rates offered so freely in Wall Street.

Harrison did not hold out much hope of a fall in the call rate; he wanted to keep other market rates down, and would do so by open-market operations if necessary, but his reason was to provide trade with its requirements without any stringency. Norman was disappointed, and told Harrison that, if he had wished to draw gold from London, he would have adopted the rates he did. He would go on supplying gold to Germany and selling dollars in New York till the end of the year, but he could not continue this policy indefinitely and would have to raise Bank Rate. Harrison replied, on December 10, that the strain was seasonal and there was no change in tendencies sufficient to justify intervention on his part. Call rate had reached 12 per cent just before he wrote. Norman's growing fears were expressed in a letter to Schacht on December 11:

Looked at broadly, the financial position to-day is strange and disturbing to any Central Banker. In New York, as it seems to me, the Central Bank has ceased to function owing to the extent of speculation on the Stock Exchange: in other words, credit has been divided into two parts, one of which rules at a low rate and covers orthodox trade: the other rules at a high rate and covers unorthodox speculation. This is a distinction which exists in the minds of our friends at the Federal Reserve Bank, but to us, thousands of miles away, it fades and there is only one effective rate — the highest. The result of this condition is that I am continually being forced to support the sterling-dollar exchange lest New York should withdraw gold from here; and really it is surprising that she has not tended to do so more persistently when we remember how great a magnet is a 10% rate of interest. I am very sorry for our dear friend George Harrison, who has become Governor at a most difficult moment, politically as well as financially.

In Paris, in spite of large holdings of devisen, the inevitable expansion of circulation at the end of the year has threatened to force down the proportion, and the Bank of France has therefore

not only earmarked a considerable amount of gold in America but
is also taking from London £2/3,000,000 between now and the end
of the year.

In Berlin, I am puzzled by the conditions. True, Germany
has a general shortage of capital and high rates for long-term
money; but the exchange has been largely in her favour for a
long time past and it is only due to the peculiar conditions in
America (I imagine) that more Loans for account of Germany
have not been issued there during this Autumn. I wonder therefore what the Reichsbank is continuing to gain by accumulating
gold rather than devisen and how am I really helping you by
losing each day £200,000 or more gold which you do not need
and which endangers my position in the near future? In other
words, I am merely a go-between; and after I shall have supplied
Europe with the gold needed for the end of the year and supplied
Germany with the gold that is in process of being taken, it looks
as if a 5½% Bank Rate would be my only remedy. Who will
benefit?

Schacht replied that Germany was borrowing too much and
that he could not secure sufficient control of his money market;
to lower his rate would not affect the inflow of funds which was
coming at that time largely from France.

Norman's rejoinder on December 22 puts Schacht's problems in the perspective of the world's:

I have long been aware of your opinion that Germany is
borrowing too much foreign money and you are to be congratu-
lated on having mainly put an end to such borrowing except
short-term Bank borrowing. I am also aware of the difficulties of
your position which, as you have often told me, lacks that freedom
which you think essential for your successful economic conditions
and your sound Central Banking policy: personally, I have always
thought that you somewhat over-estimated this lack of freedom,
not so much at the difficult moments and periods in each year as
over the period of years which you and I have to consider.

Again, in writing to you I refrained from suggesting any reduction in your Bank Rate — that is not my business — and even
when I hear it discussed I play the part of a listener and no more.

As I see the difficulties of your position, they arise partly from
the altered conditions in New York: partly from the repayment of
short loans to America: partly from large French advances to
your Banks over London and partly, too, from London advances

to your Banks, largely in replacement of American money.   The
result of these conditions is a strong Mark Exchange forcing you
to accumulate either gold or devisen.   Over the past weeks and
months you have chosen to allow gold to accumulate almost daily
in small quantities.   You could not prevent your Bankers from doing
this business any more than I could prevent mine from taking the
honour and glory, if not the profits, of exporting the gold.

When writing to you ten days ago I had it in mind that you
might be willing to give me marks for sterling (or if you like it, to
take sterling for marks) to the extent more or less that gold would
otherwise be taken from London for Germany : in other words,
the Reichsbank would acquire a deferred and profitable claim for
gold instead of an immediate and unprofitable deposit of gold.
And I think that these continual shipments of gold from London
to Berlin have made both your and my positions worse : you have
more gold than you need, while I am in danger of being left with
less than I require. . . .

I will leave you to think over what I have written.   I agree
with you that the present position is largely due to French operations in devisen : but I do not think that those operations would
have had this effect upon you and upon myself had it not been for
the dislocation of the American Money Market.   And while I
agree that the gold standard gives greater satisfaction than the
exchange standard, I do not think that either you or I during
these uncertain years (when capital as well as trade balances is
moving from country to country) can wisely rely on the former
alone : we need a gold standard protected by devisen : otherwise
movements are apt to be too sudden, too severe and too suddenly
effective on markets.

In the New Year Norman had no longer any doubt where
the immediate source of danger to the stability of the world's
monetary relations lay.   On 4 January 1929 he cabled Harrison
as follows :

1. For several months your Bank Rate has stood at 5% while
   Time and Call Money rates have ruled high and are so
   to-day.
2. For several months we have supported Exchange at the
   cost of many dollars besides supplying gold freely to Germany
   and other European centres and earlier to New York.
3. These conditions may be proper during the back end of a
   year but beginning in January Exchange should right itself

R

failing which present unnatural disparity between our rates needs correction in one way or another.

4. You will realise that I have awaited the New Year before again asking your views on a situation which has been in our minds for many weeks.

5. Now however I request your views as to conditions and prospects in order that we may decide whether we should not shortly advance our Bank Rate to $5\frac{1}{2}\%$.

6. If such advance is needful I should prefer not to await any considerable loss of gold to New York before taking action.

Harrison replied that he did not see much hope of a prompt easing of the money situation without a change in speculative sentiment, nor any likelihood of change in rates. Norman replied that he would defer action till February, when a rise in Bank Rate might affect stock market sentiment in New York; the difficulties of his position arose from the differences between the market rates in the two centres, and could be removed only by a liquidation of New York's stock market or a raising of London's Bank Rate. At the same time he decided to go over to New York. He left on January 22 and was back in the Bank on February 16.

Arrived in New York, Norman was at once impressed with the urgency of action. He communicated his impression to his colleagues in London by confidential cables:

4 February 1929

1. In July 1927 System in co-operation with various Central Banks arranged policy facilitating distribution of £80 to £100 million surplus gold.

2. Roughly speaking this gold is now spread over reserves of various Central Banks and apart from fresh gold from South Africa and Russia no important changes have otherwise occurred.

3. But with 1929 come threats of such New York imports as would require high or penal Bank Rates elsewhere as a protection. In other words a scramble for gold is threatened.

4. This threat arises from credit position in United States as shown particularly by abnormal Call and Time Rates which rates appear to be due to Stock Exchange speculation.

5. Harrison wisely ignores speculation as such but for months past has worried about credit position hoping that steady pressure would have been corrective. All in vain. Moment

has come for action which I think must be unexpected and co-operative.

6. Therefore expectation is that Boston and-or Philadelphia will recommend 1% increase in Bank Rate on 6th or 13th. Precise date cannot be settled to-night but would probably be on a Wednesday and all depends upon approval of Washington.

7. Further increases may follow if needed to adjust credit position.

8. It seems useful thus to record position which has suddenly developed.

9. You must therefore choose whether you increase on 7th or 14th and in view of your cables you may perhaps prefer to be forced on 7th. When the time comes you will doubtless make 5½% immediately effective.

10. Regret cannot be more definite.

Harrison agreed that action was necessary, but could not carry the Reserve Board in Washington with him. Norman informed his colleagues:

7 February 1929

1. I still hope one or more Reserve Banks will increase shortly, but Washington visit was so disappointing and unhelpful that no one can prophesy.

2. Instead of stating their decision or policy Board issued notice to newspapers apparently like Mr. Micawber hoping to gain time and avoid a decision.

3. In discussion Stewart [1] and I have throughout ignored credit position here except as affecting international prospects and Bank Rate. We have maintained that

(a) to achieve co-operation amongst Central Banks the international measure of any market should be its Bank Rate:

(b) here international measure is surely Call and Time Rates:

(c) a period of high or penal Bank Rates in Europe in order to defend gold reserves against high Call and Time Rates with relatively low Bank Rates here might indeed prove to be threat to gold standard everywhere.

4. Remember that we sail on Friday evening.

[1] Walter W. Stewart, an Adviser to the Governors, 1928–30. Formerly on the Staff of the Federal Reserve Board.

Without waiting for his return, his colleagues raised Bank Rate on February 7 by a full point to 5½ per cent.

The division of authority in American central banking between the New York Bank in the centre of monetary dealings and stock market speculation and the Reserve Board in the political capital remote from the market was an obstacle to early realisation of the dangers of the stock market boom, and an obstacle to prompt action to meet them.

Throughout the years of expanding trade and rising stock market speculation, the Reserve Board appears to have acted on the theory that it could discriminate between the *uses* to which credit was put by discriminating between the treatment it accorded to different *forms* of credit. It sought to make credit plentiful and cheap for the movement and sale of crops (since agriculture did not share the abounding prosperity of industry) by lowering the charge for acceptance credit. It was reluctant to raise discount and associated rates for fear of checking business activity, which was not unusually great at the beginning of 1929; and, rather than run that risk by raising the cost of credit generally, refused to accept any responsibility for the dangerous condition implied in a call rate for security loans which soared above the discount rate. The fallacy of this theory was demonstrated by events. However credit was expanded, it could not be cut off from the stock market; credit expansion increased the monetary resources of the community without in any way controlling the use of the additional resources.

To Norman, studying American conditions from the point of view of Europe, the need for a drastic tightening of credit in New York until it did affect the stock market was clear. When Harrison telephoned that he was anxious to help London by buying bills there, but could do so only by simultaneously selling securities in New York which he could not do alone, he replied that the real trouble was that rates were too far apart. Indeed, he thought it time to warn European markets. He wrote on February 16 to Revelstoke, who was in Paris with the Young Committee,[1] that he must be prepared for drastic action at an early date, though the Reserve Banks were not all agreed; the Reserve Banks in the East were thinking of 5 or 6

[1] See pp. 266-270.

per cent, and London would have to follow. A few days later
he wrote an identical letter to his friends in the Central Banks
of seven European countries :

21 February 1929

I went to America to pay a visit of courtesy to the new Governor
of the Federal Reserve Bank of New York and to obtain, if possible,
a clearer view of monetary conditions and prospects in the United
States. Actually my visit has had the opposite effect and has left
me with an even deeper feeling of confusion and obscurity, about
which I should like to write to you.

It is scarcely surprising if we in Europe are baffled by the
course of events in America, for I found that those with whom I
spoke in America were not at all clear in their own minds. Their
interpretations differ, and consequently they have had no settled
policy which they could well combine to carry out.

To my mind, the cardinal point in the American position for
six months past has been that the official rates of the Federal
Reserve System have been entirely divorced from the effective
rates which bear upon the foreign exchanges. Although the official
discount rate of the Eastern Reserve Banks has three times been
advanced by $\frac{1}{2}\%$, it remains quite unrepresentative and applies
only to a particular, specialised and restricted market. With time
money at $7\frac{3}{4}\%$ and with call money fluctuating between 6 and
12%, the real strain upon European exchanges has been intense
for many months past. Until the turn of the year we in London
were content to deal with the situation by exceptional and temporary measures, in the hope that within a relatively short time the
American position, if it were not deliberately righted, would perhaps
adjust itself. But this hope has been disappointed, and there could
be no question in the long run of interposing an effective and continuing buffer against the impact of such interest rates as have
been in force in the United States. At this season of the year too,
Europe must expect to be replenishing depleted stocks of dollars in
preparation for the autumn. But those dollars can only now be
obtained in competition with domestic American demands which
are apparently inexhaustible, even though they are only satisfied
at rates of interest far higher than those ruling in the chief monetary
centres on this side.

It seems to me that the gap which exists between the effective
rate of interest in America and the official discount rates both here
and there cannot continue indefinitely. In such a confused and
confusing situation, I would not venture to forecast the means by

which a solution may be found. But I do feel strongly that a complete adjustment by some means or other must somehow come about and will before long impose itself upon us all. The strain to which our monetary system is being exposed will then become manifest to everyone.

To Schacht, Norman wrote on March 12 that he saw no change in the American situation and little reason to anticipate that an increase to 6½ per cent could be avoided; a similar increase in New York (or elsewhere) would make change in London unavoidable. A little later he was still waiting for New York.

The position here, about which I wish to keep you frequently and fully informed, has been somewhat relieved by the addition of this week's market gold to the reserves of the Bank of England. Like you, we are more concerned about external pressure than about the technical position in our own market, though it is possible that a rise of Bank Rate in New York would so affect sentiment in London that our hands might be forced by the reluctance of the market to take three months' bills at present rates of discount. Yet it seems to me that a rise in New York would not really make much difference to the fundamental position which has existed for months past. The effective strain upon the foreign exchanges might be no higher than it has been, and if sterling were immediately to fall, I should suspect that the movement would be shortlived, like the sentimental rise which took place when we raised our Bank Rate to 5½%. If then the intrinsic position remained unchanged we should seek to avoid, or at any rate, to delay, protective action on this side. We should expect to lose gold and within limits we could afford to do so, for there is no fixed minimum reserve that has to be maintained. I take it that you also may choose to part with most of the gold added last year to your reserves, if you judge that the legal minimum proportion of cover should be more nearly approached before you raise your rate.

Moreau also he warned, and Moreau agreed that the centres under pressure must raise their rates, and he would help by keeping the Paris rate down. But Harrison cabled on March 13 that the Federal Reserve Board had again refused to sanction an increase in his rate.

In April the temporary breakdown of the negotiations in Paris over a final settlement of Reparations led to pressure on

the reichsmark.   The Reichsbank was called on to find immense
amounts of foreign exchange.   Schacht suspected Paris of being
the chief source of the pressure — it was not London — but the
French representative on the Reichsbank Council had no
knowledge of any such pressure.   The French attributed the
weakness of the mark to the refusal of the Reichsbank to put up
its rate; but Schacht was sure that raising his rate would be
ineffective.   He preferred other methods of restricting credit,
which were indeed forced on him by the fall in his reserve
against notes to the legal minimum.   Germany had, however,
accumulated sufficient reserves of gold to meet the strain.   In
Europe generally, Norman wrote to Moreau in May, the
exchange position was growing steadily worse, reserves were
falling and high rates in New York persisted; he was expecting
renewed demands for Central Bank credits.   To the Governor
of the Swedish Riksbank he wrote on May 31 that they must
expect to go through the summer with a Federal Reserve Bank
rate out of relation with the effective rate of interest in New
York; which had the worst consequences — it attracted short
funds to New York, while preventing the issue of long-term
foreign loans in that market.   To Harrison he had reported on
May 10 that he had been approached directly by Germany and
Hungary, and indirectly by Denmark and Italy, for credits —
London banks were already giving large credits to Italy.
Europe's real need was for dollars, and any Central Bank credit
would be promptly converted into dollars, transmitting the
borrower's strain to sterling.   Political feeling between France
and Germany and between Italy and Hungary was handicap-
ping European credit; either, therefore, the needed advances
should come from New York, to be repaid by the sale of bonds,
or European banks would have to make the advances and raise
their bank rates to protect themselves — unless the Federal
Reserve Bank was ready to lend to the Banks of England and
France so that they could give the credits.

On June 12 the Governor gave the Committee of Treasury
a general review of the situation as he saw it.   Abroad it was
threatening.   The high rates in New York were attracting
funds, and Europe was being drained of gold: the Gold
Standard was threatened, and domestic conditions in the
United Kingdom were being made difficult.   It was necessary

to consider how much gold to allow to go before raising Bank Rate; it was necessary also to reach some policy on the Floating Debt, the size of which, and the recurrent fear of difficulty in renewing it, had been exercising the Committee for months.

Although the credit and exchange problems of Britain were fundamental in his work, Norman had, throughout the year, been under great pressure of other problems. The difficulties of British industry had been forced on the Bank's attention — they are the subject of a later chapter — and the negotiations over Reparations centred on the Young Committee continued to impose an unusual burden on him. At the end of June he left for his favourite holiday — with old Mrs. Markoe at Bar Harbor on the Maine coast. He may also have felt again the need of personal contact with his friends in New York, and he did see Harrison.

He was back in the Bank on August 5 and gave the Committee of Treasury his impressions of America. The position was worse than in February. The Federal Reserve System was agreed on no definite policy; the Governor of the New York Bank was in favour of raising Bank Rate, but the Board had not agreed. The stock market position dominated everything, and the Federal Reserve Board was unwilling to permit any drastic rates to regain control. There was no certainty, therefore, of the situation being cleared up, and it would be useless to reduce the rate in London. The Committee agreed not to make any change in Bank Rate but, if the gold drain continued, to consider applying for an increase in the Fiduciary Issue. The Governor pointed out that, unless there was a change, especially in France and the United States, part of Europe, including the United Kingdom, might be compelled to abandon the Gold Standard. He asked the Committee to consider the policy to be pursued in that event.

Meanwhile security loans had been rising again in New York since the end of May, non-banking lenders stepping in when the banks limited advances. In June bank credit began to increase rapidly: member banks of the Federal Reserve System put their rates up, and rates on brokers' loans also rose. On August 9, to Norman's surprise, the New York rate was raised after thirteen months at 5 per cent to 6 per cent. He cabled Harrison:

9 August 1929

I await full information.   Your changes in rates have caused
great surprise here but so far have on the whole been well received.
Personally I am delighted that you have established and carried a
definite policy whatever it is and this fact should make you happy.

In fact those fears about the future of the Gold Standard which
I have often expressed to you as resulting from your monetary
conditions are aggravated by political conditions arising out of
consideration of the Young Plan.

Harrison explained that he was delayed by Washington till the
last moment and could not warn him ; whether raising the rate
would accomplish what they had in mind only time would tell,
but to the extent it gave a more effective discount rate and one
more in line with private rates it was a step in the right direction.
There should be no serious reaction abroad because open
market rates influenced the international flow of funds and
these were far above discount rate.   To the member of the
Discount Market who acted as his link with it, Norman
said that the New York rise did not necessarily force up
London's rate — they must have courage ; and explained the
position.

The differences between the European powers at The
Hague over the Young Plan overshadowed markets in August.
The Governor could pursue only a hand-to-mouth policy.   He
told Harrison frankly of his fears for the Gold Standard ;   he
hoped to be free to use Bank Rate again when the Conference
ended ;   meanwhile he sold dollars to prevent gold export, and
so postponed the danger that the market would not take up the
weekly offer of Treasury Bills.   Harrison inquired about a
rumour which had reached New York that a new American
loan was to be raised, on assurances given by Norman to the
Prime Minister (Ramsay MacDonald) that he could prevent
any loss of gold (Harrison was himself inquiring whether a
dollar credit on the lines of the 1925 credits would be helpful).
Norman replied that he never mentioned the subject when he
saw the Prime Minister on his return.   All through August and
September he was losing gold to Germany and France and running down his remaining reserves of dollars.   On September 20
he had to report a domestic shock to credit — the Hatry crisis.
Six days later Bank Rate was raised to 6½ per cent.

In New York the rise in the discount rate had not prevented the stock market from continuing to draw credit from country banks and non-banking sources, and security prices continued to rise. In September they turned downwards, and credits began to be withdrawn. The New York banks, which had exercised restraint in their own lending, expanded their credits to forestall a crisis : but these efforts were inadequate. Prices on the stock market broke precipitously on October 23, to inaugurate the great depression.

The immediate effect of the collapse in New York was to relieve Europe of the strain on its reserves and credit caused by the attraction of New York for speculative funds. In retrospect, it is surprising that the United Kingdom was not forced off the Gold Standard before this relief. Already by the end of 1928 the United Kingdom had barely maintained her gold holdings at the level of 1924, while France had increased hers (in millions of gold dollars) by 544 and Germany by 469. In 1929 the co-operative effort to moderate such movements, organised in 1927, survived but was unequal to the situation. The Governor was left to face a drain on his reserves, first by the attraction of the New York stock market, and then by the automatic pull of the restored Gold Standard in France, when the difficulties of British industry made it impossible for him to use the natural expedient of tightening credit.

Two factors in the management of sterling help to explain the Governor's success in meeting such a strain on the Gold Standard. One was the inflow of newly mined Empire gold, which on the whole he was able to use to meet the demands for gold from the Continent. The other was a provision, which he had had the foresight to make and which was sufficient to tide over the last months of strain. On 22 December 1926, in reporting an offer of gold from the Bank of France, he had raised with the Committee of Treasury the question whether in principle such 'haphazard gold' should not be 'sterilised', with a view to future needs not only of London but of Europe, at any rate so long as the United States was pursuing a similar policy. Gold, however, could be sterilised only by offsetting receipts by the sale of securities in the market, which would attract attention as deflationary. The same purpose would be served by accumulating dollars.

We have already referred more than once to the Bank preferring to sell dollars rather than to part with gold. Norman had in fact begun to buy dollars before the restoration of the Gold Standard. The Bank had been at times embarrassed by proposals from the Government to draw on Issue gold to provide for the service of the war debt to America; there might also be some strain when freedom to export gold was restored. As we have seen, there was no strain; the dollar credits arranged against the possibility were not used; but the Governor continued to buy dollars when sterling was strong — by November 1927 the holding had reached $195 million.

All through the strain of 1928 and 1929 he used these dollars to meet demands which would otherwise have depressed the sterling-dollar exchange and led to the withdrawal of gold for New York. But the sale of dollars, unlike a withdrawal of gold, was not allowed to contract credit in the London market. The dollar securities were held — in the form of dollar deposits in the Federal Reserve Bank and a member bank, U.S. gold certificates and other readily realisable guaranteed securities — among 'Other Securities' in the Bank Return. As they were bought, sterling securities in that category of assets had to be sold to pay for them, and as they were sold, the proceeds were invested in sterling securities. A purchase or sale of dollars was always balanced by a sale or purchase of sterling securities; the market was neither supplied with nor depleted of money; and the total of the Bank's assets, and therefore the credit base, was not affected.

This expedient (the Government was aware of it) was an important innovation. It meant that the Bank had found itself forced to prevent an inflow or outflow of exchange reserves from having the automatic effect on credit which traditionally on the Gold Standard it was expected to have. In effect, the country's exchange reserve had (so far as it took the form of a holding of dollar deposits and securities) been segregated from the country's monetary reserve. That this was necessary was evidence of unforeseen strains after return to the Gold Standard; that it was possible provided a precedent, when the complete separation of exchange reserves from credit base was given an institutional form in the Exchange Equalisation Account four years later.

(iv)

The formal restoration of the Gold Standard by England in 1925 had decided the aim and method, rather than achieved the establishment, of stable international monetary relations. The same is true of the League policy, with which Norman was associated, of reforming the finances of Europe and removing the disturbing influence of Reparations. The former members of the Latin Monetary Union had still to follow Britain and Germany back to legal stabilisation, and the countries of Central and South-Eastern Europe, other than Austria and Hungary, still awaited the opportunity and means of following their example. It was the same with Reparations : the Dawes scheme was avowedly an interim arrangement, securing the most that was possible at the time, but deferring the final assessment of the amount of Reparations. These two tasks continued to absorb a large part of Norman's time and energy.

He had expected more rapid progress than probably was possible. Belgium was the most obvious candidate for stabilisation next, and before the end of 1925 he was hopeful that they would produce a balanced budget on which a stabilisation credit, followed by a long-term loan, could be granted. But New York was more cautious, doubtful of the predicted balance and unwilling to grant a credit until it was certain. At the end of the year he went over to settle the matter by discussion. He found the doubts were due to a new partner in Morgans, Russell Leffingwell ; so he brought Leffingwell back with him to London. He expected that the change of scene would change Leffingwell's opinion, and wrote that at bottom there was little difference between them. In fact the difference remained. Finding Leffingwell lonely in his hotel, he brought him to Thorpe Lodge ; he never used the opportunity to press his own views, and the visit was the beginning of a lifelong friendship and a lifelong admiration on Leffingwell's part of Norman's leadership. But events proved Leffingwell right on the immediate issue. Belgian finances were not yet stabilised ; Strong, who had been 'out of sympathy with the rather austere attitude of my friends' towards Belgium, was presently writing that he was shocked to learn of large uncovered external liabilities which had not been explained ; and the chance of stabilisation was deferred for a year.

Strong's visit to Europe in the late summer and autumn of 1926 provided the opportunity for another attempt. A new and forceful Finance Minister, Francqui, had carried through the domestic reforms which were a necessary basis ; Strong met him in July in Paris, where he had been urging on Poincaré 'a full-dress program like Belgium, reducing the value of the franc and stabilising it promptly'. Francqui told Strong he was now a 'little god' in Belgium and they did everything he told them, but they would begin shooting at him in two or three months and he wanted everything settled before then. On September 14, before Strong returned, there was a discussion in the Bank of England between the Governor, Strong and members of the Morgan firm, which brought to a conclusion a series of investigations and discussions with Francqui and other Belgians, Morgans and the Bank. The bankers were not to extend any credit or make any loan to Belgium unless the Central Banks had first given a credit to the National Bank, the long-term loan should be kept small and used as a reserve, and there should be immediate *de facto* stabilisation of the franc. On October 20 the Governor was able to report to the Committee of Treasury the terms of a credit to Belgium, in which the Federal Reserve Bank of New York, the Bank of France and the Reichsbank participated with the Bank of England. The scheme from the first was successful ; the credit was quickly paid off, and by the following August the National Bank was investing in British Treasury Bills.

French stabilisation, as we have seen, was effected without outside aid. Italy was more difficult, because the Italian position, unlike the French, was intrinsically weak. New York played with ideas of a loan in November 1926 when the Government had consolidated its Floating Debt, but Norman thought the conditions were not suitable. He was for long reluctant to do anything, because Italy did not offer one condition which he had always regarded as essential — an independent Central Bank. But presently he realised that 'in Italy no one is independent', and established friendly relations with the Bank of Italy. In November 1927 its President, Stringher, proposed a visit ; shortly afterwards, Strong was arriving. When Strong arrived, the President came again; and, after eight days of continual discussion, into which first Morgans and then the chief London bankers with an Italian connection were brought, a credit to the Bank of Italy was agreed on December 20. Two days later the Stabilisation Decree was published in Rome.

There remained a number of countries which might, like Belgium and Italy, require a credit but could contribute the main effort of domestic financial stabilisation without external aid : Czechoslovakia which had taken credits from private banks in New York; Denmark which had done the same in London and New York; Finland which had a credit from the Bank of England; Yougoslavia which was negotiating for an international loan with Central Bank support; Norway, Spain. There remained also certain countries in Central and Eastern Europe in which stabilisation lagged, because the impulse of external sponsorship and guidance were needed : Poland and Romania the chief.

Over the latter a rift now appeared between London and Paris, which extended for a short time to the relations between Norman and Strong. It sprang from the restoration of French finances, and the natural ambition of the directors of French policy to use their recovered strength to restore to Paris its traditional prestige and influence. It was to assert this claim, whatever the ostensible pretext, that the Governor of the Bank of France and his colleagues had visited the Bank of England, and received Norman at the Bank of France in 1927 and 1928. The report of these 1927 discussions published ten years later by M. Moreau [1] makes this clear, and it is evidence of the sincerity and value of the understanding between Central Banks that a difference which excited deep-seated political feelings did not interrupt or weaken their regular informal consultation on common interests in the field of credit and international payments.

The difficulties of Poland had long caused concern. New York bankers had been keenly interested and on more than one occasion had discussed loans. In 1926, Kemmerer, the Princeton economist, had been invited to report on the reorganisation of banking in Poland, and Strong visited Europe while

[1] Cf. p. 228.

he was engaged on the inquiry.   After a discussion with Norman
in May 1926 he wrote to Harrison in America :

There are three possible courses—
(1) League action, which Norman favours but admits is
    impossible before the Autumn Meeting of the League and
    then only if there is a satisfactory adjustment of outstand-
    ing disputes at Geneva.   He understands that meanwhile
    the patient may die :
(2) which I favour — expand Kemmerer's mission to include
    English, French, Dutch, Swiss and Swedish representa-
    tion, and, if the Poles can be persuaded, German, for a
    full-dress international inquiry.   Control would be a
    matter for negotiation ; probably an American controller.
    Norman did not object in principle — feasible, overcame
    disadvantages of League plan, but involved setting up an
    organisation which the League had already :
(3) a pure American scheme, built up around Kemmerer's
    report.   With that Norman could not associate himself
    because he did not think an effective control possible
    under it.

The Pilsudski *coup d'état* postponed all the alternatives, and
the next initiative came from the Federal Reserve Bank in New
York with French support.   Norman was unhappy over the
departure from League precedent ; he reported to the Committee of Treasury on 30 March 1927 that the proposals involved a difference of principle with New York on the question
of European reconstruction, on which they might split.   But the
matter was discussed at his meeting with Moreau and Schacht
at Calais, and in the interest of Central Bank co-operation he
did not persist in his objections.   He reported agreement to the
Committee on April 6 ; but he was still uncomfortable, as a
letter to Schacht of April 19 shows :

I do not know what will happen next about this Polish business ;
but the following are my notes of how the matter stood when
Harrison went away a week ago :

1. In principle the importance of stabilising the Polish currency is admitted.
2. If invited by Strong to join in a Rediscount Credit to the
   Bank Polski, I should recommend that the Bank of England

accept the invitation and I understand that Moreau and yourself, respectively, would do the same.

3. The Bank of England is not competent to handle or approve Polish Bills of Exchange.

4. If a Committee is to be set up by the Bank Polski (under Clause VII of Harrison's scheme), I cannot now promise to bring such pressure on any particular person from London as might be needed to induce him to join the Committee. I think it might be especially difficult to find a suitable person — if there were to be no German member of the Committee.

This position was understood both by Harrison and Monnet, but a day or two later M. Rist came to London and rather blamed me for not being more eager to undertake, and indeed to arrange, a Credit for the Bank Polski. I asked him in return why the Bank of France did not do so, to which he answered that such action on their part would be too obviously and openly political. It therefore seems that unless (as I hope) Strong will undertake and arrange invitations for a Central Bank Credit to the Bank Polski, the Polish business on the lines explained to us may not at once be accomplished.

In any event I do not wish to be forced into the position of taking the lead in this business of which I am rather suspicious, in a manner which is not very satisfactory and without precautions which appeared essential, in order to prevent someone else from undertaking the same business on perhaps worse lines. I think you will agree with me?

However, he reported to Committee of Treasury on July 13 that the agreement had been signed for a Central Bank credit for the Bank of Poland for $20 million. Moreover he agreed to renew it a year later, although he did not like its being 'mixed up with private bankers' loans'.

The departure from precedent over Romania was taken much more seriously.

On 22 February 1928 Moreau and Quesnay visited the Bank of England and, in the absence of Norman through illness (he had been confined to his bed for the past ten days and had returned to the Bank for a couple of days before taking to his bed for another week) put to the Deputy Governor (Lubbock) the claims of the Bank of France and Paris to take the lead in a scheme for Romania. The Deputy Governor explained that in London they preferred League sponsorship, and, in answer to the argument that the request for co-operation was 'a test of sincerity and reciprocity', explained that they could not support a scheme till they had seen it. After the interview he cabled Strong:

> Quoting Italian precedent Moreau asked whether we could reciprocate by endorsing any arrangement which may be agreed between you and him.

Strong, replying, welcomed the exchange of views with the Bank of France. He had no commitment to them: but he held that Central Bank co-operation was more important than any particular transaction. A month later he cabled that he had received a scheme from Rist and Quesnay; the Bank of France had agreed with the Romanian programme of stabilisation; Romania had decided not to go to the League, but to ask the Bank of France to assume the responsibility for leadership in arranging a Central Bank credit. He would participate, but this implied no initiative or responsibility for the plan or advice to the Bank of England. Norman recognised that it would be difficult to stand out for the League solution, but, in the absence of joint responsibility by Strong, he would have to examine any plan because other banks would certainly look to him for advice. There was a technical difficulty in the way of London participation; the Romanian Government was in default on an old loan, and the Stock Exchange had removed it from its List. He went to Paris on April 27 and 28, where the matter was discussed again. In the end, he decided that his relations with the Bank of France made it impossible for him to refuse participation in a credit. He wrote to Moreau to this effect with Committee of Treasury approval on May 4:

> In thanking you for the opportunity for discussion and for the mutual understanding which resulted from my recent visit to Paris, I wish you to be assured of my belief first, that such personal contact is not only valuable but essential and, secondly, that the rumours upon which you were led to base certain allegations against certain of my fellow workers and myself were either groundless or inaccurate.
>
> Turning, as promised, to the particular question of Roumania,

s

I must repeat that to my colleagues and to myself it is a continuing disappointment that stabilisation will not be conducted under the auspices of the Financial Committee of the League. None the less, since the Bank of France has after examination definitely decided to proceed alone with a scheme of Roumanian stabilisation, I am able to say that the Bank of England will not in principle refuse to co-operate with the Bank of France. I trust that you will accept this statement as evidence of the great importance which we here attach to Central Bank co-operation and of our ardent desire to work in harmony with yourself.

But having made this statement I am bound to refer to the position of the pre-War Roumanian Bonds to which I alluded during our conversations in Paris. If, however, before the question of definite participation arises, the Committee of our Stock Exchange were to notify me that arrangements had been made whereby the quotation had been (or in due course would be) officially restored, I could then recommend to my colleagues that an invitation to participate in a Central Bank Credit (for a total equivalent of $20 million more or less) should be accepted without reservation, relying in all confidence on the close attention which you have doubtless given to the financial details of the scheme.

A fortnight later Strong came over to France to recuperate on the Riviera. Walter Stewart met him at Cherbourg, Norman joining them the following day. Strong was bitterly resentful of what he regarded as Norman's attempt to make him responsible with the French for the Romanian project, by telling Moreau that the Bank of England would participate only if the Federal Reserve Bank was 'an original and responsible party' as in the case of the Polish credit. He had no intention, he told Stewart, of acting as 'expert adviser' to the Bank of England or 'endorsing' plans of the Bank of France who were quite competent to manage their own affairs. His participation in the Romanian credit was 'a question surely between the Bank of France and ourselves' and he 'would not be jockeyed into a position of forcing Romania to go to the League'. This was clear in the letter he wrote to Moreau, before Moreau approached Norman, a copy of which he was under the impression he had sent to Norman. Stewart pointed out that participation in the credit would be taken by the New York market as justifying a Romanian bond issue, so that he could not escape responsibility; but Strong insisted he was

merely obliging an important associate by agreeing to participate in a small credit. He proceeded to assert the claims of
Paris to a restoration of its pre-war position, and to point out
Norman's folly in straining relations over an unimportant
issue, 'when London was absolutely dependent on the good-
will of the Bank of France for protection against a raid on
its gold'.

When Norman arrived, his note goes on:

He embarrassed me by claiming lack of knowledge and by the
reiteration of principles which I told him plainly were brand new
to us and never heard of. Norman relapsed into reticence, and I
was forced to say that I was telling him everything in mind and
heart with no return. . . .

After lunch I asked what his complaint against the F.R.B. was.
He said no complaints; we were justified in joining with any Bank
of Issue on such business as Roumania. He himself was committed
to a League plan because it would be more impartial than the
Bank of France could be. I said I was not interested. . . .
Roumania was only an incident : the real difficulty was the underlying relations with the Bank of France. Their attitude was correct
and co-operative, but he had no response to make.

The real difficulty may have been the underlying relations
between the two Banks. A week later in the Bank of France
Moreau, while recognising the need for good relations, explained that he wished to re-establish the pre-war status of the
Paris money and investment market and of the Bank of France,
which he was entitled to do and intended to do without permitting the introduction of any political considerations or sub-
mitting to any political coercion. Strong sympathised with
him and said he had always insisted on the inclusion of the
Bank of France in plans for co-operation but explained his own
special relations with Norman and the Bank of England :

Norman was an intimate colleague and associate of mine for
whom I had a deep affection, despite certain personal qualities of
which I heartily disapprove; but for a period of ten years we had
succeeded in maintaining a relationship with the Bank of England
of the utmost friendliness and out of which had developed some of
the most constructive work that had been accomplished in European
restoration : that there had been but one really definite dispute

between us and that had been whether Governor Norman was more obstinate than I or I more obstinate than he.

Norman was exhausted and irritable when he met Strong at Cherbourg — he went away almost immediately for three months to South Africa — and Strong was very ill. Norman was probably resentful of Strong's sudden assumption of the championship of French claims. And discussion was unlikely to resolve differences, when Strong became more eloquent and vehement when his feelings were aroused, while Norman relapsed into complete inarticulateness. As we have seen, Norman had already accepted, and acted on, Strong's argument that co-operation between the Banks was more important than the Romanian incident. The personal difference quickly vanished as misunderstandings were removed and the underlying confidence was restored. Lubbock visited Strong in France, after which Strong noted :

Of course, the difficulty which arose at Cherbourg and which has now been fully explained and, I believe, cleared up, was partly due to my defective memory as to the sequence of events, but was always due partly to the fact that I was never aware, until Lubbock reached Grasse, that it was the French themselves who had proposed that we be brought in as leaders and consequently that the origination of the idea of dragging us in as a *sine qua non* to the Bank of England participation was simply the outgrowth of a proposal of Moreau, rather than a happy thought on the part of the officers of the Bank of England.

Strong wrote a frank letter to Norman and an even more revealing letter to Stewart :

I hate special pleading and do not wish to over-emphasise explanations, but I think you must realise that in the earlier stage of this Roumanian development, for most of the time I was in bed worrying lest I were facing another serious case of pneumonia, and in its last stages I was almost incapacitated from considering anything at all, because of my later illness. You will, I hope, act as my ambassador in clearing up any misunderstanding.

As to points of actual difference between Governor Norman and myself in this Roumanian matter, you and he must understand that no difference of opinion on this or any other matter will be allowed, on my part, to qualify the importance which we attach to intimate and complete confidence between the Bank of England and my own institution, nor can any difference of opinion such as is possible to arise between Governor Norman and me, however sharp it may be, impair my friendship and affection for him.

As to the difference of view in this particular Roumanian matter, it really boils down to one very simple point. For some years past it has been more than current comment in Europe, both in political and banking circles, that Governor Norman desired to establish some sort of dictatorship over the central banks of Europe and that I was collaborating with him in such a program and supporting him. Possibly he and you do not realise the extent to which statements of this sort have come to us. Had we accepted the principle either expressed or certainly implied in the letters of interpretation which he wrote to Governor Moreau immediately subsequent to the interview between Governor Moreau and Deputy Governor Lubbock, it would have been complete confirmation in the minds of the French, whether justly so or not, that these surmises as to his intention and my own were correct.

You can understand my hesitation in expressing this so bluntly to Governor Norman, and I think you can equally understand, better than anyone on this side of the water, how far it has been from my own intention to accept or assent to any such program.

This elaboration of my letter to Governor Norman is inspired by two thoughts. The first is that no one in the Bank of England knows quite so well as you exactly what I have been driving at during the last five years. The other is to make sure that you realise that the responsibility I have personally assumed in initiating and executing a program of co-operation for the purpose of bringing about monetary reorganisation in Europe in the face of some very determined opposition at home was undertaken with no selfish purpose, but rather as an expression of what we believed to be our moral responsibility, and if at this stage it proves to be a failure, the consequences will be too serious for any of us to contemplate.

Norman replied on June 11 :

MY DEAR BEN,

We all make mistakes and I cannot complain if on the two points mentioned your memory was at fault. Indeed I did not want or expect to hear from you on this subject; but no more gracious or kindly letter can I ever expect to receive nor could I more quickly or gladly add such minor slips of your memory to the list of misunderstandings already forgotten.

I write this hurriedly and amid the inevitable pressure of the last day or two of clearing up. I rejoice to have a better account of you. . . . You know full well that I and we all desire nothing more than first of all to see you well again, and then to work with you when you are well. This needs time and patience, but, Old Friend, I fear there is no short cut. Your mill must grind slowly at Grasse while mine will be doing the same on the Atlantic; we may be separated but we need not and will not drift apart. . . . So think no more about Roumania or past remarks or misunderstandings; they are all forgotten and with more affection than ever,

I am, Yours

M. N.

This is the last letter on the file of their correspondence. After Cherbourg they never met again. Strong died on 16 October 1928, in harness.

(v)

Few of those who contributed to the Dawes agreement can have expected that the question of Reparations would be reopened within four years and the Dawes Plan superseded. Admittedly, that Plan was provisional; its authors described it as providing 'a settlement extending in its application for a sufficient time to restore confidence', and 'so framed as to facilitate a final and comprehensive agreement' as soon as possible; but it met the immediate needs of removing Reparation claims from international controversy, and enabling Germany to be fitted into a stable international community. The reopening of the question in 1928 was the outcome of a consilience of circumstances.

The confidence which the Dawes Plan restored had opened the gates to an influx of foreign, mainly American, money, first short and then long-term, through which Berlin exercised the same suction on gold as did the restoration of the French monetary system. The payment of Dawes's annuities involved no strain only because the payment could be made out of foreign borrowings; meanwhile, these borrowings were building up a burden to service them much bigger than the Dawes Loan itself. Parker Gilbert, the Agent-General for Reparations, was alarmed by the symptoms of inflation and extravagance that presently appeared. Already in his report of December 1927 he was insisting on the limitations of the Dawes Plan:

> The very existence of transfer protection . . . tends to save the German public authorities from some of the consequences of their own actions, while . . . the uncertainty as to the total amount of the reparation liabilities inevitably tends everywhere in Germany to diminish the normal incentive to do the things and carry through the reforms that would clearly be in the country's own interests.

Accordingly, he concluded:

> As time goes on, and practical experience accumulates, it becomes always clearer that neither the reparation problem, nor the other problems depending upon it, will be finally solved until Germany has been given a definite task to perform on her own responsibility, without foreign supervision and without transfer protection.

Germany had signed the Locarno Pact, and been admitted to the League of Nations. Her Government was no longer anxious about Reparations, but was deeply concerned over the continued Allied occupation of the Rhineland. The French regarded the Rhineland as a pledge for Reparations; but Poincaré was faced with the problem of ratifying the French debt agreements with Britain and the United States, in which case he would need to be assured for a long time ahead of France's share of Reparations, or of facing a demand in less than a year for the capital repayment of the debts. Reparations annuities could be assured only if they could be 'commercialised', floated on to the investing public, and this was impossible so long as they were subject to interruption whenever exchange difficulties made transfer impossible. At the meeting of the League Council in Geneva in September 1928, Germany brought up the question of the Rhineland, and this brought up the question of Reparations. It was agreed to appoint a committee of experts to report.

Norman was at once brought into consultation. On October 15 Parker Gilbert was at the Bank, discussing with him and officials from the Foreign Office and Treasury names for the committee. The next day Norman saw the Prime Minister (Baldwin) and arranged for him to see Parker Gilbert.

This time Germany was a full member, and the United States also could take part officially, with the approval of the President; J. P. Morgan was in the Bank on the 23rd to discuss the choice of Americans, and again, with Leffingwell on November 12. Owen Young who, as a stop-gap Agent-General in 1925 had charmed Schacht with his 'business experience and friendly manner which from the first moment gave everyone confidence in him so that they opened their minds and hearts', was the first choice; Morgan himself became his colleague. Norman favoured Paris not Berlin, not Schacht and Moreau but Rist, above all Revelstoke and Stamp. He was over in Paris in February, leaving Stewart behind to help Young, and in March, reporting to the Prime Minister and Foreign Office on his return. Revelstoke brought back for examination the scheme for an international bank on March 21, and Addis was continually in touch with the negotiations.

Schacht had been included in the Committee as one of the two German members. On the Committee, Addis reported, 'he bore himself with dignity and moderation'. The German Government were anxious for a settlement but they had to treat Schacht carefully as their most influential expert. The proceedings began with a detailed exposition by him of Germany's position and prospects; they indicated a possible payment, only half the French estimate. Young averted an early break by making the Committee work out the framework of a scheme, into which figures could be fitted later — the division of payments between cash and deliveries, between conditional and unconditional payments, the form of organisation to replace the Transfer Committee, the Agent-General and various Dawes Commissioners. But by April the crucial issue of the amount of Reparations could no longer be deferred.

The Allies formulated their separate claims, which were handed to the Germans. Schacht added them together, showed that the total exceeded the standard Dawes Annuity and left the Committee in triumph. Since the object of the Committee's calculation was to establish a lower figure, which would not need provision for suspension of transfer on exchange grounds, and so could provide the basis for an issue of bonds, Schacht was able to leave it to the Allies' representatives to agree on a practicable figure. The proposal they put forward was rejected by the Germans; with much greater indignation the counter-proposals of Schacht were also rejected — any chance they had was destroyed by the condition attached of purely political territorial concessions.

An interruption of the Committee's work by the sudden death of Revelstoke averted a breakdown. On its resumption the Chairman was able to carry through a compromise; claims were scaled down, an average annuity was agreed of 2050·6 million marks a year for thirty-seven years, followed by such an annuity as would cover the net liability of the recipients on inter-allied debts for another twenty-two years, with provision for postponement up to two years of the larger 'unconditional' part of the annuity. All the controls of German economic life imposed by the Dawes Plan were to be abolished. The German Government would be directly liable for the provision and transfer of the annuities; but a Bank for International Settlements was to be established into which they would be paid and by which they would be distributed. It was hoped that the Bank would be able to 'commercialise' at any rate a part of them and, by encouraging and clearing a large volume of international payments, would lessen the strain which they might impose on the exchanges. An international loan would be issued on the security of the 'unconditional' annuities.

The scheme of an international clearing bank came up early in the Committee's discussions. Norman discussed an early draft with Schacht at the end of February, and a later form with Revelstoke on March 21. While the Governments were still quarrelling over the Committee's proposals at the Hague, he was working on the functions and policy of the Bank with his advisers and Schacht. Such an institution had two attractions for him; in the first place, it might provide the machinery for bringing together and offsetting the demands on the gold reserves of Central Banks, which as things were, tended all to be converted into claims upon London. Secondly, it might provide a place in which the Governors of the Central Banks could meet as a matter of routine, and therefore without attracting the publicity and exciting the rumours that had followed in the past on his efforts to keep in touch with Strong, Schacht and Moreau. Norman could argue that opportunities of offsetting claims on gold were not at present adequately taken, and much unnecessary physical movement of gold took place; but any economy in this respect which the new institution offered was overwhelmed by the precipitous decline in international trade that began in the year it was founded. Its incidental purpose of providing a meeting place remained, and gained rather than lost in value, as the difficulties of depression overtook Europe.

Among the political problems which the Young Committee could not avoid was the distribution of such payments as were made among competing claimants. The proportions had been settled at Spa in 1920; they had to be modified now in order to bring the total within the practical limits of the total of Reparations payments. While there was a reduction in claims all round, the reduction in the British claim was disproportionate. Challenged in Parliament when reports of this came through, the Chancellor, Churchill, made it clear that he would not accept them. His successor, Philip Snowden, when the Committee's report did appear, took up the same position and said that he would defend it at the international Conference on the report, called at The Hague in August.

Snowden achieved an immediate and immense popularity by his stand, and secured the restitution of a part of the amount by which the British share of the German annuities had been reduced. It was a single-handed achievement; it does not appear that he took his advice from either Treasury or Foreign Office, nor even from his chief, the Prime Minister. Norman, back from America just as the Conference began, clearly expected that Snowden would consult him; when he did not, Norman realised that he should keep out of the way. Morgan and Parker Gilbert appealed to him; complaining of Snowden's speeches and threats, they said that His Majesty's Government was isolated, and ran the danger of precipitating a crisis in Germany and at home. Norman asked them what did they suggest; the Prime Minister did not seem to want to see him; there were now (August 9) no Ministers in London; the Treasury officials did not think Snowden wanted him at The Hague (he knew Norman was at his disposal).

The amount at stake was £2½ million, deducted from the British share of the annuities on the ground that it was not required to cover the *current* payments on the British debt to

America.   But Britain had paid altogether £200 million before
the Dawes annuities had begun, and claimed that the annual
cost of this should be included in the British share.   Snowden
recovered four-fifths of this claim.   As soon as the Hague Conference was over, he invited Norman to come down and see
him in his country cottage.   Norman made a note of their long
discussion which is quoted in the next chapter : Reparations
were not mentioned.

CHAPTER VII

THE DEVELOPMENT OF THE BANK
AND ITS METHODS

(i)

THE Bank which Norman joined in 1907 was a different institution, in a different world, from the Bank which he was to govern. Before the war, the Bank asked little of its Directors until they succeeded to the Deputy Governor's and Governor's chairs; and even then, except in a crisis, a Governor need not entirely give up his own business — a senior official in the 'thirties still remembered a pre-war Governor, head of a great wholesale business, receiving his travellers with their samples in the Governor's room. It was a different world, because its balance had not been destroyed by war. The settlement of international payments creates no problem which the various markets are unable to handle, so long as payments balance and currencies are stable. England had an assured surplus on its transactions with the rest of the world, which it put at the disposal of the rest of the world by its loans. The movement of interest-rates linked the country's domestic activity with its external relations. There were fluctuations in trade and employment and recurrent outbursts of speculation and extravagance which provoked a sharp rise in Bank Rate and the related rates; but not on the scale of the inter-war years. The Bank performed its function of providing the Money Market with additional resources in the last resort, and ensuring that the Government had the money it needed. But the part which the financing of the Government played was small by post-war standards: it did not involve the continuous contact between Bank and Treasury which war brought. The simple structure of a permanent staff, recruited at school-leaving age, a part-time Directorate to supervise it, and unspecialised Governors to direct the Bank's business was adequate. It was effectively linked with the functioning organisation of trade and finance by drawing its Directors and Governors from the ranks of merchants and private bankers, by conducting its own commercial banking business through its branches, and by the intimate dependence of the Money Market on its Discount Office.

War ended this peaceful order. Cunliffe, finding the demands on the Bank's services enormously expanded and essential to the war, shouldered the responsibility and met every demand made on the Bank. But he attempted to do so without re-casting the internal organisation of the Bank. He continued to act as an autocrat and, under pressure of events, had not time, nor perhaps inclination, always to explain to his colleagues what he was doing. It was natural for him to act as if the Bank were his own business; but his colleagues were forced to realise that responsibilities were being thrust on them of which they were not aware. Norman, coming in as a volunteer to help the Deputy Governor, had ample experience of the friction caused by unauthorised initiative, however necessary in the circumstances. He was a member of the committee appointed towards the end of the war to revise and regulate the relation of Governor, Court and Committee of Treasury; and, when Cunliffe retired, he was brought to the focus of decision and administration by his election as Deputy Governor.

By the time he succeeded to the Governorship in 1920, the war was over, the Peace Treaties signed, and the post-war boom drawing to its close. It was a world at peace; but for the Bank, a world that had lost the self-regulating characteristics of the world before 1914. The Government's financial needs dominated the money and capital markets. The Gold Standard had been suspended; the exchange value of the pound in dollars had fallen by a third and was fluctuating. On the Continent, apart from the smaller neutral countries, government finances and currencies were in greater disorder. Commercial exchanges were overhung by inter-allied debts and Reparations. New York had replaced London as the chief source of loans and subsidies. Yet the internal structure of the Bank in essentials remained unchanged; it depended still almost wholly on the Governors to initiate policy and to maintain relations with the Treasury and the City. It demanded

their full-time service in administration without giving them
the status and remuneration of full-time officers. And the
City itself, though changing and in places shaken by the war,
was still in organisation and temper little changed.

The change from the Bank of the nineteenth century to the
modern Bank can be traced in the Minutes of the Committee of
Treasury. Though quite as independent by disposition as
Cunliffe, Norman had learned from experience the necessity
of carrying with him, through their representatives on the
Committee, both the Court and the City community outside.
The chief business of the Committee was the report — introduced by the traditional phrase 'The Governor acquainted the
Committee of the following matters' — of the issues that had
arisen, the information that had reached him, the action he had
been forced to take in the week that had elapsed since the last
meeting. For urgent business, if important enough, a special
meeting would be convened, or, if that was not practicable, a
meeting of such members as could be got together. In the
Committee again, he found his chief advisers and helpers,
though there were always in addition one or two of the Clearing
Bank chairmen or general managers and partners in the larger
private banking houses on whose advice he relied. While he
was still Deputy Governor he arranged for a weekly meeting
with the Chairman of the Discount Market Committee, and in
practice he saw successive chairmen of the Stock Exchange
Committee almost as regularly. With one other agency the
Governor of the Bank was forced into continuous and intimate
relations. During the war the work of the Bank as agent of the
Treasury had grown to outweigh all its older functions. After
the war this part of its work lost little of its novel importance,
and the Governor's relations with a succession of senior officers
of the Treasury provided him with friends whom it was his
business to advise, and on whose advice he in turn drew.

The driving force which compelled the Bank and its Governors to assume new and wider responsibilities was the pressure
of problems created by the war. In its own traditional field, it
was faced with the need of assisting houses, whose bills it had
carried in cold storage through the war and a year after, and
who were still unable to meet them. In most cases an extension
of the Bank's advances for another year was sufficient; but

some concerns, whose connections were mainly with Central and Eastern Europe, had to be reconstructed and provided with new capital. Thus the Bank became interested in certain old-established accepting houses which it was necessary to re-organise, and had to take over foreign interests, for example, in the Anglo-Austrian Bank, and through a subsequent reconstruction, the Anglo-International Bank; these incidentally gave the Governor another window on the market. Some of the war-time creations, designed to capture German trade, also claimed the Bank's help, when trade depression revealed the unsound assumptions on which they had been based. The Bank became the agent for the Treasury in dealing with interests in industrial concerns, acquired by the provision of capital to expand the production of munitions or by claims for unpaid war taxes.

War had left the Bank a similar responsibility in the difficulties of one of its own customers, Armstrong Whitworth. Firms specialised to munitions production must be expected to make large profits in war, since they cannot expect to work to capacity in peace. If these war-time profits are creamed off by war-time excess profits taxation, they are likely to emerge from war with expanded equipment and no outlet for even their unexpanded capacity. Armstrong's suffered this fate, and was financed by its banker, the Newcastle Branch of the Bank of England, in its attempt to find new outlets. Other munitions firms, indebted to the Treasury, and handicapped with unwanted productive capacity, were in the same case and, as we shall see, involved the Governor in attempts to reorganise them on behalf of the Government.

The greatest change was, of course, the enormously increased weight of Government financing in the operations of the London market. Treasury Bills became the staple of the Discount Market, the chief short-term investment of banks and a favourite security for foreign holders of sterling. Their issue involved regular contact with the Treasury, and the weekly tender provided the Permanent Secretary (or one of his deputies) with a routine excuse for lunch at the Bank and a discussion of current events with the Governor. The conditions in which the Bank performed its own distinctive task of regulating credit were largely determined by Government financial policy even after the war ended. So long as an excessive amount of Treasury Bills was outstanding, the banks had the means of expanding credit, irrespective of the Central Bank's policy, in periods of commodity speculation like 1924 and 1925, new issue booms like 1928 or stock exchange speculation like 1929, and encouraging an export of capital which the country could not afford.

In the last resort the Governor could control the supply of money in the Money Market by varying Bank Rate — its price in the last resort — and by influencing its amount by sale or purchase of securities; but these instruments, as we have seen, depended in wartime on the co-operation of the Chancellor of the Exchequer, in limiting the Floating Debt and varying Treasury Bill rates to accord with Bank Rate. In effect this co-operation had been secured by the time Norman became Governor. Even then, Bank Rate was a harsh brake to apply, and Norman was continually concerned to secure the immediate objects of monetary policy, the prevention of inflationary developments and the stability of the exchange value of sterling, while meeting all demands of the Treasury for money, with the minimum of shock to, or pressure on, the market. To this end he had to know what was happening — from week to week and, at crises, from hour to hour — who was responsible and what was the underlying position of the various elements in the market. This was the purpose of his weekly talks with the representatives of the Discount houses, with Clearing Bankers and with the Chairman or other representative of the Stock Exchange. Through the Discount Office of the Bank he could follow the current needs and transactions of the discount houses; they had to have accounts with the Bank, and the Bank could regulate their business by the requirements it imposed on bills it would accept for re-discount, or as security for advances. But he sought to supplement this information by regular returns of the position of other firms in the market. Already, as a matter of established practice, members of the Court brought their balance-sheets to the Governor and informed him of any important or novel transaction in which they proposed to engage; this practice Norman extended to accepting houses and discount houses. The information was confidential to himself, the Deputy Governor and the head of the Discount Office. No one doubted that such confidence would be respected, and the information was readily given. If any reluctance was shown, Norman usually knew the reason; of one such interview he noted: 'I probably hold more of his bills than anyone else and more than I am willing to hold without seeing his figures'.

With the same object of ensuring that there was no weakness in the market, he used his influence over the years to strengthen the firms in it. He refused accounts to new firms until they had demonstrated their capacity and adequacy; if the applicants would not wait, they should join an existing firm or acquire one. He encouraged and assisted mergers of smaller firms to make more substantial units. He had the means of disciplining them if he chose. Of one who called to complain of his treatment he noted: 'I explain why I do not take his endorsement (which covers at least twenty times his capital) and he was charged an extra $\frac{1}{2}$ per cent in the Discount Office to establish a principle — but he can always get money on approved security and margin (at *a* rate)'. He pointed out to the manager of a bank operating overseas that he should not appear in the Discount Office both as a large acceptor of bills and as a borrower on his own account; and he recurred again and again in interviews to the need of caution in combining the business of accepting with the business of long-term issuing. His regular meetings with the representatives of the Discount Market also provided an opportunity for suggesting any modification of practice which the credit position called for. Thus in September 1927, when he was taking measures to deal with the pressure on London without raising Bank Rate, he noted after one such meeting: 'I urge them to maintain at all times a private rate of discount (as has been and is done in Paris, Berlin, etc.) irrespective of minor changes in gold holdings and of temporary easy money — say $4\frac{3}{16}$ with Bank Rate $4\frac{1}{2}$ as a minimum less broker's commission. They agree.'

Throughout the 'twenties he was resisting, as an exponent of the unanimous policy of the Committee of Treasury, the tendency for bills to be extended beyond their original basis, the movement of goods, into pure finance bills. Treasury Bills provided more than enough in that line, and he resisted the

T

pressure, now of a Clearing Bank to secure 'approval' of Ship-building Bills, now of an overseas banking house to grant successive renewals of what originated in trade bills to finance the holding of nitrates or coffee or some other commodity. Not until 1930, when the process of repaying and funding Treasury Bills had reduced the supply (outside the holdings of Government Departments and the Bank itself) so far that the market was embarrassed by shortage of bills as a whole, did the Committee relax its rules, to allow finance bills to qualify for rediscount, though earlier the market had at times been short of bills.

Formal representations and the use of specific powers fell far short, however, of explaining the influence which Norman was able to exercise in his market. Like the majority of his predecessors he had been brought up in it and could meet its members on terms of equality of experience. Unlike the majority of his predecessors, the range of his contacts and sources of information was far wider than that of anyone else in the market, so that his information and advice had a unique value. In addition to the information which the members of the Court, especially the members of the Committee of Treasury, brought in, and the routine reports he received from the Discount Market and the Chairman for the time being of the Clearing Banks Committee, he had his personal contact with individual bankers of all categories, with the Stock Exchange and the Government brokers; he had his intimate and continuing contact with the Treasury (the correlative contact of the Treasury with the City through the Bank was similarly novel) and with the outside world. With the new financial centre dominating the world in the 'twenties, New York, he had close personal relations and unique advice from Strong and J. P. Morgan & Co. With the centres of trouble on the Continent he had contact through his relations with Central Bankers and his co-operation with the Financial Committee of the League of Nations in framing and carrying out policies to remedy such troubles. With all Central Banks on the Continent and in the Empire he built up intimate relations. With all this he had a continual stream through his room of visitors from every branch of British economic life and all parts of the world, anxious to communicate their special information to him. Hence, when he sought information from a broker or banker, he was able to give as good as he received. His advice came to be sought, by firms and on projects where there was no formal obligation to seek it, because his advice was valuable and, being based on information which was not common knowledge in the market, often decisive.

Information of one kind it was part of his duty to collect and use — information of difficulties threatening the stability of any bank or banking house. A Central Bank is the money market's lender of last resort; but a great deal more than the offer of credit, when trouble has arrived, is needed to prevent disturbance of credit and of the regular functioning of the market. The difficulties of accepting houses and holders of bills on Central European firms we have noticed; the Governor's advice was essential here, because in the last resort only the Bank would come to the assistance of such firms if they had to be reconstructed. Equally the Governor was informed of any difficulties — though they threatened only loss of profits and not the risk of insolvency — in which the decline and misfortunes of a local industry might have involved a bank heavily dependent on the locality; or the collapse in price of a world staple, involving some new country, might have undermined the position of a British bank operating overseas. In January 1923, on the very day that Norman got back from America from the mission to negotiate the American debt settlement, he was met with the news of the difficulties into which Cox, the Army bankers, had fallen and the need of immediate assistance. Lloyds Bank was willing to take over the liabilities and assets as the outcome of urgent discussions in which the Bank participated, and the arrangement was completed, in essentials, within the week.

The process of amalgamation of deposit banks, while it had created the five great national banks operating over the whole of the country, had still left a number of banks inconveniently, if not dangerously, dependent on areas of depressed industry. The need of strengthening these was one of Norman's constant preoccupations. The obvious expedient of shepherding them into the fold of one or other of the five big banks could not be adopted, because Government and public were suspicious of a further concentration of the business of deposit-banking under only five managements; and Norman himself was distrustful of further concentration. He arranged for a confirmation of the Government's opposition to further amalgamations with the larger banks by answer to a question in Parliament on 7 July 1925, and set himself to 'marry' some of the smaller banks or, if they remained single, to strengthen their position. He resisted the acquisition by the bigger banks of banks operating branches outside the United Kingdom, even more strongly than their acquisition of English banks. Though he sought to prevent such acquisitions, it was not from any lack of interest in the countries in which they operated; he took every opportunity of informing himself on conditions overseas. When an Australian State had quarrelled with an important group of its creditors and found itself unable to borrow in the London market to meet pressing maturities, he remonstrated with its Premier and convinced him that he must meet the reasonable claims of his creditors, while at the same time he worked on the issuing brokers to meet the State's needs as soon as the quarrel had been compromised. When the fall in nitrate prices involved Chile in difficulties, he helped to organise a credit pool in which the assets of the banks and merchants embarrassed by the collapse could be held until they became sound again, or could be replaced, and in the meantime arranged credits to carry them. The great struggle to localise and check the collapse of credit on the Continent in 1931, in which he failed and England was involved, was only the last and most difficult of the actions he had fought — hitherto with success — to remove weaknesses that threatened credit and to maintain the functioning of the London market.

His information was not restricted to banking concerns. For months before the Hatry crisis, callers had been warning him that a dangerous position was being built up. He could do little to prevent the final break, but he asked the firms who consulted him what their commitments were and what security they had, and so limited the area of damage. Similarly he would warn the discount houses against taking too many of the bills of firms which he knew were dangerously straining their credit. All this was within the traditional function of the Governor of the Bank, though none of his predecessors for over a century had faced such a succession of difficulties in the market. By 1928 his attention was being drawn outside the specialised circle of Discount Market and deposit banking to the underlying difficulties of industry and commerce, but this may be deferred till later.

The leading firms on the Stock Exchange, especially the large jobbers, and those which made issues of new capital, had long had accounts with the Bank. Further, the Bank, as the Government's banker and issuer of Government loans, had been an important influence in the capital market, in close contact with the Stock Exchange through the Government brokers. During and after the war the Bank's activities and influence were on an altogether different scale; but the Governor's powers were not personally enlarged. There was no statutory control, by licence or otherwise, of new issues or stock prices between the wars; Norman had to depend on personal effort and influence to ensure that the Government's policy was carried out. His frequent meetings with successive chairmen of the Stock Exchange Committee, among whom he made some of his closest professional friends, and the daily report of the Government brokers, were his chief channels. On the other side he was always looking ahead to gauge the Government's needs and to take any opportunity of funding Floating Debt, converting maturing issues, and — at the end — raising the vast sums which were required. Similarly the Comptroller-General of the National Debt Office would warn him of his requirements and discuss the ways of meeting them.

We have seen how, without any power of forbidding them, he imposed some regulation on new issues for foreign account. Only his personal influence, based on intimate contacts with all the houses making such issues and backed by the value of his knowledge and advice and — in the last resort — his power of tightening credit generally, kept within bounds the natural tendency of an organisation like the London new-issue market, which had grown up and was organised for meeting the needs of overseas borrowers, to meet the urgent and apparently limitless demands of their traditional clients. These same houses could help him by their contacts with New York to shift some of the pressure to lend from London to America; and their knowledge and resources could be used to support the Reconstruction loans to Europe, and later the reorganisation loans to British industry, for which preference was essential. Similarly, he drilled the issuers of Municipal and Dominion loans and Trustee loans generally to get them into an orderly programme, adjusted to the need of the Government to make its issues, and to co-operate in making the terms of each issue fit in with the general credit policy of the country. This secured, he always gave all the advice and help he could ; if he could not do more, he could occasionally point out that his advice had been worth something. To a belated request for a £10 million loan on which he had suggested action months earlier, 'I say it is absurd not to have come months ago and made loans larger' ; and to a Dominion, 'They did not take my advice which would have meant 4½ per cent at 99; now they must pay 5 per cent with less good prospects'. He would not discriminate between houses, refusing to recommend an issuer to a foreign government and telling them to consult their own bankers ; on the other hand, he felt justified in warning a Dominion Central Bank, as *their* banker, that a new issuing house they thought of using was of uncertain credit standing and 'piratical' habits.

(ii)

The state of the world compelled the Governors of Central Banks to reach out to other capitals in the attempt to restore order ; Norman took the lead and made the greatest contribution to this policy, and the form it took was due to him. From the time he first met Ben Strong in 1916 it is clear that he foresaw the need of international economic co-operation and began to prepare for it, and he found in Strong an ally who shared his views. By May 1917, when Cunliffe was still Governor, the two Banks had agreed on the methods of formal co-operation, to be put into operation when mutually convenient. The heads of the agreement provided for either to open an account with the other, New York acting also for such of the other eleven Federal Reserve Banks as wished to join : they would buy and hold bills for each other, making themselves responsible for payment at maturity : they would earmark and set aside gold for each other : and exchange information on credit matters and financial conditions.

The agreement envisaged that the Federal Reserve Bank of

New York would eventually reach an arrangement on similar lines with the Bank of France : and it was hoped that a similar system of mutual and exclusive banking services would in time be generalised with all other Central Banks. For this it was necessary to define a Central Bank ; as we have seen, one of the obstacles to convening the conference proposed by the Genoa financial resolutions was the difficulty of deciding what institutions to invite. What Norman and Strong regarded as essential was embodied in a later memorandum :

CENTRAL BANKS

March 1921

A Central Bank should not compete with other Banks for general business.

A Central Bank should not take monies at interest on its own account nor accept Bills of Exchange.

A Central Bank should have no Branch outside its own country.

A Central Bank should not engage in a general Exchange business on its own account with any other country.

A Central Bank should be independent but should do all its own Government's business — directly or indirectly — including Gold and Currency.

A Central Bank should be the Banker of all other Banks in its own country and should assist them to develop its business and economic resources.

A Central Bank should protect its own Traders from the rapacity of other Banks in its own country.

A Central Bank should act as the settling agent for Clearing House balances arising between the Banks of its own country, and to the widest extent practicable.

A Central Bank should handle domestic collections for its members and so regulate the domestic exchanges.

A Central Bank should have power to examine Banks which come to the Central Bank for credits and assistance.

A Central Bank may have an Agency in another country.

That Agency should either be in its own name or should be the Central Bank of the other country : in the former case it should do all its Banking and all kindred business with the Central Bank of the other country.

And should co-operate in practice and principle with the Central Bank of the other country.

And should receive the most favoured treatment and information from the Central Bank of the other country.

And should do the Banking and kindred business of its Principal's Government in the other country.

The reality of which these statements were only a framework and aspiration was worked out during the financial reconstruction of Central Europe. The Bank of England proceeded to disengage itself from all business that might compete with the commercial banks. The branches, it was decided, should not resume their discount business. The West End Branch was ultimately sold to the Royal Bank of Scotland. Some accounts had to be carried on; but new accounts were restricted normally to members of the Discount Market, a limited number of stockbrokers and other firms essential to the working of the capital market; though the Bank could still be appealed to in the last resort by an important firm in any branch of industry, commerce or finance, if its needs could not be met by the commercial banks.

The network of relations with other centres was the creation of Norman himself. He used every opportunity to bring other Central Bankers to London, and to visit them himself. He encouraged them to visit one another, and drew them in to the co-operative schemes for reconstruction and stabilisation in which he and Strong took the lead. He had three reasons, he wrote, for his visit to America in 1921: 'to pay our respects to the Board in Washington; to point out the needs of the world for treatment and consideration on international lines; to support and strengthen your position by returning your visits and standing behind you as regards the rest'. He told the Governors of the banks in Holland and Belgium that they should help the Reichsbank; at the same time he was pressing the German Government, when it appealed to London for capital, to give the Reichsbank the independence proper to a Central Bank. He extracted from Beneš, then Prime Minister, a promise to establish a Central Bank in the place of the existing Banking Office of the Czechoslovakian Treasury. He hoped, with Strong's approbation, to use the co-operation of Central Banks to control the uneconomic movement across the exchanges of funds provided by Reparations payments and war debt settlements. He welcomed the resolutions of the Brussels and, still more, the Genoa Conference as a recognition of the place of Central Banks.

On 8 July 1925 the Committee of Treasury passed the following resolution :

For the purpose of record the Committee affirmed their acceptance and support of those Resolutions of the Financial Commission of the Genoa Conference which affect Banks of Issue, by which Resolutions the Bank have in recent years been guided and by giving effect to which it is hoped that general co-operation and exclusive relations between Central Banks may in due course be promoted.

And he looked outside Europe and North America to the other States of the Empire. In asking the Committee of Treasury in November 1920 to approve the release of a senior official [1] to become the first Governor of the South African Reserve Bank, he described its establishment 'as a matter of supreme importance to the Empire, to this country and to the Bank of England', and almost equally important that its policy and methods should accord with those of the Bank of England. He reminded the Committee that Central Bank deposits were essential to London. All through the 'twenties he was pressing the Governments of India and Australia to convert the Imperial Bank of India and the Commonwealth Bank of Australia into Central Banks, by curtailing their commercial business and putting them in a position to regulate banking conditions generally : and he assisted them with expert advisers, help in choosing staff and such facilities as he could offer in London. At the end of 1934 he provided the Bank of Canada with one of his most senior officials [2] as its first Deputy Governor. With all these new and reorganised institutions he arranged a regular system of mutual visits and exchange of information.

At the same time, he sought to maintain links with the political world which the League of Nations gave. We have seen how he clung to the sponsorship of the Financial Committee of the League in his dispute with Moreau in 1928, and even allowed the difference to disturb his relations with Ben Strong. A weakness of the League from his point of view was

[1] W. H. Clegg, the Chief Accountant. Director of the Bank of England, 1932–37.

[2] J. A. C. Osborne, Secretary of the Bank.

that the United States was not a member. In April 1927 he
had written to Strong:

After several talks with Monnet, I am wondering whether the
Financial Committee of the League could not turn itself around
somehow and join hands with some of your people, and from a
changed and wider angle, do much useful work. For reconstruction
needs an outside body of some sort, which can continue for many
years to exercise a wide and impartial authority behind anything
the Central Banks can do.

After Sir Otto Niemeyer left the Treasury for the Bank in
August 1927 one of the first tasks which he undertook was to
visit New York and discuss this possibility. But nothing came
of it.

Some of these activities took Norman into the field of the
Foreign Office. His efforts to restore economic life in Central
Europe, to clear war debts out of the way of international co-
operation, to settle Reparations in a way that made German
economic recovery possible, and to extend the benefits of stable
currencies and balanced budgets to all the disorganised countries of Europe, though economic and often technical in character, had all a political element in which the Foreign Office was
interested. Austen Chamberlain, Foreign Secretary in the
Baldwin Government of 1924 to 1929, had been a friend ever
since they worked together in dealing with the results of war-
time inflation. With Baldwin himself he had formed a closer
friendship, and often called on him in Downing Street and
stayed with him at Chequers. But he preferred to deal exclusively with the Treasury. He never approached the Foreign
Office except on their invitation, and preferred to leave it to
the Treasury to decide in any matter that involved foreign
policy what other consultations were necessary. An illustration
occurred in 1929 of a Foreign Office approach to him.

Chamberlain wrote to Norman asking if he could consult
him, and sent a memorandum of certain criticisms of British
finance which had come up in Foreign Office correspondence;
he had told the Chancellor of the Exchequer (Churchill) that
he was consulting him. The complaint made was that London
did not make its loans conditional on the placing of orders with
British firms; other countries did, with the result that British

industry was losing ground. Romania was given as an example, where Schröders had offered, after investigation, to negotiate a loan, but had made it conditional on League sponsorship; whereas the French Government had deterred them from applying to the League and supported instead a loan offered by the American house of Blair, and the Bank of England had given the French a free hand. A similar loan was pending in Yugoslavia. The Foreign Office accordingly pressed for conditional loans in place of what they understood to be the present view that proceeds of loans should be spent where costs and prices were lowest. Industry needed this help. There was also a complaint against one of the Clearing Banks giving credit to German customers on cheaper terms than English.

Norman went to the Foreign Office to argue the matter with the plaintiffs. His report to the Committee of Treasury was on the following lines:

There have been increasing complaints by the Foreign Office of the failure of Finance and Industry to keep in touch with the F.O. or with one another: so far as foreign Loans and foreign contracts are concerned, there is no team work: accordingly the French beat us every time

Therefore at A. C.'s invitation, I gave an hour's address at the F.O. last week and was afterwards questioned for an hour. It was very interesting and showed on their part eagerness, friendliness and some superiority; with a complete failure to distinguish post-War from pre-War conditions or the relative position of London or of industry.

Coming at the end to a specific point — Why had France got many orders out of e.g. Poland and Roumania to the exclusion of our industry? I said, first, because of London's loyalty to the League and, second, because of London's unwillingness to make foreign loans except for economic and financial considerations. Would H.M.G. stand behind the Bankers if Loans for political purposes, e.g. Poland and Roumania, were issued here? A. C. said emphatically no:

On this basis team-work with the F.O. falls to the ground, leaving merely information or gossip.

I was also interested to hear the opinion of A. C. and his Staff: that London should jettison the League rather than miss (financially sound) foreign Loans or other business.

He had, however, made it clear that he sympathised with the difficulties of British industry, and would not rule out conditional loans if the competition of other countries compelled it. The underlying difficulty, he noted, was that in the postwar period London no longer took the lead, her banks were already locked up in industry, and industry was too individualistic in practice to pursue a competitive policy. The explanation of the low rate given by the Clearing Bank to a German customer was that it was the charge for a credit to a bank, not the rate German industry would pay. After some further discussion he agreed substantially with a memorandum drawn up by Chamberlain: London should not lose good business in any 'fruitless' endeavour to support the League — Salter agreed with this; priority should still be given to 'League' loans — it was unlikely that there would be money to spare for much more. If the French Government persisted in its tendency to make political loans, the British Government should not make any general protest, which would be useless and at the moment dangerous, but consider the circumstance of each, and be prepared to give diplomatic support to any respectable British interest. The Government could not take the responsibility of urging a loan to the Yugoslav Government on any British house.

Although it was not thought politic to establish departmental relations between the Governor's subordinates and the Foreign Office staff, this did not prevent occasional polite exchanges. In January 1929 Norman wrote:

Last month I conspired with certain bankers — or instigated them — to send a representative to Belgrade. This was in the hope of bringing off sooner or later a stabilisation loan which has already dragged on for many months, and the object of a representative was to remind the Serbs that there was such a place as London and bankers there just as willing to do business as bankers in Paris or elsewhere — all most proper.

He had asked the Foreign Office for an introduction to the British Minister for this representative, and had had no reply. Just two years later, he had himself to reply to a similar complaint: the Minister at Bucharest had heard that the head of the Bank's Overseas Department had been in Bucharest and

had not called on him. Norman explained to the Foreign
Office that his colleague had been on tour, without definite
arrangement as to where and when he would call, solely in
connection with Central Banking contacts. He went on :

As to the general question, we (Bank of England) have made
it a practice to avoid calling at our Embassies or Legations when
any one of us happens to be in any particular Capital, and this
applies to America as well as to Europe. We have done so for the
reason that our attitude is essentially non-political and is concerned solely with Central Banking, that we have no information
to give to Ministers and that we do not expect to receive political
information from any one of them in those Capitals where we may
have dealings with Central Banks.

Our position in this respect is, of course, different from that of,
say, the Bank of France, who, along with their Government, play
a definite and united part on political lines in practically all their
international transactions, directed in every case towards a national
policy.

Our official connection in London is solely with the Treasury,
and the fact that I am endeavouring from time to time to give you
information, in case it should be useful or interesting to you, does
not in the least affect the position of the Bank of England *vis-à-vis*
the Treasury.

Whereas you (the Foreign Office) may be said to follow the
policy of the League we, since its establishment, give the first place
to the B.I.S., and therein lies an additional reason for us to encourage Central Banking and to avoid diplomatic contacts.

At the same time as he was clearing up his relations with
the Foreign Office in 1929, Norman was trying to induce the
Treasury to interest itself in a problem in which the Foreign
Office might have been concerned, though he does not appear
to have raised it with them. He was concerned over what
seemed at the moment 'a more or less deliberate attempt from
America to purchase various undertakings owned and conducted from London'. He encouraged the Chairman of a
great British engineering company who brought to him a proposal to vary the rights attaching to different shares and to
restrict those carrying control to British holders. Harrison in
New York warned him that such proposals would have a considerable effect on British shares in the New York market;

one large bank had informed him that they held $250 million worth of British shares in trust against which they issued certificates; the effect on the sterling-dollar exchange should be considered. But Norman brought together a conference of bankers, stockbrokers and the Treasury to discuss safeguards; he secured agreement that the danger should be watched, but the Treasury feared the political complications of definite action. A couple of years later Norman took action himself, with the approval of the Committee of Treasury, when one of the South African gold-mining houses approached him for advice. Their shares were a favourite investment in Paris: an attempt was being made to secure control by buying up shares, a process facilitated by the fact that many of them were in Bearer form. Eventually Norman purchased enough of the shares to defeat the attempt, selling them years after when the danger was past. The South African gold-mining industry was one of the last that he would have allowed to pass out of British control.

(iii)

Norman was well aware of the limit within which Central Banks could expect to enjoy 'independence'. The Reichsbank back in 1921 illustrated both the need and the possibility:

A Central Bank which is so much dominated by its own Government as to have no independence and initiative, and even no right of protest, is not in a fair position and therefore cannot play its part either within its own country or, still more, alongside other Central Banks. . . .

And again:

. . . No one wishes to give an independent Reichsbank the power of veto over the 'entire financial and economic programme' of the German Government. I think that what we all have in mind is . . . to make unsound finance and dangerous methods difficult though, as the State is Sovereign, not impossible.

And his advice to the President (on 6 February 1922) was consistent with this:

It is now important, I am sure, that *your* position should be strengthened . . . and that hereafter you should make a practice of objecting to any unwise economic measures or to any inflationary policy which your Government may wish to adopt. It matters not whether such policy may seem unavoidable or not. The important point is that the Reichsbank, once independent, should be known to adopt towards its Government the habit of making excessive note issues difficult, of recommending to the utmost limit contraction in respect of Treasury Certificates and other short forms of Government borrowing, and of insisting on a sound financial policy.

The limits set to the power of any Central Bank by Government needs or policy explain the complexity of the credit problem Norman had to face. So far as his personal contacts and the prestige of the Bank reached, he could use their influence; but he was faced with problems which were not susceptible to this treatment, such as the outburst of new issues for the domestic market in 1925 and 1928, or the recurrent flare-up of Stock Exchange speculation. The old-established issuing houses with which he had close contact were not yet, in the 'twenties, interested in and organised for domestic industrial issues. The Governor could exercise a personal influence only when he was consulted or warned. On the day on which Hatry's schemes collapsed, the whole matter was brought into the Governor's room at the Bank, the bankers concerned brought in, co-operation arranged with the Stock Exchange and the crisis reported to the Chancellor of the Exchequer at the Treasury the same evening. But in this field the Central Bank's main instrument was bound to be its control of credit. Norman, though he could keep the price of money up by raising Bank Rate, was handicapped, when he wished to contract its supply to check such speculation, by the simultaneous and conflicting need of ample credit for the restoration of the war-ravaged industry and trade of the country.

This persistent conflict of aims in credit policy constituted Norman's chief problem in his relations with the Treasury; it did not prevent harmonious and effective co-operation. The conflict was inherent in the country's situation — in an inflationary monetary condition, due to the vast expansion of money supply by war inflation, coinciding with an endemic unemployment problem, due to the dislocation by war of old-established firms and industries, affecting large industrial areas of the country. Because it was inherent, it was continually forced on the attention both of Bank and of Treasury, and a credit policy which took account of both needs was worked out in practice. Norman became Governor just as the immediate control of credit conditions was restored to the Bank. During the war and until the spring of 1920, the price of credit was set by the Treasury's rate on Treasury Bills; from 1920 onwards it was set by Bank Rate. But this instrument could not yet be used freely. Answering a question in Parliament on 28 October 1920 on the Brussels Conference, the Chancellor had said the Government was in complete agreement with the recommendation that Banks of Issue should be freed from political pressure. Norman took up the matter with him in a personal letter:

1 November 1920

MY DEAR CHAMBERLAIN,

I happen to have seen your answer to Major Barnes' question last week, as reported on page 1974 of Hansard, and as the intention no doubt was to put you in a hole the answer was an ingenious means of avoiding it. I recognise some of your difficulties and do not want to put you in a hole: hence this personal form of address.

But the Brussels recommendation remains. And when I call to mind your remark to my predecessor (that an independent Rise in the Bank Rate would be an unfriendly act); when I remember our continuing desire for higher rates ever since last July and indeed long before it, and your continuing unwillingness to consent, owing to political reasons . . . I wonder what (in the spirit as well as in the letter) is the meaning of 'political pressure'.

Yours very truly,

M. NORMAN.

Two further changes also were necessary before the Bank's traditional responsibility was restored — the amalgamation of the note-issues and the freeing of gold exports.

So long as the Currency Notes issue was outstanding, the supply of hand-to-hand cash could be increased by a purely political decision, and, short of that, could be increased within the limits of the Treasury decision made on the recommendation of the Cunliffe Committee without any prior augmentation of the gold reserve. Until the two issues were merged in 1928, therefore, the Governor's powers did not match his responsibilities, even after the Gold Standard was restored, and even if we ignore the difficulties arising from an excessive volume of Treasury Bills in the hands of the public.

The return to the Gold Standard did, however, restore the Governor of the Bank effectively to his traditional position. Any weakness in the currency would now once again be reflected in a tendency for gold to flow out and for the credit base to be contracted. This was an argument to which there was no answer, so long as the Government wished to stay on the Gold Standard, except a contraction of credit, either directly by reducing the supply of money, or indirectly by raising its price. Relations with the Treasury remained harmonious, because Norman was aware of the difficulties of industry and made the most sparing use possible of his final sanction, a change in Bank Rate. He used it as a threat, where a threat might deter a transaction which would put a strain on sterling; he offset its internal pressure, when he dare not reduce it, by buying securities and, as in the autumn of 1929, letting his gold reserve down; he used all his influence and ingenuity to meet demands of other centres on London for gold by securing for London the new gold coming from the Empire and any other gold he could come by; he operated a private Bank exchange equalisation fund of dollars; but in the last resort, so long as the country was on the Gold Standard, he depended on the use of Bank Rate. He took care to keep the Treasury, and if necessary the Chancellor, directly informed of the position as he saw it and his intentions. He did not always carry the Chancellor with him. At the meeting of the Committee of Treasury after raising the Bank Rate on Thursday 3 December 1925 he reported that 'he had called at the Treasury late in the evening of December 2, to leave word, as a matter of courtesy, for the Chancellor [Churchill] of a possible increase in Bank Rate. About 11.20 A.M. on Thursday the Chancellor himself had telephoned protesting against the proposed increase and threatening to state in the House of Commons that such increase had been made without his having been consulted and against his wishes. Such action on the part of a Chancellor seemed to be without precedent.'

The traditional relation was reaffirmed by the Chancellor in answer to questions in Parliament in the troubled year 1929. On February 14 he was asked whether any consultation with

U

the Treasury took place before the recent rise in the Bank Rate
was decided on : he replied :

I was, of course, fully informed beforehand. But the assent of
the Chancellor of the Exchequer to movements of the Bank Rate is
not required by law or custom.

Again on February 19 when he was asked :

What is and has been the practice with regard to consultations
by the Governor of the Bank with himself or his Treasury officials
when it is proposed to alter the Bank Rate?

he replied :

Decisions in regard to alterations of the Bank Rate are taken
by the Bank of England on its sole responsibility. It has frequently
been the practice of the Governor in post-war times to inform the
Chancellor when a proposal to alter the Rate is about to be considered.

Churchill's successor, Snowden, was equally definite. Defending, at the Labour Party Conference in October 1929, the
action of the Bank in raising Bank Rate he insisted on the
absolute freedom of the Court of the Bank from Treasury control. The Treasury had no responsibility for the increased
Bank Rate; the matter rested entirely with the Bank. The
increase had been delayed as long as possible; if it had not
taken place, it would have been necessary to abandon the Gold
Standard altogether. It was no use railing against the Bank;
National and State-controlled Central Banks in other countries
had not exempted them from high bank rates.

It may be added that Norman had reported to the Committee of Treasury on 11 September 1929 that the Chancellor
had agreed after discussion to the need of an increase at an early
date, and had asked for further similar discussions on the Bank
and Treasury's policy in financial and exchange questions,
among which the Governor's particular responsibilities would
include changes in Bank Rate and tenders for Treasury Bills.
As a rule, however, there was no clash; that this was so is to
be attributed to the relation of continuous and intimate consultation that he had created.

Before his time a visit by the Governor to the Treasury was

a formal occasion for a specific purpose ; Norman turned it into a regular routine. The traditional rule was for the Governor to be accompanied by the Deputy Governor on any visit to the Treasury ; this rule lapsed because the visits were too frequent and the Governors had too much to do to duplicate each other's functions. He would call on his way home from the Bank after five, or on his way to the Bank about ten, once, twice or even oftener in a week. There was usually some specific business pending and continual questions of persons for business and committee appointments. But if there was no specific business, the Governor's report on the City, its difficulties and prospects, was invaluable to the Treasury, although time-consuming, and the Treasury's advice on the political situation invaluable to the Governor. A comment by Strong on 19 October 1927 on an article by Snowden sums up the position :

The point he makes about co-operation is of the greatest significance, but raises the question which you and I have discussed so frequently. How can such a situation as the present one be met by any scheme or device, automatic or mechanical ? Must it not be dealt with by this species of management and co-operation such as we have been attempting to give it, and, if so, must not people generally trust someone ? And therefore does it not resolve itself to the simple question 'Do they trust us ?'

When the country had left the Gold Standard in 1931 the contact was maintained. The Governor retained his responsibility for conditions in his market ; Government finance determined the climate of credit, and it was important for the Government to be informed of the effect of its financial policy and advised on its aims by an experienced and trustworthy expert in business finance. There was a new link in the responsibility of the Bank to the Treasury for the sterling exchange which was regulated, immediately at any rate, by the Bank's intervention in the market. After 1937 the shadow of war revived the problems of war finance, and revived therefore the need for intimate consultation between the Treasury and the issuer of Government loans, a need which lasted until the end of Norman's tenure of office.

Norman created indeed the same relations with the

Treasury as the older type of private banker maintained with his customers. The oldest and still the fundamental relation between Bank and Treasury was that of banker and customer. That relation imposed on the Bank its traditional reserve in talking about its customers' business, and equally imposed on both Bank and Treasury the need of candour in their confidential relations; no system would work without this. Norman's first object was to give his customer a banker's advice and aid. He was frank in his information and advice, however unpleasant they might be; he was persistent in the advice he thought the situation demanded, however unpopular it made him. But equally he endeavoured to secure for his customer the credit he needed. Week by week he had to ensure that the market would take up the Treasury Bills which he had to offer by tender on behalf of the Government. At longer intervals he had to float loans to fund Treasury Bills or meet maturities or deficits, and ensure that they were fully subscribed. But, like any other banker, he had to warn his customer of any danger to his credit and assist him to shape his policy so as to put the least strain, at the least expense, on his credit. It was in the quite continuous intercourse arising from this relation that the atmosphere was created that made relations harmonious and smooth. And out of this intercourse came Norman's friendship with Bradbury, Warren Fisher, Blackett, Niemeyer, Wilson,[1] Hopkins,[2] Phillips [3] — and a host of junior officials and secretaries.

We have seen how Snowden, a Chancellor with whom the Governor had quickly established a relation of mutual respect and confidence, ignored him during the heated arguments of the Hague Conference in August 1929; but sent for him as soon as he returned to England. The note which Norman made of their talk illustrates well the relations of Bank and Government:

4 September 1929

The Chancellor left a message that he wanted to see the Governor who might be willing to offer to go and see him in the country. This the Governor did.

---

[1] Sir Horace J. Wilson, Permanent Secretary, 1939–42.
[2] Sir Richard Hopkins, Permanent Secretary, 1942–45.
[3] Sir Frederick Phillips, Joint Second Secretary, 1943.

The Chancellor and the Governor talked for about $2\frac{1}{4}$ hours : nearly half the time was taken up by Bank Rate and international interest levels, especially low Rate here compared with New York and Germany. The Chancellor was persistent for a long time that a higher rate was no remedy; would harm trade; would be bitterly criticised; and would itself lead to still higher rates elsewhere and eventually here.

The Chancellor and the Governor then discussed at some length the maturities in 1930 and the high total of Treasury Bills, both of which were threatening and would be expensive : even the 1930 maturities could hardly be prolonged as easily as had been done in earlier years.

The question of the occasional difficulty and danger arising from the necessity of large tenders being essential every Friday was also discussed. The Governor said that if our own people one Friday did not take the Bills, the Chancellor certainly could not expect foreigners to buy Bills or to keep a portfolio here. The Governor added that the joint interest of the Chancellor and himself in these tenders was absolutely and eminently similar — though perhaps not so eminently as regards the Bank Rate — so that they had better go into partnership, each doing his own part of the job in harmony with the other. The Governor said that his was the technical and financial side — the Chancellor's was the political and fiscal side. On this basis the Chancellor must now leave the Bank Rate to the Governor, to which the Chancellor agreed, stipulating that the Governor should see him next week; the Governor promising that he would not this autumn put up the Bank Rate for fun but only when it was essential and, rather than have any fears about a currency shortage, would increase the Fiduciary maximum too soon rather than too late.

The Chancellor and the Governor talked at some length about the B.I.S. which the Governor said frankly seemed to be the only way for Europe out of financial chaos. What was needed was a real understanding among the Central Banks, not from operations and cleverness in the early years of the Bank but from the Governors mixing on neutral soil at a B.I.S. Club. The Chancellor agreed to all this : he wondered whether the Government ought to share at all in the control but seemed inclined to be pro-Central Bank rather than pro-Government. . . .

With regard to Rationalisation (Cotton and Iron and Steel), the Governor described at length what the Bank were trying to do and stated that it was hoped to set up a separate Company to finance it and to have the best possible advice — including the best technical Steel man in the world. This was going to cost a good deal of money some of which must come from the public — it could not all come from the Bank. The Chancellor said he entirely approved the scheme and would himself at all times support it. If the Bank would take up the Worsted trade he would be especially glad to have their heads knocked together : but Rationalisation of industry was not properly his job and he could not do it. It was for Thomas [1] and Graham.[2]

Norman always attached the greatest importance to the Bank's connection with the Treasury. He was cautious in the use of his influence outside the recognised field of the Bank and Treasury's common interest, or even within it. He reported to the Committee of Treasury in November 1929 that Moreau had invited him to come over and discuss the French accumulation of sterling holdings and had added that he should first try to bring about an alteration in the attitude and policy of His Majesty's Government and Treasury; to which he had replied that he wished Moreau well in his attempt to build up again the Paris market, and that, while it was necessary for the Bank of England to keep on friendly terms with the Government and Treasury, he had no power to alter their policy.

He held very strongly that these relations depended on the traditional practice of restricting communication between Bank and Treasury to the Governors. In the 'thirties it became impossible to maintain this restriction. He reported to the Committee of Treasury on 17 September 1930 that the establishment of the Bank for International Settlements had altered the Bank's traditional relations with the Treasury. By receiving and distributing Reparations and war debt payments, the B.I.S. had established a direct connection with the Treasury, and he regretted the change. Again, after the suspension of the Gold Standard, he told the Committee that one result was to accentuate and widen the change which, in his opinion, 'involves the transfer of decisions from the Bank to the Treasury and must inevitably lead to difficulties in the future'. He was right in insisting that the position of the Bank, when the country was off the Gold Standard, was fundamentally changed ; and he had more experience than anyone else had ever had of the

---

[1] J. H. Thomas, Lord Privy Seal and Minister for Employment.
[2] W. Graham, President of the Board of Trade.

difficulties of a Governor of the Bank when the country was off the Gold Standard. How he faced these difficulties again, we shall see in the sequel.

(iv)

For the first half-dozen years of his Governorship Norman had to do his work under the unchanged pre-war constitution and organisation of the Bank. The external changes, which called for corresponding internal reorganisation, were not fully realised and thought out or, so far as they were, were regarded as transient post-war phenomena. It was left to Norman, with the help of the senior officials of the Bank, to meet them by personal efforts, wider in range of responsibility and more prolonged in time than any of his predecessors had had to make. Yet it may be doubted whether the influence and achievement of the Bank were ever greater.

One change had relieved the Governor; as soon as Cunliffe had retired, an office of Comptroller had been created, to which the Chief Cashier was transferred. It was intended that the holder, who was present not only at Court but at meetings of the Committee of Treasury, should relieve the Governors of the cares of routine internal organisation and administration. Norman was fortunate in the three holders [1] of this office, before it was dropped in a wider reorganisation. But all the chief discussions of policy and decisions were canalised through the Governor himself, not only decisions on Bank policy but on the problems of the City generally. Norman was not a practised speaker or advocate and committee-man : his early difficulties in expressing himself persisted. But his knowledge, the range of his experience, the patience with which he would listen and the clarity and courage he showed in decision drew people to him, and enabled him to impose his view without the aid of the advocate's art. And he made sure that, if he took the first impact of the problems that assailed the Bank, he secured the support of, and shared the responsibility with, the Committee of Treasury. His relations with the Court were set out in the

---

[1] Sir J. Gordon Nairne, 1918–25; a Director, 1925–31. Sir Ernest Harvey, 1925–28; a Director, 1928–29; Deputy Governor, 1929–36. C. P. Mahon, 1929–32.

Minutes of the Committee for 6 October 1926. There had been questions raised lately on what information should be given to Court. The Governor pointed out:

(*a*) To Members of Committee of Treasury available information is given regularly, and further particulars will be furnished at request of any member.

(*b*) He believed that the position of other members of Court was still as defined in the Revelstoke Report — 'that they disclaimed any desire to be particularly informed of the more confidential questions which concern the Bank, provided they are satisfied that these responsibilities, which every one of them had assumed on election, are delegated to and safeguarded by an efficient committee over the nomination and election of which the entire Court has control. '

(*c*) He would rely on members of the Committee and the Secretary for suggestions regarding what matters should go to the Court.

He early became aware of the excessive burden on any holder of his office. It was one of the subjects that recurs in his correspondence with Strong. Imploring Strong in May 1922 to take more care of his health (as he did repeatedly not only out of affection, but because Strong was 'uniquely and internationally fitted' for the work they were trying to do together), he admits that he is open to criticism himself but argues 'while I have been learning to use an old machine, you have had the job of making a *new* machine — out of nothing'. But Strong had an important influence on the development of the Bank of England by persuading Norman that an institution of the scale of a Central Bank must be run on his principle — 'organisation'; not Norman's — 'a person'. Norman may not have been wholly convinced, but he realised that, whoever the person in charge, an adequate organisation to support him was essential; or, as Strong put it, 'better so far as the comfort of the boss is concerned'.

The first steps were rudimentary; an experienced official was charged to read the Press and draw the Governor's attention to anything he should note, and to prepare charts illustrating current economic and financial conditions, modelled on those of the Federal Reserve Bank of New York which had excited Norman's interest. The decisive innovation sprang out of the Governor's work in the international field. The pressure of the work was great; equally its novel and exacting character was apparent to the Committee of Treasury. Norman took the initiative by establishing a Central Banking section in the Bank. It was to serve two purposes — to conduct the Bank's relations, business and diplomatic, with other Central Banks; and it was to provide a nursery in which selected members of the junior staff could be trained for the new responsibilities of a Central Bank. He discussed with the Committee the names of experienced bankers, civil servants and officers of the League from among whom an organising and directing head of the section might be found. He probably already had in mind the reinforcing of the Bank by the introduction of several recruits of this calibre in a new capacity, officials on a level with the Comptroller or full-time Executive Directors. The appointment actually made, in 1926, was H. A. Siepmann,[1] a former Treasury official who, after some experience in private banking, had assisted Blackett when he was Finance Member of the Council in India, and then held the post of Adviser to the National Bank of Hungary. It was this section which organised relations with other Central Banks and the systematic selection and training of staff for the new Bank which Norman was creating. To justify his innovation to the Committee of Treasury, Norman appointed a Committee as soon as the new section was working to report on the Conduct of Foreign Business.

The Committee reported in December 1926, generally approving the arrangements that had been made and rather widening their scope. Initially the section had been subdivided on a geographical (or language) principle: the Committee proposed that this sharp division should be abolished. The non-committal title 'Adviser' had been adopted for the position to which Siepmann had been appointed; it had the advantage that it was outside the existing staff-hierarchy, making it possible to go outside the ordinary field and method of appointment without obstructing normal promotion to existing offices. The Committee recommended the appointment of a second Adviser.

[1] Director of the Bank of England, 1945–54.

They also suggested a closer integration of the section's work with the Chief Cashier's Office, where banking was involved, and with the Secretary's Department, so far as correspondence was concerned. Perhaps the most significant — and, in view of the growth of the Governor's personal activities and responsibilities by this time, surprising — paragraph in the report was this :

We consider that the Governor should be provided with an efficient secretary who should be of sufficient experience and standing to be of real assistance to him. He should have free access to correspondence and cables, and be able to communicate on lesser matters with heads of departments and so relieve the Governor of unnecessary detail. He should not be changed until the position was a bar to definite further promotion.

The Governor had had private secretaries before, but usually junior officials who did not stay long ; the Committee had to recommend that his secretary should open all letters to the Governor. The first tenant of the reorganised office of Private Secretary, E. H. D. Skinner, was taken from the infant Central Banking section.

Norman had been concerned with his position ever since his first year of office. The discussion, when it began, turned almost wholly on the *term* for which individual Governors should serve, and only incidentally on the nature and extent of their work. All through the exacting years of financial reconstruction Norman had been conscious of the need of continuity in the office of Governor, but had never been sure that his own term would be extended.

The whole Court of Directors, including the Governor and Deputy Governor, came up for re-election annually, at a General Court held in March or April : and it was the custom to announce in the previous autumn the names to be proposed for Governor and Deputy Governor. Although the tradition of two years as Deputy Governor and two years as Governor had been broken for Cunliffe during the war, the exceptions to it throughout the long history of the Bank were so rare that to abandon it deliberately must have seemed a great step into the unknown. Every autumn, in response to anxious inquiries, Norman wrote a personal letter (from Thorpe Lodge) to Ben Strong as soon as he could report that he would still be Governor next year.   In 1921 he wrote on June 22 :

I have now been placed in the saddle until (say) April 1st 1922 and the future will not be even considered until November 1921 — in accordance with long custom.   But I am driven to regard it as very probable that, given health, arrangements will be made next November for me to continue for another year, till April 1923.

The following March he wrote that he could not answer Strong's question about the following year : elections were for a year only, and his forthcoming re-election for a third year was in breach of custom.   He went on :

What will happen after that I have not the least idea, but I must confess that there is no understudy at the present time ready and qualified to step into the gap.   It is difficult for me to find out about this question, perhaps more so than anyone else ;   and opinion among the Directors . . . naturally has not crystallised.

When a year later the time came to decide, Norman was again continued.   His Deputy Governor, H. A. Trotter, who had served exceptionally for three years, was compelled by the needs of his own business to retire ; he wrote to Strong that he hoped Norman would go on as Governor as long as possible, no one could fill his place, and there was no one for whom he could have had the same admiration and something more.   Norman himself wrote:

I continue as Governor (and my doing so may raise some criticism, as it will be my fourth year and people prefer the Rotation; but how swap horses just now ?).   Lubbock becomes Deputy Governor . . . clever, industrious, and charming as you will remember.   But he will have to begin at the bottom to learn in detail about the Market, Stock Exchange, Foreign Exchanges and generally the technical side.

Lubbock served the traditional two years as Deputy Governor and was succeeded in April 1925 by Sir Alan Anderson [1] who 'like Lubbock does not seem to have the training but is a

[1] Director of the Bank of England, 1918–46.   Deputy Governor, 1925–26.

masterful, strong man who becomes Deputy Governor more from duty than pleasure'.   He went on:

Thus I continue for another year from April — perhaps two. They are still holding on to the traditional two-year Governorship to which I am considered to be an exception.   We hope to return, as soon as world conditions allow us to dispense with me.   I hope that things work out that way; anything else would involve all sorts of difficulties within and without.

A year later, when preparations were being made for April 1926, the issue had become suddenly acute.   Writing to Strong on 12 October 1925 from Thorpe Lodge, Norman complains of the pressure on him, 'partly things without, and partly things within'.   Sir Alan Anderson had to return to his own business and the whole matter was reconsidered by the senior members of the Court in a private meeting in Revelstoke's house.   They confirmed their previous decision to ask Norman to continue till April 1927, but when they turned to the question of a successor they found themselves in a difficulty.   In practice, a Governor now had to give up his own business while in office, but his fees were based on the assumption that he continued to receive his normal income.   In relation to the requirements of the office, the Governor's fees — and also the Deputy Governor's — were 'ridiculously low'; they had not been changed since 1892.   Norman had been consulted and agreed that they were inadequate; but he thought it would be inexpedient to raise them, though they might be adjusted in a general re-organisation in which the higher direction of the Bank as a whole was reviewed.   In any case he insisted, as he did consistently whenever the matter was raised during his tenure of office, that any increase should not apply to him but be deferred until a successor took office.   The question was also discussed whether, 'in view of the desirability of continuing and developing the intimate relations with other Central Banks which had formed so conspicuous and successful a function of the present Governor's administration, an endeavour should be made to arrange that Norman on vacating the Governor's chair should continue to have the principal direction of these foreign relations and the superintendence of a foreign department to be formed to confirm and develop them'.   It was thought that there would be no difficulty in making such arrangements. The provisional conclusion was then reached that, with adequate fees for Governor and Deputy Governor and the continued services of Norman in the conduct of foreign business, a reversion to the system of rotating Governorship was practicable, and names were discussed.

There was a body of opinion that a return to the old system of two-year Governorships was desirable, indeed that a permanent Governor, however necessary continuity and special experience might be, would be dangerous. But those who held this view appreciated the work which they had watched Norman doing and realised his unique fitness for it. Their policy accordingly was to reserve Norman for this work by retaining his services as a special assistant to Governors appointed in the traditional way. At the beginning of 1926 Anderson had cabled Strong for his opinion; Strong's reply is an independent opinion of unique authority:

My own case is rather simple. It means staying on until 1927 — more or less — as events may determine and in the interval deciding upon a successor. With you I am clear that you must decide between a tradition and a person. As infants, we of the F.R. Bank have no tradition and may overvalue it. But I verily believe that your old ways have great advantages if the old conditions are to return — but must be modified if we are about to establish new ways in Central banking. The gold standard permitted and facilitated, possibly necessitated, rotation and all that went with it. A new standard will require more continuity and (if you please) a more technically trained management than the old tradition did. Norman combines qualities and abilities which are singularly adapted to the period of indecision as to what the world has in store for us. My guess is that the period is nearly ended and that another year or two will see the approach to normal monetary policies as we knew them before the war. Therefore is it not worth while to attempt to save the tradition, and if so, how about the person? It may be that by March 1927 the need for any particular person — Norman — will have passed. If not I fear a compromise. A plan to continue him in the rather uncertain indefinite role of advisor or specialist seems likely to deprive him of authority but leaves him with great responsibility. On the other hand — has the Bank the organisation, or can it make one — capable of dealing with highly specialized problems still

unsolved (international) in case they persist and Norman should
retire ?

On the whole my thoughts lean to a clear-cut decision — either
save the tradition or keep the person. The former if the sky is clear
— the latter so long as the clouds are about. The prognosis is for
clear sky — but it may be well to have the umbrella handy. But
this ignores my conviction that in any case you need to strengthen
the bank's staff — and change your ways internally so as to relieve
the office of Governor of a part of his routine.

In reply, Anderson restated the problem :

You say 'we must' choose between a tradition and a person.
I don't want to choose — they're both good and I want them both.
Moreover this tradition has a summary way with people who
don't keep it. It cut off Charles I's head and lost George III some
promising colonies.

I don't think it's senile yet and if we upset it it will upset us
and Parliament will name the next Governor.

As for the 'person' — he is the man for the job — the new and
hard job — so it seems a pity to lose him or to let him kill himself,
and why should we ? Why should we let our best razor blunt
himself by sharpening pencils ? Curiously enough it isn't the work
— the new and difficult work — that fags him. The work for
which he's needed this year next year and the year after doesn't
involve long hours or every day at an office. He could go on doing
that work for years without violating tradition or getting stale.

I should like him to drop the title as soon as may be and all
the daily ties that go with it : it doesn't handicap a partner in
Morgans to have no title nor I believe would M. find his counsel
less regarded because he spoke as the untitled voice of the Bank.

The problem of finding a successor to Anderson as Deputy
Governor was met by inducing Trotter to accept office again
in April 1926.

Thus the members of the Court who would effectively
decide the matter expected to return to the old system in 1927.
They met privately again in July 1926. The proposal that
Norman should continue in office, not as Governor, but in a
special capacity — responsible for foreign business — when
first put to him, was not at first rejected ; writing to Strong he
mentioned it and was obviously considering it. But before the
Committee of Treasury had to decide whom to recommend for

the following year, his mind was made up. At another private
meeting in October, Revelstoke reported his views :

The Governor said that he was persuaded that the suggestion
of a so-called 'Foreign Secretaryship', in connection with which
he should have the direction and control of matters relating to the
'Central Bank' and other foreign developments, was one which it
would be impossible to carry to practical effect: that the domestic
business of the Bank and these foreign responsibilities were so
closely interwoven that any attempt to create a watertight department would result in failure : and that a more general control,
with, so to speak, a partnership in all questions, would be derogatory
to the dignity of the actual occupant of the Chair.

The Governor went on to say that he placed himself unre-
servedly in the hands of his friends and colleagues : that in no
circumstances would he forsake or fail the Bank or the Court : that
he felt that a certain number of his colleagues would prefer an
immediate return to the rotation principle ; and that on the whole
he had thought that another Director should be selected to occupy
his Chair in April next : that he would refuse to accept any invitation to re-occupy the Governor's Chair at that date, unless he were
convinced that any such invitation was the real wish of his colleagues, so that he might continue to be able to rely, not only on
the loyalty of the Court, but also on the genuine goodwill of every
member of it. He wished therefore to give them an absolute option
on his continued services, for them to accept or to reject, as might
seem best to them.

The Directors accepted his decision. They decided to recommend him for re-election as Governor in April 1927, with
Lubbock as his Deputy, with the reservation that this implied
no decision in principle. Shortly afterwards, on November 24,
the Committee of Treasury appointed a special committee,
with the Deputy Governor, Trotter, as Chairman, to report on
'the Bank's Administration in General and the Future of the
Governorship'.

This committee's inquiry and report provide an illuminat-
ing contemporary review of the Governor's work and the problem of his future position. Norman gave evidence twice, once
at the outset of the inquiry, when he gave a description of the
Governor's work ; and again towards the end, when he developed his proposals for meeting the actual situation. His

chief aim was to make clear the increased responsibilities falling on the Governor in the post-war world, in order to make a
case for a larger 'professional' element on the Court and in the
higher staff of the Bank. He could not foresee all the changes
of the next two years; but for that period at least the executive
must be 'whole-time and professional'. This need must be
met without permanent disturbance of the traditional constitu-
tional position of the Court; therefore the large majority of
the Court must be elected as at present, the Committee of
Treasury must continue to be chosen as at present and exercise
its present powers, all authority would still flow by delegation
from the Court, and any change no longer called for could be
discarded — it was even possible that a return would be made
to the traditional system of two-year rotating Governorships.
For the duration of the present pressure, however, Governors
should be appointed for any period up to seven years, 'with
encores'; they should be assisted by not more than eight
whole-time professionals as 'Comptrollers' (the only available
office not limited to one department); these should be eligible
for the Court and for the Governorship; and their fees as
Directors or Governor should be additional to their salary as
Comptrollers. The scheme was an attempt to combine the
'Conseil Général' with the 'Directorium'; the new officials
might be drawn from the existing Court, the staff or from the
ranks of outside experts; they must be eligible for the Court
to give them authority, and to prevent cleavage between
them and the Court. The scheme was offered as a way of
'modernising the machinery of the Bank without altering the
constitution'.

The committee's report was, as might be expected, a compromise. They recognised the need for strengthening the
executive for the current work of the Bank; but refused to
regard it as permanent, or to make permanent changes. The
majority of Central Banks, they pointed out, had permanent
or semi-permanent Governors, appointed or approved by
Government. Any departure from tradition in the direction
of permanency might lead His Majesty's Government to claim
a similar control over the Bank of England. 'We believe', they
said, 'that the world-wide prestige of the Bank of England, and
in particular the assistance which it has been able to give to the

financial reconstruction of Europe since the war is largely due
to the fact that it is a private institution not dependent on
Government — in fact separated from politics. This unique
position would be forfeited if the highest appointments were
associated with the sanction of Government.' It was not easy
to reach a decision, they continued, 'when the Governorship
has been held with general approval by one man for eight
years'. They admitted the force in argument of the need for
training, and therefore for permanency, but the primary functions of the Bank were concerned with the City of London and
the country, not with foreign relations, and permanency of
appointment would attract criticism and offer a stepping-stone
to political interference.

The practical conclusion was that the Bank's organisation
should be improved, with a Comptroller taking a new and
definite responsibility in the Bank for relations with other Central Banks and international financial reconstruction. The
services of Norman as Governor should be secured for the next
three years, to April 1930; but an eventual return to the
system of two-year appointments should remain the Bank's
policy. The Committee of Treasury thanked the authors of
the report, but postponed indefinitely its formal adoption.
They resolved to report to the Court that an eventual return
to the system of rotation was desirable but the time was not
ripe for any recommendation as to the date; meanwhile the
present administration should be continued and the organisation of the Bank further developed.

Norman's policy was thus given a renewed lease. For the
time being, he was to be free to continue to devote his own
services and the Bank's resources to the cause of international
financial reconstruction, and to modify the Bank's organisation
to serve this end. But if his term was lengthened, he was still
tethered. It was what he expected and as much as, at the
moment, he needed; writing to Strong, just before the resolutions of the Committee of Treasury, he said :

The question of our internal arrangements has been gradually
coming to a head — finally by a recommendation from a committee that we return permanently to the old *system* of *rotation*
after a couple more years — during which time I should be expected to make everything ready for the return. In principle this

X

prospect is attractive to our older colleagues who were brought up on rotation and have hardly realised the inwardness and permanence of the gulf between now and 1914. . . . In practice those of us who realise the gulf (or think we do) believe that rotation may be attractive as a prospect but in reality is impossible (at least in our lifetime). So I guess the recommendation will be turned down — after it has somewhat cleared the air — and we shall continue to develop on the present lines . . . *i.e.* with Harvey, Siepmann, Niemeyer, Stewart and so on ; and perhaps with the difference that some of them may become directors. Anyway no changes are likely (in the ordinary course) so far as Lubbock and I are concerned for a couple of years or so.

The issue of principle had been deliberately postponed, but events outside the control of the Committee of Treasury were liable at any moment to bring it up again. It arose in the summer of 1928, as it had arisen three years previously, on the need of finding a new Deputy Governor, when Lubbock was unable to continue. The obvious successor, designated both by personality and experience of the Bank, and by the part he had come to play in the new functions which events were forcing on the Bank, was the Comptroller and former Chief Cashier, Sir Ernest Harvey. The opponents of a permanent Governorship realised the danger ; an official who became Deputy Governor would become a permanent Deputy Governor, and the *de facto* continuity of the Governor's office would be reinforced. When the Committee had to make the formal choice of names to recommend for election as Governor, Norman was asked to give his views fully. His notes summarise the position his own mind had reached, and forecast the course that the actual development of the Bank was to take.

We seem to have been trying to fight against the tide — a tide which is due to the changed position of London and of the Bank since the war. So long as London was dominant throughout the world the rotation system worked well in this country but was not tried in any other. With the passing of that dominance to New York, I do not think it can work well in this country. Central Banking, a more or less managed Currency, innumerable questions of Credit and innumerable problems of Reparations and External and Internal Debts, require a professional in both chairs and a professional without outside interests.

I believe a return to the rotation system next year would bring an end to the present constitution of the Bank . . .

I think it fortunate that we have had several years of political quiet in which to set our house in order by adapting, without changing, old conditions to new needs. I cannot look forward to any date when the rotation system would be safe again as well as wise.

Since I have been allowed special facilities for learning and special experiences and special knowledge, I think it would be a mistake from the Bank's point of view to get rid of me now. But so far as health and peace of mind and leisure and perhaps happiness are concerned, it would suit me. All this I have said to one or two Committees and frequently to the Committee of Treasury.

We were late in building up a body of professionals drawn from outside. We could not draw them from inside because the experience does not exist there. At present they number two permanent and one temporary and work together extremely well. We need two or three more especially with languages and outside experience. At the same time we are trying to build up an expert staff to be ready in from 10 to 15 years, with a knowledge of the problems with which we are now dealing and with a knowledge of languages.

I think we should change the constitution to the extent of allowing a few of these professionals to sit on the Court. It would improve their status. It would permit them to share the responsibilities of the Court; and it is impossible for the Court as a whole to be familiar with the technical questions or with all the business that is going on. I think, too, it will be difficult to recruit the Court indefinitely in the old way — the numbers of candidates are decreasing. . . . If we want to maintain the constitution of the Bank, we can do so partly by modernising the membership of the Court.

On October 2 the Committee of Treasury resolved to continue Norman in office and to accept Harvey as Deputy Governor; they sent the names forward to the Court and they were elected for the year beginning April 1929. Their names were recommended again in November 1929 — for Harvey's second year.

In practice, Norman's views on the future of the Governorship had been accepted; his own tenure of office was indeterminate, and he had secured the appointment of a permanent professional Deputy. But the Committee of Treasury had never yet accepted them in principle. At the end of July 1930, before Harvey was put forward for a third term, Peacock [1] ascertained Norman's views and reported them: he had two aims — to get the idea accepted that the Governor's term of office should be longer and that, therefore, he should be specially selected and give up any idea of maintaining a connection with his own business; and that the succession should be open to officials as well as to members of the Court, though the bias should be in favour of someone with wide financial and industrial experience before coming to the Bank, and not Whitehall experience which was likely to be favoured by any Government.

Just before the time for putting forward names for election, Peacock reported another talk; Norman complained that he had still no knowledge what names it was intended to put forward, and said that it was wrong that no move had been made to find people to replace himself and Harvey; the constitution ought to be altered quickly to relieve the Court of the necessity of filling up vacancies (caused by death or resignation) immediately, when it might be more convenient to have vacancies available, and to enable the Bank to remunerate properly a few full-time Directors; the matter might be taken up with the Macmillan Committee or its Chairman. Peacock had told him that the majority had accepted the idea that there could be no reversion to the two-year system, though a few still clung to it. Many accepted the view that a Governor should serve for seven or ten years, and, therefore, must be trained, and should come to the Bank to become familiar with the work. Most of the Directors still thought that Governors should be drawn from the same class as before, in order to preserve the Bank's connection with finance and industry, but officials should not be excluded. They would like to know his views on his own future, because they would like Harvey to succeed him. He agreed with Norman that they ought always to have two or three possible Governors in training in the Bank.

The outcome was that the names of Norman and Harvey were put forward for re-election. Before their actual election, Norman tried to get the Committee of Treasury to settle the

[1] E. R. Peacock, Director of the Bank of England, 1921–24 and 1929–46. Knighted, 1934.

issue of principle, and, at the same time, meet the criticism from outside of the Bank's constitution. On 7 January 1931 he asked whether they thought it advisable, with the object of avoiding unfriendly recommendations by the Macmillan Committee, for the Bank to offer now :

1. That the appointment of the Governors should be subject to the approval of some outside body or person.
2. That the period of appointment should be five or ten years.
3. That there should be some limitation on the Court's freedom of choice for Directors.
4. That an Advisory Committee composed of representatives of Finance, Commerce and Industry should be set up for purposes of consultation.
5. That the Issue and Banking Departments should be amalgamated.
6. That there should be regular publication of a Report.
7. That there should be a fixed dividend.
8. That the Higher Administration of the Bank should be reorganised.

The Committee were still of opinion that it was unnecessary to take any action. They were, nevertheless, moved by the bare possibility of such changes, and did proceed to commit themselves definitely on the immediate problem of the Governorship. On 15 January 1931 an informal meeting of the Court passed the following resolution, which Cullen communicated to Norman :

Subject to annual election, as required by the Charter, the term of office of the present Governor be regarded as not subject to any definite limitation as to time.

Further, after the formal re-election of Norman and Harvey, another informal meeting passed unanimously the following resolutions on 10 April 1931 :

(a) That the Order of Court of the 30th November 1848, be so amended as to remove the restriction upon the tenure of Office by Governors :
(b) That steps be taken to secure authority to increase the sums available for the remuneration of Governors and Directors.

On April 23 a committee was appointed, with Peacock as Chairman, to consider the Organisation of the Bank, with instructions to give effect to these two resolutions.

The committee's deliberations were interrupted by the financial crisis of the autumn, and it did not report until 23 June 1932. It carried out its instructions as to tenure of office and remuneration of Governors; it recommended also that the Court might nominate Directors to undertake executive duties and receive special remuneration; it recommended that the burden of work falling on the Governors be relieved further by the appointment of additional Advisers, by the creation of a new office of Assistant to the Governors free from Departmental duties, and by relieving Heads of Departments so far as possible of routine duties. At the same time, they sought to retain unchanged the traditional character and outlook of the Bank. While they approved of a wider range of choice for Directors, they repeated the warning of the committee of 1918 that —

the counsel to be afforded by a Director can only be of value if it is the outcome of a continuous appreciation of the atmosphere and of the conditions which rule at the Bank of England, and we consider it essential that invitations . . . should only be extended to those business men whose occupations and interest would permit them to make a constant practice of being present at the Bank, on occasions apart from . . . weekly Court or . . . Committees.

and in the choice of Directors —

the man with City experience should continue to be predominant . . . Governors, like the Members of the Court, should, whenever possible, be chosen from those with practical business experience and only exceptionally from the Officials of the Bank.

On the question of remuneration they reported :

So long as it was the practice for the Governors to be in Office for a period of four years only, and were able even during those four years to devote some of their time to their own affairs, a system of payment which was admittedly nominal and bore no relation to the responsibilities involved was not only possible but tended to enhance the dignity and prestige of the positions. This is no longer the case. We have, therefore, reached the conclusion that the Governors should be remunerated on a scale sufficient to maintain the dignity of their Offices, though not necessarily comparable with the rewards offered in similar positions in Commercial Banking and Industry.

They recommended formally that, except by direction of the Court, no Member of the Court should have any active interest in any other business while occupying either Chair, or receiving special remuneration. Similarly, while approving the principle of appointing full-time Executive Directors, they stated that the long-standing practice by which Members of the Court rendered voluntary service to the Governors as occasion arose was of great value and should be retained; and warned the Court that the appointment of a 'considerable number' of Executive Directors would tend to reduce the influence of other Members of the Court and 'diminish living contact with the commerce and industry of the Country'. They recommended only two such appointments at the moment; other appointments should wait until the effect of the changes proposed had been thoroughly tested. The chief departmental changes proposed were a strengthening of the Overseas and Foreign Department and the creation of a new Establishment Department. While commending the initiative which the Bank had taken in reorganising industry (in which the Chairman himself was particularly interested),[1] the Committee regarded it as a temporary and abnormal function, which did not require any appointments of a permanent character — 'such direct interest in industry does not under normal conditions form part of the functions of Central Banks'. Tradition was confirmed in another recommendation; relations between the Bank and Whitehall should be 'intimate and cordial', but, to avoid misunderstandings, all communication should be through the Governors.

This report ended the long debate on the position and functions of the Governor. The difference between Norman and his colleagues on the Court did not spring from any fundamental divergence over the type of institution the Bank was to be and the place it was to hold in the country. He was a conservative, not a doctrinaire reformer. But he had experience of the challenge of the post-war world earlier than they, and sought to

[1] See Chapter VIII.

adapt the old Bank to its new opportunities. They were now convinced, not by him, but by events, and accepted the conclusions which he had already drawn from events. The new tasks which faced the Bank meant that the administrative development foreseen by the Committee came sooner than they had expected. So did the State control which they — and not less Norman — feared and wished to avoid; but this was part of a larger political movement which no internal Bank policy could have diverted. It may be doubted whether any spontaneous domestic reform would have averted the political change. But, in retrospect, it is to be regretted that Norman was not allowed to unfold before the Macmillan Committee the internal reorganisation and the external adjustments which had been in his mind for years.

It will be convenient to anticipate events, and include in this chapter certain later issues that arose when Norman was re-elected. In October 1931 the Committee of Treasury informed Norman that they were considering the question of Governorship for 1932, they wished to propose him, but were forced to consider the state of his health. His reply was that he wished, before he retired, to see the future organisation of the Bank settled, and wished, therefore, to have the report of the Peacock Committee adopted by the Court, when the new Governor would be elected. He would, therefore, wish to remain Governor until April 1933 — his doctor agreed to his continuing for another year — but he would be unwilling that any further extension should be proposed. He would give his attention to handing over his work to a successor, and would be willing that it should be known that he would retire in April 1933. However, he was asked to accept election again in 1933; he did so, on the condition that he, and also the Deputy Governor, had the option of continuing in 1934 as well. He was assured that, in the absence of unforeseen change of circumstances, and the Committee knew of nothing which would lead them to desire a change, it was assumed that he would continue in office until he announced his wish to retire.

In July 1936 he did announce that he wished to retire; he did not wish to continue after April 1937, but, if it proved impossible to select another candidate that autumn, he asked them to arrange that his term of office ended in the spring of

1938. He was re-elected in April 1937, and raised the matter again in the following July, by offering to approach a possible candidate on behalf of the Committee. The Committee was less anxious about the Governorship, so long as Norman was available, than they had been since he was first continued beyond the traditional two years in 1922. The reasons are given in a letter which Peacock wrote to Norman during the negotiations over the last attempt in 1937 to find a suitable, and agreed, successor :

The Bank stands higher in public esteem to-day than at any time since the war, and what it decides to do will be more readily accepted. . . . If we come to a clear view of what would be best for the Bank and the country, we may go forward with confidence. . . . Further, the Bank as a machine is equipped as never before, and as to all the technique of the business will do its job and take effective care of any Governor. We owe both these things mainly to you. I think you may be too close to it all to realise how our strength and influence have grown and how much old prejudice and rancour have subsided. . . .

By 1938 the danger of war was apparent. Any hope of a return to 'normal' conditions was postponed. Norman was continued year after year until the election of 1944. Then he had barely recovered from a severe illness, and left the decision to his doctors. They forbade another term.

CHAPTER VIII

A CENTRAL BANKER IN INDUSTRY

(i)

THE difficulties of certain industries, expanded by war and as suddenly contracted by peace, have already required our attention. The Bank had early warning of the needs of an ordinary commercial customer of one of its branches, a survivor from the pre-war régime of combining a commercial banking business with the functions of a Central Bank. Sir W. G. Armstrong Whitworth & Company Ltd., the great armament firm of Tyneside and Manchester, had always banked with the Newcastle Branch of the Bank. The Bank had, as a matter of course, financed its expanded war-time activities and, almost equally as a matter of course, financed the new post-war enterprises by which it sought to compensate for the curtailment of armament work. Although it had a wide range of interests in engineering, coal and steel-making, the foundation of its success in the past had lain in its skill and facilities for manufacturing heavy guns and gun-mountings, armour plate and warships, for which governments were the only customers, and His Majesty's Government overwhelmingly the most important. When it is remembered that a capital ship provides as much employment as forty large tramp-steamers, employment largely specialised and highly skilled, the problem created for Armstrongs by the Government's agreement at the Washington Naval Conference to build no more capital ships can be realised.

The chief directions in which the firm sought new outlets were in commercial shipbuilding, locomotive building and in the creation of a large new pulp and paper manufacture in Newfoundland. Since the scale of the firm's operations was large, the Bank's advances were large — far larger than any advance made to assist a banking customer in its own special field. Early in his Governorship, Norman had had to draw the

Committee of Treasury's attention to Armstrongs' borrowings, when there was agreement that the Bank could not withdraw its support. Unfortunately the new enterprises, so far from compensating for the losses on the firm's traditional work, added to them. With the decline in shipping after the short post-war boom, Armstrongs' customers, mainly foreign shipowners, found it difficult to pay for the ships they had ordered, and Armstrongs found itself left with unsaleable ships or unrealisable ship-mortgages. The Newfoundland enterprise was more unfortunate. The scale on which it proved necessary to develop it, and the time that elapsed before completion, exhausted Armstrongs' resources and credits long before it could be brought into economic operation. By October 1924 Norman had to report to the Committee that their advances were now £1,450,000, to which had to be added an overdraft of £780,000, mainly on account of the Newfoundland project. An issue of £2,500,000 debentures was made in December 1924, of which the Bank took £500,000, but this gave only transient relief. By June 1925 the Bank's credits had reached £2,600,000. Either reconstruction or a receivership was necessary, and on the advice of Peacock, Norman brought in Frater Taylor, a Scotsman with much experience both of company reorganisation and of Canada, to investigate and report.

Taylor's report was the first step in a constructive approach to the problems raised by Armstrongs. It revealed a position which could only be made worse by mere extension of bank credit. The firm had already taken £3½ million; another £1 million (quickly raised to £1½ million) would be required to complete the Newfoundland scheme, and perhaps £½ million to meet further requirements in England. He feared a receivership might have to be considered, but for the moment this step was postponed. The Committee of Treasury agreed on August 28 that the Bank must continue to meet the inevitable expenses in Newfoundland and at home, but should require the approval of Armstrongs' accountants for any advance and the Bank's own approval for any new commitment by the firm. The firm should also pay no dividend except on the 1st Preference Shares, and restrict the Civil Engineering Department which was responsible for the largest losses at home. At the end of the year the Bank took a charge on £3 million unissued debentures, and required the Newfoundland Company to create £1 million of debentures as security for its loan. In June 1926 Taylor was given a temporary appointment to look after Armstrongs. A committee of creditors was formed (and met in the Bank) to co-operate with the Bank in case of a receivership. The Bank funded £3 million of its claims in December 1926, and gave a guarantee for the completion of ships building, although by the end of the year its total commitments had reached £6½ million.

The position now was that Armstrongs had no further security to offer; they could not carry on without further advances; yet it was difficult to close them down. The Admiralty had approached the Bank; Armstrongs was in debt to them, and was also engaged on contracts for them which must be completed. The Newfoundland project had a considerable value which would be lost if it could not be completed. Other banks were involved with subsidiaries of Armstrongs, who had guaranteed overdrafts for them. All through 1926 Norman was discussing with accountants and lawyers the possibilities of reconstruction. The possible lines appeared only when he approached Sir Herbert Lawrence, Chairman of Vickers, the other great armaments concern, and found that he would welcome some arrangement for working with Armstrongs. By the end of the year, some merger of interests was agreed; Lawrence was thinking of a purchase by Vickers, Norman of a new company, but in principle a policy had been found. The Deputy Governor (Trotter) was able now to explain to Court, as he did on 6 January 1927 while the Governor was on his way to America, the whole extent of the Bank's commitments to Armstrongs and the policy it was hoped to apply.

Norman had to decide what to do about the enormous debt to the Bank. Armstrongs would continue to lose money if it was allowed to go on without some reorganisation; and the Governor of the Bank, of all people, could not simply close the works down. With the help of Vickers it would be possible to preserve the nucleus, which was essential to national defence, and to put it ultimately, it was hoped, on a self-supporting basis. The other assets might be sold or, if they showed any prospect of paying their way, entrusted to separate operating companies; anything else must be closed down and written off. A large part of the Bank's advances would never be recovered ; but at any rate the drain of losses would be stopped, something would be recovered by such sales, and some security would be created for further repayment in the future. The policy of segregating the armament interests and concentrating them with those of Vickers in a new company, while closing down plant redundant to any probable demand, was called 'Rationalisation'. The same principles were to be applied to other depressed industries which brought their troubles to the Governor.

It took time to work out the agreement with Vickers. It was not an alliance of equals ; Vickers was financially strong and profitable, while the new armament company might not be able for a long time to earn profits. When this became clear to Lawrence and Peacock, who was negotiating with him for the Governor, and when Plender [1] confirmed their view, Norman asked them to prepare a memorandum which proposed a Government guarantee in view of the national importance of rationalisation generally and of armaments capacity in particular. Norman took this proposal to the Prime Minister on 21 June 1927. The Government, while approving the merger, did not feel able to give the guarantee — though their decision did not reach Norman till July 29. He had expected this answer, and already, after consulting Plender, made up his mind that the Bank should give the necessary guarantee. Sending Peacock the news, he went on :

For my part, if the proposal can be turned round the other way, I am willing to recommend the Bank to take the place of the Government in providing the necessary financial support ; by 'turned the other way' I mean that, instead of maintaining shops and yards and skeleton staffs, etc., all the assets of the Company should be abandoned unless they are economical and remunerative under peace conditions. It is important that the new company detach itself openly from the armament business to the extent that that business will not be remunerative.

He had put the same view, on the same conditions, to the Deputy Governor (Lubbock) in June just before he saw the Prime Minister (Baldwin), stressing the importance of carrying

[1] Sir William Plender of Deloitte Plender Griffiths & Co., Chartered Accountants. Later, Lord Plender.

through the merger from the point of view both of Bank and country. The Committee of Treasury gave its approval in August 'in view of the national importance of the merger' and 'as the only course affording present relief and the possibility of ultimate recovery'. Norman suggested that the object of the Bank's contribution might be explained 'as an endeavour to bring about the rationalisation of the Iron and Steel Industry and to avoid the increase of unemployment and disturbance of labour which would be involved by the closing of the works or by the receivership of Armstrong, Whitworth & Co.'.

The new armament company, Vickers-Armstrong, was controlled by Vickers, who received two-thirds of the ordinary shares, and Armstrongs, who received one-third; the superior claims of Vickers's profitability were recognised by an allocation of a still larger proportion of preference shares. The Bank accepted Vickers-Armstrong ordinary shares in exchange for the whole of its holding of debentures in Armstrongs, over £5 million; the preference shares and ordinary shares of Armstrongs were written down to a small fraction of their nominal amount. The shipbuilding business was transferred to a separate operating company, as was also the general engineering business. Meanwhile the Newfoundland Pulp & Paper Company was sold to an American company, International Paper Co. Ltd., for £1½ million in cash and £2 million preference shares, the whole of which was transferred to the Bank in settlement of debts.

Thus the waterlogged and rapidly sinking Armstrong Whitworth concern was relieved of its intolerable load of debt, the core of its business incorporated (in exchange for shares) in a new armaments company solidly based on the best works in the country, and its other assets either realised to liquidate debt or reorganised in shipbuilding and general engineering companies, which started clear of debt. The Bank incurred a new liability in the guarantee of Vickers-Armstrong profits, and it had to face further sacrifices subsequently to keep alive the operating companies and to realise the securities it had received. But it accepted both the immediate loss on Armstrongs' banking debt and these subsequent losses as justified by the salving of the Elswick works and the armament business, and by the contribution made to the better organisation of that and its related branches of British industry. Norman bought out the other First Debenture holders to facilitate the scheme, but he refused to make further concessions to other holders of Armstrong ordinary shares; 'I have made', he said, 'sacrifices all round for moral reasons, I wish to retain control for rationalising reasons, and I need the equity to give a speculative value to shares which must be sold quickly'. He insisted that all circulars on the reconstruction should be 'full pessimistic and approved by the Bank's solicitor'. By giving up *all* its prior charges 'the Bank would not only have discharged their moral responsibility to the Public but would also have supported a scheme which should serve as a model for future experiments in rationalisation'. He put this to the most conservative critic on the Court of his industrial experiments who 'entirely agreed with the decision and the reasons, *i.e. noblesse oblige*, in the case of each claim'. At the end of 1929 Armstrongs' banking account with the Bank of England was closed.

(ii)

Norman did not rush into the reorganisation of the steel industry light-heartedly. He was reluctant either to intervene himself or to encourage the Government to intervene. He told the Committee of Treasury on 8 December 1926 that the great firms of Baldwins and Beardmores had applied to the Government for financial assistance and postponement of debts in order to avoid receiverships. He had strongly advised against Government assistance to industrial concerns on the grounds that many of them needed new blood, new management and economies which could be secured only by a receiver, while the Exchequer could ill afford such assistance and would find it very difficult to limit its amount. He suspected the industry of refusing to face the need of drastic reorganisation because it was sitting waiting for Protection; but he was dragged in by the necessity of dealing with his banking customer, Armstrongs.

The section of the steel industry in which Vickers and Armstrongs were engaged was only a small part of the whole. The new company found it convenient to segregate it in a new specialised company, the English Steel Corporation, into which another great Sheffield firm, Cammell Laird, put its steel-making plant. An attempt to bring in others failed. Meanwhile the needs of the rest of that industry were being pressed on Norman, both by the difficulties of particular firms and by projects for general reorganisation. As early as May 1927 he was approached by a London stockbroker, with a proposal for a review of the industry as a whole. It began with an unfavourable comparison between the British industry and its foreign competitors, and went on to argue that the industry's difficulties could be solved only by adopting their policy, 'amalgamation and co-operation of the various units'. It would be difficult for the interested parties themselves to initiate and carry through negotiations; an independent agent would be required and this, it was suggested, the big finance houses of the City might, in the national interest, consider it almost their duty to provide. This suggestion may be taken perhaps as marking an epoch; up to this time all the great houses in London which handled issues had done so almost exclusively for overseas borrowers; since then they have more and more turned their attention to the needs of British industry; the process would have been much slower but for the Governor's initiative. At the moment, however, he could say only that the principle of the reorganisation appealed to him and he would raise it with representatives of the houses suggested. He did so, and met with a ready response; but a general memorandum was not enough to go on, and he told his visitor that his idea would have to be worked out into a concrete proposal in agreement with the firms affected before it could be put to the finance houses.

Other similar proposals began to reach Norman. A financier involved in an embarrassed iron concern thought a finance company for iron and steel, or even for industry generally, was the solution; Norman poured cold water on the suggestion. One enterprising issuing banker sought introductions to the South Wales steel firms (of which he knew nothing) with a view to a merger. Hatry's last scheme was for an amalgamation of firms producing 60 per cent of the country's steel, which he explained to the Governor. But again he was not responsive, and, when a leading merchant-banker consulted him after

Hatry's failure about taking up the scheme, Norman recorded :
'I advise him to go slow : complicated : management difficult : personal troubles : part of a larger question. He will
consider.' He was repeating his own experience.

The difficulties — and opportunities — of individual firms
proved a more effective stimulus. Opportunities were represented by the formation of English Steel ; difficulties by the
needs of Baldwins and Beardmores mentioned above. A Director of the Bank sought advice for one of the Cleveland firms and
thus raised the whole question of the relation of the three large
firms in that area. The Governor's friend, Lord Weir, reported
difficulties in the West of Scotland. Finally, Norman found
himself forced after all to deal with the firm of Beardmores. He
told the Committee of Treasury on 19 June 1929 that Beardmores was in danger under Scottish law of immediate liquidation, and he proposed to come to its help 'as an alternative to
possible Government intervention'. It was a new Government
under Ramsay MacDonald, faced with the possibility of Beardmores closing down and turning off its whole staff; Norman
had seen the Minister concerned, J. H. Thomas, consulted
Lord Weir, Sir Gilbert Garnsey [1] and two bankers, even before
the meeting of the Committee. The Government welcomed
any prompt help, and the plan Norman put to the Committee
was a loan provided that the company could carry on, had
assets to pledge and offered a prospect of earning enough in
two or three years to meet the charges on the debt. On further
examination, he found that the position was less hopeful; he
invested £710,000 in First Mortgage Debentures on condition
that the Government postponed its claims on the company and
that he was given control until the debt was repaid.

The time had come for some definition and statement of
his policy. The City was becoming interested in rationalisation
schemes. Norman had been approached by friends in the
City, not only about steel, but about coal, locomotive engine
building and other projects. Industry also was beginning to
look to the City and the Bank; the shipbuilders had made
their first approach to Norman. He had acquired a new
contact with industry in Sir Andrew Duncan,[2] former Director

---

[1] Of Price Waterhouse & Co., Chartered Accountants.
[2] Director of the Bank of England, 1929–40.

Y

of the Shipbuilders' Federation and Coal Controller and now Chairman of the Central Electricity Board, who was elected to the Court of the Bank in 1929; and came to rely on him more and more in all industrial matters. The Government, under stress of persistent unemployment, was actively looking round for help. J. H. Thomas had been given special responsibility, and freedom from any departmental duties, to deal with unemployment; in his official associate, Sir Horace J. Wilson, Norman found another civil servant, whose advice and friendship he valued, whose main interests (and wide experience) were in the field of industry.

Even before the change of Government, Norman had been alarmed by a growing demand for a new Trade Facilities Act — an obnoxious expedient to a banker because it superseded the market's judgment and usually led to loans to defaulting foreign governments whose creditors were pressing them to honour existing obligations. He reported this demand to the Committee of Treasury on 20 February 1929, and said that 'in these circumstances the Bank would find money to a moderate extent in support of any scheme of rationalisation which to their satisfaction is established on an economic and profitable basis'. The new Government needed something more public. At the end of the year he informed the Committee of Treasury that J. H. Thomas needed a statement which he could use in public. The Committee was reluctant to make any public commitment, but approved a draft, the Governor promising to ask that it be reproduced in any public speech *verbatim*. It was used by Thomas in a speech to a business audience in Lancashire on 10 January 1930 :

In considering the steps that might be taken to produce a better employment position by improving the organisation and equipment of British industries, I have found that a feeling exists that manufacturers are handicapped in bringing about the necessary reorganisation and re-equipment by the fact that the long-continued trade depression has pushed them to the limits of the credit which they can reasonably expect to obtain from their bankers or which the bankers can reasonably be expected to provide. As a result of consultations which I have had, I am now in a position to state that the City is deeply interested in placing industry upon a broad and sound basis and ready to support any plans that in its opinion lead to this end. Those in the City who have been studying this matter are convinced that a number of our important industries must be fundamentally reorganised and modernised in order to be able to produce at prices which will enable them to compete with the world. Industries which propose schemes that, in the opinion of those advising the City, conform to this requirement will receive the most sympathetic consideration and the co-operation of the City in working out plans and finding the necessary finance. In the case of individual undertakings the City will be similarly ready to help, provided that the scheme under discussion fits in as part of the general plans for the industry in question as a whole and gives reasonable promise that the changes will enable the undertaking to become an effective unit in combination and co-operation with other similar undertakings.

Until the end of 1929 Norman had handled these new relations with industry personally. He had, however, gradually collected a group of advisers, employed at first intermittently and then retained as full-time servants of the Bank. Frater Taylor, called in first to advise on Armstrong Whitworth, went on to recommend a general reorganisation of the steel industry, but was absorbed in the management of individual concerns in that industry, coming back later to undertake the care of the Bank's Newfoundland paper interest. An accountant, Sir James Cooper, was used to represent the Bank's interest on direction of companies which it had helped, particularly in textiles ; a little later a lawyer with wide experience of company matters, Hugh C. Bischoff, was added to the little team of experts ; as was Frank Hodges, a former Secretary of the Miners' Federation (recommended by some of Norman's friends in the Government), and an economist whose interests had been in industrial, not banking questions. The chief need at the moment, however, was an expert on steel ; the Governor told the Committee of Treasury on 4 September 1929 that he was looking for a leading world expert. He met his need partly by calling in a firm of American consultants who prepared a report on the reorganisation of the industry, and then, through Duncan, secured the services of the managing director of an important English firm, Charles Bruce Gardner,[1] who not only provided the intimate knowledge of the steel industry sought,

---

[1] Later Sir Charles Bruce-Gardner, Bt.

but with his industrial experience was able to fill a place which the growth of the Bank's industrial interests had created, that of manager of a specialised organisation in which these interests could be concentrated.

The Governor told the Committee on 14 August 1929 that he was thinking of forming a company for the purpose of examining schemes and, if approved, carrying them through. His team of advisers would form the directorate; the chairman, he suggested — using the opportunity to prod the Committee in its discussions of the future of the Governorship — should be the person they proposed to succeed himself. The company was registered as the Securities Management Trust on November 20 and the miscellaneous collection of industrial securities which the Bank had accumulated handed over to it for supervision, the Bank undertaking to meet its financial needs by advances. To ensure proper control of the new company's activities, a committee of Directors, with Stamp as Chairman, was appointed to advise the Committee of Treasury on all applications from it for finance, and the Governor undertook that the draft minutes of its board meetings should be laid before the Committee.

As recorded at the time, the objects of the Trust were to go much further than the management of the industrial interests which the Bank had already acquired, or might acquire in the future in solving individual problems. It was to initiate or help to develop schemes for the 'rationalisation' of whole industries, by investigations not limited to the technical or accounting field: and expressly to try and locate really capable leaders, without whom no scheme could prosper. Backed by the influence of the Bank, the approval of all interested parties was to be sought, and the risk of partial and overlapping schemes avoided. The result could then be presented as a basis for the necessary financial help.

The Governor was willing that the Bank should support financially, as well as investigate and sponsor, schemes of rationalisation; but his chief object was to encourage the flow of capital generally to this purpose, and for this to enlist the support of the City houses engaged in the issue of securities. The precise form of organisation adopted arose out of a particular need. One of the subsidiaries of Armstrongs, the colliery and iron firm Pearson & Knowles, had taken part in the formation of a new steel company, Partingtons, on the Manchester Ship Canal. This needed additional finance, and offered a nucleus for the rationalisation of the iron, coal and steel industry of South Lancashire. Norman called in to advise him on the necessary financial reconstruction Major Albert Pam, a partner in Schröder's. Major Pam advised that a considerable amount of new money would be needed to enable the reorganised concern to carry on; the existing shareholders had lost their money and must be content with deferred shares, while the new money was raised by an issue of preference shares. Norman asked him to see whether he could arrange such an issue, promising the Bank's support. Major Pam was able in a few days to collect a group of issuing houses which would assist his own firm to handle the issue. In reporting this to the Governor, he suggested that it would be a pity, having brought such a group into being, to let it break up after only a single issue. Why should not the Governor form a permanent group, which all the important issuing houses should be invited to join, to make similar issues in the future? Norman seized on the idea and proceeded immediately to elaborate the scheme. The object was a company with a small paid-up but very large subscribed capital, to include all the important public and private banks in the City, with the Bank of England as the chief shareholder responsible, through Securities Management Trust, for its management. He secured the approval of the Committee of Treasury, and, finding that every banker who called on him in the next few weeks was willing and eager to co-operate, launched the scheme, as the Bankers' Industrial Development Company, on 15 April 1930. He had summarised its purpose in reporting to Court on March 6 as being —

to examine, assist and finance the amalgamation, reconstruction and reorganisation on an economic and rationalised basis of groups of British Companies engaged in important industries.

He himself was Chairman, with Sir Guy Granet as his alternate, and the Board consisted of leading partners or chairmen of the larger merchant-banking houses, also with alternates available for continuous attention to the affairs of the company. The announcement of its formation attracted attention to the new

interest of the City in industry, to which Thomas' speech had
already referred.

This initiative in the field of industrial finance was approved
by the Committee of Treasury and Court, but only with some
misgivings. Unlike the reorganisation of Armstrongs, which
was forced on them by existing banking commitments, it was a
spontaneous incursion into a new field. They were exposed to
complaints from other banks and issuing houses that the Bank's
innovation was a renewal of competition with private banking,
from which, as the Central Bank, it had withdrawn. And they
feared commitments which the Bank had neither the organisation nor the experience of technical conditions and markets to
undertake. Nevertheless they gave the innovation in policy
their approval. The crucial discussion was on 21 November
1929. The Governor's chief argument was recorded as
follows :

He pointed out that the Bank through no particular merit of
their own had accumulated large reserves, and that in his opinion
the Directors were not so much Directors of a banking concern as
Trustees of a National Institution on behalf of the public. He was
convinced that industry at present required a helping hand from
someone entirely outside who would be able to bring together the
various interests concerned in the shortest possible time and, if
necessary, assist also by a moderate expenditure of money, and he
considered that the Bank would only be fulfilling its proper function
in endeavouring to bring this about.

And he had weighty support. The record continues :

Mr. Peacock told the Court that shortly after the War the
Governor had outlined to him his schemes for restoring and re-
generating Europe. Many of these schemes had at that time
frightened him, but he now realised that the Governor had been
absolutely right. The Governor had recently outlined to him his
views as to the steps required to restore health to industry, and it
was his view that just as the Governor was right before with regard
to Europe, so was he right now in regard to British industry, and
he was entirely in agreement with his proposals.

But the decision had been settled in principle, as such questions
of principle are settled in practical affairs, on a succession of
actual cases, each of which Norman had reported, and his

action on each of which had been approved. It was only the systematisation and publicity that was new.

Norman's plans and hopes were summarised in evidence he gave to sub-committees of the Committee of Civil Research, on the iron and steel industry on 21 March 1930 and the cotton industry on April 11 following. He began by rejecting the suggestion which had been put to the sub-committees that the Clearing Banks should finance the reorganisation and re-equipment of industry. They should face the unpleasant fact that many of their short-term advances, which had become frozen, had little or no security behind them in present conditions, and should write them off; but long-term finance was the business of other agencies. There were famous and old-established banking houses in the City which had hitherto been engaged in making issues for overseas borrowers; these houses could, and would if a case were made for it, devote themselves to finding capital for British industry. The money needed for rationalisation could be found, either by London or by our American friends; but the borrowers must put their industries in a condition in which loans would be justified. Individual firms could not raise money; he would not help them himself. The industries in which they were units must be organised in a way that ensured the scale, equipment and co-ordination required for economical production.

He illustrated these principles by references to his own experiments. He had secured the services of the greatest consulting firm in the American steel industry to survey and make a plan for the British industry. The Bank had assisted the rationalisation of the armament industry — at great loss since disarmament followed the attempt. He had obtained money for the reorganisation of the Lancashire steel industry and for the armament firm of Beardmores — in this case dealing with a single firm only because there were legal obstacles to proceeding by way of a receivership, to fit its various activities into a co-ordinated plan. He had promised finance for a scheme to reduce the number of spindles in the cotton industry and merge the separate firms in a single large-scale concern, and to the shipbuilding industry by a different route to concentrate on a limited number of berths which there was a reasonable hope of keeping employed. He believed that advice could be obtained from America and Germany if necessary, and that Protection should not be given until the attempt had been made to reduce costs by a rational reorganisation. He also outlined the ideas which were taking shape in the Securities Management Trust and the Bankers' Industrial Development Company.

(iii)

It is necessary to turn back a little to explain Norman's intervention in industries other than the steel industry in which the Bank's connection with Armstrongs had compelled action.

The cotton industry before 1914 had been the greatest of British export industries. Although other countries were gaining on it, it had retained its lead; indeed in the year before war broke out it provided 70 per cent of the world's total exports of cotton manufactures. But the interruption by war of its overseas contacts, by compelling its customers to turn to other sources of supply or to undertake manufacture themselves, inevitably weakened Lancashire's competitive position. The spread of Protection after the war continued this influence throughout the inter-war period; and again Lancashire suffered most. By the mere volume of her exports she offered the broadest target for attack; her dependence on exports was greater than that of any other producer — 85 per cent (by volume) of her production before the war. This export was dangerously concentrated : India took two-fifths of her total production, the other Far Eastern markets another fifth. India after the war used her new freedom to protect her own manufactures; in the other Far Eastern markets Japanese competition began to displace the better but more expensive products of Lancashire, and political and monetary disorder to reduce the takings of China. Lancashire maintained or recovered the markets for the finer goods, and had no reason to fear competition in the home market, even without Protection; but other markets were not capable of expansion to replace the vast markets for cheaper classes of cloth that were lost.

The organisation of the industry in Lancashire, mainly in firms specialised to a single process — spinning, weaving or finishing — which were co-ordinated by middlemen who placed

orders and handled exports, gave all the economies of mass-
production so long as the total volume of output was maintained, but became uneconomical when the volume fell to a level
at which full employment of machinery and operatives was not
possible, and, moreover, was not readily adaptable to changes
in volume, type of product and direction of export. The
impact of the decline was concentrated on the spinning section.
This was partly because it was furthest from the consumer, so
that the sections nearer the consumer were able to exploit the
competition of redundant mills to force down prices below
costs, but partly to a peculiar financial disability. The trade
was conducted mainly by public joint-stock companies; the
capital for these was raised largely on loan, and the deferred
ordinary shares were usually only partly paid up; so that
trade depression would lead to calls on ordinary shareholders,
who were usually local investors, largely engaged in the
industry, to meet losses. During the short post-war re-stocking
boom, spinning prices unfortunately had been forced up to unprecedented heights, with corresponding profits. On the basis
of these profits, a speculative re-financing boom developed.
Mill companies were bought up, at prices that gave the previous
shareholders a large profit, and resold to the public at a large
profit to the purchasers. The new companies were constituted
on the same dangerous system of a large proportion of loan-
capital, supported by a small proportion of paid-up ordinary
capital and a large liability of ordinary shareholders to pay up
the rest of the issued ordinary shares on calls. The leading
trade circular, Tattersall's, estimated that the total amount
thus called up in the 'twenties exceeded £30 million; how
much was actually paid up is unknown, but it is unlikely that
it was less than half, and the whole of this went in meeting
losses already incurred, not in purchase of improved equipment.
Thus on the ordinary strain of loss of trade was superimposed
the financial strain of meeting calls on unpaid shares. On the
security of this liability, the mills received advances from banks;
banks were also involved as creditors in some cases, because
they had advanced the money to purchase for resale, and were
left with the mills as security when the boom collapsed and
their debtors found themselves unable to effect the resale and
repay the advance.

In yet another way, the organisation of the industry in joint-stock companies intensified the strain of loss of trade. The persons who actually conducted operations were officials of the mills, with a greater interest in retaining their office and salaries than in avoiding calls on any shares they held. Hence a persistent tendency to what was called 'weak selling' — selling at less than cost in order to secure such business as was available, and financing the loss by further bank advances on the security of the uncalled liability of shareholders on their shares. The burden of indebtedness steadily mounted through the 'twenties. The ordinary operation of bankruptcy, which should have limited and wiped out indebtedness, was postponed. The industry itself became progressively less able to secure remunerative prices even for its diminished output; and the local banks became longer and longer creditors of the industry, with steadily deteriorating security.

It is evidence of the strength of the spinning industry that as a whole it continued to make profits until the world depression in 1930. The first response to its difficulties was an attempt to work short-time throughout the industry by agreement. Keynes in the *Nation* in 1926 criticised this policy as tending to raise costs and contributing nothing to meet the real difficulties of the industry; when challenged to meet the representatives of the industry, he gave his support to an association of spinners set up to regulate prices, and recommended a cartel with transferable quotas as a way of encouraging the concentration of work in mills working full time. But the association did not command sufficient support to make its policy effective, and began to work at a scheme for a large-scale merger of mills. For this principle there was in Manchester a good deal of support; the difficulty was that it involved, not only the final sacrifice of any interest many shareholders retained — and almost certainly a call on their remaining uncalled liability — but, by extinguishing a large number of independent units, the loss of their position by the persons at the time operating these units. Some means of compelling independent mills to enter the merger would be needed, and the only means (short of Government compulsion) was pressure by the chief creditors, the banks.

It was at this stage that the Bank's help was sought. The

Deputy Governor reported to the Committee of Treasury on 25 July 1928 that he had had a visit from the leaders of the spinners' price association, who explained a scheme for a large amalgamation and sought his advice on raising additional working capital; he had replied cautiously that in principle he was sympathetic, but that, 'while they would wish to be of assistance, they could make no suggestion at present as to the means by which additional capital could be provided'. A few weeks later, on September 19, the Governor told the Committee that he thought it would be necessary for the Bank to support and subscribe to a satisfactory scheme, partly to help the cotton industry, partly to keep the question away from politics, but more especially to relieve certain of the banks from a dangerous position. The growing advances of these banks to the cotton industry were already unduly large, and unless they obtained relief from them there was a danger that the Bank might be compelled to assist them. A month later, in reporting that the Bank might have to make an issue of debentures for the proposed Lancashire textile corporation, he said it should be regarded as a precaution and defence against a breakdown of credit in Lancashire or against the need for the Government to provide cash, and it might involve the Bank in some ultimate loss. He was perhaps unduly influenced by the disproportionate credits to cotton-spinning firms given by one of the Lancashire banks which were obstructing a 'marriage' he was trying to arrange with a stronger bank. He acquired a direct interest in Lancashire's problem by taking over, at a price which relieved the merger of risk, a large number of cotton securities held against these advances; on these the Bank was involved in a considerable 'ultimate loss', whereas its advances to the new corporation were repaid.

The scheme was supported by the chief Manchester bank, which had already promised to write off or fund the debts of companies merged in it (though doubtful whether the organisers would make the best managers). The other creditor banks were slower; in the end all were agreed to use their power to bring in companies, and to remove the immediate pressure of debt by accepting securities of the new corporation in exchange. But the process of organisation was slow; the Bank had to make advances to cover the preliminary expenses of forming

the corporation, and then to provide it with working capital;
and at the end one bank decided it was unable to forgo its
existing claims except in return for a prior charge on the assets
of the new corporation. But the whole basis of the plan was
the extinction of all secured prior charges, both in order to leave
security for raising new money (on income debentures) and to
avoid the danger of a receivership and liquidation if the prior
charges could not be earned in the interval before the corporation had established itself. The Governor and the promoters
of the scheme could not move the recalcitrant; he said he was
friendly but his committee and board were adamant. An
attempt to substitute a less comprehensive scheme alienated
another bank, and the Governor would not support a scheme
which included debentures for existing debts. These initial
difficulties were overcome and the company registered in
January 1929 as the Lancashire Cotton Corporation. But the
pulling in of the encumbered companies and the organisation
of a new system of regulating production and distribution was
a slow business. The Bank had to finance the company for
nearly two years before it was possible to make an issue of
debentures. By that time conditions were so unfavourable,
especially for a new enterprise in a depressed industry, that an
interest charge of $6\frac{1}{2}$ per cent was necessary and the Bank had
(privately) to guarantee payment of this for five years.

Delay threatened this scheme by disappointing the Government as well as the Governor. On 12 January 1931 he had an
interview with Graham, the President of the Board of Trade,
who was disturbed at the position of affairs, and worked, before
Parliament reassembled, to appoint a Commission of three
with power to close down, if necessary, 25 per cent of the
spindles and 30 per cent of the looms in Lancashire, and to
make such arrangements as they thought necessary about
merchanting. Norman deprecated such action, and expressed
his view also to the Chancellor (Snowden). He hoped nothing
would come of the suggestion; but he was approached a little
later by Sir Arthur Steel-Maitland, the Minister of Labour
in the preceding Conservative Administration, to ask whether
Government action in the textile industries was not possible
without causing serious disturbance. In the event, the Government left the problem of redundancy to the new corporation.

The long delay was not the end of the enterprise's misfortunes. The combination of depression throughout industry and its markets, superimposed on the peculiar difficulties of the cotton industry, with the experiments, delays and mistakes inevitable in working out a new type of organisation for an industry, resulted in trading losses which threatened to swallow up the whole of the £2 million promised, before the concern was firmly established. The head of a successful large concern, with many branches and a world-wide trade in another manufacturing industry, was called in to advise. He examined the progress made, and reported that the corner had been turned and the losses no more than was to be expected. But the change from a large loss to a profit (though a small profit), on which he based his judgment, occurred in the transient recovery of the cotton industry, which followed the suspension of the Gold Standard. He had not noticed that other firms in the industry had also turned from loss to profit, and that, just as their losses had been relatively smaller, so now their profits were relatively larger. The trade revival did not last long and by the beginning of 1932 the corporation was meeting much larger losses. The Governor now sought the advice of four independent leaders of industry in Manchester, and on their advice agreed with the Trustee for the debentures that a change of management was necessary. He regretted it on personal grounds and noted in his diary that he told the Chairman that he supported the Trustee in asking for his resignation 'as expedient and necessary rather than just'.

The new Chairman, Frank Platt,[1] was an experienced director of cotton-spinning companies, who had been working for some time on a scheme for a second merger. Under his direction, supported by the Governor's advisers, a considerable reorganisation was carried through; the administration was decentralised and its cost reduced; production was limited to mills that could be worked full, or nearly full time — the corporation hitherto had not secured this economy of combination; and more use was made of the good-will of the mills absorbed. To check the further erosion of margins, Platt reorganised the price association which, with the corporation at its core, was able to secure for spinning a larger share of the

---

[1] Later Sir Frank Platt.

price of the finished product than it had been receiving, and also to prevent the further fall of prices. Losses were gradually stopped, and in two and a half years the experiment was justifying the support it had received by earning profits as large as its early losses. In 1936 the capital was rearranged to get rid of the debentures, and in 1937 the Governor proposed to the Committee of Treasury that the Bank could liquidate its position; he proposed to arrange for the sale of its holding, in Lancashire. The sale was in fact deferred until the beginning of 1940, when the Bank's holding was realised at a book profit.

Norman had expected, when he first interested himself in cotton, that much more widespread reorganisation would be necessary. No other section of the industry, however, put forward a considered and elaborated plan which he felt it necessary to support. In the spinning section a scheme was worked out and adopted for a levy on production, the proceeds of which could be used to reduce the number of spindles; he supported and assisted this, but it depended on Government compulsion rather than on financial aid. Members of the Boards of the Securities Management Trust and the Bankers' Industrial Development Company did, on the invitation of the trade and with Sir Horace Wilson's approval, study the position of the industry as a whole in 1933, but nothing resulted. The ordinary process of bankruptcy, the rigorous concentration of the industry in order to release labour for war purposes in the Second World War and the reluctance of labour to return to or enter the industry after the war effected an adjustment of the industry's capacity to the markets it could hope to find. But much suffering and waste of resources would have been prevented if the rationalisation of the industry, with Norman's support, could have been achieved when he hoped, in 1928, and extended from the spinning to the manufacturing and merchanting sections.

(iv)

Of all the great industries, shipbuilding had had the worst record of unemployment since the war. After the post-war boom it had risen to over 40 per cent of the insured workers registered in the industry, and, although the percentage had been

brought down by 1929 to 22½, the whole reduction was attributable to the reduction in the numbers registered in the industry
from 270,000 in 1923 to 205,000 in 1929. Employment reflected
the state of the industry. As early as January 1926 the *Economist*
contrasted the figures of construction in 1925 with the last pre-
war year — a quarterly average of new tonnage commenced
of 203,000 contrasted with 467,000 in 1913 — and said 'these
bald statistics of ship-construction present a picture of deepening shadow, which, in view of the vital importance of shipbuilding . . . must necessarily occasion serious reflections. . . .
The completed construction . . . representing about 35 per cent
of the productive capacity of the existing yards.' Yet 1925
was better than the average of the four years 1922–25. After
further decline in the year of the coal stoppage, there was a
recovery in 1927 and renewed decline in 1930 and onwards.
The root of the trouble was partly the development of shipbuilding in other countries after 1914, which deprived the
expanded British industry of former custom, but partly also a
world-wide overbuilding of ships in the years 1919–21, when
the tonnage launched was double that of the three pre-war
years. The increase in international trade was too small to
absorb this increase; freights fell, and new building was discouraged. One specialised but important section suffered in
addition the loss of all new contracts for capital ships and a
reduced demand for other warships.

An approach was made to Norman. On 24 April 1929 he
noted in his diary, Sir James Lithgow called, at Duncan's
suggestion, to put to him a scheme for buying up and scrapping
redundant shipyards as a step towards rationalisation. He told
Lithgow: 'We are willing to consider, if politically non-conten-
tious, subject to approval by Deloittes, Freshfields and any
technical adviser we choose — but make no commitment'. He
reported the interview to the Committee of Treasury at its
next meeting; £2 million was wanted, to be repaid in five to
ten years. It was the same object, approached by a different
scheme, as the cotton-spinning scheme — to relieve an industry
which was ruining itself by internecine competition for an
inadequate demand, of some of the capacity rendered redundant by post-war world changes, so that it could meet the
permanent demands on it without progressive deterioration.

The shipbuilders adopted a more direct method, adapted to the type of firm engaged and to the industry's organisation — a levy on all tonnage launched to provide the service for a bond on which the money could be raised which was needed to buy up redundant yards. It was a year and a half before the scheme was complete and an issue of £1 million could be made; by that time the Bankers' Industrial Development Company was established and could sponsor the issue. The purpose of the issue was defined in the prospectus as being —

for the principal purpose of assisting the shipbuilding industry by the purchase and dismantling of redundant and obsolete shipyards, the disposal of their contents and the resale of the sites under restriction against further use for shipbuilding. . . . The elimination of redundant and obsolete shipyards will bring about concentration of building and should result in an increased output from the remaining yards with lower working costs and enable shipbuilders to compete on more favourable terms with foreign yards.

The basis was a payment to the company administering the scheme of 1 per cent of the contract price of all vessels completed in the previous half-year until the proceeds of the issue were repaid : and a list was added of the shipbuilders, including all the important firms, who had already entered into a contract with the company to pay the levy.

It was fortunate that the shipbuilders' scheme was launched before the great depression had overtaken the industry. Its aim was limited to removing the redundant capacity revealed by eight years of relatively good trade in the world as a whole and, judged by post-war standards, in the United Kingdom. The further decline in the demand for the output of the industry could not be met by the scheme, but must have involved a large part of the industry in bankruptcy if the scheme had not made some concentration of production possible. Armstrongs and Beardmores both took advantage of it to rid themselves of yards which involved them in serious continuing losses while making it more difficult for firms confined to shipbuilding to keep themselves alive. As late as 29 June 1932 the Governor had to appeal to the Committee of Treasury for approval of aid to another company in the same plight as

Beardmores. The Fairfield Shipbuilding & Engineering Company could not carry on without an advance; it was contrary to the national interest that it should close; he had seen its bankers, and if they would give no further help he proposed to supply the necessary funds. The Bank arranged a loan of £150,000 in July 1933. When it was taken over two and a half years later by a commercial bank, only £45,000 had been drawn, but this had been sufficient to save the firm. The year 1932 proved to be the lowest point in the fortunes of the industry; thereafter orders expanded, but had not reached the level of 1928–29 when war broke out again.

When the worst of the depression was over and orders were flowing in again to the shipbuilding yards, this organised scrapping of shipyards came in for much public criticism. The criticism was excited by a natural sympathy for unemployment persisting in towns in which one of the closed yards had been the principal employer. But such sympathy ignored the awkward fact of the industry's position when the decision had to be made which faced the Cabinet and the Governor. The scheme did not cause the unemployment of shipyard workers; it was itself caused by the unemployment, which was the outcome of the difficulties of the employers. The industry is one employing a large amount of fixed capital and a substantial designing and supervising class; any decline in volume of output left a burden of overhead expenses which in time made losses unavoidable; the expense of keeping in existence idle shipyards and ships was an unnecessary addition to these. The expansion of British shipbuilding, already before the war greater than the whole of the shipbuilding industry of the rest of the world, to nearly double its pre-war capacity in 1920–21, after the rest of the world had increased its capacity in shipbuilding even more, was an unfortunate response to transient boom conditions, which made it unlikely that the industry would enjoy full employment under any conditions in the foreseeable future except another war.

The criticism heard during the Second World War, that the scheme had undermined the country's strength, had as little justification. War was not a contingency for which industrialists were being encouraged to prepare in 1929. The attitude of Government to the industry had been expressed in the

z

Washington Naval Agreement in 1922 and in Arthur Henderson's fight for a limitation of armaments through the League of
Nations in 1930 and 1931, and subsequent economies. The
immediate danger which the industry faced in 1929 was a
drastic further contraction by widespread insolvency and
liquidation. Governments were doing little to prevent this;
their first thought, when faced with the imminent closing-down
of a great firm like Beardmores or Fairfields, was to ask the
Governor to make an advance that no commercial banker felt
justified in making. It is far more probable that the industry
would have been smaller and not larger when war came a
second time, had the scheme not been carried through. The
solvent firms in it had still in 1929 to face the strain on their
resources of three years of world depression. The unemployment of the 'twenties had shown, even more clearly than in
cotton spinning, that war and the post-war spread of Protection
had fundamentally changed the international position and
prospects of the older export industries, that bankruptcy was
too slow and expensive a process to rely on for effecting an ·
adjustment of capacity to probable long-term demands, and
that a surgical operation was necessary.

Even if it had had no internal problems of disorganisation
to face, shipbuilding would have reflected the troubles of shipping. On 5 January 1931 Norman was suddenly asked by the
Treasury (and the accountant who had investigated the position) to come to the assistance of the Oceanic Steam Navigation
Company, which owned the White Star Line. This company
had been bought back after the war from its American owners
(it had always remained under the British flag) by the Royal
Mail Steam Packet Company. It could not now carry on
without a temporary advance to cover its operating loss until
the summer season restored its takings, and also to complete a
new ship, the *Georgic*, which was being built for it by Harland
& Wolff. It could raise no further credits with its commercial
bankers and it was in debt to the Treasury, who were not
prepared to give further credit.

The proposal was that the Bank should buy its half-interest
in the Shaw Savill and Albion Line; if it was unable to maintain its payments to Harland & Wolff there was a danger that
the latter's creditors would insist on a receivership. Norman

arranged a temporary advance on the security of the shares he was asked to buy. On May 11 he had to report to the Committee of Treasury that further help was needed; he proposed an advance of £1 million (out of which the previous advance would be repaid), provided that Deloittes approved the security and the Treasury requested it in writing. He also proposed an advance to the White Star Line (as distinct from the O.S.N. Co.) to enable it to release its half share in the Shaw Savill Company from pledge to another shipowner. The Committee 'did not view the proposition with favour but realised that it was difficult to refuse a request made by the Chancellor of the Exchequer'.

Having met the pressing need of temporary credit, Norman called in Sir Frederick Lewis [1] to advise him. It became clear that the need was far from being temporary and self-liquidating. Some permanent reorganisation was called for. On Lewis's advice, he approached first the Chairman of the Cunard Company, who considered sympathetically the possibility of purchasing the White Star North Atlantic fleet, and he asked the Committee of Treasury to continue the Bank's credit (at the Treasury's request) until the negotiations were complete. But the Cunard at that time decided against the purchase; there was no alternative buyer, and no chance of an early repayment of the Bank's advance; and the Governor had to take the responsibility for a reorganisation of the White Star, with Lewis as chairman, and an indefinite extension of the credit. It was reconsidered in August 1933, but continued on the ground that to insist on repayment would involve a receivership, the very thing the original advance had been given to prevent. The advance was not finally repaid until October 1937.

In 1934 the whole complex of Royal Mail interests was forced on the Governor. He had resisted it in 1931 and had carefully kept clear of any responsibility for the Royal Mail Company's affairs — he accepted it for the White Star only at the Treasury's request — but a three-year moratorium on the Royal Mail obligations had been arranged with his reluctant help and without his financial participation. When this expired at the end of 1934 the Company was not yet able to meet

---

[1] Chairman of Furness Withy & Co., Ltd.   Later, Lord Essendon.

its obligations. Norman had already put the situation to members of the Committee of Treasury on June 5; some £2½ million would be needed to make it possible for the lines controlled by the group to carry on and avoid liquidation. But the scheme put forward by the Company's representatives was rejected on legal grounds. Other schemes proposed, which the creditors might have accepted, did not satisfy the Governor on wider grounds. The Treasury, when approached, was unwilling to provide the new money on which any continuation of the lines depended; it was indeed a principal creditor in respect of Trade Facilities loans to some of the subsidiaries. On the other hand, the principle of the scheme — the formation of a realisation company or companies to take over the assets of the group, mainly shares in operating lines, and to sell these in order to meet the creditors' claims without liquidating the operating lines — offered the best hope of meeting the creditors' claims, maintaining the shipping services, and retaining such balance of earning capacity as survived for the ordinary shareholders. When all alternatives had failed, the Governor finally agreed to act and asked the Bank to take responsibility.

The complication of the Royal Mail's interest in and obligation to the Oceanic Steam Navigation Company and White Star Line had already been eased by the absorption of the White Star by the Cunard Company in the previous year. The remaining assets consisted of holdings in the main Royal Mail Company's services, and other lines, of which the most important group was associated with the Elder Dempster Line and the West Coast of Africa, and the most valuable was a large holding in the Union Castle Company. Two realisation companies were formed — R.M. Realisation Company and E.D. Realisation Company. The West African interests and half the Union Castle holdings were transferred in exchange for shares to the latter, the rest to the former. The two realisation companies took over the liabilities of the group with the assets. They raised loans of something over £2 million from the Bank which, with cash produced by the realisation of some of the non-shipping assets, enabled them to pay off the Company's bankers and the O.S.N. Co., thus releasing the First Debentures pledged to them; other creditors were given the Realisation Companies' debentures and shares. The Bank had control and appointed an identical board for the two companies; the Deputy Governor, Sir Ernest Harvey, was Chairman of both, Sir Thomas Catto [1] Deputy Chairman.

The scheme avoided liquidation at a time when the assets could have realised an amount insufficient to meet the claims of secured creditors and nothing at all for other creditors and ordinary shareholders. By making it possible to carry on the operating units, with skilled and patient financial direction, the group secured the advantage of reviving trade after 1934. By the end of 1937 enough had been raised by sale of office buildings, shares in subsidiaries and other assets to meet the creditors and still leave a valuable equity for the shareholders, which included the Union Castle holdings which were distributed among them. Three years of hard work by the realisation companies had been rewarded.

(v)

It is necessary to turn back to the steel industry. Norman was not content with responding to isolated appeals from embarrassed firms. He aimed at a comprehensive reorganisation, which his intervention in particular cases would support, but which the industry itself would carry out. The lines of such a reorganisation were laid down in two reports. The first was made by an American firm of consultants in January 1930. It extended to only half a dozen pages, much of which was occupied by summarised history and description, and attributed the loss of economy to the multiplicity of plants, each manufacturing a diversity of products on a scale far too small for economic production; but it pointed out that existing grouping was aimed at financial consolidation rather than technical co-ordination and integration, and urged the need of a 'regionalisation' of the industry by centring new developments on integrated plants in each of six regions, based either on local ores (*e.g.* in Northamptonshire) or ores imported to plants situated on tide-water (*e.g.* in South Wales and on the Clyde). The second was a much more detailed report compiled by Bruce

[1] Later Lord Catto, Director of the Bank of England, 1940. Governor, 1944–49.

Gardner, surveying the industry area by area and product by product, and relating its proposals to the needs and possibilities of the existing firms. It aimed at a similar regional concentration and integration of processes, but indicated also the route by which such a rationalisation could be achieved with least friction and most economy.

Without any statutory powers, Norman's advisers were able to influence the development of the steel industry in the course of the next eight years in the direction of a more rational and productive organisation. The Lancashire Steel Corporation provided the most important engineering area in the country, and also the chief centre of wire-drawing, with a modern steel plant. The concentration of the armament steel producers in the English Steel Corporation has been noticed. On 21 January 1930 the Governor had a long talk with the Chairman of the firm which dominated the manufacture of steel pipes, Stewarts & Lloyds, and in April, on the same day as the Bankers Industrial Development Co. held its first board meeting, received from him a scheme for a new steel-works on the Northamptonshire ore-bed at Corby which would become the centre of the concern's operations. His technical advisers investigated the scheme and gave it their approval and advice. It fitted in with the general plan for the industry; it would exploit ore similar to the *minette* ore of Lorraine and provide the country with a modern Bessemer plant — the process invented in England and then neglected, though used predominantly on the Continent and in America. It promised to cheapen production and to reduce imports. But it involved a large initial capital commitment, at least £4 million, and the new issue market was not likely to provide any such sum. The examination and elaboration of the plans took some time; then, in November 1932, arrangements were made by which the firm's ordinary bankers would provide most of the money needed to construct the new plant, with the B.I.D. providing the balance, the whole to be repaid out of the proceeds of a debenture issue to be made when market conditions changed. Such a venture required courage. The Governor's closest colleague and supporter doubted the practicability in 1932 of a credit of the size required through the B.I.D. Did the outlook justify them, he asked, in encouraging the firm to embark on a great programme of expansion involving an expenditure before they were through of £5 million or £6 million? Even if it did, were they justified in encouraging the bankers to finance the scheme by advances, on an undertaking to repay by a future issue, and in promising a B.I.D. guarantee? He suggested widening the B.I.D. by bringing in some of the larger industrial and commercial concerns, and consulting the existing Consultative Council on the possibility. The Governor thought that such consultation would not be fair either to the borrowing company or to their bankers, and that the Bank must follow the precedent of its advances to the Central Electricity Board in anticipation of long-term issues. The success of the scheme exceeded anticipation. It gave the country the most modern and cheapest steel-producing plant in Europe, so much so that the firm was able to repay the temporary credit before it had all been drawn; and this section of the industry was equipped to meet all the demands on it as they expanded after 1934.

Another project included in the plan and assisted by the Governor's advisers and by a temporary advance from the Bank was a new plant constructed jointly by Guest, Keen & Nettlefolds and Baldwins at Cardiff to replace obsolete plants inland. A smaller project, originated and organised by the Bank's technical adviser in 1937, and designed to fill a gap in the country's equipment, was the establishment of an electric steel-works at Jarrow, which had been left the most depressed of the Tyneside towns by the decline of Palmers's shipbuilding company. The neighbouring iron and steel firm of Consett joined the Bank in finding the initial capital — £1 million might be needed — and, when the scheme was working and well established, took over the Bank's share in it.

The Bank's other interventions in the steel industry were forced on it. On 4 May 1938 the Governor reported to the Committee of Treasury that Richard Thomas & Company had applied to their bankers for an immediate advance to enable them to continue the construction of their new works at Ebbw Vale; £6/7 million would be needed to complete them, and their bankers had refused to advance more than was needed for current business. Through the Securities Management Trust the Governor had advanced £400,000 to enable the contractors to continue their work, making it payable to the firm's bankers for them to hand on, and bringing in as participant the issuing house which had financed the scheme originally by an issue of debentures. It was natural that the Bank should help; the firm was the largest producer of thin sheet and tinplate, it had shown great technical enterprise by introducing the first continuous strip rolling-mill in the country with a new steel plant to feed it, and it was the essential basis for any rational reorganisation of the tinplate industry. But further advances had to be made, while an inquiry was conducted, and in the end a larger sum was required than for any previous scheme. This was provided by the Bank and the five biggest Clearing Banks contributing to a pool sufficient to assure the completion of the new plant; most of the money was provided against debentures, of which the Bank took £1 million. In addition the Bank provided £½ million against ordinary shares, and was given in return control of the business until the debentures were repaid. Again, a technically sound scheme, aided by the increased demands for the industry's products which followed, given time justified itself financially. After the Governor had retired, the business was merged with another large plant in its field, Baldwins, the debentures were paid off and the Bank gradually disposed of its ordinary shares at a profit.

A few months after Richard Thomas & Company appealed to the Bank, another steel-sheet producer, John Summers & Sons, found itself in a similar difficulty. It was engaged in putting in a continuous strip-mill and had exhausted its liquid resources and available credit with the work only half done. The Governor reported to the Committee of Treasury on 5 October 1938 that they needed additional finance to the amount of £3,600,000; they had been improvident in not assuring themselves of it first, but Thomas's difficulties had made it difficult for them to go to the market, and in any case the completion of this scheme was of national importance. The B.I.D. investigated the position, and brought the firm into contact with the United Steel Companies, which by this time had completely re-established its prosperity and had considerable surplus liquid resources. By January 1939 a scheme was worked out in agreement for a debenture issue of £2 million and the subscription of £1 million ordinary shares, for which the Bank took responsibility through the B.I.D. (as well as for any needs not met by the debenture issue), and of £1,288,000 by United Steel. The Bank was to have control; this, the Governor told the Committee, was necessary because the Bank had assumed 'moral and financial responsibilities' towards the joint-stock banks and others in connection with the money provided for Richard Thomas. To protect these interests and to ensure co-operation with the British Iron and Steel Federation, the same degree of control was necessary as the Bank possessed over Richard Thomas. The new plant was completed and was profitable from the first; co-operation with Richard Thomas was arranged.

One project in the plan for steel was not realised — the union of the three great steel firms on the Tees. Bolckow Vaughan was merged in Dorman Long, with the help of the Governor's advisers and the provision of some additional capital through the Bankers' Industrial Development Company; but the legal constitution of the third, South Durham, prevented the completion of the scheme. There were many other projects brought to the Governor on which he and his staff gave such advice as they could (if they were worth consideration at all) but which went no further. Some of the largest houses in the City wished to assist amalgamations in the coal industry; Norman encouraged them, but no concrete scheme emerged. He was approached with proposals for a merger of firms building railway locomotives; he made some inquiries and found that one of the chief firms refused to consider the project. Various sections of the woollen and worsted industry submitted schemes; the only one that had any result was a scheme for eliminating redundant machinery which the wool-combing section carried through without assistance. His advice was sought by the Government when the British film-making industry ran into financial difficulties; but it was the ordinary Bank staff that was involved in the lengthy and complicated investigations to which this led.

Inevitably, in a period of great trade depression, the news that the Bank had set up special agencies, in S.M.T. and B.I.D., to provide finance for industry which it could not get from ordinary sources, provoked a stream of applications from firms in difficulties, which could be fitted into no such schemes of rationalisation as these agencies were set up to assist. Isolated firms — which had not the national importance of Beardmores or the White Star; small amalgamations, aimed principally at improving the credit-standing of the constituent firms; technical projects, which could find no support in the then condition of the capital market; owners of private businesses who wished to sell out while there was still something left to sell — all sought out the Governor.[1] But many quite reasonable proposals were investigated, which it proved impossible to help. An example was the proposal brought to the Governor by a Labour Member of Parliament for a new company to be formed by Imperial Chemical Industries and other concerns in the relevant field of chemical industry, to investigate and develop the production of synthetic petrol and so to reduce the country's dependence on imported supplies. The Governor received the proposal sympathetically, secured a report on it from one of the leading scientific advisers in the government service and took it to the Treasury; but his efforts led to nothing.

(vi)

The interest which Norman found himself forced to take in industry — in the customers of the Clearing Banks and banking houses who were his own customers — drew him into a number of tentative essays in devising new or modifying old financial institutions, to supplement the existing machinery of finance, and incidentally to relieve him, in his position of Governor, from appeals for help which were outside the Bank's normal business.

The earliest in point of time was an institution to provide farmers with additional facilities for borrowing. It was promised in the King's Speech on the opening of a new session of Parliament in 1926. The Governor drew the attention of the

[1] One of the Governor's industrial advisers, meeting a Director of the B.I.D. at dinner with a medical scientist, naturally fell into conversation with him on their common interest. Presently their host broke in with the question, 'What on earth are you people talking about B.I.D for?' They explained, and received the reply, 'B.I.D. is short for Brought in Dead, and it means two guineas for the House Surgeon on duty'. When this story was told at the Bank lunch table the Governor was not amused; for many of the proposals brought to him the description was only too apt.

Committee of Treasury to it on February 3, adding that the joint-stock banks (with whom he had been consulting) were discussing it, and that the Bank should subscribe to any scheme. The banks' discussions were slow and difficult. They were doubtful of the need; certainly the farmers would not get better terms than they got from the banks. If short-term credits (mentioned in the Government's statement) were included, they would largely replace existing sources in the banks and dealers. The Government would have to guarantee the bonds issued by the new institution if the rates were to be kept low, and provision would have to be made that the borrowers could not anticipate repayment if interest rates as a whole came down. Moreover, the banks were not all equally interested in farmers' loans, and one of the five biggest banks was unwilling to participate at all unless the Government guaranteed a return on the institution's own capital. It was not until the end of 1928 that agreement was reached. All the banks except one agreed to contribute capital, as did the Bank of England; the Bank agreed to make advances to the new institution in anticipation of its issues of bonds to the public. It was confined to long-term loans and called The Agricultural Mortgage Corporation; the Governor proposed Sir Otto Niemeyer, who with the Governor had assisted in the negotiations, as a member of its first Board. By March 1931 the Governor was able to report that the Corporation was working well. The Scottish banks found it expedient, owing to their different legal system, to form a separate Scottish corporation, and had asked the Governor to arrange for the Government's brokers to do the underwriting for their issues. Towards the end of the war, when the movement among farmers to buy their farms was growing, the banks increased the resources of the Corporation, and the bank which had stood out came into the scheme, taking over some of the Bank of England's shares.

The second innovation was an experiment in meeting an alleged deficiency in the provision of medium-term credit. To meet a shortage of bills available to the market, the Bank had considered in February 1929 relaxing the conditions on which it would discount instalment finance bills. This came to nothing, but in October the Governor referred to it and suggested that he might be asked for additional capital by an

approved company providing instalment finance, whose bills
might be made eligible for re-discount at the Bank. He had
been discussing the problem of financing re-equipment of
industry with Gibson Jarvie, the Managing Director of an instalment finance company, the United Dominions Trust, who
thought that he could do something to meet industry's need.
The Governor offered him additional capital, provided that it
was used 'for productive purposes, no luxuries'; and secured
the Committee of Treasury's approval to subscribing £250,000
'subject to satisfactory understanding as to policy and personnel'. More capital was put in in November 1935, but the
Bank's whole holding was sold over the next three years.

The same agency was used to help with another problem.
The Macmillan Committee had called attention to a gap in
the existing provision for industrial finance — the needs of
firms which were too small to make a public issue, but needed
finance for a longer period than would properly form the subject of a bank advance. In 1932 one of the Clearing Banks was
discussing the need with a merchant banker — an 'Industrial
Mortgage Scheme' they called it — and brought it to the
Governor. He entirely approved and offered his moral support; he urged them to bring in the other Clearing Banks,
though he did not feel he could act as their spokesman. The
scheme did not mature; the demands for credits in the condition of trade at the time confronted the banks with problems
enough without seeking new responsibilities. But schemes were
put forward in various quarters, and in February 1934 the
Governor did appeal to the Clearing Bankers, at their quarterly
meeting in the Bank, to give their financial support to a scheme.
At this point the United Dominions Trust offered to set up a
company for which it would find the capital itself, provided that
the Clearing Banks would give it banking facilities. This they
were very ready to do, and the company, Credit for Industry,
was set up with the purpose of providing finance for the smaller
industrial concerns, where the amount required would not
justify a public issue; normally the maximum for any one
concern would be £50,000. The Governor suggested Bruce
Gardner as a Director, and the company performed a useful
service until war broke out.

A special case of the problem of small concerns was found

in the Special Areas, scheduled by the Government as in need of new industries to relieve the endemic unemployment caused by the loss of older industries. The Governor reported to the Committee of Treasury in October 1935 that the Commission for Special Areas was being pressed to provide medium-term credits. After discussion with the Chancellor (Neville Chamberlain) and with financiers with experience of such financing, he proposed to the Board of Trade at the end of the year a scheme for a company with a capital of £1 million and a life of four years to make advances with a maximum of £10,000 to any one concern in the Special Areas. The capital was provided as to nine-tenths by insurance and other large companies, as to one-tenth by the Clearing Banks and Bank of England; the Government met the expenses of administration and bore a quarter of any loss. When it was put into liquidation in 1947 no dividend had been paid on the shares, but the capital was repaid; loans for £300,000 were still outstanding, but only if there was very extensive and unexpected default would the Government be involved in any loss. The company was administered from the Bank, and served incidentally to advise and assist the trustees to whom Lord Nuffield had given £1 million also for the help of industry in the Special Areas.

The Governor was approached also in February 1932, when the banks were cumbered with frozen industrial advances accumulated through the depression, with a proposal for a liquidation company to take them over; but it did not come from banking quarters and he refused to consider it. He would favour, he said, a B.I.D. to unfreeze generally the banks' present industrial lock-ups, but not a securities company tied to one bank. On the other hand, he encouraged a group of merchant-bankers who discussed with him in November 1931 a scheme for a re-discount institution to relieve accepting houses of some of their commitments: but again the pressure was not great enough to secure general support, and the scheme went no further.

After all attempts to devolve them on new agencies, there remained industrial and financial troubles which were brought to the Governor, sometimes via the Treasury, in the same way as the steel and shipping companies that occupied so much of his time in the 'thirties, just because they had reached, or threatened to reach, the dimensions of a political issue, and there was no one else ready and equipped to handle them. In this way the Governor's immediate advisers and helpers were engaged on the difficulties of the film industry and of tin companies, as well as those of banks and accepting houses involved in the Standstill on German and Austrian credits.

It remains to record the subsequent history of Norman's own creations—Securities Management Trust and the Bankers' Industrial Development Company. Both were devised to meet a particular situation. The Bank was not in a position to undertake a general reform; it could only respond to initiative on the part of industry, and to appeals from particular trades or firms. But these were numerous and promising enough to call for special agencies, on the one hand to relieve the Governor and his colleagues in the Bank of the day-to-day supervision of these new interests, on the other to link the existing agencies for providing capital with the Bank's initiative. By 1934 the situation had changed. In universal depression bankruptcy cuts many knots. The Government's general financial policy, relieved of the obligations of the Gold Standard, aimed almost exclusively at relieving and reviving industry. The demand of industries like steel and engineering, which had suffered from the competition of countries which excluded British competition from their own markets, had been met by Protection. Unemployment had forced a great shift of labour out of coal and shipbuilding into building and such new industries as motor manufacture and electrical equipment.

Early in 1935 the B.I.D. was due under its articles to be wound up, unless special steps were taken to extend it. At the same time the engagement with the Bank of the specialist advisers, who constituted the Board of S.M.T., also came to an end. In June and July 1934 the Governor reviewed with the Committee of Treasury the progress of the schemes to which they were committed, and particularly the prospects of finally liquidating the complex of interests springing from Armstrongs. The conclusion to which the review pointed was that there was little scope for active initiative, though the Bank must still expect to be called on for special assistance for particular firms. The number of public issues had been small; an organisation for systematic planning of industrial reorganisation and making public issues to finance them did not seem justified. A personal change, which weighed heavily with Norman, was the resignation from S.M.T. of Sir Andrew Duncan. This left him, as he noted, with no one else who knew the Bank's investments and commitments in industry except Bruce Gardner, the Managing Director of S.M.T. These constituted an excessive burden for one man, who ought to be relieved of legal and accounting contacts and of much resulting correspondence, though he should see it all. The burden was, it may be noted, undoubted, since in addition to specific tasks Bruce Gardner was the point of contact for the whole of the group of Heavy Industries with the Bank. The decision come to was to retain the services of Bruce Gardner alone among the industrial advisers. The B.I.D. was extended for another five years, the capital structure being modified so that the full amount of the shares held by the Bank would be called up before any call was made on the shares held by other banks and finance houses.

Five years later the same questions came up again. The need of an agency in the Bank to deal with the Bank's financial relations with industry, and of an agency through which capital could be raised in large amounts to meet the needs of reorganisation and re-equipment, had been demonstrated again by the Bank's part in the reorganisation of shipping, and in steel by the needs of Richard Thomas, Summers and Jarrow. There was again a personal question involved : the Government were asking for the services of Bruce Gardner for rearmament. It was again decided to keep the two companies in existence, the B.I.D. with a capital of nominal amount, and the Bank was looking for a successor to Bruce Gardner when the imminence of war postponed further plans. Finally, during the war, when the question of the needs of small firms for new capital was under discussion, the future of the B.I.D. was again discussed. It was, however, virtually superseded by the Finance Corporation for Industry, in the formation of which the Bank took the initiative. In August it was decided, in view of government policy in regard to industry, that its useful life was ended. Securities Management Trust survived as a convenient agency for holding the remaining Bank interests in industry.

When in January 1931 Norman invited the Chairman of the
United Steel Companies to call, the latter expressed his surprise
that the Governor of the Bank of England should trouble
himself about the problems of the steel industry. When on
July 22 in the same year the Chairman of the Cunard Company wrote to confirm the undertaking he had given to study
the position of the White Star Line, he began : 'I thank you
for your courtesy in according me an interview last Thursday,
when your mind must have been full of matters of more
primary importance even than British North Atlantic Shipping
as represented by the Cunard and White Star Lines'. Other
callers, though less appreciative, were equally surprised ; one,
whose chairmanship of a family business was in question,
brought a shorthand writer with him and earned an entry in
the Governor's diary — 'unreasonable and overbearing — I
stone-walled'. But the Governor's interest was natural, indeed
inevitable. As he put it himself, he had been faced with two
tasks in office, first the restoration of normal commercial life
in Europe, and then the restoration of stable currencies with
Banking as the foundation ; with these accomplished he found
British export industry in no condition to take its part in the
recovery of world trade. He did not presume to say how
industry should be run ; but if there were weaknesses which
depended on finance he felt justified, if not compelled, in taking
an initiative.

He used the term *Rationalisation* as a convenient label for the
policy he wished to further. It was a current catchword,
which, strictly applied, indicated what was aimed at. Industry
is continually in process of readjustment to changes in its
technical or commercial conditions. It is liable to cling to
traditional and existing methods, which change has made
obsolete or inept. War and the post-war boom had checked
the normal piecemeal process of adjustment, while at the same
time they created new commercial conditions vastly different
from those of industry before 1914. After the war low profits
or losses in the industries most in need of readjustment — the
older export industries — and high taxation had further handicapped and delayed necessary changes ; while government
policy had been directed rather to relieving the resultant unemployment than to creating conditions in which employment

would expand. For some industries markets had suffered a permanent contraction, with excessive competition for what was left; in others technical advance had rendered much existing equipment obsolete or inefficient.

Popular usage identified Rationalisation with amalgamation; amalgamation was only an incident or means. If an industry suffered, like shipbuilding or coal or cotton, from capacity excessive in relation to any probable demand for its product and an organised contraction was necessary, some merging of existing units, and still more some united action by the industry as a whole (as distinct from efforts by isolated firms) would be essential. Again, if an industry were in need of expensive re-equipment, as the steel industry was, joint action might be needed to secure an economic volume of output, and the acquisition and employment of the new equipment might be facilitated by a merger of existing firms. But in every case the first need was a rational criticism of the existing organisation of the industry (as distinct from the single firm), some measures to assure a market and then finance for such technical improvement as the scientists could suggest.

Norman was aware of the limits of what could be done, and distrustful of sweeping measures of amalgamation. He insisted that an amalgamation might be too large, especially if it aimed at covering a whole trade; that it was dangerous unless there were in sight men capable of managing the new concern; and that it could not be considered except on the basis of an expert examination of the firms to be absorbed and the plants they would contribute. Again and again he insisted at interviews that the process was troublesome and technical, involving questions of methods, materials, markets and persons. At the same time he was impatient at the slow progress made. He complained to the Committee of Treasury of the individualism of existing firms, the 'embedment' of existing directors and officials, unwillingness to admit new men (and ideas) from outside, and the reliance of investors on the false security of prior charges; and, on another occasion to the Chancellor, of the unwillingness of the joint-stock banks to use the power they possessed, as creditors of the most embarrassed industries, to compel reorganisation.

2 A

On the other hand, he feared compulsion by the State. One constant motive in his efforts was to relieve the Government of the necessity for intervention. It was the first impulse of many students of the depressed industries to turn to the State, and the natural reaction of a Socialist Minister. Norman was willing to use any influence by interview and exhortation, to strain the customary practice of the Bank in providing loans, and to encourage creditors to insist on reorganisation ; but he regarded the actual task of reorganisation as too delicate and technical to be solved merely by government compulsion. Compulsion might give control of an industry ; but, when control had been taken, every question of personalities, regional claims, choice of technical alternatives, selection of plant for expansion or closing, securing of outlets, as well as creating a new management capable of a novel and greater task of administration, and new relations with labour, would still have to be faced. But the aims of reorganisation were not in dispute ; Norman arranged a private meeting on 7 July 1931 to discuss the steel industry with some of the Union leaders, and noted 'Complete agreement — except on nationalisation !'

The obstacles to government action were, however, less doctrinaire than practical. The Socialist Governments did not command a Socialist majority in Parliament, and the Conservative and National Governments were not disposed to Socialist experiment ; but the critical position of the major export industries was such as to override doctrinal differences, if government action had been practicable. Government was not organised — as it had been during the First World War and was to be again in the Second World War — to act quickly in an emergency, and to administer complicated enterprises dependent on markets and under managements that had enjoyed independence. Norman was called in because he would act quickly, knowing that in an emergency the Bank's Committee of Treasury and Court would support him. Especially where it was a matter of meeting a sudden need for additional credits or new capital, he could and would act. His intervention was prompted by a succession of emergencies : in responding to such appeals the Governor was fulfilling the primary rôle of a Central Bank — acting as lender of last resort. The rôle was novel only in being extended from the banking to the

industrial and commercial field. But the fields were continuous, and the normal restriction to the Money Market a
matter of expediency, economy of resources and practical convenience rather than a sharp distinction of principle.

Thus his initiative was similar in principle to the initiative
he took in financing the recovery of Austria and other Central
European countries, in providing credit when the market was
difficult for the Governments of certain Empire territories and
in helping to get a settlement of German Reparations and
inter-allied debts. All were, on a comprehensive view, credit
problems, and all made their effects felt on the Bank of England.
The resources he could command were small compared with
those at the disposal of governments; but he could use them
with less delay, and he never lacked courage. Considered as an
exceptional and abnormal task, undertaken with an improvised
policy and an improvised staff, limited by the co-operation he
could secure from a reasonably suspicious capital market and
a properly cautious Court and Committee of Treasury, and
lacking any powers of coercion, to have saved the armament
capacity of Armstrongs and Beardmores, established one efficient large-scale unit in the cotton-spinning industry, restored
a large part of British liner traffic to profitable operation, helped
to save the greater part of shipbuilding from bankruptcy and
closing down, and prevented from collapse the experiment of
establishing a modern, technically efficient steel-sheet industry,
not to mention the minor activities described in this chapter,
was a considerable achievement. It is even more remarkable
when it is remembered that its author's main work — the
maintenance of stable monetary conditions — was at the same
time requiring his care and attention for the effects on sterling
of the New York stock market boom, the world decline in trade,
a flight from sterling and the working out of a new system of
international payments based on a freely moving exchange
rate.

CHAPTER IX

DEPRESSION AND CRISIS

(i)

THE collapse of the New York stock market boom in October 1929 relieved London and the Bank of a strain that had pre-occupied the Governor for more than a year. The fall of specu-lative profits in New York, the repatriation of French foreign balances, the return of flight money to Germany once the Young Plan was accepted, had called for all the resources a Central Bank could deploy to defend its currency. He had been handicapped, if he wished to restrict credit and make money dear, by the domestic claims of depressed industries, struggling exports and a rising Floating Debt; and the local preoccupations of other Central Banks had limited the co-operation he could secure from them. Now he could respond to domestic claims. Beginning on October 31 the Bank reduced its rate, in step with New York, from $6\frac{1}{2}$ to 3 per cent by May 1. The Bank replaced the gold it had lost since June 1929, and, although the Clearing Bankers' balances with the Bank of England were not expanded, their total deposits expanded by December 1930 to their highest point. But the removal of the abnormal difficulties with which the Governor and his fellow Central Bankers had been faced in their own special field of monetary policy, only threw into relief, as 1930 advanced, the intractable economic problems of world-wide depression in trade.

The relief from the necessity of high rates led observers to expect too much. Harrison in New York shared this optimism; he had telephoned on October 31 that he was well satisfied with the course of events, thought the market was through now and no bank failures likely. On November 15 he had more hope than ever and thought the bottom might have been reached. In the New Year he visited London and Paris; he found plenty of short money available, but a dearth of long-term funds for capital investment in various parts of the world. His policy was to make short-term rates sufficiently low to be unattractive and so to encourage a shift into long-term investment. He hoped Paris would soon be open to long-term borrowing, to share the burden with New York.

His policy, within its limits, was effective; the Federal Reserve Bank helped the New York banks to meet the pressure put on them to finance the liquidation of stock-market loans, and his cheap-money policy helped the revival of foreign lending in the first half of 1930, which (including the Young Loan) resulted in larger issues than in 1929. It also encouraged short-term loans to other centres, and the withdrawal of foreign money, employed in New York, to its country of origin, where it could ease the pressure for liquidity. London similarly maintained the volume of its foreign loans, long and short, though it is unlikely that in this case the current balance of payments, unaided by foreign credits, was sufficient to finance such lending. It was not in the tradition of London to cut off sharp, at the first sign of difficulty, the accommodation it gave to its debtors; by helping them to meet their needs, London might lessen the ultimate pressure on itself. If the current surplus of the United Kingdom had shrunk, it could be supplemented, if necessary, by the proceeds of maturing loans and the investment of overseas funds normally entrusted to London for reinvestment.

In the world as a whole, production and trade were declining. Indirectly and after some delay the effects began to appear in the United Kingdom. Unemployment, which in 1929, apart from the chronically depressed industries, had been relatively low, increased seasonally towards the end of the year, but, instead of the usual recovery in the spring, continued to increase throughout 1930. From the beginning of that year, it overshadowed every other economic and political question. The Government was criticised, and offered advice, as if the growing unemployment was a domestic matter within the area of its control; in fact the depression was world-wide and overtook the United Kingdom comparatively late. The fall in the level of activity and income was not so great in Britain as in Germany, the United States and many other countries. The full impact of depression was not revealed by general index-numbers; the most serious change was in agricultural prices, which declined earlier and further than industrial prices. Critical conditions appeared first in agricultural countries — in the Dutch East Indies, Australia, Canada and British India — a year before the United Kingdom. In the United Kingdom, the volume of employment reached its highest point in 1929, after prices had turned downwards, in spite of the monetary problems which were causing the Governor such anxiety. In the United States production reached a peak in the middle of 1929, at the same time as prices, and fell precipitously in the last quarter of the year; a fall which continued until the spring of 1933. Exports and imports turned downwards a little later than production, but then followed the same course. Thus the shock of the stock market collapse fell upon an economy in which a general decline had already set in, and helped to give it the cumulative character which made it so profound.

The same cumulative effects were seen in international relations. The depression of the overseas primary producers was presently reflected in declining markets for British exports; the export industries, depressed already by the effect of war-time changes in shutting them out of their customary markets, were the first and chief sufferers in the general depression. In America, trade depression, following on the shock given to the credit of so many of their customers by the collapse of security prices, forced many banks into bankruptcy, and after 1930 put a stop to American foreign lending. The American market for the exports of primary and other products of other countries contracted, intensifying their difficulties, while the artificial prosperity of Germany, other European countries and South America, which had been built up and sustained by the spending of American loans, abruptly collapsed. America itself suffered by this cessation of lending, because the volume and prices of its exports needed the support of foreign loans; more serious for the rest of the world was the strain on the Gold Standard imposed by an American excess of exports (without lending) which had to be paid for in gold. The Labour Chancellor of the Exchequer (Snowden) early in 1930 contrasted ruefully the conditions with which he found himself faced, when he took office in June 1929, with the state of affairs when he had first assumed responsibilities of office in 1924; they were conditions which no Minister or Government of a single country could control.

The decline in employment and profits intensified the criticism of the monetary policy with which Norman was associated. Just before the American crash he warned the Chancellor to resist at the Trade Union Congress the temptation to treat the depression as soluble by monetary expedients — not that Snowden was so predisposed; even the promise of a committee of inquiry might threaten the maintenance of the Gold Standard. He wrote afterwards to congratulate him on the results of his speech, 'indigestible and unattractive' as it looked at the time. As we have seen, the Central Bankers were not disposed, either in theory or in practice, to accept the responsibility for the level of prices which current opinion sought to put upon them. When, as money became cheaper and cheaper, only to be accompanied by deeper and deeper depression, opinion shifted from interest rates to the quantity and distribution of gold as the cause of the world's troubles, they still looked to government finance, political payments, and the inadaptability of industry for the explanation both of their countries' difficulties and of the unequal gold distribution accompanying them.

The Bank continued its policy of making money as cheap as the strain on the sterling exchanges allowed, and maintaining the supply of money in the London market with as little variation as possible by offsetting any decline or increase in its Reserve by adding to or reducing its Securities. In reducing Bank Rate it was following the market rate. There was a big reflux of funds from New York to Europe from October 1929 onwards. Although most of the gold movement which this involved was to France, and London in 1930 had to meet a drain to France and Germany, the strain was mitigated by distress exports of gold from Australia and other primary producers, and by the cessation of India's competition for South African gold. The country's gold reserve was a continual anxiety; but it was not until the more gradual strain of depression was reinforced by a flight from sterling in July 1931, and the Bank was not unwilling to impress the public with the seriousness of the position, that the Bank's gold was run down.

Throughout 1930 the first claim on Norman's energies was

made, not by his normal preoccupation with credit and exchange, but by the attempt to help with the reorganisation of
industry, with which we were concerned in the last chapter.
He was driven to this by his view of the long-term need of the
country for stronger and more efficient export industries, if a
stable exchange was to be possible. Like his colleagues in the
Bank, he regarded this intervention as something exceptional
and temporary, forced on the Bank by the abnormal conditions
of industry after a war. But it brought him into closer relations
with the Government. The Labour Cabinet was pledged to
an attack on unemployment, and predisposed to a policy of
expenditure on public works, such as Lloyd George was pressing on the country. The influence of the Chancellor and
Treasury limited it to schemes that were economically sound
and ruled out spending merely for the sake of spending. The
Governor's interest in industry, and his undertaking to find
finance for approved schemes of reorganisation without calling
on the Government, made it possible to attempt something
more than bare relief.

In addition, there were the fruits of the Hague Conference
to be garnered — the organisation of the Bank for International
Settlements to receive and distribute Reparations, and the issue
of the Young Loan. This was to be the first stage in 'mobilising' or 'commercialising' Reparations; that is, raising the
amount needed to pay off Reparations by loans from private
investors, issued on the security of the German Government's
Reparations annuity payments. Such loans provided immediate cash payments to the recipient Governments and to that
extent changed Germany's debt into an obligation to the private
investor, to whom, it was thought, Germany was less likely to
default than to political creditors; and it was even hoped by
some that the Young Loan would be the first of a series. The
Bank for International Settlements was also in a way the
product of this policy of 'commercialisation', a neutral agent
which would be interposed betwen ex-enemy Governments and
ex-Allies, and so strengthen the claims of the Loan to be
regarded as an ordinary obligation in the world's capital
market.

At first Norman had great hopes of the new institution. It
would be a valuable centre for meetings of Central Bankers and

so assist co-operation ; it might be able to facilitate clearing of
international debts, earmarking gold and so reducing the need
for actual movement of gold ; it might develop banking and
issuing business supplementary to its handling of Reparations
payments. Schacht discouraged such hopes. A centralised
system for accounting for gold transfers and earmarking, he
argued, was unnecessary ; Central Banks could more simply
make their arrangements direct ; existing opportunities for
arbitrage were not adequately used, and he would much prefer
direct Central Bank initiative when any export of gold other
than through the market was necessary. Schacht was doubtful
whether he would make any deposits with the new Bank ; if he
did they would be callable. When Norman asked him whether
the B.I.S. was not entitled to the same support, irrespective of
profit, as any national Central Bank, he got no response.

Norman seems to have been convinced ; his note of possible
policy for the Bank was limited, in addition to its primary function of handling Reparations, to facilitating co-operation and
such banking, other than commercial banking, as it could
find scope for. National Central Banks should be free to impose
such limits on the B.I.S.'s transactions in their markets as they
thought fit, though obviously they must leave it some scope for
business. Even so, he took immense pains to assist in launching
the new institution on right lines, securing the Chancellor's
assent to his selections for the English members of the Organising Committee, Addis and Walter Layton,[1] and keeping in
touch with Schacht who was the German member. Because
they both attached primary value to the use of the Bank as a
meeting-place, they wanted a large Board, an international
staff, and a chief executive who would be regarded as neutral
in European controversies. The head had therefore to be an
American ; even when he was found in G. W. McGarrah, a
banker who had been a member of the Reichstag Board
under the Dawes Plan, they were nervous of excessive French
influence, and insisted on an American Vice-President, if there
was to be a French General Manager. Subsequently Norman
secured the appointment also of an English Manager.

The first business of the Bank, when it came into being in
April 1930, was to make arrangements for the issue of the

---

[1] Knighted, 1930. Lord Layton, 1947.

Young Loan. The details of the Reparations Plan had been worked out at a second Hague Conference in January, agreement reached, and signed by Germany (in spite of Schacht's opposition) on January 20. The Loan was an ambitious and complicated essay in international finance. The date — before October, the amount — $300 million, and the nature of the guarantees, had been decided at The Hague. The term, thirty-five years, and the nominal rate of interest, $5\frac{1}{2}$ per cent, were embodied in a B.I.S. draft. The Bank then convened a meeting on May 1 in Brussels of bankers from the markets in which the Loan was to be issued. This was followed on May 6 by a meeting of representatives of the Treasuries of the countries which were to participate in the proceeds of the Loan. Finally a committee of four — Norman, who had taken a leading part in the Brussels meeting, Luther, who had succeeded Schacht as President of the Reichsbank when the latter resigned in March in protest against the burden put on Germany, an American and a Frenchman — working almost continuously from May 30 to June 3, completed the scheme in detail. The General Bond was signed by the German Finance Minister on June 10, just a year after the Young Plan had been completed; the issue followed on June 13.

The issue was made on nine markets in as many currencies, and the proceeds were to be distributed among seven countries, not all included among the issuers. The United States took just under $86 million, France just under $85 million, Great Britain $49 million, Sweden and Holland $25 million each, and Switzerland $15 million. It was a further charge on the same German revenues as had been charged with the Dawes Loan, but it came at a time when the financial climate was very different. The Dawes Loan had been issued in an atmosphere of hope, in order to restore Germany's industry and contribution to Europe's economic life. The Young Loan, though it was the crown of a plan which was accepted as a final settlement of the Reparations problem, came at a time when the financial sky was overcast, economic depression was deepening, and the flow of international loans drying up. Markets did not respond, the bankers who had taken up the Loan could not dispose of it to more permanent holders, it went to a discount, and the Bank for International Settlements had no means of supporting it. The burden of the annuities fell heavily on Germany with the decline of her trade and the cessation of foreign credits. But the settlement of the Reparations problem remained an achievement. In the disorder and difficulty of world depression, Reparations would otherwise have embittered political relations again and aggravated the world's economic difficulties.

The Bank for International Settlements, if it did not realise the high hopes of providing a 'Central Bank for Central Banks', able to expand credit to any limit needed to revive international trade, settled down to the useful function of providing a regular meeting-place, at which the Governors of the national Central Banks could meet, without attracting excessive attention and exciting unreasonable hopes or suspicions, could discuss their common problems and develop the habit of looking at them from the point of view of Europe and the world. In this they were aided by a staff which was varied in its national composition and forced by its position, and by its systematic studies, to take that point of view. Norman was the most loyal of the Bank's supporters and the most regular attendant at its Board and other meetings. It was enabled to engage in normal banking operations by the deposit with it of considerable sums by Central Banks, notably the Bank of France, which supplemented the deposits representing the temporary custody of Germany's Reparation payments. Norman's loyalty did not deter him from vigorous criticism of the technical conduct of these operations when he felt they were not of a character entirely appropriate to the new institution.

(ii)

For the Bank of England's normal business, though not for its Governor, the year 1930 was quiet compared with the preceding and succeeding years. Norman returned from a month in Egypt, whither he had been driven by the cumulative strains of the previous autumn (a request from the Macmillan Committee for oral evidence being the last straw), to find that the great Clydeside armament firm, Beardmores, was again needing his intervention. The movement which he had started for the reorganisation of the export industries had excited hopes, and new schemes were being pressed on him from all sides. Depression made the completion of certain schemes for merging or strengthening local banks in the affected areas more urgent; he told the Committee of Treasury in August that he was relieved to be able to report one more merger. Demands for credit and loans — from Argentina, India, Chile, Austria, Australia — were being pressed on London. The Committee approved a credit to the Commonwealth Bank of Australia to meet a temporary need of sterling. Norman did not rule out foreign loans; but, to keep some control, secured the Chancellor's agreement to a policy of allowing only loans approved by the Governor. He was anxious to bring down the price of money quickly, but wished to do it by agreement with other centres. He failed to secure common action when he visited Rome in February for the B.I.S. Organising Committee, and the Bank reduced its Rate to 4 per cent on March 6 independently; as it did again a fortnight later to $3\frac{1}{2}$ per cent. Rome was a disappointment also, because the committee refused to consider the project of making the B.I.S. into a 'Central Bankers' bank' or anything but a Reparations bank. At the end of April the Governor of the Federal Reserve Bank of New York cabled that he would probably reduce his rate to 3 per cent; there had been some recovery of stock prices and industrial output in America. Norman hoped that France and Belgium would follow suit, and it was decided to reduce Bank Rate to 3 per cent. Thus London was ready for its *tranche* of the Young Loan on June 13; it was also possible to issue in July a long-delayed Austrian Loan, to which the Chancellor attached importance.

In the second half of the year world depression began to dominate people's minds. The growing demand for Protection of British industry and Imperial Preferences was supported by a bankers' manifesto (signed among others by McKenna and by a Director of the Bank) on July 4. The Governor had to make it clear that it did not emanate from the Bank, indeed his own feeling was that the demand for Protection at that moment deterred industry from facing its problems itself. In Germany the combined strain of growing unemployment and the Administration's attempts to maintain balance in its budget and a surplus on its external trade excited growing discontent. The Reichstag election, which took place on September 14, resulted in a disconcerting increase in the representation of the National Socialists and the Communists. International confidence was shaken and at once there began a flight of capital. Germany had built up its gold reserves, aided by its share of the proceeds of the Young Loan, to the highest point since 1924, and had not reduced short-term interest rates to the extent that the other great powers had; but from this time on her finances were in difficulty and her currency under strain. The first important discussion, on October 10, of the Board of the B.I.S., was on Germany's difficulties.

Shortly afterward the first reports began to reach the Bank of distrust of sterling. On November 19 the Committee of Treasury considered, but decided against, raising Bank Rate. The Governor told the Committee that he had discussed the dollar rate with Harrison, who was of the opinion that if it fell far enough to lead to gold shipments to America, this would be partly due to the domestic and budget situation in the United Kingdom. A fortnight later the Governor pointed out that the American and French exchanges would have been more unfavourable but for the support given by the Federal Reserve Bank and the Bank of France; but it was unlikely that the latter would continue its purchases of sterling. Harrison had told him that he was much disturbed over the position in Europe (where in his opinion 'there was no good borrower'), and was not prepared to hold more than a limited amount of sterling, but thought it might be possible to induce the Bank of France to ease the situation by a simultaneous lowering of discount rates and some foreign lending. Co-operation between the most important of the Central Banks survived; and New York on December 23 and Paris on January 2 reduced their rates to 2 per cent.

Norman had had to tell Harrison that, while a reduction in the French rate would be useful, he could not pledge himself not to follow suit, and he doubted whether a policy of capital export by France was practicable. He went on to tell the Committee that the Chancellor had consulted him on the stream of questions, in and out of Parliament, about gold, and the need of a definite plan of action. He had replied that the

Chancellor could ask the Bank of England to summon a conference of bankers, as proposed by the Genoa Conference, but the invitation would be declined (bitter complaints had reached the Bank from the Federal Reserve Bank and the Bank of France on the publication of the League's Gold Report); or he could make use of the Gold Delegation of the League; or he could ask the B.I.S. to summon a conference, or summon a governmental conference himself. But the Chancellor was not prepared to adopt any of these suggestions.

Norman knew that direct discussions of the drain of gold to France had been initiated by the French Treasury. British Treasury officials discussed with him the line they should take, and subsequently the actual course of the talks. The debate followed much the same lines as had Norman's discussions with Moreau in 1927. The British spokesmen argued that France exercised an excessive pull over the world's gold, because she had undervalued her currency when she stabilised her exchange. The French replied that the influx of gold was due to the normal working of the Gold Standard; England should apply the orthodox remedy of a higher Bank Rate. The obstacle to expanding foreign lending was the doubtful credit of borrowers; but loans were being made to Romania, Poland and Yugoslavia, and Paris was quite ready to buy British securities. Norman had discussed with the Treasury the possibility of a loan in France, but it had been agreed that the political objections were too great. He objected to French purchases of British Government securities even more, and his reports led him to doubt whether Paris still thought well enough of the British political outlook to buy them.

While the Bank of France and Bank of England had preferred not to be drawn into the Treasury discussions, Norman had discussed this subject with Moret, the Governor of the Bank of France, who had warned him of the political difficulties of expanding foreign lending, but said that the French Government might welcome a British proposal for a loan in Paris. The Committee of Treasury shared Norman's dislike of this expedient. The Bank of France were only too anxious to check the influx of gold, but attributed it to 'natural' causes — the withdrawal of French funds from other centres because the depressed conditions there left no employment for them, the

lower cost of France's raw material imports reducing her need
for foreign exchange, and political fears leading to a withdrawal
of balances from London in spite of the favourable interest rate.
In the spring of 1931 Moret put forward a proposal for a syndicate to encourage the resort to Paris for short- and medium-
term credits, for which Paris had ample funds. Norman promised to support such a movement by interesting London
bankers in it, which he did; but there was no significant
result.

On 14 January 1931 Norman raised with the Committee
of Treasury the question of their policy if the drain of gold from
London continued. He had discussed it with the Chancellor,
and had told him that if there were any signs of a flight from
sterling, he would consider it necessary to raise Bank Rate; it
would be unpopular, but, he believed, necessary, and it would
draw attention to the unsatisfactory position. He had been
surprised at the lack of resilience in sterling at this time of year.
A week later he had to point out that the position had deteriorated, and the New York exchange was below gold point. His
inclination was against earmarking gold in New York or trying
to arrange a loan in France or the United States. He did not
advise raising Bank Rate yet; but would try to tighten the
market rate, and would suggest to the Bank of France that they
take from him dollars in exchange for francs to support the
sterling-franc rate. This action proved temporarily effective;
London, in spite of a worsening balance of payments, gained
gold, thanks to other countries' greater difficulties until the
second half of the year, and Bank Rate, when it was changed
on May 14, followed the market and New York down. Nevertheless, Norman's anxiety over sterling was never relieved, and
he reported that his fellow Central Bankers in Basle thought
that London could no longer be relied on as a capital market.
The reduction in Bank Rate came in the same week as he
reported to the Committee of Treasury the difficulties of the
Credit-Anstalt.

By this time it was apparent that the depression in industry
was something far more profound than could be explained by
the shock of a stock market collapse or a strain on industry's
liquid resources. In the United Kingdom the number of registered unemployed, which had been 1,344,000 at the end of

1929, had increased to 2,500,000 by the end of 1930, in Germany from 2,851,000 to 4,384,000; in the United States industrial production had fallen by a fifth; in every country prices had fallen steeply and were still falling. Agriculture was in greater straits than industry, and industries dependent on export than the sheltered trades which worked exclusively for a home market, but the depression had now spread to every branch of economic life. Wage-rates were maintained as prices fell, but earnings were reduced by unemployment; products with their prices maintained by price agreements found their markets disappearing. The weaknesses left in the economy of the world by the war were aggravated and reacted on the economy as a whole. These depressive elements in the world were no longer offset by the expansion of building, automobiles and other new industries, based on inflationary profits in America and the stimulus of Protectionist nationalism elsewhere, and the outcome was visible in world-wide depression. For the Central Banker the effect was seen in a general strain on government finances, and a renewed threat to the stability of currencies and exchanges.

It had been a principal aim, and one of the chief results, of the restoration of the Gold Standard and stabilisation of exchanges to restore the free flow of capital between countries. By this means the burden of Reparations and other debt, which had held back the return of Germany and Central Europe to normal commercial activity and to stability in government finances, had been lifted; the rapid expansion of the new countries outside Europe — the British Dominions and the Republics of South America — had been financed; London and Amsterdam had been able to resume their traditional function of world-bankers, America to use its enormous surplus resources to supplement them. But this flow of capital assumed a world restored to normal industry and trade, with countries in balance, industry and agriculture properly related in the world as a whole, and the great industries expanding together, so that the process of exchange could go on smoothly and without check. The world was still far from this condition. Agriculture was only intermittently prosperous. Industries like coal, steel, shipbuilding and textiles, overstimulated by war or Protection, were highly vulnerable to any recession in world demand. The free movement of funds might also take the form of a drain from centres which were short of capital to New York where large and quick profits were offered, or to Paris in anticipation of the stabilisation of the franc. London, the world's chief middleman and clearing centre, was enabled to resume its overseas lending, long and short, but the proportion of its own savings, available through its own favourable balance, to funds temporarily deposited in London by other centres, had declined. Once doubts began to arise of the ability of borrowers to repay, creditors sought to withdraw their funds, and the very success of the movement to restore capital movement became a danger. The deepening of trade depression justified such doubts; great industries and whole countries became doubtful debtors. The check to the flow of loans, on which the new countries outside Europe had come to depend, had the same effect as a contraction of credit. The inflated supply of funds, long and short, since the war had led to much extravagance and misdirected investment which any check to lending revealed. Even in England, where the price of credit had been kept up, supplies had been ample enough to finance speculative booms on the Stock Exchange and in the new issue market. Depression created budgetary problems for governments, and recalled the danger of inflation only recently brought under control. When to all these economic elements in a disturbed and anxious world were added political fears, the danger appeared of the movement of funds from motives of panic and the transition from trade depression to financial crisis. Such political fears were excited by the September election to the Reichstag, and it gradually became clear that the policy of the Labour Government in the United Kingdom, with however little reason, was exciting similar fears in other countries.

The impact of world depression outside the United Kingdom was illustrated earliest and most clearly by Australia's misfortunes. There the fall in the world price of the country's staple products, wool and wheat, following a period of inflationary expansion based on foreign borrowing, had reduced the income of the country by a fifth and left the Government faced in 1931 with a deficit in its budget, unemployment, the need to reduce wages (which were regulated under statute by

Australian Courts), and a large short-term external debt.   The
crisis was precipitated by a statement from the Commonwealth
Bank of Australia — a Government-owned institution — that
it could not make advances to wheat growers in excess of the
realisable export price of their wheat, and a decision by the
Commonwealth Court of Arbitration that wages should be
reduced by 10 per cent.   Scullin, the head of the Labour
Government, made a public declaration against any attempt
to deal with the situation by further inflation.   When pressed
to do so by the Trade Unions Conference, he refused to override
the award of the Arbitration Court and the left wing of the
party split under the leadership of Lang, the Premier of New
South Wales, who proposed the suspension of payments to
external bondholders and the reduction of interest on internal
debt.   Scullin replied that the Commonwealth Government
would meet any default on its debt by New South Wales.   On
February 13 the Commonwealth Bank refused to finance State
Governments further unless expenditure was reduced.   After
the failure to carry through a plan to balance the budget by
means of a three-year programme, the Bank informed the
Commonwealth Treasurer that it could provide no further
finance unless there was an improvement in the economic
situation.

However, the British Government postponed for two years
Australia's payments on its War Debt.   Continual pressure had
been maintained on the Government by the Loan Council,
representative of both Commonwealth Government and States,
through which all plans for external borrowing had for some
years been canalised ;   in April it agreed to the raising of an
external loan, and discussed ways of reducing expenditure.
It recommended also a reduction in bank interest, and a conference of State Premiers and Treasurers to formulate a programme for restoring financial stability.   The plan, drawn up
with expert advice at the end of May, was drastic and effective.
The chief measures were a reduction in the global amount of all
government wages, salaries and pensions by 20 per cent below
the previous year's figures and a voluntary conversion of
Government Debt to a 4 per cent basis.   The Loan Council
approved ;   the Labour Party itself finally accepted the necessity ;   and the opposition to releasing enough of the gold reserves

to meet maturing bills in London was withdrawn. Even New South Wales fell into line. The necessary legislation was passed, the banks, the largest holders of Government Debt, gave a lead in accepting the conversion — with the Commonwealth Bank, which refused further loans for unemployment works, they also justified the Administration's resolution by notifying it of the limit beyond which no further credit could be given. By October the deficit had been brought within manageable terms, and the crisis was over.

On March 21 Norman left for America, on a visit Harrison had suggested earlier in the year. He returned just a month later, having visited Washington and seen the President, Mellon, the Secretary of the Treasury, and the Federal Reserve Board, as well as the Federal Reserve Bank in New York. His report to the Committee of Treasury was that the United States was concerned only with American securities, and no longer with foreign lending ; its costs needed bringing down, but any reduction in wages was opposed ; existing rates for money were likely to persist indefinitely. It would seem that the purpose of his visit was to discuss the ominous shrinking in world trade, and the possibility of reversing it. There was as yet no urgent sense of crisis, and he was concerned on his return to the Bank with the needs of industry and the national finances.

(iii)

The collapse of the Credit-Anstalt on May 11 was a turning-point. The strain of economic decline was revealed, no longer on the periphery of the Western World, in countries like Australia, the Argentine and the United States itself, with immense natural resources and potential reserves, but at the heart of the closely integrated financial system of Western Europe. It appeared in the country in which a breakdown had come first after the war, and the efforts of international co-operation had been called for first. The policy of the Allied Governments in breaking up the Hapsburg Empire into separate national States had weakened the trade and finance of all the territories affected, without making them independent and self-dependent. Each was tied to others by credits or debits, investments and contracts, and a failure of one must threaten the stability, if not the solvency, of its creditors and suppliers. The Credit-Anstalt was the most important bank in Austria, with a large part of Austrian industry dependent on it for finance. Like other Continental banks, its resources were largely tied up in more or less permanent investments in industrial firms; yet, again like most Central European banks, these resources were derived in part from deposits made and credits given by foreign banks. If declining trade destroyed industry's ability to repay the bank, the bank could not meet its own recurring liabilities, and its difficulties would be transmitted to other banks in other countries.

Norman reported to a special meeting of the Committee of Treasury the Credit-Anstalt's difficulties the day it announced its inability to meet them; the Austrian Finance Minister had appealed to him to send one of his Advisers; he had refused because the B.I.S. had already sent representatives to investigate. But the business of the special meeting was domestic — an appeal from the Government to the Bank to come to the assistance of a great shipping line. At the ordinary meeting on the 13th Norman reported that the Austrian National Bank, Austrian Government and Rothschilds had arranged to give the Credit-Anstalt the support needed. The following week, it was reported that the Credit-Anstalt was trying to arrange meetings of creditors in different centres to extend credits and had asked the Bank to take the lead in London; this it was not yet prepared to do. Norman was in Basle at the time for the Board and General meetings of the B.I.S.; he returned two days later to learn of proposals for an informal committee of creditors and shareholders. At Basle he had had the reports of other European bankers; he had also had a visit from Schacht. On Whit Monday, May 25, he came into the Bank, calling at the Treasury on his way but finding no one there, collected his advisers on Central Europe and telephoned his friends in the chief Continental centres; the rest of the day and evening he spent at Thorpe Lodge with his advisers working on the problem. The following day, he agreed a committee (and announcement) with Rothschilds and the other banking houses concerned. At the Committee of Treasury on the 27th he reported his approval of this committee. He said that the

National Bank was apathetic and the B.I.S. too slow; the
Credit-Anstalt was the dominant bank in Eastern Europe; he
feared a moratorium which would destroy Austrian credit;
the bank's future lay with its foreign creditors.

A week later he reported that the position was better; an
international committee of creditors had been formed. He
had refused a B.I.S. suggestion of a credit to the National Bank,
until he had the results of a proper inquiry to go on; but the
Committee should consider its attitude to further support —
their present commitment was £350,000. If the position in
Eastern Europe worsened, Germany would be involved, and
the trouble would ultimately spread to this country. If the
Bank decided to help, the Federal Reserve Bank would co-
operate. The Committee decided to support any co-operative
scheme sponsored by the B.I.S. *pro rata* up to $5 million.
Norman had been telephoning Harrison in New York, Luther
in Berlin, and Stewart in Basle, and had discussed the position
with the London committee. He had agreed with the creditors
that what was needed was to put into the Credit-Anstalt 'a
foreign butcher' — he had to explain to the Bank of France
that in adding that 'Schacht was the right type', he was not
proposing to bring Schacht back into a position of authority.
A Dutch adviser was put in, and a credit was arranged for the
National Bank by the B.I.S. At the same time the Austrian
Government tried to arrange a loan from private bankers to
the Credit-Anstalt; the negotiations broke down when the
Austrian Government resigned rather than accept the political
terms attached to the loan by the French. The Bank of England
provided a credit to meet the deficiency. But long before this
time Austria's difficulties had infected Germany.

There was a run on the banks in Germany at the end of
May. Germany was in no condition to meet any strain. As a
result of the great inflation in the 'twenties, industry and the
banks had lost their liquid resources. The banks replenished
them by attracting foreign deposits and drawing on acceptance
and other credits in foreign centres; it has been estimated that
about 45 per cent of German bank deposits at the end of 1928
were foreign-owned and even at the end of 1930 this proportion
was little changed. Thus Germany was dependent on foreign
capital to a critical extent, and, once the foreigner had any

reason to doubt the solvency of German industry or German Government, or the liquidity of German banks, exposed to withdrawals which the banks could not meet. The banks would transmit the strain to the Reichsbank by discounting with it, and the Reichsbank had been able to strengthen its reserves by a strict credit policy when Germany was enjoying the benefit of foreign loans. But there was no margin if large demands were simultaneously made on industry, Government and banks for immediate repayment of foreign credits. Such demands inevitably followed from Austria's difficulties; the economic relations of the two countries were close, and foreign creditors would expect a drain on Germany and seek to anticipate it.

The German banking system was a fair-weather system. Long-term investments in industrial and commercial concerns were a normal part of the banks' lending policy; such loans were not callable, and could not be made liquid in a crisis, least of all when the pressure came from foreigners whose claims had to be met in foreign exchange. Even the proceeds of acceptance credits were frozen in such illiquid loans, thus indirectly endangering the solvency of foreign banks which had given them. It was an unfortunate coincidence that when bad weather came, in the form of falling prices and falling tax receipts, the full weight of the obligations assumed under the Young Plan came into force. An unbalanced budget was added to an external drain to alarm the foreign creditors, and the pressure on the Reichsbank's exchange reserves was more than it could meet. There was a political obstacle to prompt help by other Governments. On March 19 the German Foreign Minister had revealed in a meeting at Geneva that Germany and Austria had agreed on a Customs Union. This announcement aroused the fears of France and the Succession States of the Austro-Hungarian Empire of a German political revival. The French Government had obstructed the grant of credits to Austria, so long as this agreement stood, and, although the British representatives at Geneva proposed that the question of the legality of the agreement be referred to the International Court at The Hague, and the German Foreign Minister accepted the proposal, the suspicions excited continued to obstruct international economic co-operation.

The German Chancellor (Bruening) and Foreign Minister

came over to London the first week-end in June. Norman was asked to the Foreign Office on the Friday night and to Chequers on Sunday to meet them. The British Government were not prepared to modify the Young settlement, the main object of the visit, though Norman thought it was inevitable. He mentioned these conversations to the Committee of Treasury, and cabled after them to Harrison in New York. He was being pressed by London bankers to know whether they should call in their credits to Germany; he deprecated such action. Germany was still a good bet in the long run and deserved help, not worrying. But Austria was still his main concern, and he was not prepared to encourage private bankers to grant credits there.

Once the joint Central Bank credit to Austria was arranged, however, he gave his whole mind and energies to Germany. Bruening used his emergency power of legislating by decree when the Reichstag was not sitting to do all that was practicable internally to reduce the strain on the Reich budget. He reduced the salaries of all government officials, reduced war pensions, cut all departmental estimates, increased indirect taxes and imposed a 'crisis tax' on salaries and wages. State and Communal budgets were also reduced, and economies introduced into unemployment insurance. The political opposition excited stimulated the outflow of foreign funds and the Reichsbank rate was raised — without much effect — on June 13 from 5 to 7 per cent. On June 19 there was panic in Berlin and the Reichsbank prepared to take more drastic means to protect its exchange reserves.

In London already by June 13 the Treasury and Foreign Office were discussing a postponement of German payments, and Leith-Ross [1] and Norman took to Chequers that week-end the draft of a message to Washington suggesting postponement. Mellon, still Secretary of the American Treasury, arrived in London on June 17. Norman saw him at once and explained to him his view of the Austrian, German and general situation, 'omitting no facts or fears, especially the threat to currencies; there was need of a suspension for three years — on stringent conditions'. The same afternoon he took Mellon to the House of Commons, where he went over the ground again with the Prime Minister (Ramsay MacDonald) and Foreign

---

[1] Deputy Controller of Finance, H.M. Treasury, 1925–32. Knighted, 1933.

Secretary (Arthur Henderson) and raised the question of
action — 'Hoover might take the lead? Suspension of *all*
inter-Government payments for 2-3 years? What about
France? Urgent? Could Mellon go to Paris? He will get
in touch with Washington this evening.' Norman himself rang
up Harrison in New York as soon as he got back to the Bank.
On Friday the 19th he saw the Chancellor in the morning
and in the evening first Vansittart [1] at the Foreign Office and
then the Prime Minister, returning later to 10 Downing Street
with an agreed statement for him to telephone to Washington.
President Hoover returned from a political tour to Washington
on the 19th; he had been in consultation with his financial
advisers, and on the evening of the 20th announced his proposal that for a period of one year there should be a postponement of all payments on inter-governmental debts.

If a chance of checking the slide into general international
insolvency ever existed, it was offered by the Hoover proposal;
the slow process of international diplomatic agreement destroyed it. Germany immediately and gratefully announced
its acceptance; a day later the British Government gave its unconditional agreement. The French Government on June 26
offered its agreement on conditions which President Hoover
could not accept; only on July 6 was French agreement
secured. In the interval the atmosphere of the world's markets
had changed. On June 22, the Monday after the Hoover
announcement, the drain on German foreign exchange reserves
had ceased; the immediate danger of a further fall leaving the
Reichsbank note-issue uncovered was met by a credit from the
Bank of England, replaced on June 25 by a $100 million credit
from the B.I.S. and the Central Banks in London and Paris
and the Federal Reserve Bank of New York jointly. But foreign
withdrawals began again on July 1; on July 6 nearly 100 million
reichsmarks of foreign exchange was lost, and the next day the
Reichsbank's last reserves were exhausted. The same day the
failure of the largest German textile firm was announced,
ominous because it revealed the weakness of the internal credit
situation as well as the external; and on the 13th the first
of the great bank failures took place. Luther, President of

---

[1] Sir Robert Vansittart, Permanent Under-Secretary of State for Foreign
Affairs, 1930–38. Later Lord Vansittart.

the Reichsbank, still insisted to his colleagues at Basle that fundamentally the economic position of Germany was sounder than in 1929, but Norman did not believe that any early recovery was possible. Luther visited London and Paris in the endeavour to secure further credits; the French continued to insist on political concessions, though the B.I.S. and Central Banks renewed their credit. The German Government was forced to deal with its difficulties by emergency decrees, temporarily limiting internal payments and establishing a strict exchange control, which proved not to be temporary. Norman advised the Prime Minister that a proposed meeting of experts was no longer useful; a conference of Ministers was the only hope. It met in London on July 20, but reached no agreement.

Norman had explained the position to the Committee of Treasury, on June 23 and 24, when he asked approval of the two credits given to the Reichsbank, and more fully on July 8 — the position of the Reichsbank had deteriorated; he expected demands for further credits for Eastern Europe to maintain currencies when he went to Basle; the Bank of England had already given credit amounting to $53½ million, yet there would be collapse if there were no further assistance and there would be none if London refused. He had told the Treasury that Austria and Hungary could be successfully dealt with only by the League. The Committee agreed that it would be impossible to refuse further credits. But again, at Basle, he insisted that credits could not meet Germany's difficulties unless there was a clearing up of the political situation. To the London banks with credits outstanding on Germany who came to him, he urged the importance of maintaining such credits; an attempt to call them in would probably fail and precipitate a worse collapse. This led to an agreed policy, organised by a committee of Clearing Banks and Accepting Houses. Through Norman and Harrison, New York bankers were approached, and an identical policy adopted there. An exchange of cables on July 15 and 16 confirmed the arrangement:

231/31   Confidential for Norman

1. Following my telephone conversation with you this morning I asked the heads of 11 of the principal New York banks to meet with me to discuss the desirability of their agreeing

upon some concerted action to be taken by the New York banks and Bankers with respect to the payment of check and cable orders against German dollar balances and the acceptance of bills for German account.

2. It is of course their general belief that it would be desirable to have a uniform policy with respect to these matters in this and the London market as well as other markets if possible. Having reported the substance of our conversation to-day about the London position and after some discussion here it was generally agreed that whilst the situation is very uncertain and difficult of analysis and must be watched from day to day nevertheless for the present at least check and cable orders will be honoured to the extent of existing credit balances. This I understood from you is about the position of the London market. With perhaps one exception it was also agreed that acceptance lines now outstanding would be maintained for the present at least at about the amount actually in use, assuming that the Germans will continue to take necessary steps to prevent the flight of German capital and provided that the London, and if possible other markets, will take about the same position. This position of the New York bankers about acceptances means that bills drawn prior to or after the holiday began would be accepted unless their acceptance involved a substantial increase in existing used lines.

Confidential for Harrison

1. The London Bankers are glad for the present in accordance with your 231/31 to adopt a uniform policy for New York and London generally as follows :

A. Acceptance lines now outstanding in London will for the present be continued at least at about the amount actually in use, and

B. In accordance with the practice in London cheque and cable orders will be honoured in New York to the extent of credit balances and New York action in regard to acceptance lines now in use will follow the course referred to in paragraph A.

2. Of course this is a friendly understanding and not a binding commitment.

3. Thus I think you have done a fine job.

Norman refused, however, in any way to guarantee the bankers against any resulting loss. They proceeded with their negotiations through the international committee of creditors of Austria, and through a new committee of experts, with an American chairman in Albert Wiggin and an English expert in Sir Walter Layton, to negotiate with their debtors. The outcome was the Standstill Agreements, under which credits to Germany were frozen but their service guaranteed. Norman had promised that if the position of the accepting houses, or the Clearing Banks which gave them credits, came into such jeopardy that it constituted a national crisis, he would take it up with the Government, as it had been taken up in 1914; but that would involve legislation. In the event the London bankers were able to handle their own problems, with losses but without disaster, and without sacrificing the reputation of London for statesmanlike banking, or contributing to the collapse of Central Europe into National Socialism. The support given by London and New York to German clients, added to the credits given to the Reichsbank by the other great Central Banks, and the suspension of payments on the Young and other loans, reduced the external pressure on Germany to manageable proportions. A resumption was made possible of the normal internal banking essential for trade. The banks were reopened (with government aid or guarantees in some cases) on July 16, and on August 1 all restrictions on withdrawals for domestic payments were withdrawn. But the strain had gone too far to permit a return to the freedom of banking and external payments, which had been established by the Dawes Plan. All exchange transactions were concentrated in the Reichsbank. New government agencies were established for internal clearing and for giving credits which the Reichstag's rules would not allow the Reichsbank to give, and an office of Reichskommissar for Banking was established for the supervision of all banks by the Government.

(iv)

On July 15, the day on which he organised with Harrison their arrangements for a common line on Germany, Norman had a forcible reminder of the weakness of London's own position. In the same cable as Harrison summarised his negotiations with the New York bankers, he added: 'We are concerned and surprised at sudden drop in sterling exchange to-day. Can you throw any light on this?' Norman replied:

... 2. I cannot explain the drop in sterling in relation to dollars and most European currencies. It was sudden and unexpected and resulted in engagement of over £7 million gold for these days including £4 million for Bachmann.[1]

3. We were perplexed this morning about a change in Bank Rate because exchanges are still so disorganised that $2\frac{1}{2}\%$ is hardly justified. But to cope with such disorganisation would require 7% or 8% rather than $3\frac{1}{2}\%$ and as no more gold is being withdrawn we hope to ride at least another week. By that time the Conference of Ministers called for Monday evening should have put the position of Central Europe on a more satisfactory and permanent basis.

4. There is a rumour that we first decided on a 4% Bank Rate and went back to $2\frac{1}{2}\%$ a few moments later. This is wholly untrue.

There had been recurrent signs of weakness in sterling. In the New Year, instead of the usual seasonal strength against the dollar, the exchanges had remained against London. The exchange on Paris had been strong, but this was probably due to Paris lending to London, for London to lend to Germany. From early in June the Continent showed its distrust by an appreciation of the Dutch and Swiss currencies and a rise in the forward premium on dollars and francs, but the South African gold was still coming to the Bank. The break on July 16 is explained by the breakdown in German banking, in which London was deeply involved, coming just after the publication of the Macmillan Committee's Report in the Press of July 13, which gave for the first time an estimate of London short-term foreign indebtedness. Already the sterling exchanges were at or below gold export point; on the 15th the Paris rate fell more than a franc below the lower gold point, on the 16th the dollar fell to 4·84. By July 22 the Bank had lost £22 million of gold, and this heavy flow was ineffective to bring the sterling rates back. The Committee of Treasury decided to recommend that Bank Rate should be raised if the Ministers Conference sitting in London was without result; it was raised the next day to

[1] President of the National Bank of Switzerland.

$3\frac{1}{2}$ per cent, and a week later to $4\frac{1}{2}$ per cent, and the Bank began to intervene in the exchange market.

The Bank's holdings of dollars and francs were not sufficient to hold the sterling rate for more than a few days; and gold transfers did not have a quick enough effect. Any reluctance to borrow was swept away. Kindersley crossed to Paris and found the Governor of the Bank of France very ready to give a credit. The Bank sought a Government guarantee. The Chancellor was unwilling to give this; the Bank should be prepared to use its gold, and the London banks must be free to withdraw their credits from Germany. The Committee of Clearing Bankers were willing to help the Bank by providing commercial bills to serve as security for credits, but preferred a New York to a Paris credit, unless credits could be raised in both quarters. Harrison's response was to offer a credit with the Federal Reserve Bank of $100 million. The credits, of £25 million each, were arranged on the Saturday before Bank Holiday and announced on August 1. At the same time the Fiduciary Issue was increased by £15 million.

At the meeting of the Committee of Treasury on the previous Wednesday, Norman collapsed and had to be taken home. With the exception of one day, August 5, when he came in to the Bank, he was confined to his house, most of the time in bed, until August 15 when, on his doctor's advice, he sailed to Canada for a complete rest. He did not return until September 23, when the crisis was over.

By a coincidence, his withdrawal came just when the last attempt to deal with the crisis by Central Bank co-operation had been arranged. But the coincidence is not probably significant. Already he had insisted that the difficulties of Central Europe went beyond the possibility of handling by monetary policy and Central Bank credits alone, essential as these might be. He had insisted that the German problem was political, to be resolved by Ministers in conference, not by financial experts. And already in agreeing to arrange the two Central Bank credits to support sterling, the Committee of Treasury had informed the Chancellor that, in their view and doubtless also in Norman's, their use was limited to giving the Government time to deal with its budgetary problem. The policy which the Bank continued to carry out, of defending sterling against the strain of continued withdrawals until the resources it could draw on were exhausted, was the Governor's.

It had been expected that the announcement of the credits would stop the drain on London, and when the markets opened after Bank Holiday the Bank withdrew its support of sterling, thinking it better to allow any withdrawal to show itself in its gold holding. Unfortunately, the same day as the credits were announced, the Report of the May Committee on the national finances was published. This confirmed in the minds of foreign observers their worst fears. The credits were interpreted as a sign of weakness and the increase in the Fiduciary Issue as evidence of inflation. The franc rate moved to 123·50 and the Bank lost £4½ million in one day. The Bank immediately reversed its policy and used the credits, helped by the Bank of France, which provided dollars against francs when the demand for dollars rose faster than the dollar credit became available. But the drain of money from London had attained a volume that threatened to take the situation out of the Bank's control. Reporting to the Chancellor on August 6, the Deputy Governor (Sir Ernest Harvey) said that £60 million of gold and foreign exchange had been withdrawn in four weeks, and the Bank could not meet such a drain for long. All the reports received showed that foreigners expected a readjustment of the budgetary situation, and the time available for decisions, as a means of safeguarding the value of sterling, might be much shorter than had seemed likely. He asked whether the Chancellor would see any objection to his meeting the Opposition Leaders and telling them in confidence the facts of the loss of gold and his apprehensions. An example may be cited — the report of an interview with the Governor of the Bank of France; he had been surprised at the loss of confidence on the Continent, the break in the rate was fairly positive evidence of a flight from sterling; three weeks earlier, it would have been easy to float a long-term British loan in Paris, now it was impossible; he compared the British position with the position of France in 1926 before Poincaré came in and the finances were restored. Sir Walter Layton, writing to the Chancellor from Geneva, reported the alarm of the Continental members of the Committee on German Debt. The stability of sterling was the one sheet-anchor for Europe, and Britain the only country that could help Europe to weather the storm; the British Government should borrow abroad and reassure its creditors by publishing at once a programme for dealing with the budgetary situation to be submitted to Parliament.

Quite apart from such advice from abroad, the Bank was concerned over its statutory obligation to pay gold for sterling on demand. By using the credits, it postponed a drain of gold, but only postponed it; the credits would have to be repaid, and meantime they concealed from the British public the seriousness of the situation. Of this the Chancellor needed no convincing, and the Prime Minister quickly appreciated it on his return to London on August 11. Arrangements were made for an immediate meeting of the Economy Sub-Committee of the Cabinet, and on the 13th the Opposition Leaders were informed of the exchange position. The same day the Treasury asked the Bank to sound New York as to the possibilities of a credit, not this time to the Bank of England, but to the Government. The movement of funds was now too large to be handled by temporary inter-Central Bank credits; yet the danger of a drain on the Bank's gold, following on the exhaustion of the credits and exercising a sudden and large deflationary effect on internal credit, was imminent. Of this again the public had not been warned by any further rise in Bank Rate, since the Bank's advisers in New York, Paris and Zürich had advised it that such a rise would only increase distrust of sterling, and its contractionist effect could not operate fast enough to check the drain. But the negotiation of Government credits, unlike the support given by one Central Bank to another, raised explicitly the issue of Government financial policy, on which the lenders would expect to be assured, and so brought the defence of sterling into a controversy which had divided British domestic politics almost since the Labour Government took office.

The Labour Party had fought the General Election of 1929 very largely on the issue of unemployment. In office it had found itself confronted with a slide of the world into depression, which made any remedy difficult. The first and chief impact was on the Chancellor, who found himself faced with declining revenues, increasing expenditure, and a deteriorating external balance. These his orthodox convictions drove him to seek to

correct, which brought him early into conflict, not only with
the Conservative Party, which wanted Protection, and the
Liberal Party, which wanted Public Works without much
regard to economy, but with a large section of his own followers,
who had promised the unemployed 'work or maintenance'.
Almost the first measure the Government carried through Parliament was a Bill to amend the Unemployment Insurance Act,
increasing rates of benefit, transferring from the Insurance
Fund to the Exchequer the cost of 'Transitional Benefit' (the
continuation of benefit after the right to it based on insurance
contributions was exhausted) and abolishing the condition of
'genuinely seeking work' hitherto attached to benefit.   The
result was that, as unemployment increased, not only had the
borrowing power of the Unemployment Fund to be extended,
but a new burden was placed on the Exchequer to finance more
than proportionately increased numbers on transitional benefit.
It followed that Snowden's 1930 Budget was a conservative
measure, which gave as little satisfaction to his own Party as
to his political opponents.

    Before the next Budget the Cabinet had abundant warning
of the serious condition of the country's economy.   The number
of registered unemployed increased from 1,761,000 in April
1930 to 2,593,000 in April 1931.   At the end of January 1931
Sir Richard Hopkins, Controller of Finance, H.M. Treasury,
giving evidence before the Royal Commission on Unemployment Insurance, drew attention to the increasing cost of the
scheme to the Treasury and the increasing amount of borrowing
by the Fund from the Treasury.   The following week there
was a debate on national economy in the House of Commons.
The Chancellor concluded his speech :

    I say with all the seriousness I can command that the national
position is so grave that drastic and disagreeable measures will have to
be taken if Budget equilibrium is to be maintained and if industrial
progress is to be made.

The debate ended with a resolution calling for the appointment
of a small and independent committee to make recommendations to the Chancellor of the Exchequer for 'effecting forthwith all practicable and legitimate reductions in the national
expenditure consistent with the efficiency of the services'.   The

Chairman of the Committee appointed on March 17 was Sir George May,[1] from whom it took its name.

The unemployment issue was forced on the country's attention again when an interim report which the Government had requested from the Royal Commission on Unemployment Insurance was published on June 4. This showed that the income of the Fund was sufficient to meet only half of the charges on it, and its debt was increasing by £1 million a week. The Commission recommended the removal of certain anomalies, an increase in contributions and reduction in rates of benefit, and a qualified means test for transitional benefit, which together would reduce the annual deficit on the Fund from £39 million to £7½ million. The Government postponed serious action until it should have received the Commission's further report, but the unpopularity of the proposals among the Government's supporters in Parliament was made clear. The Report of the Macmillan Committee, published nearly six weeks later, gave considerable space to the examination of unemployment, its relations with monetary policy and the inter-relations of domestic and external payments; but it was received by opinion at home as a specialist's report on a rather esoteric problem, and probably did little more than confirm the unreflecting view that no change in the Gold Standard was conceivable.

Very different was the political impact of the May Report, published on August 1, the day after Parliament adjourned for the Summer Recess. We have seen how it alarmed foreigners; in the domestic political area it opened wide the rift between the conflicting elements in the Government's own party. On the eve of the adjournment Neville Chamberlain, after consulting the Chancellor, raised a discussion of the position. His speech was not a party utterance, though it demanded vigorous action, and Snowden, thanking him for his restraint, warned the House once again of the seriousness of the position, told them of the unparalleled withdrawals from London, and promised that he would do his utmost to deal with it, however disagreeable the consequences. The May Report predicted a deficit on the Budget of £120 million, and proposed reductions in expenditure amounting to £96 million, nearly

[1] Later Lord May.

two-thirds of it on unemployment insurance. It was an alarming and a provocative document; unfortunately, while it alarmed the foreigner, it only provoked the Government's supporters.

The rapid deterioration of the exchange situation compelled the Government to press on with its plans for meeting the Committee's challenge. The critical discussions occupied the week beginning August 17; the Economy Sub-Committee's proposals were presented to the full Cabinet on the 19th, to the Consultative Committee of the Party and the General Council of the Trades Union Congress on the 20th and to the Leaders of the Conservative and Liberal Parties on the following day. The Prime Minister and Chancellor, reminded daily of the international strain, could not secure agreement on their proposals from colleagues who were not informed of the strain and did not share their sense of external danger. Still less was the General Council of the Trades Union Congress ready to agree to any reductions in social services or wages. The Opposition Leaders, on the other hand, promised their support for the Government's proposals, once they were satisfied that they were adequate.

The reply of Harrison to the Bank's tentative inquiry on the 13th had been that the British Government should raise loans in New York and Paris of, say, £50 million each, and that such a loan would be practicable in America, provided the programme of economy was adequate and received the approval of Parliament. When, a week later, the drain on reserves made the question of a loan urgent, Harrison had to point out that he could only advise, the Statutes of the Federal Reserve Bank precluding loans to foreign governments, and the British Treasury should put themselves in touch with their New York Agents, Morgans. When, on August 22, the Prime Minister was ready with proposals, he asked the Deputy Governor again to obtain Harrison's opinion. Harrison replied that if the programme was approved by all three parties it would be possible to raise a loan, but again referred the Government to Morgans. They had cabled on the 21st that a public loan would require prior Parliamentary action, though agreement of Party leaders on a supporting programme might be adequate for a private credit transaction; but, they added, 'it is going to take a great deal more than simply the joint declaration of three Party leaders to convince the investment and banking public here that real amendment has been undertaken and that the Government is in a position to command heavy foreign credit favours'.

The final scheme of economies put forward by the Prime Minister and Chancellor was to be submitted to a Cabinet meeting at 7 P.M. on Sunday, August 23, with a view to an immediate decision as to its adoption. The Prime Minister thought it desirable to know whether it would ensure the necessary credits, and asked the Deputy Governor that morning to obtain an answer before the meeting. The Deputy Governor explained that the difference in time between London and New York and the necessity of coding and decoding would make it difficult : but immediately had a cable sent to Morgans setting out the scheme of economies and the suggestion for loans or credits in New York and Paris. The cable went on :

I am assured that if as the result of the adoption of the Government's scheme the loans and credits are likely to be obtainable the other political parties will promise support to the Government's programme as a minimum, they however reserving to themselves the right if they think fit of moving amendments in Parliament with a view to increasing the amount to be provided by means of economies.

The Prime Minister is anxious if possible that I should be able to advise him by 7 P.M. our time as to whether there is a likelihood that the loans and credits would be forthcoming if the rest of their programme is adopted.

It is understood of course that you could not at such short notice give anything in the nature of a binding commitment and could do no more than express your own personal opinions.

Morgans' reply, sent through their partners in London, was as follows :

We are considering very carefully here the tentative suggestion made by the Deputy Governor as to the bare possibility of the British Government desiring to arrange some form of joint French and American credit. It is of course quite impossible to give any assurance to-day. Please tell your friends in the event that they should desire financial co-operation we shall as always do our utmost to meet their wishes. If the suggestion were to take the form of a public loan offering we are confident that until Parliament convenes and acts and until we have had an opportunity to feel out our own investment community we could render no favourable opinion whatsoever. If the suggestion however were to take the form of a short-term Treasury operation that would be less difficult and if the British Government should desire us to canvass among ourselves and our immediate friends such a suggestion we should take up the matter vigorously tomorrow morning and be able to give you an answer by our closing tomorrow afternoon.

Kindly let us know subsequent to the results of the Cabinet Meeting which you say will be held this evening whether the Government wish us to explore promptly this possibility. The furthest we have gone to-day has been to discuss merely among ourselves the possibility of a short credit in this market of from 100 to 150 million dollars and we have as above indicated assumed that as a condition the French banking market would do an equivalent amount. When we speak of short term we have roughly in mind 90 day Treasury Bills subject to renewals for an inclusive period of one year.

In the foregoing we have as always given you the precise trend of our thought. Let us know promptly as indicated above what the Government's desires are and within 24 hours we shall be able to give you our final judgment. Are we right in assuming that the programme under consideration will have the sincere approval and support of the Bank of England and the City generally and thus go a long way towards restoring internal confidence in Great Britain. Of course our ability to do anything depends on the response of public opinion particularly in Great Britain to the Government's announcement of the programme.

The Deputy Governor went with this to Downing Street. The Prime Minister took it from him and apparently read it to the Cabinet. He left the discussions which followed to hand in to the King his resignation.

There is little in the cable to explain the excitement it caused; clearly it was the occasion of a break in the Cabinet only because it assumed — and was understood to assume — a programme of economies on which compromise or agreement was impossible. There may have been an element of hope deferred; the Cabinet had been waiting for nearly two hours, and the message when it arrived offered no solution of their differences. Among the proposed economies the reduction of unemployment benefits was the one both that the rank and file of the Labour Members were most determined to resist and that foreigners with funds to lend had taken as the test and symbol of a change in British finances. But there was nothing new in this. The programme of economies itself was the occasion only, not the cause, of the political explosion which the cable from New York set off.

Seen in perspective, the cause of the split in the Cabinet was a fundamental conflict between Snowden's policy, supported in the last resort by the Prime Minister, which was actuated by deep-seated fear of inflation, consciousness of the weakness of the country's external economic position and a knowledge of the dangers of the political situation in Europe, and a policy which looked only to domestic needs and aspirations. The conflict had shown itself early in the Administration's life and had appeared in every economic debate — in the criticisms of the moderation of the 1930 Budget, in the controversy over a policy of 'public works' to relieve unemployment, in the bitter criticisms of Snowden's warning that the financial position was serious, in the debate that followed the Treasury evidence to the Unemployment Commission in February 1931, in the renewed disappointment over the 1931 Budget, above all in the reaction to the May Report, the general tendency of which was widely known in advance and inspired the debate on July 30, the day before Parliament adjourned. If any one thing split the Cabinet, it was its inability to decide what to do about the May Report. No alternative policy to that followed by the Chancellor for dealing with the country's external difficulties was formulated. Even the people who had been opposed to the return to the Gold Standard in 1925 were not prepared to reverse that decision in the conditions of 1931 ; yet an inflationary policy designed to increase employment in the home market was not practicable so long as the country's credit conditions were linked by the Gold Standard with those in other countries. Keynes and Bevin with some other members of the Macmillan Committee, while signing the main Report, had attempted in an Addendum to work out what would now be called a 'Reflationary' policy within the limits imposed by a fixed rate of exchange and freedom of capital transfer ; but it came too late, and does not seem to have been studied by Snowden's opponents.

The hasty adoption of an explanation of the crisis, which

attributed it to an attempt by foreign financiers to impose their
own reactionary principles on British domestic policy — the
'Bankers' Ramp' — suggests a belated realisation of the
dependence of England on the rest of the world and resentment of the fact. It was a natural reaction; but the record of
negotiations does not bear out this explanation. It appeared
first, on August 25, in the *Daily Herald*, which reported that the
Government had been informed by the Federal Reserve Bank
of New York that further credits to the Bank of England would
be granted only if economies were introduced into the Unemployment Insurance Scheme. In fact Harrison, the Governor
of the Federal Reserve Bank, had not been asked for further
large credits to the Bank of England but for advice on raising a
loan or credit for the British Government. He had not refused
such a credit, but had given his opinion that the New York
market would not consider a British loan unless there was a
change in the British budgetary position; so did Morgans,
even before they were approached by the British Treasury.
Morgans, as their cable of August 23 shows, when approached
by the Treasury as to the possibility of a short-term credit (not
a market loan), on the assumption of the economies proposed
by the British Chancellor, offered to canvass their New York
banking friends, and considered the possibility of giving a credit
by themselves, on the scale of the Federal Reserve Bank's previous credit to the Bank of England, provided a similar credit
were raised in Paris. The attitude of Paris was the same as
New York's; they could not organise credits for His Majesty's
Government unless they could show that British finances were
being reformed. The markets in Amsterdam and Zürich made
their opinion equally clear by massive withdrawals of funds
from London. Morgans, like Harrison, were replying to a
request for advice on the attitude of the New York market to
any approach for credit from the British Government; they were
giving an expert opinion, though they did not conceal their
agreement with the market's view. In the discussion of terms
after the credit had been settled in principle, Morgans cabled:

There is not a single institution in our whole banking community
which actually desires the British Treasury notes on any terms
either as to commission or interest. If they go into the matter it
will be because of their becoming convinced that it is important

and necessary for the whole banking community here to co-operate in the support of sterling. You are aware of the large volume of frozen credits that many institutions hold here, those along the Atlantic seaboard being burdened with frozen German and other credits, those in the interior being tied up with frozen local loans. Every institution is probably making strenuous endeavours to get its position more liquid.

Subsequently they were subjected to as much criticism in their own country as they were in England; but the criticism at home was not for failing to satisfy themselves that the foreign borrower was a good credit risk, but for giving credits to foreigners at all.

A criticism with more relevance to actual conditions was the charge that British bankers had 'borrowed short and lent long'. It is true that the country was not able to meet its foreign liabilities, which were mainly short, but the implication that the British bankers were solely to blame is too simple an explanation. London, it is true, had borrowed short on a scale for which there was no precedent before 1914. The chief borrower was the Government and the chief form of short borrowing was the unprecedented volume of Treasury Bills. Some of these were held directly by foreign firms and foreign banks with London offices; more were held by the British banks as a means of employing the deposits of foreigners. There were substantial holdings by foreigners of long-term British Government securities also. Some of these non-resident bank balances and bill holdings were the correlative of London's function as the world's chief clearing centre for international payments. Foreign banks with London branches as agents, and Empire banks with head offices or branches in London, held sterling balances in order that they could supply their customers with sterling to make payment for merchandise, services and debt charges due to Britain. Of the large amount of such balances revealed by the Macmillan Committee's Report, it was not realised how much consisted of the necessary sterling reserves which non-resident bankers and businesses were compelled to hold in the ordinary course of business. It was the inflation of such balances by Government short-term borrowing, offering an ideal bankers' investment in the Treasury Bill, that constituted a novel problem. Norman had been pressing for its reduction ever since he became Governor.

In some of their credits the English bankers may have been unwise. They gave short-term credits to German and other foreign bankers, who did not use their resources with the same regard to their liquidity as is the custom in British banking. When, therefore, German banks found the industrial concerns whose re-equipment they had financed were caught by the depression, there was no possibility of their meeting the demands of their London creditors. Accepting houses, pursuing their traditional practice with their usual care, were similarly caught. These foreign liabilities to London, if they could not be collected, and had to be continued under the Standstill Agreements, did not involve the London credit-givers in bankruptcy; what they did was to lessen the means which the banks had expected to be available to London and, so far as their form went, were legally available, for meeting foreign claims on London. Long-term loans were issued in London for overseas borrowers in excess of the current ability of the country's export claims to transfer them. Norman had continually sought to restrict them, while meeting the needs of the Empire. The neglect of any attempt to control them by law was the outcome of the general state of opinion which did not yet regard exchange control as a possibility.

The statistics of foreign balances published by the Macmillan Committee, the publication of which the Continent regarded as one of the turning-points in the crisis, did not deserve that prominence. They were large figures, but no one had any criterion by which to gauge their potential threat. They showed a reduction in the liability, both gross and net, each year since 1928; they did not distinguish between the banking reserves of banks operating overseas, especially in the Empire, and less stable elements; they did not distinguish between liabilities to other sterling countries, which did not normally threaten London's gold reserves, and liabilities to countries with different currency systems, which did. On the other hand, the decline in agricultural prices, and the consequent difficulty over external payments which overtook some parts of the Empire before the depression reached Britain, may have involved a demand for gold and foreign exchange, which would be met by drafts on London.

Again, it may be doubted whether gold and exchange

reserves were large enough. Norman never thought they were, but had few opportunities of increasing them. The historical form in which the English note-issue was cast in 1928, with a normal backing of gold for any issue in excess of the Fiduciary amount, and the fact that no use had been made of the power to increase the Fiduciary part, until use was so abnormal that it excited alarm, was unfortunate. It tied up £130 million of the gold reserve in the Issue Department, where it could not be used to meet the drain of gold except with violent deflationary effects. Whether the gold reserve was 'adequate', and whether — another doubt sometimes expressed — the level of the credits sought was pitched high enough, depended on the possibilities of flight from sterling. The possibility of flight by non-resident holders was less than the figure of non-resident balances, because a substantial part of these could not be run down to zero without disrupting the business of the holders ; on the other hand, it was increased by the opportunities for selling sterling securities and selling sterling itself forward. If to these possibilities is added the possibility of flight from sterling by resident holders, British citizens, no reserve would be 'adequate'. In the official statement announcing the suspension of the Gold Standard, it was said that 'His Majesty's Government have no reason to believe that the present difficulties are due to any substantial extent to the export of capital by British nationals'. But His Majesty's Government were unlikely to be informed of any such movement. Many British enterprises had interests in other countries which would make export, or the deferring of import, of funds easy, but the ordinary businessman without such connections never during the crisis showed any distrust of sterling. More important than any errors of judgment of bankers was the slow pace of Parliamentary democracy, which made every step taken in the crisis too late to effect its object, and, underlying the crisis, the destructive action of world depression.

The Sunday papers of August 23 had revealed the existence of a Cabinet crisis : its resolution by the formation of a National Government under Ramsay MacDonald was announced on the following day. The reassurance given by this was offset by *The Times* letting out a few hours earlier that the two Central Bank credits were nearly exhausted. Credits for the equivalent of £40 million each were secured from New York and Paris, and announced on August 28. Monetarily the drain was relieved, but the flight from sterling had acquired too much momentum to be stopped even by additional reserves of this magnitude. Messages from the Bank for International Settlements and elsewhere reported that the formation of a National Government had given new hopes, for Europe as much as for Britain : but these were weakened by what seemed unnecessary delay in taking action to countries accustomed to action by decree in an emergency, and by a Manifesto published jointly by the Labour Party and the Trades Union Congress on September 3, threatening 'embittered conflict and industrial chaos' if any attempt were made to reduce wages, and making it clear that the new Government was something less than a National Government.

Parliament reassembled on September 8 and Snowden presented a drastic and courageous Budget on the 10th, followed the next day by an Economy Bill to cut expenditure by £70 million. A report by the Admiralty on September 15 of 'unrest' over some of the cuts in pay included in the Economy Act was exaggerated out of all proportion to its real importance, and on the Continent had an effect corresponding to the political prestige of the Navy. On September 16 the losses of gold and foreign exchange were over £10 million and on September 17 £18¾ million. The same day inquiries were made in New York and Paris as to the possibility of further credits; the replies though friendly offered no prospect of assistance on the scale that was by that time obviously necessary. By Saturday, the 19th, the credits were exhausted — £200 million of gold and foreign exchange had been lost since July 13 — and the Bank's holding of gold was reduced to the equivalent of the obligations incurred under the credits. The Deputy Governor reported the position to the Prime Minister and Chancellor on the 19th, and asked to be relieved of the obligation to sell gold on demand. They replied that the Bank should impose such restrictions on the supply of gold as it thought expedient, and promised to introduce a Bill of Indemnity. The announcement to the public of the suspension of the Gold Standard was made on the evening of Sunday, the 20th.

CHAPTER X

A FRESH START

(i)

NORMAN landed in Liverpool on the morning of September 23. Only then did he learn that the Gold Standard had been suspended.[1] Nothing could have been a greater blow: he was profoundly depressed and for a time his temper showed it. The morning after he landed he called on Baldwin and the Chancellor, and left that evening for a long week-end at Much Hadham. On Monday he resumed work at the Bank. There were questions enough waiting for him: Lancashire cotton losses, the White Star Line, the Standstill on German and Austrian short-term debts, his own future in the Bank — an entry in his diary for November 12 reads 'Selection as Governor 1932/3 final'. Most pressing of all were the immediate questions raised by the suspension of the Gold Standard; arrangements with Morgans for buying and selling dollars ('a nest-egg and free forward dealing essential'); visits from Central Bankers embarrassed by the fall in the value (in their own currency) of their sterling holdings — his second week-end after he resumed work, he spent at the monthly meeting in Basle, 'unpleasant days'; the uncertainties of the exchange market and of his own money market. He was quickly back in his normal routine of continuous conference with officials and continuous interviews with visitors.

The suspension of the Gold Standard caused no panic in London. Markets were confused and hesitant, and the Stock Exchange was closed for a couple of days; but there was no

[1] The Deputy Governor had tried to warn him; but he had gone away for reasons of health and without taking a cable code, and any radiogram had to be sent *en clair*. The Deputy Governor devised a message which he thought the Governor alone would understand — 'Sorry to go off before you arrived' but the Governor, not expecting the news it was intended to convey, understood it as merely an apology for absence.

suggestion of a run on banks and no signs of any flight of capital. A Bill amending the Act by which in 1925 the Gold Standard had been restored was passed through Parliament on September 21 ; it relieved the Bank of its obligation to buy and sell gold on demand, and gave the Treasury general powers to protect the exchange. The same day Bank Rate was raised to 6 per cent, the reasons for restraint having lost their force. The Treasury used its powers to restrict the purchase of foreign exchange to normal trade and travel, and arrangements were made with the banks and the accepting houses to refuse credit for speculative purposes. By the end of the month, the exchange with New York had settled down at a rate around 3·90. Opinion at home and abroad was reassured by the balancing of the Budget and by the return of a National Government at a general election on October 27 by a large majority.

Frequent and rapid movements in the exchange value of sterling marked the change. The revival of confidence abroad in the British Government was supported by a large covering movement by speculators who had been bears of sterling before September 20, and by the beginning of a movement which was to lend contraband support to sterling, the attraction of gold from Indian and other hoards by the higher sterling price obtainable — a movement which surprised the Government but had been expected by Norman. The Treasury and Bank were able to begin accumulating foreign exchange against the credits they had raised in Paris and New York; it was announced at the end of October that two-fifths of the Central Bank credits to the Bank of England had been repaid, in advance of the due date, and the rest renewed for three months. But the rush of imports in October and November, coming on the top of the normal seasonal weakness of the exchange, depressed sterling, and the balancing action by short-term credits which met seasonal strains under the Gold Standard, no longer operated. Other countries were offsetting the depreciation of sterling by additional import duties, quotas and exchange restrictions, and the Continent was still looking for signs of inflation in England. Sterling fell sharply in New York at the end of November to 3·38, and a day later to 3·27. It was supported and recovered by December 14, on fears of inflation in America, to 3·44, but fell again by over 11 cents in one day

on the reaffirmation by Congress of its opposition to any reduction of war debts. In the New Year the seasonal movements
of trade gave sterling support ; confidence was strengthened at
the end of January by the repayment of the balance of the
Central Bank credits, and on February 18 Bank Rate came down
to 5 per cent. On March 2 arrangements for repaying the
Treasury credits were announced, the restrictions on foreign
exchange dealings were removed, and on the 10th Bank Rate
was reduced to 4 per cent. On March 31 sterling touched
3·80 again.

These months were a time of difficulty and anxiety for the
Bank. The Governor had explained to the Committee of
Treasury on 4 November 1931 his view of sterling. He hoped
that *de facto* stabilisation would take place at some natural level,
which would be revealed after a satisfactory balance of payments had been secured ; but he thought this would be achieved
only gradually over a long period. In the meantime the volume
of credit should be kept under strict control and speculation in
securities and commodities discouraged. The situation in many
parts of the world was threatening, and the outlook uncertain.
Bank Rate might be regarded as unnecessarily high, but it was
important to avoid any step that would give the market a false
impression of the situation. The fall in sterling in December
alarmed the Government, and disinclined them to do anything
to ease credit. He discussed exchange policy with the Committee again early in December, and on December 8 took a
memorandum to the Chancellor (Neville Chamberlain), which
shows the development of his views. The fluctuations in the
exchange were more serious for trade than the actual level ;
the Bank could moderate these fluctuations, but had not the
resources to peg the rate or even to withstand a determined
speculative attack ; attempts to arrange with the holders of large
sterling balances to retain them would only suggest that the
United Kingdom was arriving at a standstill, as would any
approach to other Central Banks ; they had not enough gold
and foreign exchange to carry through a long-term policy, and
the Government should avoid any statement that seemed to
commit it to stabilisation. It was agreed that the Bank should
do what it could to iron out fluctuations, that a committee of
officers of the Bank, representatives of the banks dealing in

exchange, and the Treasury should meet regularly and that some 'academic study' should be given to the measures needed if things came to the worst and there was a flight of capital.

The Bank used three commercial banks as its agent in the exchange market; but their interventions were watched and tended to give an exaggerated opinion of official activity. Sir Henry Strakosch advised the Bank in March to develop its own exchange department, big enough and specialised enough to deal with big movements, and acquiring a real knowledge of the underlying forces of the market, which could be obtained only by constant and actual touch with dealings. Machinery was, however, subordinate: the real difficulty was lack of resources. The Bank was placed in a dilemma when supplies of gold and foreign exchange were offered. It could buy these only by increasing the supply of money by its payment for them, thus increasing the Bankers' Balances with the Bank of England and enabling (and encouraging) them to expand loans and advances. Any such credit expansion, in the still suspicious temper of foreign money markets, would weaken sterling and thus tend to reverse the flow of funds to London. Large speculative movements of funds into and out of London could not be prevented from having their full effect on the exchange value of sterling, unless the Bank absorbed or released them. With its existing resources, the Bank could not absorb them without inflating credit, nor release them without corresponding deflation.

It was to meet this difficulty that the Exchange Equalisation Account was devised: the Governor told the Committee of Treasury on April 13 that provision would be included in the forthcoming Finance Bill. As passed, the Act provided that an Exchange Equalisation Account should be established under the control of the Treasury, to be invested in securities or gold in such manner as the Treasury thought best adapted 'for checking undue fluctuations in the exchange value of sterling'; and that £150 million should be issued to the Account out of the Consolidated Fund, and also the assets of the existing Exchange Account. The Account's endowment was invested in Treasury Bills, which the Bank, as operator of the Account, sold as it needed sterling to pay for gold or foreign exchange, and replaced by buying other Treasury Bills when it acquired sterling

by selling gold and foreign exchange. As its purchases of gold
and foreign exchange were always balanced by its sale of
Treasury Bills, they had not the effect of increasing the market's
supply of cash and the commercial banks' cash reserve; similarly its sales of exchange did not deflate credit, because they
were offset by purchases of Treasury Bills. Thus the domestic
market was insulated from the immediate effects of influx and
efflux of speculative funds — so long as the Account's resources
held out. The Account came into operation on July 1.

The limited aim of the Exchange Equalisation Account did
not meet the expectations of foreign observers; especially in
America, after that country went off gold itself in 1933, wider
political and commercial aims were attributed to it. The
simple explanation of its origin — that the Bank itself had not
resources of its own adequate to the task of preventing disconcerting fluctuations in sterling — was not appreciated, and the
declared object, to moderate fluctuations, did not seem sufficient
to justify its establishment. Two charges (mutually incompatible) were freely brought against the Bank and Government
— that sterling was deliberately depreciated to secure an advantage in international trade; and that sterling was depreciated
to force America off gold. Both were repugnant to the aims
Norman set himself and consistently followed. The first was
supported by a simple phrase in the speech with which the
Chancellor introduced the measure. After referring to the large
accumulations of liquid funds, he said that the tide had set
strongly in the direction of England and added: 'This is
flattering to our vanity, but at the same time it is sometimes
a serious embarrassment to our trade'. It is at least as probable
that he referred to the inconvenience of sudden changes in the
value of sterling as to the loss of the element of transient protection given by exchange depreciation. The second assumed
that the British authorities had complete control over the
world's exchanges. The actual experience of the Bank in its
interventions in the exchange market would quickly have dis-
countenanced any such idea.

When in April the establishment of the Account was settled,
the dollar had weakened to 3·80 owing to the suspicions excited
on the Continent by the Goldsborough-Fletcher Act, passed
through Congress but subsequently vetoed, which aimed at

raising commodity prices by devaluing the dollar. Both New York and Paris joined in a speculative bear movement; and in May the Bank found itself, in its endeavour to hold sterling as steady as possible on the dollar and the franc, defending the dollar and accumulating a mass of dollars with very few Continental currencies. In self-defence it shifted its purchases from dollars to francs and began gradually to earmark gold against its dollars. Later in the month the passing by Congress of the Revenue Act and the vetoing of the Soldiers' Bonus Bill restored confidence in the dollar; bear-covering helped the reaction, and the dollar strengthened by the beginning of June to 3·68. The Bank resisted the decline in sterling, but the market was influenced by fears that foreign holders of War Loan would take the opportunity of conversion [1] to withdraw their money. As confidence in the dollar returned, and doubts of sterling spread, the drain on the Bank's and Account's resources in gold and foreign exchange continued. The Bank was forced to let the rates for sterling fall, though it spread the fall over six months by continued support. The lowest point, 3·14½, was reached on November 29 under the influence of rumours that the United Kingdom intended to default on its war debt. An announcement to the contrary reversed the current, and the Bank had to intervene to prevent too sudden a rise in sterling. The rise was spread by the operations of the Account over three months; but it was feared that a sharper or larger rise would have had such a psychological effect that the resulting speculation would have embarrassed the American authorities. Already it was clear that large reserves were needed if fluctuations were to be moderated and no one could yet judge where the equilibrium rate for sterling would settle.

In 1933 a new situation developed. The obvious approach of a banking crisis in America undermined confidence in the dollar, while political fears affected also the franc. On March 4 American banks were closed, the Administration proceeded to put a complete embargo on gold exports, and Congress gave the President powers to devalue the dollar with a limit of 50 per cent, and to inflate the currency by $3000 million. Consistently with its previous action, the Bank allowed sterling to appreciate on the dollar, though intervening to moderate the

[1] See Chapter XI.

violence of the movements in the rate; in March the rate had averaged 3.43, in November it averaged 5·15.

In June and July the only exception occurred to the rule that the Account did not peg the rate. The Bank was requested to hold sterling while the World Economic Conference was meeting in London. At the Conference a successful attempt was made by a committee consisting of representatives of the Central Banks of England, France and New York, in consultation with their Treasuries, to work out a scheme for stabilising their exchange rates. It was experimental, since there was a limit put on the gold which any party to the agreement was pledged to sacrifice before allowing his rate to fall; but rates were agreed, methods of co-operation worked out, and a beginning could have been made. President Roosevelt rejected the scheme — and any scheme of stabilisation of exchanges — by cable. The hopes excited by the Conference had been unreasonable, but this rejection destroyed any chance of an early agreement on stable exchange rates.

The failure of the attempt to reach some agreement on exchanges reacted to the disadvantage of sterling. The Continent expected that sterling would move with the dollar and depreciate on the European gold currencies. The Governments and Central Banks of the latter took the opportunity of the Conference to agree on a policy of consultation and co-operation. The Account lost heavily in supporting sterling between July 3 and October 5; from then on sterling was stronger and some of this loss was recovered.

The actual practice of the Bank, therefore, both before the Exchange Equalisation Account was established, and as the operating agent of the Account subsequently, through the troubled years of America's strain and departure from the Gold Standard, was consistently that which Norman urged on the Chancellor on 8 December 1931, and maintained throughout the period between the suspension of the Gold Standard in September 1931 and the outbreak of war in 1939. To refrain from dealing unnecessarily; to ignore the question of profit and loss; to avoid deliberate depreciation of sterling — even at the risk of allowing reserves to fall dangerously low; to allow sterling to find the level which economic circumstances would dictate in the absence of transient speculative pressures; and

2 D

to avoid any attempt to fix the rate prematurely — these were the principles on which he thought the country's exchange policy should be based, and on which, in practice, it was based.

The message by which President Roosevelt torpedoed the project of a provisional stabilisation of exchange rates by co-operative action crystallised an opinion which was widely held :

The world will not long be lulled by the specious fallacy of achieving a temporary and probably an artificial stability in foreign exchange on the part of a few large countries only. The sound internal economic system of a nation is a greater factor in its well-being than the price of its currency in changing terms of the currencies of other nations. . . . So, too, old fetishes of so-called international bankers are being replaced by efforts to plan national currencies with the objective of giving to those currencies a continuing purchasing power which does not greatly vary in terms of the commodities and need of modern civilisation. Let me be frank in saying that the United States seeks the kind of a dollar which a generation hence will have the same purchasing power and debt paying power as the dollar value we hope to attain in the near future. . . .

The technique he proceeded to adopt was, however, novel — the purchase of gold at rising dollar prices. A mystical belief in a causal relation between the price of gold and the price level of commodities — even when the link between gold and currency had been severed by the suspension of convertibility and the prohibition of the use of gold for foreign payments — took the place of any more sophisticated theory. At first the purchases were restricted to the product of American gold mines ; when it was found that there was no effect on commodity prices in America (at any rate none that could not be explained by other measures such as the simultaneous Government purchases of American wheat and other commodities) nor outside, his agent proceeded to buy gold in London and Paris. In spite of substantial purchases the effect on commodity prices outside America was not great ; but in the first three weeks of the policy the dollar price of gold was forced up from \$29·80 to \$33·56, and the dollar-sterling rate rose by November 16 to 5·53.

While this was going on, the Federal Reserve Bank of New York — hitherto the normal agent responsible for exchange policy — was excluded by legislation from any participation in foreign relations, except under direction from Washington, and by current political feeling even from consultation. But the President found it difficult to dispense with the Bank as an agent, and came to value the opinion of its Governor, G. L. Harrison, not only on exchange but on general financial questions. In November Harrison approached Norman with the suggestion, which he said he was authorised to make, that an arrangement on the lines of the London Conference proposal for the provisional and experimental stabilisation of the chief exchange rates be revived. His hope was that it would lead to definite stabilisation by America before long. Norman was sympathetic; but there were two obstacles. The franc was weak and was not likely to recover unless a more stable Government came into office; and the American proposal was conditional on the British Government pledging itself not to allow sterling to depreciate on gold more than the dollar was depreciated. Norman did not himself think that Britain should give this undertaking: he distrusted the effect of capital movements and did not share the view of his American correspondents and visitors that the British balance of payments was safely restored. Nor did he think that his Government would give such a pledge — and he ascertained that they would not. On this the suggestion broke down; the U.S. Administration believed that the British Government had stolen a march on America by going off gold and by using the Exchange Equalisation Account to prevent sterling from appreciating, and were not prepared themselves to sacrifice the advantage which they believed they had obtained by depreciating their exchange, without an assurance from the British Government. In the middle of December the dollar strengthened and Harrison reported that it was impossible to press the scheme. The Administration went on with its gold-buying policy until they had raised the dollar price of gold to $35 per fine ounce. They then desisted from further depreciation and stabilised at that rate on 31 January 1934. This was not, however, a return to the Gold Standard, for the restrictions on purchase and export of gold were retained. Other Gold Standard countries did not regard the dollar as being on gold, and the possibility of a further devaluation of the dollar was a recurrent cause of unsettlement

in exchange markets. The gold value of the dollar could be
varied by proclamation by the President, but it could not be
raised above 60 per cent. or lowered below 50 per cent of its
old parity; the $35 value chosen being 59·06 per cent, there
was little room for appreciation but much for further depreciation.

The supersession of the Federal Reserve Bank of New York
by the U.S. Treasury in the control of exchange policy involved
a suspension of the customary intimate relations between the
Federal Reserve Bank and the Bank of England. Norman took
holidays at Bar Harbor in 1933, 1934 and 1935 ; during the first
of these he met Harrison and also President Roosevelt, though
they do not seem to have talked business ; but he subsequently
avoided Harrison for fear of causing him embarrassment. It
was, perhaps, fortunate that he was freed from this claim on
his time, since the strain of the task of industrial reconstruction
thrust on him and the new problems confronting him in his
own market were as much as even his capacity for work could
bear. He kept himself informed of the position of the Exchange
Equalisation Account and its operations, particularly in relation
to the Bank's principal in the matter, the Treasury. On one
occasion, for example, when the Account was losing reserves
heavily, he warned the Treasury and reported : 'Spoke fully
about this. Asked if Treasury were aware of impending difficulties over losses in gold and dollars, and he said "Yes". Asked
if Treasury wanted more facts as to the E.E.A/c. : he said
"No". Asked if Treasury wished to have a forecast as to how
far *down* the Account would go by a certain date at present
pace of loss : he said "No". So we rest in peace pro tem !'

It was not until the spring of 1935 that relations with the
dollar again compelled his continuous attention. The Bank,
in operating the Exchange Equalisation Account after 1933,
was forced to regulate sterling mainly by dealing in francs or
gold. It was able to secure dollars by putting gold into the
Federal Reserve Bank; but the facility was under licence
revocable at any moment and did not extend to the correlative
right to take gold out by paying in dollars — this latter being
restricted by the U.S. Treasury to countries still on the Gold
Standard. Paris, on the other hand, would always provide
francs against gold or gold against francs. To support sterling

when it was weak on the dollar, therefore, the Bank had to sell dollars in Paris for francs, earmarking gold in favour of the Federal Reserve Bank and paying the francs it received into the Bank of France who earmarked gold in its favour. Relations with other European Central Banks were close. They found it convenient to buy their gold and dollars in London; London recovered its importance as an active exchange market. The Governors met regularly at Basle, where, although the representatives of countries remaining on the Gold Standard did not treat England, nor even Germany, where Schacht [1] had returned to the Reichsbank, as equals, they welcomed their Governors in conference. Norman was therefore continually concerned with conditions on the Continent, and relations with the currencies of Belgium, Holland, Switzerland as well as France.

(ii)

It will be convenient at this point to turn to another consequence of England's suspension of the Gold Standard.

Its effects in other countries had been striking. With the exception of Canada and South Africa, the other Empire Governments followed sterling off gold. South Africa, under the impression that it had been directly on the Gold Standard, did not follow sterling and its pound appreciated on sterling; but the attractions of cheap sterling for South African investors, short and long, led to such a withdrawal of capital that South Africa was forced to come back on to sterling, and so off gold, 15 months later. Canada, with less dependence on London than on New York, imposed an official embargo on gold exports on 19 October 1931 (there had been an unofficial embargo intermittently since January 1929) but allowed its exchange to float.

Outside the Empire, other countries dependent on the British market for their exports and using sterling for their foreign payments, such as the Scandinavian countries, most of South America, and ultimately Japan, followed sterling without establishing any official link. On the other hand, the independent gold currencies — the French and Swiss francs, the

---

[1] Reappointed President of the Reichsbank, March 1933.

guilder, the lira, the belga, the mark — adhered to their gold parities, and found themselves handicapped in export trade to the sterling area and associated markets. So much of British imports came from Empire and other countries which followed sterling off the old gold parity, and the pressure for export markets in the prevailing conditions of world depression was so great, that Britain had to pay little more in sterling for its imports. Sterling prices exercised a depressing influence on gold prices all through the 'thirties, accentuating the depression in particular of agriculture, and extending industrial depression from the existing depressed areas to countries hitherto relatively immune.

The break-up of the stable exchange relations established between 1924 and 1928 had other effects. No stable system of rates could be constructed to take the place of gold parities; embargoes and restrictions on foreign payments, bilateral payments agreements, and systems of exchange control, whether by restriction of imports or by discriminatory rates of exchange for different purposes and different countries, spread rapidly. The world economy which existed in 1914 and which had been painfully reconstructed in the 'twenties, was again disrupted. Britain's inability to maintain the Gold Standard was a shock both to the functioning of a world economy and to the ideas on which it was based. The return of Britain to Protection in 1932 was an equal shock to ideas, since it extended the régime of protective tariffs to the greatest, and hitherto the most nearly free, of markets for exports. Though the change in policy can be traced back to the dislocation of Britain's external trade by the war and its effects, the actual legislation marked the end of an epoch. Britain continued to admit more imports than any other country, but Protection in old and new forms was intensified during the eight years to the outbreak of war.

Had His Majesty's Government and the Bank been seeking any competitive commercial advantage, they would have resisted as far as their influence extended the policy, so quickly adopted by a large part of the world, of following sterling off gold and attaching their currencies to sterling. By devaluing with sterling they deprived British traders of any advantage in their markets from devaluation; by devaluing further than sterling, as many countries did, they raised additional obstacles to British exports and facilitated their own entry into British markets. So far from resisting this tendency, the British authorities encouraged it. Norman's aim from the first was to restore the movement of international trade and to maintain as much freedom of payments as possible, and the widest possible use of sterling and of London's facilities was the chief means at his disposal. As early as January 1932 he was encouraging the Governor of the Central Bank of Sweden to base his foreign transactions on London ; in June he gave the Danes a revolving credit for the same purpose.

The chief result of going off gold was to throw into relief the financial and monetary links that bound other Empire countries to London. Hitherto these had been obscured by the maintenance of sterling at a fixed parity with gold ; now it was made clear that sterling was the currency in which the Empire, with the partial exception of Canada, conducted its external transactions, and in which it held its external reserves. With this came a clearer realisation also of London's responsibilities : sterling was an interest wider than the United Kingdom, its stability and availability were important to the greater part of the Empire and beyond, and London was still the clearing house of a large part of the transactions of the rest of the world. As such, it was the centre to which other countries looked for credits and loans. Norman recognised London's responsibility. The difficulties of the overseas territories, dependent on sterling balances to meet their external obligations, had contributed to the United Kingdom's difficulties in 1931 ; from 1932 onwards, the Bank looked at the balance of payments of the Sterling Area rather than that of the United Kingdom in estimating its liabilities and the probable course of the sterling exchanges.

The other territories of the Sterling Area shared the relief from the deflationary pressure on both government and private expenditure which the defence of fixed exchanges had involved. In the middle of 1932 a rise in sterling prices began which, with two or three temporary checks, has continued ever since ; but it was too slow for traders and primary producers. When discussions began over the agenda for the Imperial Conference at Ottawa, there were signs that the Conference might be used for the propagation of inflationary policies. New Zealand proposed the addition of Monetary Policy to the agenda ; the

Dominions generally cherished excessive hopes of what the
United Kingdom could achieve. There was a danger of disappointment creating a sense of grievance if the Conference did
not result in an improvement. At the same time the fall in
prices was world-wide and attributable to world conditions;
while British monetary and credit policy, though important for
and through sterling, was local and limited in its scope.

Norman's position is indicated in some notes he made during the discussion of the line to be taken at the Conference by
the United Kingdom. In general, he thought that too little
emphasis was being laid on the world-wide nature of the problems facing the countries represented at the Conference: he
sought to clarify the monetary problem with which the British
authorities were faced, and the possibility of co-operation in
the Empire. Thus, it would be going too far to say that Great
Britain's power to lend abroad was destroyed; the Dominions
did not regard themselves as being 'abroad', and lending to
them had not stopped. Again he thought it was possible to
exaggerate the volume of the mobile short-term capital fund
which might affect the exchanges, for which a figure of £2000
million had been mentioned: a large part had been lost or
withdrawn in the crisis year. On the other hand, it would be a
mistake to suggest that the sterling exchange had required
little management; that sterling could be regarded as an
adequate substitute for gold until conditions changed; and
that if they did not change, a sterling standard could become
a satisfactory alternative to a gold standard. The object must
be to return to gold; and in stressing the fundamental importance of sterling prices, it was desirable to stress their relation to
gold prices. He was particularly concerned to avoid any suggestion that being no longer tied to gold would remove many
of the contingencies which in the past had necessitated high
money rates. Conditions which had to be remedied by high
rates when on the Gold Standard were quite possible off the
Gold Standard, and would have to be remedied somehow —
presumably by putting up rates. Even if Central Banks should
not intervene to check a rise in prices from a depressed level,
they might be forced to by, for example, a European stock-
market boom.

The decision whether to attach their currencies to sterling

lay with the individual governments; it was for the United
Kingdom to decide whether it could assist them with loans.
London's position was not easy; the favourable balance of
payments of the 'twenties was gone, large short-term resources
were tied up in Europe; it was necessary to avoid any strain
on external payments which might revive distrust of sterling
and start a renewed flight. On the other hand, the territories
dependent on export of primary products were still in danger
of default on their debts, and further depreciation; London
was their only resort, New York bankers (as Norman wrote to
a Dominion Central Banker) were 'as buyers of bonds flat on
their backs'. In 1932 London made external loans to an
amount of £29 million compared with New York's £8 million,
all but half a million to the Empire. London could not reject
the Empire's claims; significantly, Canada, an Empire country
not attached to sterling, turned to London when New York
would not meet her needs and took more than half London's
external loans in 1932 and 1933. Australia made very big
demands for conversion and re-funding of existing loans. Norman insisted on the necessity of meeting these needs; but he
exercised a banker's right to criticise. He objected to the
practice of Crown Colonies borrowing on Bills in the London
market, and reminded their agents that 'they are all one family
with one cow to milk and in view of the condition of the cow
must exercise restraint'. India's needs were a continual preoccupation; they were large and pressing, but they had to be
adjusted to the varying capacity of the new-issue market. He
had to explain to more than one Government that they must
take their chance of borrowing when he offered it.

One territory incensed the issuing bankers, which had
always met its needs, by talking about re-funding sinking funds
and by pursuing a policy of domestic inflation which made it
very unlikely that it would be able to meet its external debt
service. When its Finance Minister arrived in London with
very large maturities to re-fund, he found his former friends
all disinclined to lend him anything. Norman sympathised
with the issuing bankers; but he could not let an Empire
Government face default. For a week he kept bankers and
Ministers in conference, putting the case of each to the other
and extracting concessions from both, until agreement to float

the re-funding issue was — with a large undisclosed subscription from the Bank — agreed. The Adviser who had assisted
him remarked as they left the last meeting, 'I do not know how
even you stand a strain like this last week's'. 'I could not have
done, ten years ago', the Governor replied.

Characteristically he appreciated the qualities of the Minister
as much as he disapproved of his financial policy, and, when
asked for an introduction to Schacht, whom the Minister wished
to see on a mission to sell his country's produce in Germany,
he wrote as follows :

I must not let Mr. —— come to see you without first giving
you a private warning. He is at once charming and dangerous —
an extreme Socialist and a complete Christian. He is a Minister
not because he likes politics but because through politics he wishes
to benefit first his own country and then the whole world. Sooner
or later the schemes he is arranging . . . will bring trouble to
[his country]. But in the meantime he is perfectly honest and is
doing what he believes to be right from all points of view. Thus,
you will find him serious even if misguided and I myself have
enjoyed many conversations with him this year though I have
found it difficult to agree with him in any particular.

A great advantage of the Gold Standard is that it provides
automatically answers to so many questions raised by international payments. With currencies severed from gold the
need developed for more conscious and deliberate consideration, and gave a stimulus to the activities of Central Banks at
the same time as it involved Treasuries in the business of
exchange. In the Empire a Central Bank had been opened in
South Africa in 1921 ; the Commonwealth Bank in Australia
combined some of the functions of a Central Bank with those
of a trading bank ; while in India, as long ago as 1926, a Commission had recommended a Central Bank. Norman's policy
had been consistently to foster this development. He had
released one of his most valued officials, W. H. Clegg, to become
the first Governor of the South African Bank ; he had encouraged first his Deputy Governor, Sir Ernest Harvey, and later
Sir Otto Niemeyer, to accept invitations to Australia and
explain the functions of a Central Bank ; and he had been in
touch with successive Finance Members of Council in India in
forwarding the policy of establishing a Reserve Bank. The

three years following the suspension of the Gold Standard saw
the realisation of his hopes.

Australia did not follow the South African precedent of
modelling its Reserve Bank on the Bank of England. The
Commonwealth Bank was a going concern, meeting special
needs of the Australian situation, but it was modified after
1924 to fit the purpose of a Central Bank. Its relations with its
own Government depended much on the personality of successive Governors who, in the difficult years from 1929 to 1936,
welcomed Norman's help and advice; but relations with the
Bank of England, already close, acquired more formal importance, when the law governing the Commonwealth Bank's
reserves was altered to allow it to hold them in 'English sterling' as well as in gold. The bank took advantage of this to
sell most of its gold and invest its reserves in the permitted
classes of British bills — a doubtful procedure to Norman's
mind — and to maintain the sterling exchange standard at the
parity existing just before Britain's suspension.

New Zealand proceeded to establish a Reserve Bank in
1933, which opened the following year. The advice and help of
the Bank of England was sought, and a Deputy Chief Cashier
of the Bank, Leslie Lefeaux, was appointed first Governor.
Norman urged them not to wait for a general return to the
Gold Standard; he would have wished them to stabilise on
sterling, but short of that welcomed the link between the
two pounds — a line of policy he agreed with the Treasury.
When the English banks which operated in New Zealand protested against the law requiring them to give up their gold in
exchange for New Zealand Reserve Bank notes, he told them
that he regretted their action, that it amounted to a demand
for special treatment and that such discrimination was not
reasonable. There was an idea in New Zealand, the Governor
of the new Reserve Bank wrote, that the new Reserve Bank
would be 'a branch of the Bank of England'. Nothing could
be further from Norman's view; he had always taken the view
that the responsibility for a country's credit position rested
with that country, and had opposed the system by which
deposit banks in England, dependent on British credit conditions, operated in overseas territories. The new Reserve
Banks were in his view a necessary step as soon as the countries

establishing them were able to take control of their own credit. He recognised that they could not duplicate the London market; but they could develop a market on lines suitable to their economic arrangements.

India's Reserve Bank, recommended by a Royal Commission in 1926, was not opened till 1935. It was given the powers of most Central Banks — note-issue, credit control by re-discount and open-market operations, and acting as the commercial bankers' bank. It was required to keep the rupee at a stable rate on sterling. Norman was consulted on the choice of the first Governor, and recommended a commercial banker, Sir Osborne Smith, whom he had previously recommended as head of the Imperial Bank of India. Finally Canada revised its banking system in 1933, and established in 1935 a Reserve Bank, the Bank of Canada, which turned to the Bank of England for its first Deputy Governor, J. A. C. Osborne. There could be no question of basing Canadian currency on sterling; but it was a great advantage to London to have an institution in close relations with the Bank of England while controlling a market closely linked with New York. The Bank of Canada pursued an independent policy in regulating the value of its currency; but the opportunity it afforded to the Bank of England of discussing Canadian loan requirements, and, perhaps as important, an independent opinion on American monetary conditions, were of great value in maintaining stable currency relations with North America.

The stability established after 1933 in the exchange rates between Empire currencies and sterling was the best evidence of success. It implied confidence of the Dominions in sterling, which made them ready to hold sterling though it was no longer tied to gold, and confidence of London in the Empire, for which it continued to act as banker and capitalist. For Norman it meant continuous attention to Empire business. No class of appointments figured more frequently in his diary than visits of issuing brokers and bankers to discuss the needs of Empire territories for loans, and the means of making them. He maintained contact with the other Empire Central Banks by exchange of visits of Governors and officers, regular correspondence and telephone. The contraction in London's available resources was met by an embargo on overseas lending (an expedient Norman disliked, though ready in the circumstances to have it enforced by legislation if necessary) from which the Empire was exempt. The Empire applicants had to take their places in the queue which was enforced to prevent overcrowding of the market, and smaller demands, from provinces and municipalities in the Empire, were brought under the same control. On the other hand, the Bank would supplement this access to the long-term markets by credits of its own to Empire Central Banks, the basis being to conserve use of sterling as an international currency.

(iii)

Early in 1935 a stream of indirect messages began to reach the Governor that the Washington Administration was disturbed by British exchange policy. American visitors to the Bank, American economists in London, correspondents in Ottawa and Geneva, all brought the same report; American fears of the Machiavellian manœuvres of the Exchange Equalisation Account were reawakened.[1] Sterling had declined on gold currencies through 1934 under the strain of the depreciation of the dollar and the simultaneous transfers of funds through London to America. After some recovery there had been another fall, in February and March 1935, which affected the sterling-dollar rate through the franc and brought it below the old par of exchange for the first time since the American policy of raising prices by bidding up the dollar price of gold had been inaugurated. There was no significance in the fall; but it helped Belgium to decide to devalue the belga, and it may have influenced the Secretary of the U.S. Treasury to put out feelers on the subject of stabilisation. The British Treasury reported to the Governor suggestions through the American Embassy that the U.S. Treasury was not, and in its opinion should be, informed of the operations of the Exchange Equalisation Account; while in Washington Mr. Morgenthau, Secretary to the U.S. Treasury, made the same suggestion to a British

[1] The writer had a call from Dr. Harry White on 9 May 1935 who urged the possibility and importance of an early agreement to stabilise, and hinted that America would make things awkward for England if England resisted. He said, however, when challenged, that he was not speaking officially on behalf of the U.S. Treasury — none of the visitors were !

Treasury official, attached to the British Embassy there. In an address in May, Mr. Morgenthau said publicly that America was always ready to stabilise, but, if the great trading nations elected to continue under the present absence of rules, was no longer at a disadvantage.

Norman replied at length to the Treasury on May 27. He agreed that they should try to disabuse Morgenthau's mind of the belief that they were maliciously less forthcoming than the French, but of course they were not informed about the operations of the U.S. Exchange Account. It was true that the Federal Reserve Bank had an account in the books of the Bank of England, but the Federal Reserve Bank might have other accounts, in London or elsewhere, of which they knew nothing, and they had no knowledge of the transactions of the U.S. Treasury, for example, in silver and currencies. Every now and then the Federal Reserve Bank telephoned them, but such conversations were casual, personal and accidental, not complete or represented as authoritative. As for the Exchange Equalisation Account, they would claim that it was not used in a way to damage any other country or to depress sterling, but solely to steady fluctuations. They did not think it necessary to inform the Federal Reserve Bank of their operations; they did not operate in the Reserve Bank's market and had therefore neither regular communication with them nor need of it. As soon as America went off gold they had sold the dollars they held and had not attempted to deal in dollars since or used their account with the Federal Reserve Bank except to execute orders for third parties, such as other Central Banks. On the other hand, they talked and consulted freely and regularly with the Bank of France, simply because they were continually operating in their market and using them as their sole and active agent. However, he concluded, the Bank kept the Treasury fully informed of the operations of the Account, and it was for the Treasury to decide what to communicate to the U.S. Treasury. Nothing seems to have come of the interchanges.

Another approach was made in November 1935. The U.S. Treasury's representative in Paris called on the Governor at Morgenthau's request, and 'spoke vaguely of co-operation'. Norman did not think that the visit was more than a little mild propaganda, but, the following July on his annual holiday in

North America, made arrangements to meet the Chairman of
the Federal Reserve Board, Marriner Eccles. However, he
learned that a visit by him to Eccles in Washington would be
unwelcome to Morgenthau. Eccles came to New York to see
him, but, as Norman said on his return, this visit did and could
produce no result. The difficulty of renewing the intimate
collaboration which had existed between Norman and Strong
lay, it is clear, in the prevailing *étatisme* of American economic
policy; Morgenthau intended to keep exchange transactions,
in detail as well as in broad policy, under the control of his
Department, while Norman understood by co-operation the
continuous intimate and confidential contact of dealer with
dealer in a market, which was practicable only between Central
Bankers operating in their markets, and preferred by the British
Treasury as much as it was by the Bank.

With Norman the issue was also one of policy as well as
procedure. There were voices raised in England for an immediate return to the Gold Standard, and the Continent had
never relaxed its pressure to the same end since 1931. Norman,
with a conviction of the need of a common international standard for trade — and an experience of the value of the Gold
Standard for the control of inflation which none of his critics
and advisers could equal, nevertheless was not satisfied that
the conditions were ripe for restoration. His reasons he explained in a letter to the Governor of the Bank of Canada on
19 June 1935:

The 'panic' money which grew to such large proportions in
the 'twenties, and which was the prime agent in wrecking the
gold standard at that time is still (as recent events have shown)
capable of putting a severe strain without warning and perhaps
without adequate cause upon almost any currency.

This, I take it, is the main reason for the existence of equalisation funds in several countries; and if the publics could be made
to realise how necessary to domestic peace and quiet is the counter-
action of these 'panic' movements, a great deal of the popular
distrust of all equalisation fund operations would be removed.

The dangers inherent in the mass movement of balances from
market to market are still as great as ever. The same irrational
forces which played havoc with us a few years ago are quite capable
of playing havoc with any of us again. An attempted stabilisation,

with inadequate safeguards against these forces, would simply give them added strength.

In the second place (and apart from 'panic' movements) the continuous drifting of large quantities of gold into the United States is itself evidence that a stabilisation agreement which was limited to currency matters only would have a very temporary life. I need not insist that a prerequisite of exchange stability must be the stabilisation of international accounts generally; for you know this just as well as I do. Such a stabilisation must begin by recognising the United States as a creditor which (at present) refuses *either* to forgo payment, *or* take merchandise in payment, *or* make new loans. Such a situation is impossible: and so long as it exists, I regard a real stabilisation as no less impossible.

Thirdly (and quite apart from the *present* lack of balance in other countries' accounts with the United States) there is a large uncertain element in their future exchange relations with that country. If a sustained revival of business were to make its appearance in the United States, so much investment money might, as a direct result of such revival, be drawn to New York from other centres, that the balance would very likely be thrown out of equilibrium again.

If it were no more than a question of choosing appropriate parities (and then stabilising at those parities) there would obviously be much to be said in favour of immediate discussions. Unfortunately, however, the selection of appropriate parities is only part of the problem. Whatever parities were to be discussed we could have no reasonable hope of maintaining them unless at the same time we could have some assurance that the great disturbing forces which threaten us — of which I have already mentioned some of the most important — could be brought under control. And I see no reason as yet to suppose that the rest of the world is prepared to envisage the problem as a whole. Your American neighbours show no signs of such a disposition. The process would need quite a period of public and political education. For our part, I wish to take no risks with partial or temporary solutions.

There is, lastly, this further consideration to be borne in mind, quite apart from the question whether *de facto* stabilisation is practically possible or not. When any of us speak of making a *de facto* settlement as a prelude to a *de jure* stabilisation it is of the essence of any such *de facto* settlement that there be no leakage in advance or at any time of the plans that are to be discussed, and possibly carried out, or else forthwith abandoned.

In our general experience with the Bank of France we have found that we can count upon discretion being observed; and the success that we have in our day to day co-operation with them is absolutely conditioned by this.

You have your own contacts with the United States. . . . For our part, we consider that the risk of a leakage is so great as to render very dangerous any serious discussions with this end in view.

The recovery of the British export industry lagged behind the general recovery of the country, but Norman had never countenanced the use of exchange depreciation as a means of stimulating exports, and had no wish to use it now. It was the risks of a fixity of exchange rates, at any level, that he refused to take. Tied to a fixed rate he could not have persisted in the policy of cheap money and lower interest rates, nor allowed the free movement of funds into and out of London, nor avoided exchange control (as distinct from intervention in the market to smooth out abrupt fluctuations), nor resisted clearing arrangements, and proposals to stop all overseas issues. He was at one with the Chancellor who, in spite of his reiteration that the ultimate aim was a restoration of the Gold Standard, always found himself compelled to reply to specific questions in Parliament that return was out of the question at the moment.

Outside the United Kingdom Norman found conditions no more encouraging. In France a stable government was needed to check the steady and large movements of money from Paris to New York. Germany maintained a nominal connection between its currency and gold, and had brought back Schacht to make the system work; but it was not possible to expand government expenditure and imports and allow freedom of private imports and foreign payments, without forcing up prices and openly depreciating the mark — two consequences which no German Government would contemplate. America pressed for stabilisation; but Norman told an American visitor in May 1935 that the one essential, assuming some settlement of war debts, was that America should accept the responsibility of a creditor country, and either admit imports or resume foreign lending, or both, and immediately it would help if she discontinued her silver buying policy. He disliked the Ottawa Agreements; they cut across his policy and tended to separate Britain from Europe. At the same time he had to ensure that

2 E

London still met the capital needs of the Dominions. It was
not surprising that he wrote in March 1935 to the Governor of
a Dominion Central Bank :

> On this question of stabilisation we must distinguish between
> what is practical and what is desirable. There are very few here-
> abouts who deep down do not long for stabilisation. . . . But I
> do not know anyone who is brave enough at this moment and under
> present conditions to advocate stabilisation on gold at any feasible
> rate.

The advisers of the U.S. Treasury — and experience — had
convinced the Administration that there was something in the
'old fetishes of so-called international bankers'; but the Secretary (Morgenthau) was not ready for an unconditional return
to the Gold Standard. His position was that President Roosevelt
had saved America from chaos, that America was the last
country to devalue, that he was always ready to stabilise if
others were. He made it clear that the particular 'rule' which
he made a condition of definite stabilisation of the dollar was
an undertaking by the British Government to agree to limits
on the fluctuations in the exchange value of sterling. He would
attach the same condition to extending to the United Kingdom
the freedom to sell and buy and export gold which countries
still on the Gold Standard enjoyed, though it was pointed out
to him that the U.S. Treasury made frequent use itself of the
facilities of the London gold market and the correlative freedom
to take gold out of Britain. The strain on the Gold Standard
countries, springing fundamentally from the devaluation in
gold, first of the pound and then of the dollar, was now to
compel a change.

In the course of 1936 it became clear that France would be
unable to maintain the franc at the 'Poincaré' parity on gold,
while observing the obligations of the full Gold Standard.
Apart from temporary interruptions, Paris had continued to
draw gold from the rest of the world until the end of the first
quarter of 1935. The monetary authorities made no attempt
to sterilise this addition to their reserves, and prices rose; but
the expansion of monetary supply had little effect in stimulating
production and trade, while the handicap to French exports of
an over-valued currency exerted a cumulative pressure on the

country's industry. The devaluation of the belga in April 1935 added to this strain. The sterling-franc rate was in fact kept within a narrow range of fluctuations from May till the end of the third quarter of 1936; but beneath this superficial stability there was a progressive weakening of the franc. In May and November 1935 France suffered heavy losses of gold, and in the first three quarters of 1936 the Exchange Equalisation Account alone was virtually holding the franc. The accession of a Left-Wing Government under Blum had excited fears among the holders of volatile funds and offset such progress as had been made in bringing French costs into line with the external value of the franc.

In June 1936 M. Vincent Auriol, the Finance Minister, announced a series of measures aimed at inducing the repatriation of French funds and a cessation of hoarding; while admitting that deflation had failed, he still rejected devaluation. Close observers of the exchange market did not expect his proposals to do more than check the efflux of funds from France, and that only temporarily. Blum, visiting London for another purpose in July, raised independently with Chamberlain the question of devaluation. He had already raised it with the Secretary of the U.S. Treasury. His aim was to be able to present devaluation to his countrymen as the result of an international agreement; he sought assurances that French devaluation would not be a signal for devaluation of other currencies, and with this in view asked the British Government to agree to limits on the fluctuations it would permit in sterling. On the understanding that France returned immediately to gold on a lower parity, Chamberlain was prepared to give his approval; but he refused to promise, in any way, to put definite limits on the value of sterling, and for the moment the French Government decided to postpone action. The pressure on the franc had been relieved, but it was recognised that a change of policy was unavoidable; what was undecided, until the eve of devaluation, was whether it would be a unilateral or an agreed act, and whether it would be devaluation to a lower gold value with immediate resumption of Gold Standard practice, or suspension of the Gold Standard and the adoption of a free rate for the franc on the British precedent, which might in practice be pegged on sterling.

The possibility of a fluctuating franc created a new situation. So long as France maintained a fixed parity with gold, and interposed no obstacles to the free purchase and movement of gold, the fact that America confined the privilege of converting dollars into gold to Gold Standard countries did not prevent the Account from regulating sterling by reference to gold ; it could operate on the fluctuating sterling-dollar rate through the franc-dollar rate which was fixed. If this became impossible — and in that case it was unlikely that the bigger currencies still on the Gold Standard could maintain free transfers of gold — it would be difficult to maintain any effective control over the sterling gold price or over the dollar exchange. The British authorities would have no adequate market in which they could buy and sell gold and gold currencies, while America equally would be helpless, since it could control its exchanges only if it was prepared, which for domestic political reasons it was not, to buy and hold floating currencies.

Early in September 1936 the French approached Morgenthau on the subject of 'stabilisation', who was anxious that any action should be taken simultaneously with the British Treasury. The French were still hoping that the British Government would agree to stabilise, at any rate within a limited range of rates. This the British were determined not to do, and Morgenthau now accepted this position. He replied to the French Government to substantially the same effect as His Majesty's Government — that he sympathised with their aims and wished to help but did not believe any commitment as to rates or publication of a 'pre-stabilisation' arrangement to be necessary. He did contemplate the simultaneous publication of a 'statement of intentions' by the three Governments. From this time on, the Bank of England was in continual discussion with the Bank of France, though the discussions were handicapped by the French Government's inability to make up its mind. Finally, on September 25, the decision was taken to suspend the convertibility of the franc, but at the same time to give the Government authority to re-attach it to gold within limits representing 25·19 per cent and 34·35 per cent devaluation. Until convertibility at a new rate was established, an Exchange Fund would be charged with maintaining the rate within those limits. The market would be closed from September 26 to

October 1 to allow time for the necessary legislation, and the French Government relied on the agreed announcements by the three Governments to assure support and allay fears.

The British Government, in its statement, after referring to its consultations with the Governments of France and the United States, and the claims of domestic needs which all three recognised, reaffirmed 'their purpose to continue the policy they have pursued in the course of recent years, one constant object of which is to maintain the greatest possible equilibrium in the system of international exchanges and to avoid to the utmost extent the creation of any disturbance of that system by British monetary action'. They welcomed the 'readjustment' of the French currency; and declared their intention to continue to use the appropriate available resources so as to avoid any disturbance of the basis of international exchanges resulting from the proposed readjustment : they would arrange for consultation for this purpose with the other two Governments and their authorised agencies. They joined in an invitation to other countries to accede to the agreement and trusted 'that no country will attempt to obtain an unreasonable competitive exchange advantage and thereby hamper the effort to restore more stable economic relations'.

While the three Governments agreed on the statement they should publish, they diverged somewhat in their views of its significance. Morgenthau described the Agreement as 'a new type of gold standard . . . one more move towards our general objective, the restoration of world trade', and regarded the dollar as the 'coping stone' of the new system. The British view was that it was purely a technical arrangement to facilitate co-operation in moderating exchange fluctuations. The Bank of England had been discussing the necessary arrangements with the Bank of France even before the announcement, and complete agreement had been reached within forty-eight hours. The Bank of England asked only for the continuation of the facilities hitherto available; the Bank of France was in complete agreement on procedure, though nothing was put on paper 'ni accorde, ni entente, uniquement coopération journalière'. A generalisation of these facilities was made possible by the undertaking of the U.S. Treasury, announced on October 13, to sell gold for export or earmark to exchange equalisation or stabilisation funds of countries which gave reciprocal facilities to the U.S. Treasury. The Bank quickly worked out arrangements with the Central Banks in all the chief centres, the basis being that each would supply its own currency to the other against gold, and give gold against its currency; exchanges of information and consultation should be continuous, and intervention in the market of either would be with the full knowledge and agreement of the other. In practice, frequent movements of gold were rendered unnecessary by the practice of earmarking gold by the country taking its own currency in favour of the country selling it.

There was one exception to the general accession to the new agreement. The Bank sent emissaries to the other Central Banks after September 25. In Berlin Dr. Schacht told his visitor that he did not believe the understanding meant anything; neither England nor the United States had committed themselves to anything, and France's difficulties remained; if, however, the rest of Europe would stabilise on *sterling*, irrespective of sterling fluctuations on gold, he would regard that as amply sufficient stability, and would join in the general stabilisation. But there was no prospect of that, and he was quite able to hold the mark at whatever level he chose for as long as he chose.

It is true that the United Kingdom remained uncommitted to any fixity, and the United States remained free to devalue further to 50 per cent of the old gold value of the dollar. But the declaration of 'intention' — to co-operate, and to avoid competitive devaluation — was an advance in currency relations. It may be doubted whether the subsequent devaluations of the franc could have been carried through without serious dislocation in other markets had the practice of co-operation not been developed. It was what Norman, Ben Strong and other central bankers had been trying to establish for nearly twenty years. Nevertheless, Norman found that the Central Bankers in their monthly meeting at Basle derived small encouragement from the Agreement; no financial arrangement, in their view, could take the place of political appeasement.

The first effect of French devaluation was a repatriation of French money. Most of this was only a liquidation of speculative positions taken against the franc, and before the end of

the year it was exhausted.   In the New Year the flight of
capital from France was renewed, and took the form, no longer
almost wholly of temporary transfer of liquid funds to other
centres, but to a considerable extent of investment in industrial
securities and commodities in other countries.   The new
arrangement between the countries which adhered to the
Tripartite Agreement for clearing by transfer of gold took some
time to settle down into a smoothly working routine.   The
U.S. Treasury's power to sell gold was subject to legal restrictions which led the other parties to the Agreement to prefer
London as a clearing centre ; a handling charge of $\frac{1}{4}$ per cent
imposed by America on all gold dealings had the same effect
by making America the dearest centre for gold dealings — the
result was that clearing was concentrated on the British Exchange Equalisation Account.   Since the bulk of exchange
transactions were now cleared through Exchange Accounts and
Central Banks, the gold markets of London and elsewhere lost
most of their arbitrage work ; if all net balances on external
transactions were to be settled daily in gold, only Treasury
funds could cope with the demands for gold and absorb the
gold transferred.   At first, also, the desire of the French and
Americans to give the Agreement a political complexion —
'Co-operation between the three great democracies' — caused
some confusion : the first deal — for Russia — in dollars for
sterling in the New York market was undertaken by the U.S.
Treasury and announced in the Press as the defeat of a Russian
attempt to depreciate sterling, whereas the Bank of England
had asked the Federal Reserve Bank of New York to handle
it outside the market, knowing that the Russians wanted it to
meet a maturity in Sweden.   In the course of 1937, however,
the routine of intervention was established, and the necessity of
settling accounts by earmarking gold at the end of each working
day compelled continuous consultation between the operating
Central Banks.

(iv)

In retrospect the absorption by the United States of about $6000
million worth of gold in the three years after the Tripartite
Agreement, following on $4000 million in the three preceding

years, suggests that there was little scope for the regulation
of exchange movements — even by the most harmonious
co-operation in the most skilful control.   American current
account payments called for no such inflow of gold, but over the
period 1934–38 as a whole — and the movement was intensified
in 1939 — there was a continual pressure for dollars on capital
account by the rest of the world and for the repatriation of
American capital.   The forces behind it were the devaluation
of the dollar, a strong currency backed by ample reserves, to
under 60 per cent of its former parity, at which level it was
then pegged again on gold ;   and later, when the influence of
devaluation might have exhausted itself, the deterioration of
political conditions in Europe and the growing fear of war.
This trend was, however, not continuous ;   fear of American
financial policy at times outweighed political fears for Europe.
Contemporaries, who could not know the results of the movements as a whole, and who faced a market situation subject to
continual changes (which annual figures conceal), found ample
scope for technical — and sometimes political — intervention
in exchange markets.

This very movement of capital called for continual activity
on the part of the authorities controlling exchanges, if it was
not to invoke dislocation and alarm.   But Paris was too much
absorbed in its own troubles to act effectively as an international
currency clearing centre.   The smaller Gold Standard countries — Belgium, Holland and Switzerland — did not offer
large enough markets ;   Germany found that its own problem
of foreign payments made a free market impossible.   New York
was the natural centre by virtue of its resources, its stable gold-
based currency, and its ability to lend abroad.   But loans to
governments in default on their debts to the United States
Government were illegal under the 1934 Johnson Act ;   private
loans and credits were still discredited by the experiences of
the 'twenties.   New York was not an important foreign exchange market :   in the main it dealt with Europe through
London and sterling.   Its monetary authorities adopted a passive policy.   They regarded the dollar as on the Gold Standard ;
any country which wanted dollars could get them in exchange
for gold and vice versa ;   the remedy for a deficit or surplus of
dollars in the world's money markets was not an active policy

of supplying or supporting the dollar, but a movement of gold to or from America, or a change by other countries in their rates on the dollar. It followed, therefore, that the bulk of the work fell upon the Exchange Equalisation Account, already committed to an active policy of intervention in the exchange market (though the amount of intervention was normally exaggerated) by the refusal to fix any limits to the fluctuations of sterling on gold and other currencies.

Moreover, its administrators were assailed by problems not foreseen in the Tripartite Agreement. The devaluation of the franc in September 1936 gave France only temporary relief, and by January 1937 the French Government was seeking permission to borrow in London again. Norman advised the Chancellor against any credit; it would be used to relieve the French budget deficit without effecting any permanent improvement in the exchange position. The Government decided, however, on broad political grounds to permit the credit. The drain of money from France was not stayed; the credit was used up as quickly as it became available, and early in February the Foreign Office felt it necessary to warn the French Premier, Blum, that control of exchange and gold would be inconsistent with the Tripartite Agreement. Norman had more sympathy with French difficulties; a little later, in June, he was saying that if Blum chose to sequester French nationals' overseas investments and currency holdings, it was an internal question with no relation to the Agreement. The Bank discussed the possibilities of a joint gold loan to France by the other parties to the Tripartite Agreement, but Norman decided that was not practicable. In the event Blum did not impose exchange control, and it was agreed that some further devaluation of the franc would not be inconsistent with the Agreement.

In the first half of 1937 also there was a disturbance from another quarter. On April 7 the Gold Market was scared by a sudden rumour, originating in America, that the official American price for gold was to be reduced. President Roosevelt had recently declared that commodity prices were too high, and there were other signs that the authorities feared inflation. The effect of the scare was to reverse a rise in sterling on the dollar, to check purchases of gold on the market and to

stimulate dis-hoarding. Commodity markets with speculative
positions were badly shaken, and the French took the opportunity
to let the franc depreciate. But no announcement came from
Washington, the Exchange Equalisation Account bought gold
as it supplied the demand for dollars, and by the end of the
week the scare had died down. Its seriousness lay not in any
immediate effects, but in the implication of a widespread distrust of the current price of gold. This distrust had been
growing for a year or more and was justified by the change
in the available supply. Production was stimulated by the
higher price and supplemented by a large and continued dis-
hoarding, with the result that total supplies would have been
far more than adequate, on any basis hitherto put forward, if
they had been distributed in proportion to need. There was,
however, a disproportionate concentration of the increase in
the United States and, to a less extent, the United Kingdom,
which excited fears of inflation in their two key currencies. In
the United Kingdom the influx of gold was offset by sales of
Bills by the Exchange Equalisation Account as it paid for gold;
but this did not exclude all inflationary effects, and the Account's sterling resources were not sufficient to cope with an
unlimited influx. In America precautionary measures were
taken by increasing the required reserves of banks, and sterilising part of the incoming gold; but again without reassuring
the world.

Norman's first reaction to the rumour that America was
about to reduce its buying price for gold had been to say that
gold was in fact over-valued, in view of existing supplies and
demand, and that the rumour was based on this fact. He
favoured a reduction in the price by agreement with the
U.S.A., but any action must wait for a decision by Ministers,
to be followed by an exploratory visit to Washington — sooner
rather than later. Another scare flared up in the first week
of June, but nothing was done and the Chancellor of the Exchequer allayed fears by an answer in Parliament on June 8
that there was no change contemplated in the Government's
policy on gold and exchange. The sterling resources of the
Exchange Equalisation Account were reinforced on June 25 by
an addition of £200 million and there was still no action in
Washington. By the end of June the people who had been

getting out of gold found that they had more dollars than they were willing to hold; conditions in America had changed and fears of inflation were giving place to fears of recession; foreign purchases of American securities died down; and the world's appetite for gold revived.

The gold scare brought out a difference in the attitude of the British and American authorities to working the Tripartite Agreement. Under the influence of the scare a European Central Bank had used the facilities of the Agreement to sell a large amount of gold to America for dollars. Morgenthau resented their action as contrary to the spirit of the Agreement and pressed the British Treasury to join him in presenting to the other adherents a Code of Rules. This provided that Central Banks and Treasuries should not add to the international movements of capital by unilateral decisions to transfer their gold reserves into foreign currencies; holdings of currencies should be restricted to working balances; and Central Banks and governments should make investments in other countries only after consultation with and perhaps at the invitation of the governments concerned. Norman, habitually averse from lecturing in public associates with whom he had to work, knew from experience that the culprits would act on their own view of the market situation irrespective of codes (even though it involved them in a loss as did their recent deal in gold), and advised the Chancellor (Sir John Simon) to excuse himself from any formal protest. He did so, saying that he did not disagree with the general principles set out in the proposed code but thought it better to let principles of working emerge gradually from day-to-day experience rather than at this early stage to lay down a hard-and-fast code. He was doubtful also of the expediency of throwing any doubt on the willingness of America and Britain to take gold.

The French Ambassador in September 1937 showed some faith in the powers of the Exchange Equalisation Account, when he asked the Governor what he proposed to do to prevent a further fall of the franc. A new French Government on June 28 had decided to remove any peg from the franc and let it 'float'. The British Government was informed late that evening and the Paris markets were closed on the 29th and 30th. There was some question whether this short notice was adequate 'consultation' in the terms of the Tripartite Agreement, but the Bank of England by arrangement with the Bank of France supplied the London market with francs at 110-111 while the Paris market was closed, and when it opened assisted it to establish a new rate of 129. In September the weakness of the franc was again causing alarm; Norman, with a more modest opinion of the Exchange Equalisation Account's powers than the French Ambassador, said that he saw no remedy and could advise only to wait and see; to one of his colleagues he confided that there were only two alternatives — a Government of the Right, and Exchange Control. He was concerned over the repayment of the credit given to France by London in February; but the French Treasury repaid in gold. At the end of the year no further fall in the franc had taken place, but its balance was felt to be still precarious.

(v)

The change in the outlook of industry and trade at the end of 1937, and the recession which developed in 1938, have been overlaid in popular memory by the rearmament and war-induced expansion which succeeded it. The threat of war was already overshadowing 1938, but it did not counteract the transient influences operating on markets until the second quarter of the year. These were mainly concerned with speculation in the franc, associated with political crises in France between January and April: and they caused little change in the sterling-dollar rate in the first quarter. The Exchange Equalisation Account's gold holdings reached their peak in the second week of the year: and when they began to fall after a few months the immediate reason was a large reflux of capital to France. But from May 1938 the Account was losing gold, and the dollar rate fell to 4·92 by the end of July and by another 30 cents in August and September, what time a newspaper agitation was being carried on for reflationary measures to stimulate industrial recovery.

The crisis of September provided a rehearsal of exchange and monetary problems on the outbreak of a war. Since March the Bank had been drafting plans for control of the

exchanges on the outbreak of war : but it had received no new
powers, and could meet the increased drain on London only by
buying sterling offered, and discouraging flight by lowering the
rates at which it would do so. The Governor thought that the
sooner the rate fell below 4·86 the better ; we should yield to
pressure and merely slow down the movement. The movement
out of sterling was arrested only momentarily by the Munich
settlement on September 30, and accelerated in October and
November, causing a drastic fall in the gold holdings of the
Exchange Equalisation Account.

The only source from which they could be promptly replenished was the gold in the Issue Department of the Bank. As
long ago as 1935 the Bank had raised the question of revaluing
the gold in Issue at the current price and transferring the
surplus, leaving the circulation and the Fiduciary Issue unchanged. In April 1936 the Governor had pressed the matter
again, but had not taken it up formally with the Chancellor or
Treasury. Since then Exchange Equalisation Account gold
had been transferred to Issue to a large amount, when the
Account was running short of sterling assets to mop up an
influx of funds. Now in 1938 it was proposed to reverse the
process and to transfer gold from Issue to the Account, simultaneously increasing the Fiduciary Issue to maintain the volume
of the circulation. At first a transfer of £60 million was discussed. Then his colleagues pressed on the Governor a much
larger transfer and simultaneously a revaluation of Issue gold.
He pointed out the difficulties — revaluation meant a long and
bitter debate — it had been pressed two years before : altering
the Fiduciary Issue required legislation, or without it the
amount of gold which could be released from Issue was insufficient to re-establish the Account ; the war debt (it had
been suggested that the profits of revaluation might be used to
effect betimes a settlement with America) was 'political and
unapproachable'.

On the other hand, he recognised the urgent need of action.
On 1 December 1938 he had put to the Chancellor (Sir John
Simon) a number of suggestions for curtailing business which
increased the drain on reserves — restricting forward dealings
in exchange, forbidding advances against gold, tightening the
restrictions on issues for foreign borrowers, prohibiting the

purchase of foreign investments, shutting down American brokerage firms in London, registering all holdings of non-sterling securities. But the Chancellor objected that most of these expedients required legislation and would not be water-tight. He thought it might be necessary to make a patriotic appeal to all citizens to keep their money at home, and event-ually it might come to exchange control, but sufficient unto the day! The Bank had raised the question of 'crisis' powers of exchange control, in discussing plans for war, without any response. To let the pound slide was no solution — the Gover-nor had been warned at Basle that some Europeans would come on to sterling if sterling dropped much below $4.65, so that a falling pound would impose no check on the drain of funds and gold to the Continent. The prospect of outside help in the form of a gold or dollar loan was small, since it would require the grant by Congress of new powers to the U.S. Treasury. Never-theless Norman thought an approach should be made and meanwhile a limited transfer of gold from Issue should be arranged.

The response from the Treasury proposed a much more logical and effective approach. Experience of the working of the Account had removed the fears that led them to discourage the Bank's proposals of 1936. Now, it was possible to start from the premises that the note-issue no longer depended on gold, but within wide limits on the agreement of Bank and Treasury; and that the proper place for *all* the gold was in an exchange account. Some gold should, out of respect for con-servative opinion, be still held in Issue, but at something like its current value, and the bulk should be transferred to the Exchange Equalisation Account. The Bank welcomed the new approach and the change was effected by a new Act, which received the Royal Assent on 28 February 1939; but in antici-pation of it £200 million of gold (at the statutory price) was transferred from Issue on January 6.

Even before 1939 the subordination of market to political considerations had begun to be felt. Norman had protested against a 'good-will' mission to Brazil, on the ground that Brazil was in default on debts to the United Kingdom, but he was overruled. On the other hand, he raised no objection to a normal credit to Japan, which was vetoed by the Government.

He had given at the Government's request a credit to the National Bank of Czechoslovakia; he was to protest, in the week before war broke out, against loans to Eastern Europe, but he accepted the Government's decision. Similarly, when the Committee of Treasury, on January 4, urged the use of Bank Rate to support sterling, he accepted the Treasury's view that there should be no change; the Chancellor was still wedded to cheap money. On January 25, at the urgent request of the Foreign Secretary (Lord Halifax), he and Stamp attended a meeting at the Foreign Office when they were asked to attach their signatures to a propaganda appeal to be broadcast to Germany; although he thought that this form of propaganda might well lead to increased bitterness he felt that he had no option but to agree.

He reported faithfully to the Chancellor the 'increasing dis-repute' in which sterling was held, and warned him frequently of the weakening of the Bank's power to support it. The Chancellor agreed in January to the reimposition of restrictions on forward dealings in exchange, and gold and foreign loans were discouraged. In the first quarter, though the flow of funds to America continued, the exchange market was not very active, and gains from the smaller European countries offset losses of gold to France, where Reynaud's financial reforms and an under-valued franc were attracting money. But the Government's policy, since the transient relief offered by Munich was exhausted, had been to take no drastic measures, political or financial, leaving the Exchange Equalisation Account to fight a rearguard action. After March 15, when the Germans invaded Czechoslovakia, the Account lost gold uninterruptedly. This was no mere speculative move; it was the deliberate transfer of resources out of the United Kingdom and almost wholly to the United States. By June the whole of the gains of the previous three years had been lost, and the operators of the Account estimated that the Account's gold would be reduced to £210 million in three months. They warned Norman that, if they held the rate, they facilitated withdrawals, but that, if it was assumed that violent depreciation and credit restriction were both barred, the only practical question was whether there was any point beyond which the Government were not prepared to let resources be further diminished without protective measures of control. That point was reached on August 22, when the market was informed that in view of the international outlook the Government had decided that the nation's gold resources must be conserved intact : further sales of gold and foreign exchange by the Account would be suspended, and the value of sterling left to be determined by the market without official intervention. The public were asked to reduce their demands for foreign exchange and to refrain from any transfer abroad of capital. Norman, summoned by telephone, flew back from the Isle of Man the next day and went straight to the Treasury. On August 24 Bank Rate was put up to 4 per cent. Control followed on the outbreak of war on September 3. At the same time the rest of the gold in Issue (except a token amount) was transferred to the Exchange Equalisation Account.

Thus the revolution initiated by the suspension of the Gold Standard in 1931 was carried to its logical conclusion. The severing of the link between internal credit conditions and external relations was confirmed by the concentration of the country's whole gold reserve in an exchange account, from which internal credit conditions were insulated. Chamberlain's repeated assertions, which annoyed other governments so much, that the Government's policy was to restore the Gold Standard were quite sincere ; but he was concerned with domestic recovery, while the Governor was continuously aware of external difficulties, so that restoration was continually postponed. The Chancellor clung to Cheap Money, while the Governor built up gold reserves and perfected the technique of moderating exchange movements by intervention in the market. They learned empirically the lesson that a country with a weak and uncertain external position cannot commit itself to a fixed rate of exchange, because a fluctuating rate is the only safeguard (except Exchange Control) against undue depletion of its currency reserves ; and the corollary that with a floating rate control of domestic credit conditions must be even stricter than it is when the danger signal of a weak exchange automatically compels credit restriction.

The change entailed the separation of two functions, the union of which gave Central Banks the power they exercised under the Gold Standard. Norman was fully conscious of the change and slow to reconcile himself to it. He told the Committee of Treasury of his fears soon after the suspension of the Gold Standard in 1931; it involved the transfer of decisions from the Bank to the Treasury and must inevitably lead to difficulties — significantly, at the same time, he spoke of his alarm at the size of the Floating Debt. Four years later he was still complaining that the credit policy being pursued was not his, circumstances had put the control — as in other countries — into the hands of politicians, and he had to play second fiddle. By 1937 he had reached a more balanced view. Explaining the relations of the Bank and the Treasury in the management of exchange policy to the Governors of the Empire Central Banks, meeting in London, he said:

I am proud to think that I am a Central Banker talking to Central Bankers; but I would also ask you to remember that I am an instrument of the Treasury. The two are, of course, not incompatible, especially in these days, and I would not say that I am in any way embarrassed by divided loyalties. But the money in the Exchange Equalisation Account is public money, and those who administer the Account are responsible primarily to the Treasury who, in turn, are responsible as an Administrative Department to the Executive, and so to Parliament. . . . When the Gold Standard was abandoned, there took place an immediate redistribution of authority and responsibility, which deprived the Bank of some of its essential functions. Foreign Exchange became a Treasury matter, and perhaps it still remains to be seen what other responsibilities pass with it from Threadneedle Street to Whitehall.

So far his view was unchanged; but he went on:

. . . Some people might have expected that the result would be friction. The exact reverse is true, largely — I daresay — because we have been fortunate in the particular individuals and personalities with whom we have had to deal. In managing the Exchange Equalisation Account, we are given an extraordinarily free hand. This is not merely because the Treasury have a great many other things to think about. It has been done, I am convinced, of set purpose. In actual practice it means that the Treasury are kept currently informed about the operations of the Account, chiefly by means of a Statement, which covers only one sheet of foolscap, and is rendered to them once a week. They keep their own records, which are subject to inspection by the Comptroller and Auditor

2 F

General. He is, of course, entitled to raise any questions he likes, and he has in fact made occasional enquiries about particular transactions which did not explain themselves to him. The Bank are naturally willing and anxious to give the fullest possible explanation and we are enabled to do this by the completeness of our records. Without very complete records it might be difficult, as you may imagine, to explain and justify particular deals which may depend not only on the circumstances but even on the atmosphere and the temper and prospects and anticipations of the moment. As to the general trend and outlook, the Treasury are kept in touch by regular personal contact with the Governors, and all questions of policy are discussed with the Treasury by the Governors alone. The importance of having this single and exclusive channel of communication has been proved in practice again and again. This does not mean that the Treasury may not telephone when anything out of the ordinary occurs, to find out what is happening and what we are doing. But the executive management of the Account is normally left entirely to the Bank, and beyond rendering the regular Statements *ex post facto*, we are not called upon to explain our interventions or our failure to intervene, nor to justify the complete discretion which the Treasury allow us in matters of day to day practice.

The legal change in the distribution of authority was thus not reflected in the distribution of actual work. The same was true of relations with other Central Banks :

The other subject which I should like to mention is that of our relations with Central Banks. When I say 'our relations' I mean, of course, the relations with the Exchange Equalisation Account. . . . Paris and Amsterdam are on our doorstep. Ten years past we have known — I might almost say we have known intimately — the people who are responsible for foreign exchange in the Netherlands Bank and the Bank of France. Whatever may be the congestion on the overseas telephone lines, we have special arrangements which enable us to speak to our friends in Paris and Amsterdam within a couple of minutes. We regularly speak three or four or more times a day, and in the course of such a long series of conversations we naturally exchange information and opinions about a great variety of subjects. We have found that we can rely absolutely upon the discretion of those to whom we tell what we have in mind ; they in turn have learnt to tell us what they would probably tell nobody else. When we do business together, we

never haggle for a moment about terms, we are all accustomed
to leaving our own interests in the custody of one another for a
period, as, for example, during the lunch hour every day in Paris
or when one or other market is closed. If it is a question of intervention on the exchanges, we generally do not trouble to give limits
of rate or amount, because each is content to leave the other to
operate at his discretion, in the light of what he already knows
about the wishes and intentions of the control served.

In this way, foreign exchange management has certainly opened
up a new field of Central Bank co-operation which has been developed intensively and with extremely satisfactory results. . . .
Not quite the same can be said about those controls which are
more distant from us. In the totalitarian countries, control is
indeed so complete that close and intimate relations, though they
may be possible, are not necessarily in practice. Again in Belgium,
which practises an orthodox gold standard, questions of management do not normally arise. We have a very good working arrangement with the National Bank in Brussels, . . . but there is seldom
any occasion to make use of it. Switzerland is another rather
special case. The Swiss are not much more remote, physically
speaking, than our neighbours but their ideas of co-operation are
limited by their temperament. . . .

With countries within the sterling area the relationship remains
what it used to be : that is to say, it is a direct Central Banking
relationship with which the Exchange Equalisation Account has
very little to do because management is exclusively at the other end,
and the immediate link with sterling is a substitute for other forms
of co-operation. With the United States distance begins to be a
factor. The two markets are open simultaneously for only three
hours during each day, we have not the same personal acquaintance
with the people in charge and the mechanics of communication
are more cumbersome. What we actually do is to send a daily
cable to the Federal Reserve Bank of New York in order to reach
them direct. This cable describes shortly the condition of the
market here during our morning and gives an estimate of the
turnover involved. It practically never happens that the Federal
Reserve Bank do any intervention while both markets are open.
At the close of our business day, we report to them what we have
done and leave it for them to carry on, if necessary, in the same
sense. I think we have only once given them any limit of rate or
amount and that was at midday on the Saturday on which the
French devalued. They report to us by cable daily at the close
of their market, giving us the same kind of information as we have

given them at the close of ours. We telephone fairly freely and
thus we remain as closely in touch with one another as is necessary
for practical purposes.

It is easy to exaggerate the effect of the legal change on
actual practice. Central Bank co-operation was more intimate
and continuous than it had been on the Gold Standard, at any
rate when exchange operations were left to the Central Bank;
when they were kept strictly under government control, in
detail as well as on broad questions of policy, co-operation
was difficult. This was so with Nazi Germany, Communist
Russia and New Deal America; but even with these countries
the daily communications involved in dealing created personal
relations which eased differences of principle.

Nevertheless the administration of the Exchange Equalisation Account differed from the practice both of other adherents
to the Tripartite Agreement and of Germany, and reflected
the difference between London and their markets. Germany
dare not let the mark slip; therefore it imposed a strict control
of exchange. France and America were, like London, opposed
to control (and, for differing reasons, ill adapted to administering control), but had not London's active interest in exchange
dealing and foreign credits; accordingly they followed the
passive policy of a more-or-less automatic Gold Standard. The
British policy was based on the importance of maintaining a
free market for currencies and, so far as possible, securities, in
London. A fixed rate of sterling on gold currencies was ruled
out, because it involved a danger of a deflationary drain
of currency reserves; but sufficient stability, or at any rate
continuity, would be given to the exchange value of sterling
to maintain a free market. As the notice to the market on
22 August 1939 said, 'Hitherto, gold and foreign exchange
have been sold in London, through the Exchange Equalisation
Account, *to all comers on demand*'; or, to quote the Governor's
'prescription' in one troubled period, 'don't hesitate to take
gold and, if anyone wants dollars, let him have them at descend-
ing rates'. The maintenance of such a market was a benefit
to Britain's foreign trade, to the imports on which her economic
life depended and the exports by which she paid for those
imports. It was of importance also to the rest of the world;
at the last meeting of Central Bank Governors at Basle before

such meetings became impossible, his colleagues urged on Norman the value to Europe of the London market, as the one place in which international payments on a large scale could still be negotiated and as, therefore, an indispensable element in maintaining an international economic community.

Norman accepted the political direction of exchange policy, but was not happy under it — even when his difficulties would have been just as great under the Gold Standard. When fear of war began to overshadow every other influence in 1939, he resented the limits set by purely political conditions to the Account's power; he was not, he declared, going to sit with his hands folded seeing his assets go and waiting for control, sacrificing everything London stood for. He wanted to counter-attack when the Account's gold reserves were replenished from Issue; and he put to the Chancellor, but without results, the alternative policy of ending Cheap Money and facing some sacrifice in the domestic field for the benefit of preserving London's international market. Nevertheless he confessed that he had never felt so confused and baffled and did not know which way to turn.

The system of regulating exchanges by intervention in the market was, indeed, dependent on political conditions. When these were not threatening, it achieved an astonishing success, limiting for over a year the movement of the sterling-dollar rate within two cents and effecting the transition from one level to another — in 1934 and in 1938 — with a minimum of disturbance; this in the face of an under-valued dollar and an over-valued franc for most of the time. But it provided no answer to the avalanche of capital movements, which the fear of war released, and for which no reserves could be big enough. Norman was warned by the bankers in May 1939 that it was English money that was leaving the country as well as foreign money; but without reserves, and with an unwillingness to control the domestic credit situation, intervention in the exchange market could do little. To the domestic credit situation we must now turn.

CHAPTER XI

SOME PROBLEMS OF THE 'THIRTIES

(i)

CHEAP Money was maintained until the eve of the Second World War. The economy of lower long-term rates was extended, as maturities made it possible, from War Loan to other Government securities, to Local Authority loans, to the Dominions and Colonies, and, as they were able to replace bonds and to fund short-term borrowings, to industrial concerns. The process accompanied and helped a steady expansion of trade and industry. The Chancellor, so Norman complained in 1934, was quite satisfied that Cheap Money and the Ottawa policy had solved the country's economic problem. The course of recovery, studied in retrospect, shows that Devaluation, Cheap Money and Protection, though they attracted most attention at the time, were only a part of the explanation. Employment recovered in the last quarter of 1931, but relapsed and reached its lowest point in the third quarter of 1932; thereafter it expanded steadily, reaching the level of 1929 in the latter half of 1934 and continuing to expand till 1937. The proportion of insured workers unemployed did not recover to the same extent, because the population of working age was growing; the unemployment percentage did not fall as low as it had done in 1927 and 1928 until after war broke out. Wholesale prices, on which so much attention was concentrated, similarly rose after the suspension of the Gold Standard, and relapsed, reaching their lowest point in March 1933. A short and sharp rise was then followed by a very gradual and moderate rise until the third quarter of 1935, after which there was an acceleration until the autumn of 1937, which did not, however, bring prices to the level of 1929. These general averages conceal the more significant changes.

The expansion of employment was accounted for mainly

by two groups of industries — service industries, like distribution, which were expanding rapidly in the 'twenties and continued their trend ; and building, with its associated industries,
furniture and building materials and road transport. Engineering also recovered from the deep depression into which it had
fallen and resumed its long-term expansion. The introduction
of Protection helped iron and steel and other industries ; whatever the long-term effects, in the short run the introduction of
Protection for the first time, at a time, moreover, when a large
part of a country's productive resources are unemployed, is
likely to increase employment and to increase total income by
more than any increase caused by it in the cost of commodities.
Nevertheless the old depressed industries, which had accounted
for the persistent unemployment of the 'twenties — coal, textiles, agriculture, shipbuilding, shipping and docks — made
little contribution to recovery, and in 1937 were employing
fewer workers than before 1930. Building benefited from the
lower rates at which loans could be raised ; but the expansion
preceded the lowering of rates (representative rates on mortgages being 6 per cent in 1932, 5 per cent in 1933 and 4½ per
cent only in 1935). The mainspring in the vast expansion of
house-building must be sought in the increase in the number of
separate families seeking homes. Between the censuses of 1921
and 1931 population increased by 4½ per cent, but the number
of separate households by 17 per cent, while in the 'thirties the
number of separate households continued to rise as the high
birth-rates of the years before 1910 were reflected in high
marriage rates.

     That this great output of houses could be paid for and at
the same time demand expanded for the relatively new industries such as automobiles, radio and a variety of luxury services
is explained by the movement of prices. The catastrophic fall
after 1929 had affected the materials and foodstuffs which
Britain imported far more than the manufactures which provided the bulk of industrial employment and exports. Even
after the recovery of prices in 1933 the level of the former
remained below that of manufactures until boom conditions
appeared again at the end of 1936. Thus, as employment in
industry expanded and yielded a higher income in wages and
profits, the cost of food and raw materials lagged behind

and left a growing margin of income for housing and other new wants. The depression of the world's agricultural and raw-material producing countries enabled Britain to secure a rising volume of consumption without a corresponding rise in expenditure.

The influences on industrial activity were then numerous and varied. To attribute a decisive influence to any one of them — Cheap Money or Protection — would be fallacious. Recovery came in other countries which followed policies differing from that followed by Britain; in America, where even Cheaper Money and ampler credit expansion were used, recovery was slower and employment did not recover fully until war demands in the 'forties made themselves felt.[1] Money becomes cheaper in depression even without aid from Central Banks, and long-term interest rates fall. By 1932 some progress must have been made in restoring the underlying conditions of recovery — reduction of costs, exhaustion of stocks (especially stocks in consumers' hands), cancellation of debts, the elimination of uneconomic producers, and the re-direction of industry to new outlets.

What was distinctive in the influences assisting recovery in the United Kingdom in the 'thirties was their concentration on the home market. The expansion of distribution and other service industries, of house-building and its associated industries, protection by tariffs, quotas and a depreciated exchange, all stimulated expansion for the home market, and the provision of cheap and plentiful credit and long-term capital was naturally used by the industries expanding most. On the other hand, the cheapening of imports, which sprang from the depression of the food and raw material countries, had its corollary in a decline in the demand of those countries for British exports. Hence the industries mainly dependent on exports lagged behind the general recovery, and the problem of depressed areas which had troubled the 'twenties was unrelieved and compelled attention still. The real nature of the adjustment

---

[1] The writer received a call in 1936 from one of President Roosevelt's economic advisers, who complained bitterly that, whereas America had unbalanced its budget, devalued its currency, expanded credit and done everything English economists advised while Britain had balanced its budget, controlled credit expansion and followed a relatively 'orthodox' policy, recovery in Britain had preceded recovery in America and gone much further; it was, he said, 'very embarrassing'.

by which unemployment was reduced is shown in the diminishing proportion of total industrial production directed to exports. Two-fifths in 1912, it was still over a quarter in 1924; by 1930 it had fallen to little over a fifth, by 1935 to a sixth and by 1938 to a seventh. As imports continued to grow, the country's balance of payments deteriorated; from 1927 to 1929 it had averaged over £100 million surplus, in 1937 and 1938 it averaged over £50 million deficit. On the eve of the war the country was meeting a part of the cost of its normal imports by realising overseas assets; the seriousness of this change became apparent only after the war.

Norman never reconciled himself to the decline in the relative and absolute importance of the country's external trade and services. He still thought of the United Kingdom as fundamentally a part of an international economic community, dependent on the rest of the world for the satisfaction of a large part of its needs, and earning the means of payment by services to other countries. His inclination was always to shape his policy to maintain export industry, international banking and London's connections with the Empire and other overseas customers. He spent actually more of his time and energy in his, on the whole successful, attempts to salvage trades and firms in the steel, textile and shipping industries, which depended most on exports, than he did on the management of the money and exchange markets; but his first concern was always for the London Market and the esteem of sterling, and his recurrent fear the undermining of it by some inflationary excess.

(ii)

Revolutionary as was the Exchange Equalisation Account, it left intact the links that bound London to the other financial markets of the world, and it did not of itself diminish the dependence of British industries on foreign markets and the British market on imports from overseas. This dependence on the outer world left Norman and the Bank confronted with problems which, if different from the maintenance of the Gold Standard, were no less perplexing and exacting.

One group of problems, it is true, which had occupied

Norman throughout his Governorship, ceased to be a responsibility, the problems of inter-allied debts and Reparations.
Reparations were never resumed after their suspension under
the Hoover Moratorium. The recipient Governments, realising that the whole problem of inter-governmental obligations
was involved, began to discuss them almost at once. They
were encouraged by certain phrases used by President Hoover,
though he always insisted that he was bound by Congress's
decision and opposed to cancellation. Arrangements were
made for a conference at Lausanne on the whole question
in January 1932, which, with the ill-fortune that dogged every
attempt to deal with Reparations, was delayed till June 16.
The delay was in part due to the German Chancellor's statement on January 9 that Germany could not possibly make any
further political payments; but was due more to the difficulty
of finding sufficient common ground to make a conference
useful. When in June the conference was held, agreement was
ultimately reached to terminate Reparation payments, Germany undertaking to deposit bonds to an amount of 3000
million reichsmarks, redemption of which was deferred for
three years. But a simultaneous agreement among the creditor
powers made the scheme conditional on a satisfactory settlement of their obligations to their own creditors.

The Chancellor (Chamberlain) announced that the British
Government would suspend its demands on France and Italy
on the same conditions as German Reparation payments were
suspended, but this implied a suspension of the British debt to
America. Norman saw Baldwin during the conference and
had a long conversation with Chamberlain before he went out
to Lausanne in the middle of the conference; Chamberlain
also called him up unexpectedly at midnight on July 10 in
Basle. Norman was more concerned with Germany's need of
additional credits than with extracting further Reparation payments; there is little doubt that he agreed with the committee
of experts summoned to London in July 1931, the International
Committee of Bankers which reported in December, and the
Special Advisory Committee required to consider any application by Germany for the deferment of Young Annuities, and
his friend Schacht, who all reported that Germany could not,
in the present conditions of world depression, sustain the burden

of Reparation payments. But an agreed settlement depended on American agreement to suspend claims to debt repayment. American public opinion regarded European agreement as merely a 'ganging up' of debtors against America. Hoover could do nothing because his term of office was running out, and Roosevelt nothing because the issue was governed by Congress legislation. The result was that the Lausanne Agreement was not ratified, and Reparations went by default.

On the debts Norman's opinions did not change. He put them to the Committee of Treasury on 25 November 1932 — we should pay at all costs and in full; if we defaulted to the U.S. Government, the world would default, beginning with our own debtors; the difference between commercial or private bonded debts and debts to governments meant nothing to the uninitiated; the debt was a debt of honour; payment would improve the exchange while default would depreciate it; and he was ready to provide the Government with the necessary gold. He was reinforced in his opinion by his American friends — though reports reached him that many Americans would welcome a British default as ending an impossible position which no American action was likely to end. He had already, a month earlier, offered to provide the dollars or gold for the December payment, only to be told that the Chancellor had no intention of making provision. The exchange fell to its lowest point, $3·14½, under the combined pressure of repatriation of War Loan repayments by foreign holders and of rumours of default. The Government was finally brought round to Norman's view and early in December announced that payment would be made. The exchange recovered, but feeling had changed. The debtor Governments sent notes to Washington of their intention to make only token payments, and the United States Government accepted such payments in June 1933 on the eve of the World Economic Conference. Norman had told his American friends, when he was uncertain of the 1932 payment, that 'we choose the Old World by keeping faith with France'. The end of Reparations ended war debts. The British Government, after seeking some modification in the terms, made a token payment in 1933 and again in 1934, after which American legislation made token payments impossible and the British Government made no attempt at more. Early

in 1939 Norman was pressed from a number of quarters to urge
the Government to reopen the question. He reported to the
Committee of Treasury, but refused to take any initiative; the
debt had become purely a political matter, any payment would
be merely an expedient for qualifying under the Johnson Act for
access again to the New York issue market, no longer a question
of sustaining the credit of London by honouring an obligation.

For one element in the London Market, in which Norman
was always vitally interested, the financial collapse of 1931
had effects similar to those of 1914. When international trade
recovered in the 'twenties and currencies were stabilised, the
banks and specialised firms which gave acceptance and other
short-term credits had renewed their connections with Germany
and Central Europe, not on the scale of pre-1914 but to an
amount approaching £100 million. Such credits, given to
finance the movement of commodities and secured on the
commodities themselves, were the safest of all forms of credit;
and they seemed little less secure when granted for similar
purposes to banks of the borrowing countries. But Central
Europe was not in a position in 1931 to maintain any external
payments. The creditors recognised their debtors' difficulties.
They were interested in maintaining the financial stability of
the different countries and their banks, and were prepared to
maintain the existing volume of credit in order that means of
payment should be available for trade as it recovered. An
International Committee representative of Germany's short-
term creditors met representatives of the German banks in
July 1931 and, with the approval of the Conference of Ministers
in London, reached agreement to extend the credits beyond
the due dates.

Similar arrangements were made with Austria and Hungary. At first the extension was for six months only; it was
extended then for another year, but it was already clear that
the difficulties of the debtor countries were not temporary and
transient. Any repayment must be slow, and the agreement
provided for the replacement by new credits of debts repaid.
Norman had encouraged accepting houses, when the crisis first
developed, to continue their facilities to Germany, but had
refused then to seek a Government guarantee for outstanding
bills on the lines of the 1914 arrangement. He did, however,

discuss the possible need of such help privately with the Treasury, and at the end of 1931 he prepared with the Treasury a 'cold storage' scheme. This was held in reserve and never used. The Standstill was extended again and again, the credits being gradually reduced. Norman was in continuous touch with the Committee through a Bank Director, F. C. Tiarks;[1] he was directly concerned, since the Bank held many of the bills which represented the greater part of the credits given by London. So far as London was concerned, his willingness to re-discount Standstill Bills was the necessary basis of the arrangement.

The maintenance of this large volume of acceptance credits was one reason why Norman was opposed to a clearing with Germany in 1934. As Tiarks said, 'I cannot see how a Standstill *credit*, given to a German concern by a Banker, can be brought into any form of Clearing agreement, which is presumably created for the clearing of *cash goods* transactions between German buyers and sellers and English buyers and sellers direct without the intervention of a banker's credit', and it was feared that Germany would impose a moratorium. Norman told the Committee of Treasury that a German Clearing would jeopardise the present arrangement for carrying market bills accepted under the Standstill; direct support of several acceptors might be necessary. A Clearing was not avoided but was soon replaced by a direct arrangement between the Governments of the two countries, which the Chancellor, who himself did not want a Clearing but was pressed by the Board of Trade, could accept and Schacht could arrange. A certain proportion of the receipts from German exports to the United Kingdom was to be allocated to payment for British exports, leaving another part available for financial claims. A credit to the Reichsbank was necessary to launch the scheme, and to liquidate outstanding debts to British traders; this, with the Chancellor's approval, Norman gave.

Some two years later Norman felt justified in requiring the acceptors of the outstanding bills to absorb a proportion of them; some help might be necessary in a few cases and this he was prepared (without announcing the fact to the market) to give. He urged on the Clearing Banks the duty of carrying

[1] Director of the Bank of England, 1912–45.

their clients, rather than relying on a government-supported 'cold storage' scheme; though again in the last resort he would have asked for a government guarantee to make it possible for them to do so. In fact no guarantee was sought and the required reduction in outstanding bills was effected. But for the outbreak of war in 1939, the whole of the credits frozen in 1931 would have been absorbed, without government assistance.

The Standstill agreements provided no solution for the collapse of credit which called them into being; time and the recovery of trade were the only remedy, but the agreements held the position until time could effect a cure. Other expedients were suggested. At the end of 1931 Norman was approached with a proposal for a National Acceptance Bank by some of the accepting houses. He did not much like the proposal, but suggested a Discount Bank as a possible means of meeting the difficulty of maintaining Standstill credits, and privately commissioned a leading private banker to canvass the banks and discuss the scheme without commitment. There was not the response needed to make anything of the proposal. Early in 1932 he was approached by one of the Clearing Banks, in conjunction with an issuing house, with a proposal for an Industrial Mortgage Bank. It was to serve a double purpose — to relieve the banks of some of their industrial commitments, and to meet the demand, supported by the Macmillan Committee, for an institution for providing long-term capital to industrial concerns too small to go to the new-issue market. Norman encouraged the promoters. What he favoured personally was a 'B.I.D. to unfreeze the Clearing Banks' present industrial lock-ups'; but he was opposed to a security company tied to one Clearing Bank, and thought that the new institution should be supported by all the Clearing Banks, or at least the Big Five. At the same time he was seeking means of meeting the need diagnosed by the Macmillan Committee. Again there was not the unanimity needed for action, and again, in the domestic as in the foreign field, time and the improvement of trade relieved the strain on the banks.

A more difficult credit problem was presented by the deterioration of conditions in the South American countries with which London had intimate links; more difficult because the world depression only aggravated a situation already serious, and more urgent because the pressure was concentrated on a small number of banks. The decline of the Chilean nitrate industry had been met by the co-operation of the chief creditors, with the Bank's support, in a special agency, Cosach, to provide a pool of credit to support the debt-laden trade and to prevent the breakdown of any of the creditors involved. Now the rapid deterioration put a strain on the supporting banks greater than had been anticipated. The Bank was approached in September 1931, and Norman reported to the Committee of Treasury that the position of the chief English bank involved, the Anglo-South American Bank, had worsened, and that there was a danger of Cosach breaking down. Some of the bankers indirectly affected demanded a government guarantee for the outstanding creditors and approached the Chancellor direct. But the Treasury impressed on Norman the importance of the banking community, in its own interest, dealing with the issue rather than relying on the Government. The Committee agreed that the Anglo-South American Bank must be supported, and that the Clearing Banks should be brought in. Norman found that support from American interests could be secured, though only by a large further commitment by the Bank. A new agency was formed, Chilnit, which took over a large part of the liabilities of the Anglo-South American Bank, the Clearing Banks providing 49 per cent and the Bank of England 51 per cent of the capital required. Norman was fairly confident of government help if, in the last resort, it was necessary ; the Government was already implicated under the previous scheme and the Bank took over its liabilities. The liquidation of this frozen position took years. The Governor secured the appointment of a new Chairman to manage the Anglo-South American Bank, until ultimately it was taken over by the other English bank operating in South America. It was not until the end of 1937 that he was able to report to the Committee of Treasury that the reorganised pool had been closed — a year after he had reported that the last of the foreign government securities taken up in the reconstruction of Europe in the 'twenties had been sold.

In another way, Norman sought to relieve London of the strains due to the collapse of so many of London's overseas customers. In May 1932 he called the attention of the

Committee of Treasury to the unsatisfactory position of League
Loans. These had been made (often against the wish of the
market) on the express recommendation of the League and with
the approval of the Government — he might have added with
the strongest personal pressure by himself. One was in default
and others threatened. The Government was doing nothing to
compel respect for them, and he proposed to form a League
Loans Committee, with the backing of the issuing banks concerned, for this purpose. He induced Sir Austen Chamberlain
to act as Chairman and the Bank to pay the expenses of the
Committee. At the same time, he impressed on the issuing
houses their obligation to put the claims on them of loans they
had sponsored before any other business. Subsequently he
took steps to strengthen the Council of Foreign Bondholders,
inducing the Earl of Bessborough to take its Chair, and placed
Sir Otto Niemeyer on both committees. It was a matter of
great regret to him that in 1937 the League of Nations assimi-
lated its Financial Committee to other technical committees
by limiting the term of membership of any person to three years.
Norman attached great importance to the continuity of membership and the prestige and influence which the permanent
core had given the Committee. He protested, but in vain. The
change was made, and the four banker members showed their
sympathy with Norman's position by resigning.

With Schacht's assistance, when he was President of the
Reichsbank, it was possible to maintain the transfer of the
interest on the Dawes and Young Loans, and to avoid a Clearing in which commercial claims excluded pre-existing financial
claims. But, in Germany as in the United Kingdom, political
considerations played an increasing part in determining international payments. The Payments Agreement worked out by
Norman in consultation with Schacht in November 1934 was
modified and extended from year to year; the modifications
were not always to Norman's mind — in October 1936 he
wrote to the Treasury: 'I am now going to Basle where I shall
say No to every suggestion from Schacht, in loyalty to Downing
St., but in the long run I fear this may turn out to be foolish
and perhaps merits fresh consideration'. When the Agreement
of 1934 was replaced by a new Agreement in July 1938, providing for the transfer of Dawes and Young payments to British

holders (at a lowered rate) but not to other holders, Morgans
wrote to him protesting; they deplored the breach of the
obligation to treat all bonds of all *tranches* alike; they regretted
the part played by the British Government at whose request
they had issued the Dawes Loan in New York, and in expressing
these views they were speaking for the whole American banking
community.   Norman sent a formal acknowledgment, but
expressed his own feelings in a personal letter to Thomas W.
Lamont :

I should not wish to let this drop without saying to you personally a word more than I felt able to say in formally acknowledging
the official letter.

I regret as much as you do that these loans, which were issued
on an international and financial basis, are now treated piecemeal
on a national and political basis.   This is indeed politics and not
ethics but it has been the general trend of recent years and I do not
think we can do more than regret it.

But, without wishing to be controversial, may I say that your
official letter hardly seems to take the position of my Government
in a fair light.   They, as you may know, at the outset clearly and
formally expressed the view that the recent negotiations ought to
be on an international basis and I do not think they can properly
be blamed because the German Government refused to agree.
Nor, surely, can they be blamed for proceeding on a national basis,
which was the only solution open to them.

Agreement on an international basis could, I think, have been
reached only if your Government had been willing to take a firm
stand alongside all the creditor Governments concerned.   For few
debtor countries are nowadays willing to treat debts from the
standpoint of ethics and equity and not from the standpoint of
politics and convenience.

You cannot answer this because I am going away for a long
time to heal my wounds and I only write to clear your views and
my conscience !

(iii)

The depreciation of currencies on gold, while it relieved the
countries which permitted it of the necessity of restricting foreign
payments or domestic credit in order to protect the exchange
value of their currencies, necessarily increased the difficulties

2 G

of countries which did not follow suit. The effect was not, however, confined to Gold Standard countries. A few countries, of which China was the most important, had adhered to the older metallic standard, silver. For other than monetary reasons, the value of silver, as represented by its price in sterling or dollars, had fallen all through the 'twenties and Chinese commodity prices, being based on silver, had risen relatively to prices in the outer world. This rise had afforded a steady stimulus to Chinese commerce, but the drop in the exchange value of the pound, followed by that of the Indian rupee and the Japanese yen, reversed this influence. Chinese internal prices ceased to rise relatively to external prices, Chinese exports were handicapped and imports encouraged, and China began to experience the same sort of difficulty in maintaining its currency as other countries had done. But China, unlike England, had not a highly organised banking system and central financial administration ready to operate an inconvertible paper currency.

The depreciation of the American dollar on gold in 1932 and 1933, by forcing still lower the exchange value of the currencies which had devalued, carried this external pressure on China further. The following year, for domestic political reasons, the American Administration proceeded to force up still further the world price of silver, and in June Congress passed a Silver Purchase Act aimed at raising the proportion of silver (valued at $1·29 an ounce) in total monetary stocks to one-quarter. At first purchases were confined to American-mined silver, but presently extended to London, the chief world market. Having depreciated its own currency by reducing the exchange value of the American dollar, the United States was now forcing up the exchange value of the Chinese dollar by raising the world value of silver on which it was based. The Chinese Government protested in October to Washington without effect, and then sought to restrict the effects of the rise in silver by imposing an export tax on silver and imposing some control on foreign transactions. If, however, the Administration persisted in its policy, China would be faced with the alternatives of drastic deflation or 'going off' silver by severing the link between Chinese currency and silver.

The rise in the price of silver reacted on London in two

ways; it threatened to produce a dangerous speculative movement in the silver market, and it undermined the stability of a
country with which the United Kingdom had intimate relations
by virtue of past investments and current trade and banking.
Norman turned to China's difficulties first. The London
manager of the chief Eastern bank had approached him as
soon as the Americans began to put up the price of silver with
a proposal for a formal protest. Norman saw difficulties in
objecting to American action in raising the price of an American
commodity, but put him in touch with the Treasury and
Foreign Office, who were equally averse to any protest. In
October he came back; the Chinese Government wished his
bank to explore the possibility of raising a sterling loan in
Shanghai for supporting the exchange. Norman noted in his
diary, 'Inadequate, wasteful. China needs comprehensive
treatment — not drops in the Washington Silver Bucket.' He
urged the same objections when the Bank of China two months
later approached him direct, and warned private bankers who
consulted him on possible loans. But he proceeded to press on
the Chancellor the need of a policy, and persuaded him to set
up an inter-departmental committee, with his own Bank
Adviser among the members, to examine China's needs.

Already the effects of the price-raising policy were alarming
the experts; the banker referred to told Norman privately that
he was out of his depth and feared chaos, and his principals in
Shanghai shared his fears and would welcome any palliative
to gain time to think out a policy. The Bank's representative
on the inter-departmental committee argued that an inconvertible note-issue must fail in China because of the pressure
which needy Governments would exercise on the note-issuing
authority, and suggested to the Governor that for China the best
policy was to adopt a sterling exchange standard, at a lower
value than its present silver standard, and to seek a sterling
credit. Norman agreed; but China was seeking a large loan
to replace the silver it had lost with the object of removing the
export duty on silver and returning to a free silver standard.
The Committee felt unable to recommend a loan, but the
British Government did approach the Governments in Washington, Paris and Tokyo with a proposal to concert international
assistance to China. Japanese opposition prevented any such

action, and in August 1935 the British Government sent out to China Sir Frederick Leith-Ross to investigate and report.

Norman had proposed some such move. After consultation with the Chancellor he had earlier in the year tried to persuade Blackett to go out as adviser to the Chinese Government. He had long talks with Leith-Ross before he went out and, it would seem, still thought that the best course for China would be to associate itself with the sterling bloc. He was concerned also that any loans should have the approval of the Consortium of Bankers, formed earlier to prevent international disputes over loan contracts with China. Leith-Ross was not, however, given time to help in shaping a permanent policy. The raising of the American price for silver in March and April stimulated speculation and raised silver to a price at which the Chinese Government could not prevent the export in large amounts of silver, smuggled out especially through Japan. In May the Secretary of the U.S. Treasury stated, 'We are endeavouring to restore silver to greater usefulness as a monetary metal. It is the money of a large part of the world's population': but Mexico sent an urgent deputation to Washington to point out that it was being drained of currency. The U.S. Treasury apparently became alarmed by the speculation its policy had excited; when the price reached its peak the Secretary described his attitude as that of a 'spectator'; and in the second half of the year, the price was allowed to fall back, with intermittent support, to the level from which the rise had started two years before. The fall brought down the exchange value of the Chinese currency, and on 4 November 1935 China formally severed its age-long currency link with silver; Hong Kong followed suit.

The fears that China could not operate an inconvertible paper currency were not realised at once. The Administration was helped by loans, and purchases of its silver by Washington. Leith-Ross and Norman pressed on them the importance of making the note-issuing central bank independent, and an adviser from the Bank of England was brought out. The United States gave credits for the purpose of exchange support in 1937 and 1938; and in the latter year an Exchange Fund, under independent control with a British adviser, was constituted by means of a £10 million loan, to which a British bank operating in China contributed. But the strain of Japanese oppression and interference continued (Norman had used his links with the Bank of Japan to appeal for Japanese co-operation, but without effect); later it was intensified by civil war. In the end the situation became impossible to control and the currency lost its value. Chinese experience confirmed the maxim attributed to Lenin that the shortest way to bring in Communism is to destroy the value of a country's money.

(iv)

In home finance, the most important operation affecting the Money Market in this period was the conversion of the 5 per cent War Loan. So long as it was callable, as it had been since 1929, its mass, over £2000 million, offered an obstacle to any lowering of long-term interest rates, and the Bank and Treasury had begun to discuss its conversion long before 1929. A scheme was worked out in 1931; but the crisis postponed action in May and again in September. Snowden was not able to undertake the conversion, but his September Budget, by restoring the balance of revenue and expenditure, prepared the way, and work on it began again as soon as the Budget was through. Norman sought the advice of experienced issuing brokers like Glendyne,[1] large investors like Sir George May of the Prudential, and bankers like McKenna. Compulsory conversion was discussed but rejected. The Government had to give three months' notice of repayment, and in that time political changes might undermine the conditions on which the terms of conversion were based, but it was decided that the Government must take that risk. The scheme finally adopted, for which the Deputy Governor, Sir Ernest Harvey, was mainly responsible, was based on the assumption that most holders would accept conversion; their assent was assumed if they did not demand repayment, and inducements were offered to convert. The Governor and Deputy Governor agreed that the whole amount of the Loan should be dealt with in a single transaction, and that the rate of interest on the stock offered in exchange could be as low as 3½ per cent; the Chancellor (Neville Chamberlain)

[1] Lord Glendyne of R. Nivison & Co.

was so advised on June 7; he announced the scheme in Parliament on 30 June 1932, the day that Bank Rate was lowered to 2 per cent.

Success depended on favourable conditions in the market. There were many overseas holders of War Loan; if they refused to convert, and repatriated the money they received on repayment, the exchange value of sterling could not be held. It was necessary to secure their confidence — by a balanced budget, by refraining from any suggestion of inflation (for example by premature reduction of Bank Rate, or expansion of the Fiduciary Note Issue), and by convincing them that lower rates of interest were likely to persist. With all their care the Treasury and Bank did not prevent an amount of repatriation which put a strain on sterling towards the end of 1932; but it was delayed, and any serious speculative movement was prevented.

So far as domestic support went, it was necessary to keep the issue market clear of competing claims until the conversion was through. Other government issues had either been dealt with beforehand or were postponed, and an informal but effective embargo on all issues for overseas borrowers was imposed. The Chancellor, in making his announcement, appealed to the patriotism of holders of the Loan; the Treasury and Bank supported him by direct appeal to the chief classes of holder. Norman assured the Discount Market that the Bank would overlook an exceptional investment in long-dated securities if it was the result of accepting conversion stock. He interviewed brokers and jobbers brought together by the Government broker. The Treasury called a conference of the bankers, who agreed to convert their holdings *en bloc* — with one exception; him Norman invited to the Bank and appealed to privately. The banker argued that he needed the cash when repayment was due; he would convert only if Norman would buy from him the larger part of his considerable holding at the price of the day which was above par. Norman said, 'I'll take the lot': but the banker retained a part of his holding and shared the credit of converting.

As we have seen, the reflux of funds after the suspension of the Gold Standard made credit conditions easy, and the Bank had delayed lowering Bank Rate only until provision had been made for the repayment of the crisis credits. The purchase of the foreign exchange and gold provided by this inflow, in order to make the repayment, increased the Clearing Banks' balances with the Bank of England, and the Bank had not sufficient resources, even if it had wished, to offset this increase by sales of securities. These balances were brought back first to the level from which they had been reduced in August and September 1931 by the drain of money abroad; then from the £65 million or so of 1930 and early 1931 to about £75 million. The Exchange Equalisation Account gave the Bank power to offset the effect of any further inflow on domestic credit conditions; but the power was not fully used and bankers' balances were allowed to rise to £85/90 million. When the current turned and money began to flow out again in the second half of 1932, the gold and exchange accumulated by the Banking Department and the Exchange Equalisation Account were used to meet the drain without allowing it to deplete the Clearing Banks' balances with the Bank. There was a temporary draft on Issue gold to meet the American debt payment in December; but the opportunity offered by the reverse flow of money from America to London in 1933 was used to replace this and to build up gold reserves to a higher level than ever before. Gold in Issue was increased by a half, making possible a note-issue large enough to meet a growing demand for currency without expanding the Fiduciary Issue; while the Banking Department increased its holding of securities until bankers' balances were brought up to £100 million, about which level they were kept until the eve of the Second World War.

The Governor did not regard the suspension of the Gold Standard as a reason for relaxing the control which the Bank and Treasury together exercised over domestic credit. Rather the reverse; he was alarmed by the increased scope given to political exigencies by the increased influence in the money market of the Treasury. He felt the loss of the compulsion exercised by an adverse movement of the exchanges on the Gold Standard, and missed the traditional warning signals which then operated. The danger that speculation would force up prices and lead to misdirected production and unsound commitments seemed to him if anything greater. A floating exchange rate, if a convenience, was also an added danger; when there was any pressure on the country's external payments, a fall in the exchange rate might increase the alarms which caused the flight from sterling which the lowering of the rate was designed to check. The exchange value of sterling was the value which other countries put upon it, and Norman was always conscious of the other countries' opinions; his outlook was European and Imperial, never narrowly domestic.

It followed that, while he accepted and developed the policy of Cheap Money which trade depression and the suspension of the Gold Standard inaugurated, he relaxed none of his caution. His first aim was to restore confidence in sterling abroad. For this reason he avoided increasing the Fiduciary Issue and took every opportunity to increase the Bank's holding of gold. He continually stressed the importance of exports, at a time when the tendency was to rely for increased employment on the expansion of the home market, and for this reason struggled with the difficulties of making international payments in the absence of a common international standard. He was helped by the policy of successive Chancellors in balancing current expenditure by taxation, or accepting only a modest deficit. His chief fear was a large Floating Debt; it was the danger he called attention to first when he resumed work after his return from America in September 1931 — he even suggested that a compulsory funding of a part of it might be necessary. He impressed on the Committee of Treasury the importance of letting the bankers' balances with the Bank fluctuate, otherwise it would be impossible ever to reduce them; the price of money, he argued, depended less on its volume than on its use. Bank Rate had ceased to be available or effective but 2 per cent should be regarded as the minimum. Years later, in 1937, he suggested that the only important figure in the Bank Return was the size of the note-issue, which had steadily risen — as it has done ever since.

The general problem of credit control, as it faced Norman, was thus to give effect to the Government's policy of Cheap Money without encouraging speculative activity in security and stock markets or checking the recovery of confidence in sterling in the minds of overseas holders. He was anxious to give trade and industry the advantage of low interest rates, but not to maintain low rates by mere weight of money. The influx of money from other countries, which, with occasional set-backs, continued from the beginning of 1933 to the first quarter of 1938, was an embarrassment; it tended to inflate Clearing Bank deposits, the Bank could not refuse to increase its note-issue if more currency was required, and the Treasury Bills, which the Exchange Equalisation Account sold to pay for its purchases of the incoming gold and foreign exchange, threatened to weaken the Bank's control of the market. The conflict of aims was resolved by a policy, congenial to him, of steadily reducing the volume of Treasury Bills. If the available volume were reduced, the market would be prevented from securing such a holding that they could at any time force the hands of Treasury and Bank and, by refusing to renew Treasury Bills, compel them to create more cash. At the same time their competition for the limited supply would force down the Treasury Bill rate. Moreover, as Treasury Bills became less remunerative and less plentiful, there would be an inducement to acquire more long-term investments, thus forcing up the price of these and forcing down the long-term rate of interest also.

The Bank could lessen the expansion of Treasury Bills when money was flowing in by taking some of the gold acquired by the Exchange Account into Issue, as it did at the end of 1936. So far as the Account sold Treasury Bills, the Bank could do something to keep them out of the market by acquiring them for Government Departments and Central Bank clients, or holding more of them in Issue. But the chief means was the steady progress of funding Bills by a succession of medium-term Funding Issues. This was the customary safeguard of Central Banks; as Norman pointed out to the Treasury, every reconstruction scheme in Europe had insisted on the reduction of the Floating Debt; in no stabilised country was our figure of Treasury Bills equalled; we ought to reduce it by funding, not maintain it for the convenience of the bankers, who might then substitute commercial bills. This policy not unnaturally attracted criticism. When the banks' holdings of Treasury Bills had been brought down to the pre-crisis level by an issue of £150 million of 2½ per cent Conversion Loan 1944–49 at the end of 1933, and there was the possibility of a further funding issue, the Chancellor asked the Governor privately to explain the policy and Norman saw him on 19 March 1934. It can be inferred from various notes of the time that he would stress the danger of a large amount of outstanding Treasury Bills; there were nearly £400 million of maturing bonds to be met in the next five years and any emergency might require sudden borrowing on Treasury Bills. It might be difficult to increase these, it might even be difficult to maintain the present volume, as the demands of trade for credit expanded, without forcing up the rate. Funding, it is true, involved some increase in interest on the debt as a whole; but Funding would be at a lower rate now than the Government could count on in the future, so that, if Funding was desirable, it would be most economical to effect it now. On a long view Funding was a safeguard of Cheap Money.

The issue of £150 million 3 per cent Funding Loan 1959–69 which followed in April prevented the banks' holdings of Bills from increasing as normally they do after March and criticism revived. The *Midland Bank Review* insisted that the conventional cash ratio of the banks assumed a steady daily inflow of cash, to ensure which an adequate supply of Bills was necessary as a second line of defence. But all through 1935, 1936 and 1937 the Exchange Equalisation Account was absorbing gold, and therefore selling Treasury Bills; and the policy of funding was continued to prevent any danger of losing control in the money market. Early in 1937 there was a marked fall in the prices of long-term government securities. Keynes, in his speech at the annual meeting of the National Mutual Assurance Society in January 1938, attributed this to the Exchange Equalisation Account producing a shortage of Treasury Bills for the market, which made the cheapening of long-dated stocks necessary to induce holders of sterling to change from liquid or short-dated to long-dated stocks. In fact the Account had not departed from its normal practice; the Treasury Bills supplied by it to the market maintained the supply from October 1936 to March 1937, when there was a seasonal surplus of revenue tending to reduce the supply, and again from May to July 1937, when the use of the receipts of a Defence Bond issue in April was offsetting the normal increase in Bills due to the seasonal deficit of revenue. The last of the funding issues, in November 1936, no doubt helped to depress long-dated issues; but it was only one in-fluence among others, the reaction from the new-issue boom of 1936 and the deterioration of international relations having also their effect.

Norman was a little more disturbed by an article and corre-spondence in *The Times* in August 1938 — at a moment when the Bank was preoccupied with war plans and had just found that marine war risks might be uninsurable — not criticising the authorities for deflation but advocating an active policy of 'reflation' to reverse the depression into which trade was falling. It was argued that there was the danger of a 'vicious spiral'; low rates by making the long-term capital market more favourable would induce business to make additional capital outlay; a repetition of the 1932 manœuvre was called for — Bankers' Balances with the Bank of England should be increased by £10/20 million and supported by the provision of an additional £30/40 million Treasury Bills, so that the banks might increase their holding of investments by the amount required to revive the stock market. So far as the Bank's observation went, busi-nessmen's decisions on capital expenditure were not determined by small changes in the cost of raising capital, but by considera-tion of the prospects of earning profits, nor was the new-issue market an important source of capital for new extensions, as opposed to the transfer of the ownership of existing businesses. Conditions were very different from 1932; then political changes had revived confidence, now the political outlook was overshadowed by fear. Even more to the point, then the Clear-ing Banks held between £300/400 million of Investments, now they held between £600/700 million. Norman was not opposed to expansion but 'from a low level'. The banks were unlikely to increase their holdings further, after their experience of loss of value of Investments between 1929 and 1931 — at any rate with their present figures of paid-up capital; they always had in mind the appearance of their balance-sheets, even if eco-nomists ignored it. Without any expansion of their Invest-ments the collapse of gilt-edged values on 13 September 1938, two days before the Prime Minister flew to Berchtesgaden to see Hitler, was enough to wipe out the whole of the published capital and reserves of the Clearing Banks. Values recovered with the relief which followed that visit, but it was now clear

that the country was faced with something more serious than
a slight cyclical readjustment.

The issue of the first National Defence Bonds in April 1937
marked a turning-point. Until then Norman had taken advantage of the opportunity market conditions gave him to press
on with the reduction by funding of the Floating Debt. He had
been concerned to preserve control of the volume of money,
although the automatic safeguard provided by a fixed parity
with an international standard had been lost. He had drawn
the Committee of Treasury's attention to every symptom of
incipient inflation — the danger of a multiplication of small
industrial new issues which the abundance of money encouraged. He urged his friend the Chairman of the Stock Exchange
to bring all the security business possible into his own recognised and properly organised market and to apply for a Charter
for the Stock Exchange. He had deplored the excesses into
which speculation in commodities had been carried, as reflect-
ing on the good name of London, not only in the Committee
but in his speech at the annual bankers' dinner at the Mansion
House in 1935.

This episode illustrates his relations with activities of London
outside the Money Market. He was warned on 26 November
1934 by the Chief General Manager of one of the bigger banks
that a serious position existed in the shellac and pepper market :
there had been wild speculation, financed mainly by one of the
other banks, and the position of the chief firms in the market
was jeopardised. His first response was to note, 'I do nothing,
leaving the trouble to the Chairman of the "other bank"'.
But he found quickly that he could not disentangle himself.
He was appealed to, and ascertained the extent of the commitments of the Clearing Banks and accepting houses — both
were negligible with the one exception, and the chairman of
this protested ignorance. Then the chairman of a finance
company explained that his company was involved. Norman
learned from the biggest broker in the produce market what
the position was. The broker explained, and made proposals
for a pool to carry the firms in difficulties till they could liquidate their position ; they wanted some help from the bankers
and Norman promised to contribute. There was a public
inquiry into certain irregularities, which Norman welcomed ;

after its report he pressed the members of the produce market to regulate their practice for themselves, which they proceeded to do.   In the same speculative movement the position of the tin-mining industry came up.   Again he was consulted and supplied with confidential information.   He brought the finance houses interested together, and secured the reorganisation of the board of the chief firm in the industry.   He was similarly drawn in to the finance of film production.   The Committee of Treasury had already agreed, on his motion, to refuse to treat as eligible for discount at the Bank bills drawn under agreements to finance films, when he was asked by the Government to make an inquiry into the whole subject.

These symptoms of inflation explain his persistence in attacking the Floating Debt.   Without any deliberate policy, the Government had by 1937 completely offset by its funding operations the effect of gold purchases in increasing the volume of Treasury Bills.   Thereafter the Bank and Treasury were preoccupied, not merely with financing a programme of re-armament before they could impose on the country a wartime budget, but with the necessity of limiting current demands for loans, both in the short-term and the new-issues market, and on overseas account even more than on domestic account, against the time when the Government had to meet the unlimited claims of war finance.

The Clearing Banks were not the only sufferers from the scarcity and low rates of Treasury Bills.   Treasury Bills were now the staple of the Discount Market's business, and the policy of reducing them, in the absence of an expansion of commercial bills, threatened the existence of some of its members.   Norman had much more sympathy with these sufferers.   The Market was an essential and characteristic feature of London's organisation, which he used to describe with such pride to overseas bankers, a great convenience as an intermediary and buffer between Central Bank and Clearing Bankers.   Defaults, Standstill arrangements, the decline of the use of the commercial bill, all restricted its opportunities ; now the competition for Treasury Bills and the exiguous return from handling them threatened its livelihood.   The tender rate fell to its lowest point, 3s. 10·91d. per cent, on 25 January 1935.   Norman raised the matter with representatives of the Clearing

Bankers on February 15; on the 21st they came back to report a temporary agreement among the Clearing Bankers on bill rates; nothing below ½ per cent and no tendering by the banks themselves, money rates to be unchanged. Though temporary, the agreement lasted and the minimum was observed.

More was, however, needed to secure the Market's future, and Norman applied the same principles as he was applying when forced to intervene in industry generally — concentration in fewer firms, with larger capitals and therefore greater capacity to face the difficulties of the time. The Committee of Treasury supported him; he began by advice to the Market and mediation between firms, but had to proceed to warning and finally coercion, by refusing to re-discount at the privileged rate the bills of firms which he regarded as too small for safety. He reported to the Committee in March 1936 that the number of firms in the Market had been reduced from 22 to 18 since January 1933. The Committee agreed towards the end of the following year to refuse the Bank's special facilities to firms with less than £300,000 capital and reserves. At the same time he was supporting the Market by taking Standstill bills, and he did something by asking the Committee on Advances and Discounts of the Court to widen the range of domestic bills which the Bank should take — though at the same time he was warning accepting houses not to provide domestic credits merely to repay bank debts and overdrafts or provide working capital. He recognised that the persistence of low short-term rates threatened the Discount Market. He told some of the members privately that they were doomed; but he could not contemplate the elimination of the Market. If it went, it would be the end of the short money market; London would be like Paris and New York, 'with no outlet for short funds except the Stock Exchange and no rate except the rate resulting from the banks' telephone conversations'. He could only maintain the ½ per cent minimum, help the Market to avoid complete dependence on the Clearing Banks, and trust that its members' 'cunning and smell' would continue to find a use. Some small firms went out of business voluntarily; but there were no bankruptcies and the Market continued to fulfil its function.

The present chapter has been devoted to some of the domestic and overseas questions, apart from the specialised

field of exchange management, in which Norman was involved
in the 'thirties.   To convey an adequate impression of his
working life is difficult at any time.   Merely to describe the
functions of the Governor of the Central Bank gives no account
of the actual changing situation and the continuous pressure
in which he lived : while the method of dealing successively
with particular problems not only omits much, since it is impossible to deal with all, but fails to bring out the wide variety of
problems which were always coming upon him at the same
moment.

THE SECOND WORLD WAR

WHEN the Second World War broke out in September 1939, Norman had in the Bank of England an instrument, largely of his own creation, already experienced in the problems of war finance, equipped as it had never previously been with a personnel accustomed to meet problems of the kind involved, and imbued with the Governor's spirit. Norman could, therefore, leave much of the daily tasks which had absorbed his predecessor in 1914–18 to his leading assistants. He could lay down the main objectives while leaving their detailed application to others. This remained true even though many of his Directors became absorbed in war work outside the City and even in some cases outside the United Kingdom.

The country also had the experience of the 1914–18 war behind it and there was little of the makeshift policies and delays in decision and organisation which were inevitable, after more than two generations of peace, in 1914. Both knowledge and expectations were very different in 1939. Many things, strange and abhorrent in 1914 and only slowly introduced as that war proceeded, were in 1939 accepted as a matter of course. Many decisions had already been taken, and thanks to very thorough preparation in the interval between Munich and the outbreak of war, much was ready for immediate application. The main City markets continued to function. The Stock Exchange was never closed, though minimum prices were fixed. Such controls as were required, including Exchange Control, with the dollar at 4·03 to the £, were applied at once. Rationing started almost from the beginning. For the moment even Norman's recent preoccupations with exchange, now reinforced as time went on by the mobilisation of dollar securities and eventually by Lease Lend, and with Bank Rate faded into the background. Bank Rate, which had been raised to 4 per cent in August 1939, was reduced, as Norman had anticipated, to

3 per cent in September and to 2 per cent in October, at which it remained throughout the war and indeed till 1951. One result of the greater preparedness was that whereas in the six years between 1913 and January 1919 wholesale and retail prices rose from 100 in each case to 246 and 220, respectively (and were to rise a year later to 375 and 276), in the six years between September 1939 and August 1945 they only rose to 173 and 132.

Absence of ideological dogmatism and native quickness in perceiving the inevitable realities of a practical problem had always been Norman's characteristics and never more than in the war, when every kind of financial question, national, industrial, public and private, found its way to his room.

War conditions necessarily reduced his European foreign contacts, except with those institutions in particular, for instance, the National Bank of Belgium, whose representatives had come to this country to escape German occupation. His monthly visits to the Bank for International Settlements at Basle could no longer be made, and in fact during the war no such meetings were held.

But the stream of other visitors to the Governor's room was in no way diminished. He was constantly occupied with the numerous personal adjustments required by war conditions: arranging contacts with Whitehall and its new war activities (Lord Catto to the Treasury, Sir P. Ashley Cooper [1] to the Ministry of Supply and others to the Ministry of Economic Warfare) and, like others of his colleagues, sleeping sometimes two or three nights a week at the Bank. Apart from the particular functions of the Bank of England in the general scheme of war finance, he was throughout the intermediary between all the various City interests and the Government; the interpreter of one to the other; the reconciler of differences; and the remover of difficulties. To use his own phrase he was 'the bridge' between the City and Whitehall. It was through him that special indications were given to the banks on the financial needs of various war activities, for instance government contractors and sub-contractors in November 1939.

There were the commitments or loan maturities of large borrowers to be arranged for in an unwilling market: and a

[1] Director of the Bank of England, 1932–55.

number of special problems both financial and personal arising out of the Bank's pre-war industrial investments. These were frequently matters of difficulty and took much time and thought. The brief entries in his private diary are eloquent of the diversity and complexity of his daily round and the incessant calls on his energy and resourcefulness.

Throughout, however, besides these varied topics, two dominant thoughts occupied his mind, the finance of the war and the post-war position of British industry.

From the first Norman, who had been a critic of the 6 per cent Exchequer Bonds of 1917, was a determined advocate of moderate interest rates for the inevitable war borrowings. He also realised from the beginning that both in view of the large amounts involved and for the purpose of controlling inflation more was needed than the typical market issue. As early as the first days of September 1939, he was actively engaged in expounding these ideas to the Treasury. He aimed at a 3 per cent war and used all his influence and power to secure this end. His success is reflected in the much lower cost per million pounds of Government borrowing during the war than that incurred between 1914 and 1919.

The first War Loan issued in March 1940 was £300 million 3 per cent 1955–59. Norman insisted on a public statement that no more favourable terms would be offered for later loans to be issued during the war. It was followed by a series of tap loans — 2½ per cent National War Bonds and 3 per cent Savings Bonds — at roughly six-monthly intervals right down to the end of the war, without the general mode and conception being substantially changed.

To achieve these results, the market had to be carefully organised and to this object much of Norman's time was devoted. The informal Committee, which had for some time been advising on large (mainly overseas) loan issues, was formally constituted (under the name of the Capital Issues Committee) with much enlarged powers to advise the Treasury on the uses of its statutory powers under the Defence of the Realm Act [1] to control issues. Issues of new capital for other than purposes connected with the war were heavily restricted and, in due course, reduced to a trickle. In September the

[1] Replaced in 1946 by the Borrowing (Control and Guarantees) Act, 1946.

first of many requests was made to the Clearing Banks to limit their advances on similar lines. Parallel to this, voluntary agreements were reached with the main institutional investors, in particular with the insurance companies, on the degree to which they would invest ('all surplus funds') in new War Loans, to which they pledged full support. To organise the small savings for which bond issues were not suitable, Sir Robert Kindersley returned in the autumn of 1939 to the Chairman-ship of the National Savings Committee.

A further development (as from 1 July 1940) was the intro-duction of the Treasury Deposit Receipt for making use of the surplus funds accumulating in the Banks. This was in substance a six-months Treasury Bill though not negotiable, at an interest rate originally of $1\frac{1}{8}$ per cent with the right, however, to repayment within the six months for the purpose of subscribing to long-term war issues. At its highest, in September 1945, the total of these Deposit Receipts substantially exceeded £2000 million.

Of all these activities the Governor was the leading and, at times, the masterful instigator; and right through the war they were necessarily a constant preoccupation.

Norman's second main preoccupation during the war and increasingly as the war progressed was the position which he foresaw British industry would have to face when the war was over. He had throughout been concerned through all the necessary strains and emergencies of the war to preserve for post-war use the general structure of the financial market. Early in 1943 he was much occupied with Sir Harold Hartley in urging on industry and on the banks the importance of Industrial Research and he preached this doctrine incessantly to all and sundry.

In March 1943 he set up an internal committee in the Bank to consider the best methods in the immediate post-war period of ensuring effective co-operation between the Govern-ment and the various lenders in meeting the financial needs of the community, having regard, *inter alia*, to the necessity for effective control, for judging the validity of demands especially for new industries, for co-ordinating the allocation of capital with the allocation of materials and for dealing with the needs of industry so as to encourage maximum employment and the extension of research. The committee reported late in the autumn of 1943.

They were preoccupied with the inevitable competition between the Government's future demands on the capital market (including the funding of excessive Floating Debt), and the demands which would come from an industry relatively starved during the war and now faced with competition under peace conditions. There was a danger that this double demand would result in inflation. The committee assumed, therefore, in the immediate post-war period the maintenance of some measure of the war-time controls (exchange, capital issues, materials) with a certain order of priority in the demands to be met.

The committee went on to suggest certain improvements in the machinery by which available capital could be directed to the points in industry where it could be effectively used, having in mind particularly the sound borrower whose needs were too small for the normal market issue, and the sound borrower, large or small, who needed money when market conditions were temporarily unfavourable. To meet these particular cases, they suggested a scheme for an Industrial Development Corporation. Much further thought was given to these suggestions, out of which (though they actually came to birth shortly after Norman's resignation and under the aegis of his successor) with the financial support of the banks and insurance companies, came the two finance corporations known as the Finance Corporation for Industry and the Industrial and Commercial Finance Corporation.

As time went on Norman's health — he was now over seventy-two—became increasingly uncertain. Early in 1943 he was away for some weeks, and, at the beginning of the following year, a chill caught at a draughty junction near Much Hadham brought on a serious attack of pneumonia, which did not wholly yield to very drastic medical treatment. Early in 1944 it was known that his doctors would not allow him to stand again for election to the Court.

Norman attended the Bank Court for the last time on 13 January 1944. His colleagues in April recorded 'their profound appreciation of the manifold services rendered by the Rt. Hon.[1] Montagu Collet Norman, D.S.O., as Governor during twenty-

---

[1] He had been sworn of the Privy Council in July 1923.

four years of unprecedented change and stress. They are deeply sensible of the ability, industry, uprightness and resource with which he has carried the heavy burden of his Office : and they trust that he may soon achieve a complete recovery from the severe illness which has led to the loss of his guidance and counsel.' When, as part of the celebration of the 250th Anniversary of the foundation of the Bank in 1694, the Court decided to devote £100,000 to the encouragement of economic research, they joined his name with that of the first Governor, John Houblon, in the designation of the Houblon-Norman Fund.

He was with some difficulty persuaded by his colleagues to accept on his retirement in 1944 the Peerage which he had declined some twenty years earlier for the characteristic reason that 'he could be of more use without it'. His increasing ill-health after his retirement precluded him, though still maintaining an active interest in world affairs, from any further public activities; and on 4 February 1950 he died, in his seventy-ninth year.

'THE MAN'

THE tracks of a man across the sands of time are, as a rule, not difficult to trace : where he went, what he did, how much he accomplished of his declared objectives and by how much he fell short of them. His actions tell that part of the story ; they can be recorded, and the actions of men who live in the public eye are watched and known, at least in part. They may not always be fully understood by contemporaries, however complete the record ; and posterity is likely to reinterpret their significance for the world. But the course of a man's life is fixed within comparatively narrow limits by established facts, and although historians and economists may still differ, the outward evidence with which they deal has to be accepted rather than questioned.

But, when historians and economists have had their say, there still remains something more which contemporaries and even posterity may wish to know about a man whose life deserves to be remembered for what he did. His actions may explain themselves or be explained, but what manner of man was he in and for himself? This is a different question altogether, and the full story has not been told unless some attempt is made to answer it.

The question is, no doubt, a natural one and it may be legitimate enough so long as it is not too intrusive. But it deserves to meet, at the outset, with two formidable objections. The first is that what a man was can never be made known in the same way or to the same extent as what he did. The second objection is that those very few, who came as near to knowing the answer as it was possible to come, are almost certainly thereby disqualified from giving it.

Yet an attentive reader of these pages will have gathered many useful clues to the nature of Montagu Norman, and may even have formed some composite picture of him as a man.

Two of his leading characteristics have been referred to again and again : his vehemence and his passion for work. His 'eager and expansive energy', his 'ardent and impetuous temper' were, no doubt, partly responsible for 'the intensity that characterised all his activities'. But his 'restless energy' was not merely temperamental; it was rooted in a strong moral conviction which finds expression in several of his letters. From South Africa he wrote : 'One's so-called happiness depends upon occupation irrespective of place and people', and ten years later we find the same thing repeated in different words : 'Without some sort of work it's hardly possible to get along'. These revealing sentences show what it was that drove him mercilessly throughout his life, to the limit of his physical capacities and often beyond. Not, as many thought, the crusading spirit of a man with a gospel and a mission; not the opinionated self-assurance of a man who cannot believe that he is mistaken; nor yet a desire to dominate and to impose his will; but a firm belief that life is wasted or misspent if it is not fully charged and lived at high pressure all the time. He could, on occasion, be light-hearted, but never frivolous; he could relax, but he could not prevent himself from taking everything, in some measure, seriously : the good and the bad things, the great and the small.

This helps to account for 'his passion for concrete detail', his 'accurate memory for persons' and his irrepressible inquisitiveness. But the 'restlessness of his mind' was not the pathological restlessness of a mind which roams indiscriminately and is never at peace with itself. On the contrary, it was highly concentrated and focused upon a purpose of which he was well aware and which is repeatedly formulated in his early correspondence. He travels with his eyes wide open and his attention constantly alert, because he wants to learn and can never learn enough about anything and everything. Yet learning was not for him an end in itself. Avid as he might be for information and, still more, for understanding, he regarded them as instruments, valuable only in use; and although he had a respect for the 'learned' in an academic sense of the word, his respect was untouched by envy. In his view, they arrived nowhere; or, at best, they made it easier for more practical men to take advantage of their labours by putting them to better use.

Here, then, lay the triple mainspring of his character. He was passionately eager to work in order to learn, and to learn in order to act; 'his mind was the type that solves its problems in action': all this because of an intense vitality which was not physical nor perhaps chiefly intellectual, but spiritual, and firmly based on a profound conviction about the meaning and value of life.

This settled, some other characteristics which might otherwise seem incongruous fall neatly into place: for example, his humility. He was frequently called an autocrat or a tyrant, and the element of truth which underlay these often biased charges will be considered later. What first needs to be said, if he is to be inwardly appreciated, is that any kind of arrogance, self-importance or pretentiousness was insufferable to him in other people and utterly foreign to his own nature. Modest he may not have been, for he had taken his own measure; but his deep humility found constant expression in his attitude towards men and women in all the relations of life. Reference has been made to 'the patience with which he would listen' and to the fact that he always sought not only responsibility but advice. There might, after all, be something to learn; indeed, there probably was, and it would be a pity to miss it. So he would listen, generally without comment, and certainly without argument (which he detested) but always on the tacit understanding that he was being spoken to straightforwardly and not cleverly, or for effect. On those terms he would attend, gravely and willingly, to the naïveties of the young and the stupidities of the old, sifting and gleaning silently in his own mind. After all, quite apart from the possibility of finding some grain among the chaff, such naïveties and stupidities were themselves facts to which a practical man would have to accommodate himself; and were they necessarily less important than the rights and wrongs of the case, so often difficult to distinguish and sort out?

His essential humility also found expression in the personal courtesies for which he was famous. Superficially, they might appear to be no more than good manners carried to perfection by a man whose physical graces and inborn courtliness made it natural for him to be charming without effort and considerate without a trace of condescension. But there was far more to

it than that. At a rather deeper level, his courtesy expressed
respect for outward forms and procedures of all sorts. He
attached fully as much importance to the manner in which a
thing was done as to the mere doing of it, and he never considered a practical question settled until both had been attended
to with equal care. Deeper still lay the humanity which led
him to look upon all fellow-creatures as literally his fellows, so
that despite his regard for quality and station he would place
himself at once on exactly the same footing with a coalheaver
or a railway porter as with the City magnates who came to see
him in the Bank parlours. It was this responsive humanity
which so endeared him to his professional colleagues abroad,
especially perhaps to the governors of less important Central
Banks, whose troubles he was always ready to enter into sympathetically and to make his own.

Nothing has yet been said about his personal appearance,
which in later life made him an ideal subject for the photo-
grapher and the caricaturist. Earlier photographs, without
the beard (which he first grew in South Africa but discarded
for a time after his return) show little that seems arresting or
impressive, and it is curious that the obscurity of lips and chin,
giving a kind of sculptural quality to his profile, should also
have made his features more strikingly expressive. He was
small-boned, with noticeably delicate and shapely hands ; but
the simple dignity of his bearing added several non-existent
inches to his physical stature. He exercised a power of
magnetic fascination which was certainly in part physical,
although features and bearing combined were not enough to
account for it entirely. He was quite conscious of it, and not
above employing it deliberately on occasion ; but he probably
never asked himself where it came from. His attire, except in
one respect, was always extremely sober and correct. It bore
evidence of some old-fashioned personal valeting, of some
military regard for 'spit and polish', and of a meticulous
observance of social proprieties. The wearer proclaimed himself fastidious to a degree, sensitive to every detail of appearance,
but obedient to the conventions. A hint of richness and splen-
dour was given by the fine emerald with which he ringed his
tie ; otherwise, there was nothing to indicate a strongly marked
individuality. To all this, the one great exception was his hat,

and even his hat need have attracted no particular notice on a
hat-peg : an orthodox black felt, somewhat wide in the brim,
but quite at home with its neighbours. Yet, when he put it on,
it suddenly became vocal. To say that he put it on is to give a
false impression of what actually happened. He would sling it
into the air, somewhere in the neighbourhood of his head, and
it would land miraculously, as in a juggling trick, but at any
sort of angle ; and so he liked to leave it, as though to illustrate
his principle that responsibility should always lie where it falls.
His hat gave him an appearance of reckless irresponsibility, of
Bohemian eccentricity, which helped to foster the common
belief that he was more of an artist than a banker ; and, inevitably, it caught the eye more readily than other features of his
outward appearance. Of course he was well aware of this too,
and if he refrained from correcting it, the reason may well have
been not (as some suspected) a rather theatrical affectation but,
contrariwise, an assertion of his natural right to behave, in
such small personal matters, quite naturally.

A word should perhaps be said about his voice and manner
of speech. The voice (of which there is an extant record, made
in broadcasting) was resonant and manly, without a quaver,
and not unmusical. The articulation was almost laboriously
clear, deliberate and slow. He was painstaking and exact in
his choice of words ; interested, too, in the finer shades of
meaning and philology. His natural vehemence conveyed
itself in timbre, emphasis and intonation, as well as in his
preference for vivid juxtapositions. He gave the impression of
practising a severe economy of words, and of having carefully
framed, before he spoke, the structure of what he had to say.
When he embarked upon what was obviously going to be a long
and involved sentence, one could be sure that he would thread
his way through it and bring it triumphantly to a close. 'You
know — that man A — is one of those people — who meet a
sudden and a violent end ; — and then there's an inquiry —
and some poor fellow is hanged — for giving way — to what
was not only a natural — but a meritorious impulse.' In his
pronunciation there were peculiarities which it was difficult to
account for : with obvious zest, he rolled an exaggeratedly
Italianate R, and occasionally a vowel would be so strangely
enunciated that the hearer might be left guessing at all sorts of

far-fetched explanations to account for it : America, Dresden, an echo of the linguistic past or just caprice ?

Some of his pithier sayings were often repeated : blunt phrases like 'spitting against the wind' or characteristically vivid comments, always freshly coined in his own Mint. Much of his language, like his life, was supercharged and he constantly loaded a few words with almost more than they would bear — as, for instance, when speaking of a debt, 'forgiven but not forgotten'. He relied upon other people to attribute to the words he used, in speech or correspondence, precisely the amount of weight which he had given to them, and when they failed, as they often did, he felt disappointed and a little hurt.

It has been said above that 'his powers of explanation and advocacy . . . fell far short of his powers of insight and decision' ; and also that 'he was a bad witness'. There can be no doubt of it, nor of the fact that this shortcoming was mainly attributable to another characteristic which has been referred to more than once in the preceding pages : the intuitive quality of his mental processes. It is true enough, that his mind was 'orderly' as well as 'acute' and that he had a 'logical grasp of principles' ; but his thinking did not proceed consecutively in measured stages from a weighing of evidence to a balancing of conclusions The steps of an argument by which he might have justified himself had never been taken in his own mind, and it was therefore useless to ask him to retrace them. Consequently he 'never found it easy to explain and justify'. But when a proposition was put to him, or an unfamiliar situation ex-plained, for the first time, he had an uncanny knack of putting his finger straight onto the crucial spots, and discarding what he called the 'frills'. He did it by means of a penetrative insight, born of imagination and experience combined, to which he gave the name of 'vision', and which he looked for and admired in others because it was supremely exemplified in himself.

This may have been, in part, why 'he always found women easier to talk with than men' ; and indeed there were other feminine streaks in his character — (anyone interested in secondary characteristics might be amused to measure the angle of his ear in a profile photograph). Or again, his reliance upon intuitive insight might be associated with the fact that 'even in business his intellectual processes were more those of a creative artist than an economic man'. Yet it was a mistake, commonly made, to regard him as primarily an aesthete. His appearance and, in some ways, his temperament, lent colour to the notion, but anyone who had occasion to come to terms with him soon found that brass tacks were the only thing that mattered. A visionary he may have been, and an idealist he certainly was; but he was also, and above all, a realist, and a hard-bitten realist at that, whose judgments could be, when necessary, stern to the point of cruelty. 'I need a butcher', he said, for a task of financial reconstruction; and he meant it. His early letters from America show how, even when his sympathies had been enlisted, his critical faculties remained cold and hard. This led him to incline often towards the more pessimistic forecasts and to foresee the dangers at least as clearly as the opportunities. 'Every cloud has a silver lining, a platitude I detest' was characteristic. He never under-rated the difficulties of anything he undertook.

That he had an active and powerful mind is beyond dispute. Not only was he endowed with it by nature, but his conviction that life had little meaning apart from strenuous activity, led him to exercise and cultivate his own mind ceaselessly and deliberately. A natural inquisitiveness reinforced his thirst for knowledge, but what made him intellectually voracious was his character, much more than his intelligence; and, in this as in so many other respects, he was essentially English. He never could have believed for a moment that important questions can be solved by looking up the right answers or that practical conclusions can be derived from purely theoretical premisses. Not only before the Macmillan Committee but on every other occasion he 'refused to commit himself to any simple criterion or formula. . . . He always had in mind an actual situation' and 'explained his action as a series of responses to particular market situations'. 'He deliberately refused to generalise. . . . He was not doctrinaire.' His 'untiring attention to detail' was the logical and necessary complement of his general approach.

That kind of mental make-up is perfectly compatible with a certain indifference to theoretical implications. If Norman was not recognised at school as a 'clever' boy or at the University as a 'promising student', there is no need to quarrel with the verdict, any more than he would have quarrelled with it. If by Continental standards his *formation* had been deficient, with results that could never be quite overtaken by his own efforts, it may be that the standards, or the judgments to which they led, were at fault, rather than the man or the system of education which had failed to bring out his capacities. His colleagues abroad may sometimes have been disconcerted by meeting a Central Bank Governor who was 'not interested in history', and who scorned the acrobatics of debate, but there were never two opinions about his mental calibre; though from their own relative inexperience — for he became the doyen of them all — they may sometimes have concluded (wrongly) that, as he put in one of his South African letters, it was all 'a question of experience, and not of ability'.

He found life infinitely variegated and exciting; full of subtleties and complexities in which he delighted — fine shades of meaning, significant distinctions and, especially, strange vagaries of human character and motive. All these he could appreciate and would insist upon, sometimes with a vigour which, to blunter minds, might seem incongruously like formalism and pedantry. He was often perplexed, but he could never have been bored (except by enforced idleness when he yearned for 'the luxury of occupation'). He was a practitioner, an innovator, an experimenter of such astonishing resourcefulness that he was seldom quite baffled. It was no accident that he was always interested in any kind of genuine craftsmanship.

But, however active and able a man's mind may be, his life will be filled not merely with problems but with people, and his relations with his fellow-men will largely determine the verdict of his contemporaries, perhaps also of posterity. He had written as though his own happiness were dependent entirely upon occupation, 'irrespective of place and people', yet people mattered to him tremendously, not only as they affected him personally but for their own sake. How he regarded his position at the head of a great organisation, staffed with men and women of all types and of all ages from sixteen to sixty, was conveyed by what he once said of his own Deputy Governorship: 'You cannot think what it means to be the father and mother of five thousand souls'. Personality meant to him something which ought to be both preserved from within, by its own integrity, and respected from without for its inviolability. He was not censorious, for he cared less about what else a man was than about whether he was wholly and genuinely himself; so that an outspoken difference of opinion or attitude, so far from repelling, intrigued and attracted him. He could not abide a 'yes-man', and if he were to be accessible to flattery it had to be flattery of a very indirect and unobtrusive kind.

It has been said that he was shy and that 'he did not make friends easily'. In later life this was perhaps attributable to the fact that most people were afraid of him, and he did not like them to be. He was certainly 'sensitive to the personal relations involved in work' and wished them to be harmonious, if only for the sake of efficiency. Yet he did not always himself contribute to the harmony, for it could not be said of him that he ever suffered fools gladly. He could excuse a misdemeanour much more readily than a crass stupidity.

The personal interest he took in everybody who came across him, even casually, gave more than a polish to his perfect courtesy. Countless stories were told of how he had recognised undistinguished people or remembered a trivial occasion in a manner so considerate and complimentary that it endeared him for ever. But these stories were matched with others not so pleasing. Almost all those who worked in his immediate neighbourhood had reason, at one time or another, to complain of his tantrums. In retrospect, it is not difficult to make allowances for a man, by nature highly strung, working continuously under a strain which hardier nervous constitutions might well have found unbearable. But this does not get over the fact that he could be childishly violent and cruelly unjust towards those very people whose loyalty and affection made them put up with treatment they would not normally have tolerated. They sometimes compared him to a *prima donna*, but they were unlikely to make the mistake of attributing his excesses to mere vanity or egotism. The truth lay deeper in his emotional nature, which not seldom revealed a streak of implacability that was aggressive and pitiless.

The fashionable explanation to-day would be that he was corrupted by power. Dictators are expected to be violent and capricious, and it was commonly thought that he came near to being a dictator. Inside the Bank, the charge was more true than the critics themselves perhaps realised, for Norman inherited and maintained a tradition of long standing, that 'the Governor governs'. Even in the course of a two-year term, a man of such marked individuality would be expected to assert himself, and in the course of twenty years he could easily become an autocrat without wishing to. But what concerns us here is the question whether the concentration and exercise of so much personal authority led to its abuse in this instance ; and the answer lies partly in the narrative of what actually happened, partly in an appreciation of the Governor's character as a whole.

It has been shown that he repeatedly went out of his way — more often than was strictly necessary — to place himself and his office at the disposal of his colleagues ; and it has been suggested in this chapter that his whole life proves him to have been a man dedicated not to himself but to a task which he willingly undertook but would as willingly have laid down again, if it had seemed to be for the best that he should do so. He was as masterful as a great leader is bound to be and his general outlook, in this and other activities of life, could be called authoritarian (not dictatorial). But, for that very reason, he was always himself ready to bow to legitimate authority and careful, while preserving his own, not to challenge or usurp that of others. The idea that he tried to set up a kind of rival Foreign Office in Threadneedle Street, or to override the policies and decisions of the Cabinet, was never anything but moonshine.

But how masterful does a great leader have to be ? The question is badly framed, because what matters is not the degree of compulsion exercised but the manner in which it is brought to bear ; and the appropriate manner varies according to circumstances. On the barrack square the bark of a Sergeant-Major is in place ; in the presence of a monarch the lightest wish may be interpreted as a gentle command ; and a tyrant, in any walk of life, is a plain bully. Nothing is more distinctive in a man than the way he sets about getting those things done which, in his opinion, ought to be done. Norman could bark ; and there was truth in the claim that the drill and discipline of the Bank of England could be compared only with those of the Brigade of Guards. But what he preferred was to cajole. He did not easily persuade, because he would not and could not argue; yet he somehow managed to get a great number and a great variety of people to do just what he wanted them to do, although very often they did not want to do it. Sometimes he would take advantage of their personal devotion, asking as a favour what he had no right to exact, and perhaps even accepting conditions or limitations which he already knew would prove, in practice, to be inoperative. Sometimes he made a tacit appeal to loyalties which were impersonal and scarcely conscious. Or again, he would accept, almost as of right, services voluntarily offered as a tribute of admiration or respect. The upshot was that he could mobilise, in effect, an army out of the ground, and did so, time and again. In his later years his prestige was so high throughout the financial world that few would risk doing anything which might fall short of his standards, and fewer would deny him any support for which he asked.

But there was some excuse for popular misrepresentations. Not only did he have some difficulty in explaining himself to more than one person at a time : he actually resented having to do so and avoided the necessity whenever possible. No remark he ever made was more damaging (and also more misleading) than his famous quotation at the Mansion House of the Arab proverb : 'The dogs may bark, but the caravan moves on'. It could be taken as offensive to his listeners and insolently contemptuous of warnings and restraints. Yet nothing was more foreign to the speaker than any wish or inclination to be insolent or offensive. Indifferent to uninstructed opinion he always was; he merely ignored it as of no account — and this, for a man in his position, may have been a tactical or diplomatic mistake. He had, perhaps too obviously, an aristocrat's contempt for the vulgarity and pretentiousness of ignorance. But enough has been said here to show how he always sought advice and listened to it, how he strove for conciliation and suffered acutely from 'the strain of disagreement'.

It remains to chronicle some of the human characteristics and foibles which marked his individuality — an individuality which he was never at pains to disguise : the way he had of inquisitively fingering everything within reach; the odd slips

of paper, tucked away in his waistcoat pockets, which recorded
his ruminations at all hours of the day and night, and served
him as a reminder of the different things he intended to contrive ; his dislike of what he called 'essays', by which he meant
any statement covering more than one or two pages, for he
seems to have shared Arthur Balfour's belief that half a sheet
of note-paper is enough for any subject. He needed to take
nourishment at frequent intervals, and after a couple of hours
he would complain of being 'faint for want of food'. His hand-
writing was beautiful ; he wrote, slowly and firmly with a broad
nib, an upright hand, the letters clearly modulated and well
rounded, but without flourishes of any sort. He smoked, but
very moderately, an occasional cigarette or a small cigar ;
and for many years he made it a rule not to smoke in the Bank
until after lunch. Unless pressed for time, he liked to walk
rather than take a vehicle, and while he walked he was constantly observing and exploring. In one respect, if memory
serves — for it was not noticeable at the time — he was most
un-English, for although he often smiled enchantingly, he never
laughed aloud. He may have agreed with Lord Chesterfield
that laughter is a vulgar noise.

No doubt he made things worse for himself than they need
have been by his cult of secrecy, and this was such a prominent
trait in his character that it deserves some closer consideration.
It is not to be accounted for by the fact that the traditional
policy and practice of the Bank of England had been never to
explain, or even to comment. On the contrary, Norman himself was responsible for what seemed like a startlingly new
departure, when the Bank introduced regular arrangements
for making information available, under a whole-time senior
official. His secretiveness was personal, and to those (especially
foreigners) who had to do with him only occasionally, it seemed
like deliberate and needless mystification : they would have
found him quite enigmatic enough in any case. There may
indeed have been a mischievous and puckish element about it,
especially as time went on and it became a settled habit. He
sometimes even made sure of being found out, as when he would
hand back a memorandum with the words : 'I have not read
it', and then proceed to discuss the subject, knowing full well
that his pencil annotations in the margin would be discovered

2 I

later on. But such rather childish naughtiness was merely
the outcrop of a deep-seated propensity which, if he had been
given to self-analysis, he might have justified on three different
grounds, all consistent with his principles, and rational. In the
first place, he had a banker's respect for confidences and knew
how much they contributed to clarity and efficiency, whenever
trouble threatened. Perfect discretion was an essential condition of his becoming, as he was and meant to be, the trusted
confidant of the whole City; and when the Bank for International Settlements was founded, he thought of it as a
'confessional' through which a similar relationship might be
established between all Central Bankers. In the second place,
experience told him that most people will not allow themselves to be guided for their own good. The best of reasons may
fail in face of vanity, stupidity or ill-will, and then it becomes
necessary to resort to guile. Achilles was a doughty fighter but
the comparatively innocent deceptions of Ulysses resolved many
a situation which would not have yielded to more direct treatment; and they required secrecy. Thirdly, and not least
important, Norman, with his 'orderly mind', his artist's respect
for form, his courtly regard for outward observances, his precision and his exacting standards of practical efficiency, could
not help paying the closest attention to what may be called, for
want of a better word, function. Each person has his proper
sphere, each thing has its proper use, and nothing but confusion
results if their functions are not differentiated and circum-
scribed. So easily can they become smudged and merged that
it requires unremitting care to keep them separate, and the
only way is not only to store them in distinct compartments
of the mind, so that no irrelevancies may intrude, but also to
preserve and insist upon a proper recognition of them in all
outward behaviour. Whether a letter is to be marked 'Private'
or 'Confidential' may seem a matter of no importance : but
for Norman the two words had different connotations. Whether
one procedure is followed or another may not matter much if
the effect is the same ; but with him, every step had to be
taken as exactly and delicately as in a minuet. None of this
would have been possible for a man with such multifarious
contacts and concerns unless frankness and openness in one
direction had been doubled by secrecy in every other. But the

effect sometimes was to give him the appearance (not contra-
dicted by his outward aspect) of being engaged in a perpetual
conspiracy.

This brings us to a cryptic statement, faithfully recorded
in the preceding narrative, by one of his closest friends, Ben
Strong. It refers to 'certain personal qualities of which I
heartily disapprove', but no clue is offered as to what these
were. It is only fair to recognise that Ben Strong was, in
some respects, an observer from a distance which, at that
time, was comparatively remote. But the impression remains
that there were facets of Norman's character which even a
sympathetic observer might well find unsympathetic. What
they may have been appears clearly enough from what has
been said here : a tendency to dramatise, and over-dramatise ;
perhaps an inclination to surprise and shock, *pour épater les
bourgeois* ; an independent self-reliance carried to impracticable
extremes, considering the trend of the times. On every one
of these counts, only a plea of guilty — perhaps rather of
touché — could be entered, with reservations. The reservations
would have tended to show that all these minor characteristics
were rightly described as facets : namely, as the obverse and,
at least to some extent, the inevitable correlative of qualities
less obvious but more real. Turn the whole complex round
and look at it from the other side, and it would reveal splen-
dours of a very different order.

But there remains one unanswered question, deliberately
deferred, which must have been present to the mind of any
attentive reader of these pages. Norman has been described
here as a highly complex but fully integrated character, and
not (as he was often supposed to be) a bundle of irreconcilable contradictions. His philosophy might, in its general
outlines, have been reduced to terms of a mathematical
formula : occupation means work, work means learning,
learning means experience, experience must issue in action
and action is life. So far so good ; but what sort of action,
and for what purpose ? The springs of action having been
determined, what is its goal ? The answer is not easy to
give, and he would never have attempted to formulate it
exactly. What seems clear enough is that the goal was universal
and remote. It transcended the limitations of geography and

nationality, for 'by training and experience he was international in outlook'. Even to begin with, his outlook was 'European and Imperial, never narrowly domestic'; and it came to be universal, as his humanity was, so that he could make friends with Schacht and try to be on terms with the Japanese representatives in London or in Basle, whatever might be said of such associations. But to what purpose? If pressed, he would probably have said no more than that the best any of us can attempt to do is to get on with the job which, in our own sphere of action, most needs doing. He would not willingly have associated himself with any such remoter generalisations as that the preservation of good government at home and peace abroad were what he was actually, if not consciously, engaged upon promoting. Yet those who worked with him were made to feel that the ends they served through him were, in some undefined and unclaimed way, sublime. He had eternal longings; he founded a professional brotherhood which survives him unimpaired; and, even when he failed to carry conviction, he radiated inspiration.

An account of a man, such as has been attempted in this chapter, cannot be complete, because the facets of a fully developed character are too numerous; it cannot preserve due proportion and perspective, because these vary with the point of view; it cannot even be truthful because it has to present in static terms what is essentially dynamic and organic. But, whatever the whole truth about Norman may have been, it is clear enough that his mind had a grasp and power in practical affairs which made him a living force on a historic scale; and that his life affords a rare example of single-minded, unsparing devotion to humanist ideals — ideals perhaps unformulated by himself, and certainly difficult to pinpoint, yet perfectly apparent in the consistent trends of his tireless activity. He had two outstanding qualities, so obvious in the narrative of his life at every stage that it has not yet been necessary to mention them by name: a lion-hearted courage and an unrelenting tenacity of purpose. His temperament was both a disturbing and a stimulating factor — the one, indeed, implies the other: it put an emotional head of steam behind his driving force, but it also sometimes hampered his effectiveness by exposing him to misunderstanding and facile misrepresentation. If he had written his own ten commandments, they might not have had a great deal in common with the Decalogue but they would have been a safe guide to any man with high public responsibilities. All in all, he was a man of such a stamp and stature that any country may deem itself fortunate if it is served by more than one in the course of a single generation.

INDEX

THE END